THE VALUE OF CREATIVITY

The Value of Creativity

The origins and emergence of a modern belief

JOHN HOPE MASON

ASHGATE

Published by
Ashgate Publishing
Gower House
Croft Road
Aldershot
Hampshire GU11 :
England

Ashgate Publishing
Suite 420
101 Cherry Street
Burlington, VT 05
USA

Ashgate website:

British Library Ca.
Hope Mason, John
   The value of creativity : an essay on intellectual history,
   fromGenesis to Nietzsche
   1. Intellectual life - History 2. Creative ability 3. Creative
   ability in science 4. Europe - Intellectual life - History
   I. Title
   306.4'2

Library of Congress Cataloging-in-Publication Data
Hope Mason, John
   The value of creativity: an essay on intellectual history, from Genesis to Nietzsche/
   John Hope Mason.
      p.cm.
   Includes bibliographical references (p.) and index.
   ISBN 0-7546-0760-7 (alk. paper)
      1. Creative ability–Philosophy. I. Title.

B105.C74 M37 2002
128'3c–dc21

2002074462

ISBN 0 7546 0760 7

Printed and bound in Great Britain by Antony Rowe Ltd.,
Chippenham, Wiltshire

Contents

Preface

This book — an essay in intellectual history — arose out of a mixture of bewilderment and curiosity. I was bewildered at the confident assumption of many of my contemporaries that the future they believed in, or would like to see, would be one in which every person could be creative; and I was curious about the reasons for this assumption. The fact that I was perplexed was due to the disparity I saw between the confidence with which the belief was held and the mass of evidence which seemed to undermine it or call it into question. This then led me to want to discover both the grounds for the confidence and the reasons for my scepticism. I was therefore led to the past.

It soon became clear that behind the confidence lay both ancient beliefs and modern developments, but how could both these be incorporated within a single study? The parameters and stringencies of intellectual history today are such that to try and deal in one work with a range of texts spanning the period from the Book of Genesis to the writings of Nietzsche would be to invite ridicule, if not contempt. No matter. The subject was too interesting to be abandoned. But it would need to be handled in a particular way; it would need to take the form of an extended essay, and that is what this book is. It provides a narrative which has a clear focus but many omissions, examining certain aspects in detail while treating others summarily. Since the subject is so large different readers will have different disappointments at what is omitted, whether in terms of topics covered, or of levels of detail, or of discussion of scholarly debates. Such omissions are inevitable in an essay of this kind, since its aim is not to be comprehensive but rather to combine selective analysis with an overall coherence.

At the heart of this book there is a puzzle. The modern value of creativity began to appear in Western Europe in the middle of the 19th century, as the age-old sense of reliance on a non-human Creator began to give way to a belief in human creativity. But the main factors which brought about this change and which can be seen to have given rise to the new value — scientific, technological, economic and political developments — were not reflected in the value itself, for that was applied almost exclusively to artistic and cultural activity. The explanation of this puzzle is the subject of this book.

Acknowledgements

Much of the work for this book was made possible by research grants from the Leverhulme Trust Fund and the Stiftung Volkswagenwerk, a fellowship at the Wissenschaftskolleg zu Berlin, a writer's bursary from the Arts Council of Great Britain, and sabbatical leave from Middlesex University. My thanks to them all.

An early version of Chapter 2 appeared in *History of European Ideas* 9 (1988), pp. 697-715, 'The Character of Creativity: two traditions' (reprinted here with permission from Elsevier Science); the first section of Chapter 3 was published in *Defending Politics*, edited by Iain Hampsher-Monk (British Academic Press, London, 1993, reprinted here with permission from I.B. Taurus); and aspects of Chapters 6 and 7 appeared in *Eighteenth-Century Aesthetics and the Reconstruction of Art*, edited by Paul Mattick Jr. (Cambridge University Press, New York, 1994, reprinted here with permission from Cambridge University Press) and in *Rousseau and the Sources of the Self*, edited by Timothy O'Hagan (Avebury Press, Aldershot, 1997).

To write a short book about a large subject takes a long time. For their support over this period I am especially grateful to Christopher May, Manjeet May, and John Lloyd Smith. For many different kinds of assistance I also owe thanks to the late Helmut Becker, Romana Blacher, Bernard Crick, Peter Gilbert, Pam Hall, Iain Hampsher-Monk, Eva Hoffman, Alan Hollinghurst, Daniel Javitch, Hector Laing, Keith McClelland, Jonathan Rée, Simon Richardson, Ariane and Gerd Sattler, Brian Vickers and Igor Webb. Finally, my particular thanks to my stepsons Felix and Ferdy; it is to them that I dedicate this book.

CHAPTER ONE

Prologue: the divine wanderer

I

A vision filled his mind, radiant and compelling. Everything he saw, everything he cast his eyes on, seemed dull in comparison. The vision glowed; it was another sun, his sun, his own source of life. In its warmth he was intact, no longer needing the warmth of other people. In its light new forms took shape, rare, brilliant, rich in meaning. The vision pulsated; it wanted to live. And such was the strength it gave him that he knew that he could make it real. The vision could be made flesh, as radiant and compelling as he saw it now.

It was not to be. His name was Victor Frankenstein, and what he created was a monster, a creature of such repellent ugliness that everyone who saw it was disgusted. After disgust came fear. For the monster, meaning well but rejected by everyone, refused to accept his lonely fate. He took revenge, killing those dear to Frankenstein — members of his family, his closest friend, and finally, on his wedding-day, his wife. The vision of beauty led to a nightmare of terror; the thrill of creation ended in hideous destruction.

Frankenstein was first published in 1818 and was an immediate success. Within a few years stage versions had appeared in both London and Paris and the story was as popular throughout the nineteenth century on stage as it has been over the last century on film. One early version of the story was called *Presumption*, another, a burlesque, was called *Frank in Steam*. These titles reflect obvious aspects of the book: the ancient theme that human beings should recognize their limits and not trespass on areas traditionally reserved for the gods (or God), and the modern theme of the dangers of science. Given the immensity of these latter dangers today it is not surprising that *Frankenstein* is generally taken to be a story about a reckless scientist.

To see it as such, however, is to miss the central significance of Mary Shelley's work. For Frankenstein is not simply a scientist, he is a man of vision, and as such he could be a poet, or an entrepreneur, or a statesman. Mary Shelley's father, William Godwin, was in his way such a man, and her husband the poet was pre-eminently that. The idea for the story came to Mary Shelley in the summer of 1816, when she and her husband spent time on Lake Geneva with Byron. The poems of that summer — *Manfred, Prometheus, Mont Blanc* — and Mary's experience of both her father and husband can be seen to have contributed to, or to echo, material in the novel. Its scope is wider than the problem of science, and its implications are correspondingly more far-reaching.

Not only does Frankenstein have a vision, he also realizes his vision. He is, to the utmost extent, creative. And the unwelcome truth which the novel presents is that creativity may be both irresistible and undesirable. Frankenstein is not evil or malevolent; even at the end of his life he is described as 'noble and godlike', 'a celestial spirit', a 'divine wanderer'.[1] There are times when he attributes his work to the desire for power and 'boundless grandeur'[2] but his principal impulse is to achieve something novel and significant, the desire to 'pioneer a new way, explore unknown powers, and unfold to the world the deepest mysteries of creation'.[3] It is the belief in this possibility which becomes an obsession and takes an 'irresistible hold'[4] on his imagination. Ambition played an important part but he was not moved by ambition alone. The vision had its own radiant attraction.

Where then did it all go wrong? Could Frankenstein have succeeded in his aim? After all, the monster was not malevolent. He had a tender heart — 'my soul glowed with love and humanity'[5] — and it was only when he was rejected by everyone that he became destructive — 'my vices are the children of the forced solitude which I abhor', 'misery made me a fiend'.[6] Is it not possible that he could have been accepted, at the very least by Frankenstein himself who knew the situation? In the answer to this question lies the bitter truth of the book. For there is an intrinsic connection between Frankenstein's creation of the monster and his rejection of it, between the initial glorious vision and the eventual catastrophic destruction.

The crux of the matter is Frankenstein's isolation. To do his work he has to shut himself away from the living world, from the beauties of high summer, from friends and family. All his 'feelings of affection' to others, or to the charms of nature, were put in abeyance.[7] It is not painful for him to do this, because the vision had such compelling power. He feels no loss or emptiness or absence. He immerses himself in his great task and becomes wholly self-absorbed. To be able to be this is essential to achieving his goal, but being this he is then incapable of accepting reality. The real world is different, it is not self but other. To create another being is precisely to create something different from oneself, and the ugliness of the monster displays this difference with melodramatic effectiveness. Frankenstein never admits, let alone accepts, the reality of this otherness. He cannot even bring himself to give the minimal recognition that is conferred by a name; all his emotions have become concentrated in himself. That is why his rejection of the monster is not fortuitous but inevitable.

On only one occasion does he show pity. The creature pleads with him to end his loneliness by creating a female companion. Frankenstein is moved by this plea — 'I compassionated him'[8] — and agrees to the request. He sets about repeating his work, travelling to the remotest Orkneys to find the solitude which he needs. But his efforts are fruitless; he is unable to summon up the same 'enthusiastic frenzy' of his first creation.[9] He starts to think of all kinds of possible consequences and this leads him to abandon the attempt. This failure confirms what had been shown earlier. As obsessive ambition and self-absorption can enable a vision to be realized, so, by the same token, compassion is unproductive.

Mary Shelley emphasises this theme further by duplicating it. The account of Frankenstein and the monster is set within another story, that of the young explorer Robert Walton who is on a voyage of discovery to the unknown regions of the North Pole. Walton is convinced that he will find there 'a land surpassing in wonders and beauty every region hitherto discovered', not a 'seat of frost and desolation' but 'the region of beauty and delight'.[10] He has learnt to endure the cold and hardship so as to be able to pursue this dream, spurred on by 'a love for the marvellous, a belief in the marvellous', to go beyond 'the common pathways of men'.[11]

It is as Walton's ship is sailing among the ice-floes of the Arctic that he comes across Frankenstein, then in the last stages of his pursuit of the monster. He immediately recognizes the latter as a kindred spirit and confides in him his dream.

> [I told him] how gladly I would sacrifice my fortune, my existence, my every hope, to the furtherance of my enterprise. One man's life or death were but a small price to pay for the acquirement of the knowledge which I sought; for the dominion I should acquire over the elemental foes of our race. As I spoke, a dark gloom spread over my listener's countenance ... I paused; at length he spoke, in broken accents: 'Unhappy man! Do you share my madness? Have you drunk also of the intoxicating draught? Hear me — let me reveal my tale, and you will dash the cup from your lips![12]

In this context, as a cautionary tale to someone 'pursuing the same course, exposing [him]self to the same dangers',[13] that Frankenstein tells his story. When it is finished, Walton again takes up the narrative. His crew do not want to proceed further north and come to him asking that the voyage be abandoned. Hearing this Frankenstein intervenes: 'Be men, or be more than men. Be steady in your purposes and firm as a rock ... Do not return to your families with the stigma of disgrace marked on your brows. Return as heroes'.[14] But the crew are not moved; and Walton is not self-absorbed like Frankenstein. He has always been conscious of lacking a true friend and he recognizes now his crew's feelings. He rejects heroism and agrees to turn back.

When Frankenstein is told this he wants to be left on the ice for his final encounter with the monster, but he is now too weak to move. As death approaches he bids Walton farewell. 'Seek happiness and tranquillity', he advises him, 'and avoid ambition'.[15] It is wrong, he had said earlier, to pursue any course which 'has a tendency to weaken your affections'.[16] The moral could not be clearer.[17] Yet even at this final moment Frankenstein does not regard himself as in any way to blame for what has occurred, and his final words reassert the validity of what he attempted. 'I have myself been blasted in these hopes', he exclaims, 'yet another may succeed'.[18] The vision remains irresistible.

The sight of Walton's ship sailing north into the ever colder, ever bleaker Arctic emptiness, driven on by the belief that there they would find a rich beauty, is a powerful image of futile ambition. But when Mary Shelley wrote, the North Pole had not yet been discovered and the idea that it would be a region of abundance had a long history. Frankenstein's search was similar in that it had been in graveyards and charnel-houses, among death, that he had found the source of life.[19] But his labours were not in vain. Unlike Walton he ignored the claims of everyone else and did not turn back. As a result he succeeded. The vision was made flesh. It was not his creative impulse or faculty which was frustrated. On the contrary, his creativity operated at full stretch. The problem was that it could do so only at the expense of other equally (or more) essential feelings.[20]

II

This book is about the way in which 'creativity' became a value. When *Frankenstein* was published no such value existed; that is to say, there was no general belief that to be 'creative' was, in the words of Matthew Arnold writing half a century later, 'the true function of man'. To be sure, there were many individuals who had achieved fame for abilities which we would now call 'creative', and as Mary Shelley was writing that word was coming to be used in an increasingly wide variety of ways. But only in the middle years of the 19th century do we begin to read statements that 'man is made to create' (Disraeli),[21] or that real human fulfilment lies in 'positive, creative activity' (Marx),[22] or that 'the exercise of a free, creative power...a free, creative activity, is the true function of man' (Arnold).[23] In other words, only then did creativity start to hold a place which gradually became as central to our society as heroism, honour, piety, or virtue (in different forms) had been in earlier societies.

The aim of this study is to provide an answer to two questions about this development: first, why did this new value emerge *then*, at that time? and second, why did *this* value arise? why did it take that particular form, being applied almost exclusively to artistic and cultural activity?

The answer to the first question relates this development to the general transformation which occurred in Western Europe between the early 17th and the late 19th centuries, as a rural, agricultural, tradition-bound society gave way to one which was urban, industrial and increasingly open. Although we may assume that one of the distinguishing features of human beings has been their freedom to act in new and self-chosen ways, throughout most history that freedom was contained within an overall dependence, and the sense of dependence (expressed in religious beliefs and rituals) was pervasive. 'The earth is the Lord's, and the fulness thereof', wrote the Psalmist; 'it is He who hath made us, and not we ourselves'.[24] In general, people saw themselves as relying on external, non-human forces which (or, in the case of a Creator, who) provided the essentials both of material well-being and of intellectual and metaphysical coherence. Only in the 17th and 18th centuries did it gradually begin to become apparent that they were moving out of a condition of dependence into a world which, in the most important respects, they were making themselves. This change took time to register. Locke wrote in 1690 that 'if we will rightly estimate things...and [assess] what in them is purely owing to nature, and what to labour,...ninety-nine out of one hundred are wholly to be put on the account of labour';[25] but it was only two hundred years later that May Day, the annual festival of the earth's fertility, became a celebration of human productivity.

There were three aspects of this change which seem to be particularly relevant to the emergence of creativity as a value. The first was the way in which scientific and technological advances began to make a sense of human independence *possible* (Chapter 4). The second was the fact that with the introduction of free-market economics there was not only gradually accelerating economic growth, but constant innovation became inescapably *necessary* (Chapter 5). Then, in the last quarter of the 18th century, the impact of these two (and other) developments reached as it were a critical mass and led to a new perception of history, namely, the modern idea of progress (Chapter 8). This notion of continuing improvement (so that not only will tomorrow be better than today, but the day after tomorrow will be better than tomorrow, and so on) had the effect of making the new not only possible and necessary but also *desirable.*

However, if this account is broadly correct, we are then faced with a puzzle, one which seems to have gone unnoticed and which this study sets out to explain. If it was the case that it was mainly these factors which enabled human beings to regard themselves as not being dependent on a Creator, but as being themselves 'creative', why did the value which subsequently appeared have nothing to do with technology or economics? Why was it applied instead to the non-material realm of aesthetic activity, with the paradigm of the 'creative' individual being not an inventor or an entrepreneur but a poet or artist?

The principal reason for this anomaly is that there have been two radically different ways in which the creative attribute has been perceived in European thought. This book opened with *Frankenstein* because that work stands in a long tradition, as Mary Shelley acknowledged by giving it the subtitle *The Modern Prometheus*. The myth of Prometheus, in its original form and many subsequent versions, portrayed the creative capacity as amoral, dangerous and disruptive, associated always with conflict (and sometimes with physicality or sexuality). By contrast, there was another perspective exemplified by the figure of God the Creator in Judaeo-Christian theology and by the originating One in neo-Platonic philosophy. This identified the creative attribute with moral goodness, with harmony and spirituality. Throughout European history these two views have been present. In two chapters which serve as an introduction and background to the ensuing analysis I show how they existed in Antiquity (Chapter 2) and in the Italian Renaissance (Chapter 3).

In the modern period, as the decisive transformation was beginning to occur, we find the same contrast or opposition in discussions of 'genius', as that word began to take on the meaning of an outstandingly gifted and creative person. In the writings of Blackwell, Diderot, Rousseau or Goethe genius is characterized in quasi-Promethean terms (Chapter 6); in the works of Shaftesbury, Young or Kant, it is described in quasi-neo-Platonic terms (Chapter 7). This second view came to dominate German thinking on this subject and this in turn exerted a major influence on such figures as Coleridge, Carlyle and Arnold, as well as Marx (Chapter 9). For all of them the creative was synonymous with an aesthetic and ethical dimension which set it apart from, and in opposition to, the ugly and morally offensive aspects of the new world taking shape around them. In other words, an idealized view of creativity made possible a wholly admirable kind of value.

In the last decades of the 19th century the assumptions which sustained this belief were subject to a fierce attack by Nietzsche, and in his writings we find the most complete elaboration of the Promethean view (Chapter 10). But Nietzsche himself remained a prisoner of the notion that creativity was essentially artistic; while he could be said to have de-moralized the attribute he did not de-aestheticize it. It is perhaps his influence, more than any other, which can be seen to underlie the esteem for creativity in Western society today, and this study ends with a brief consideration of the implications of that fact (Chapter 11).

III

The definition of creativity on which this book is based is that *to create is to act in the world, or on the world, in a new and significant way.* To act in the world is to perform an action, (and it is important to be aware that creativity can be manifest as much in an action as in an artefact); to act on the world is to form or make something.

The verb 'to create' (French, *créer*; German, *schöpfen, schaffen*) is different from 'to make' (*faire*; *machen*) or 'to produce' (*produire*; *erzeugen*) as neither of these necessarily involves innovation. What in Latin differentiated *creare* from *facere* (to make) was the sense of bringing something into the world which did not previously exist. The former was used of generating a new entity (e.g. Lucretius' *'natura creatrix'*), or of begetting a child, or of establishing a new legal status,[26] and it was therefore adopted by Jerome in his translation of the Bible to describe the action of the Judaeo-Christian God in making the universe.[27]

A distinction is sometimes made between the creative process as 'creation' and as 'procreation', using metaphors which describe what are taken to be distinctly male and female modes of action. The former is seen as being the imposition of humanly-determined form on inert or submissive matter, working upon nature and being outside nature, in the manner of the Judaeo-Christian God. The latter is the generation of new life from within the body, according to the processes of nature, reproduction rather than production. *Frankenstein* provides an example of this contrast, depicting a man's attempt at reproduction which, being forced and unnatural, has disastrous consequences. From this perspective Victor's hubris is not that of attempting to be like God but rather that of trying to appropriate the specifically female role. In a broader sense Mary Shelley's story can be seen as an attack on the assumption which has dominated European thought about creativity, both divine and human, namely that it is a distinctly male attribute.[28]

This aspect of the subject is not pursued here, not because I regard it as insignificant — on the contrary, I believe it to be of great importance — but because in the period covered by this book the subject was rarely discussed in these terms. For the same reason, this study has little to say about the psychology of the creative process. In part this is due to the lack of direct evidence about this before the 19th century. What we have is a number of beliefs or attitudes about creative activity which show a fairly consistent pattern; and such beliefs play an important part in understanding the ways in which the modern value emerged. But the purpose of this book is not to analyse the creative process (or processes) as such. It is concerned rather with the ways in which creativity became a value.

The fact that the word to 'create' involved some kind of innovation initially set it apart from to 'invent' (*invenir*; *erfinden*) and 'to discover' (*découvrir*; *entdecken*), for both of these verbs originally meant finding or uncovering something which already existed. This sense still applies in the case of to 'discover'. A geographical discovery is an 'uncovering' of something which had existed previously but had not been known about or seen; a scientific discovery, likewise, usually relates to a problem which is already recognized, (hence the phenomenon of simultaneous discoveries, like Darwin and Wallace on natural selection). The verb 'to invent', on the other hand, has lost most of its associations with finding, and is close in meaning to 'to innovate'. But whereas both 'invent' and 'innovate' share the sense of novelty with 'create', they lack the element of significance. An action or artefact has significance if it has a meaning which is widely shared, or profoundly experienced, if it is recognized as being cogent or important or convincing (i.e. not superficial or transient or trivial), occupying a distinct place within a broad field of understanding or experience. It is always possible that an invention or innovation may achieve significance. But something is no less 'inventive' if it lacks this dimension; whereas an act or work is not 'creative' if it is not significant.[29]

Drawing attention to these differences between 'create', 'invent' and 'discover' is one way of trying to identify what has come to set 'create' apart from the other terms. But the meanings of all three words have altered over time and (over the last three or four centuries) the distinctions have not been hard and fast. Scientific discoveries and technological inventions have introduced knowledge and techniques which have been both new and significant, and as such they played a major role in altering perceptions of human capacity and potential. This in turn was a key factor in leading to the rise of creativity as a value. In addition, both science and technology could be seen to be as problematic as other 'creative' activities, as the story of *Frankenstein* demonstrates. The fact that they have not received more attention here is a reflection partly of the limited amount of evidence, but much more — given the vastness of the subject — of the need to be selective.

Another reason for omitting scientific innovation is its high degree of impersonality. The verification of a new theory or the validity of a new technique is established by criteria which are matters of general agreement, and the end-product is not seen as a reflection either of its maker or of the process of discovery. This means that such activity is not susceptible to one of the misapprehensions which have clung to works of art or literature — the ergonic fallacy. I use this term to describe the opposite of the genetic (or intentional) fallacy, the belief that the essential character and/or meaning of a finished work is determined by, or is a reflection of, its origin (*genesis*).[30] The genetic fallacy assumes that to know the original purpose is to understand the end-result. The ergonic fallacy, by contrast, assumes that the work (*ergon*) embodies the character of its creator; the qualities present in the completed work are assumed to have been present in the originating agent. In other words, it suggests that we can know the character of the creator, or of the creative act, from what we see in the end-result.

This fallacy has an ancient lineage, because it provides one of the oldest arguments for the existence of God — the argument from design. 'The heavens declare the glory of God', wrote the Psalmist; 'ever since God created the world', stated Paul, 'his everlasting power and deity — however invisible — have been there ... to see in the things he has made'.[31] The same idea occurred in the works of Plato and assumed central importance in both Stoic and neo-Platonic thought: the order, harmony and beauty of the heavens above (or on earth around us) was taken as evidence of an orderly, harmonious and benign first principle,[32] to which we owe our existence and in accordance with which we should conduct our lives. This idea was also applied to human artefacts, usually works of art, in a variety of ways. It could be in terms of aesthetic principles of intelligence and harmony,[33] or a matter of emotional effect,[34] or an instance of moral benefit.[35] In all cases there was the assumption that the distinct qualities of the end-product must be present in the agent in the act of making. It is of course possible that that could be the case, and that might become probable if there were independent evidence to hand (i.e. about the making distinct from the result). But without such evidence such an assumption cannot be sustained, and what we have then is the ergonic fallacy. In the twentieth century it became less common to claim (or to see) a direct relation between the person and the work,[36] but in the period with which this study is concerned the projection of the qualities of the end-result on to the originating process — in particular the assimilation of the aesthetic and the creative — was an important element in promoting an idealized view of creativity.

IV

While the noun 'creativeness' was used in English from the end of the 18th century the word 'creativity' did not appear until the late 19th century and only became common in the 20th century.[37] In French and German the nouns *créativité* and *Kreativität* only came into general use in the second half of this century, and were derived from Anglo-American usage (principally in psychology).[38] This book is not concerned with either the 20th century or modern psychology (except briefly, in Chapter 11). But that does not mean that this noun cannot be applied to previous centuries, like other terms (such as 'aesthetics' or 'ecology') which we use in discussing periods before these words existed. Though the noun 'creativity' is new, what it refers to — creative activity or ability — is not, and to use the word in this way does not seem a cause for contention.

What may give rise to difficulties is the broad span of time covered by this study. While it makes no claim to be comprehensive the book does assume that different debates, in different contexts, have been addressing a recurrent problem, and have shown striking similarities. It indicates how continuities can be seen to have existed, and suggests that awareness of these helps us to understand why certain developments in European thought took a particular form. In recent years it has become common to assert that this kind of history is no longer valid; that assumptions of continuity are wrong (and discontinuity should be the norm); that the broad view ignores (or distorts or suppresses) individual qualities; that there are no essential, persistent or universal human attributes; that past texts can be understood only within the terms of a specific and limited context; and that we should write about micro-cultures, rather than mountain peaks.

There are good arguments to support most of these claims and our understanding of the past has been much enriched by studies in which they have been applied with precision and insight. But there have been losses as well as gains; when the focus becomes too restricted it can generate a new set of problems. For the moment it is only necessary to make the following points. First, this study concentrates on, and is concerned almost entirely with, European thought; it does not assert therefore that features which it describes as recurrent or general were also universal. Second, it examines not only what certain individuals thought but the intellectual traditions within which they operated (openly or tacitly); this could of course be as much a matter of misreading (on their part) as what we might now regard as a historically more precise and accurate reading. The assumption is not that such traditions were fully coherent, or unified, (or even necessarily recognized as what we can now see as a tradition). Rather, it is that there were transmissions, influences, and debates with the dead as well as with the living. This study has dealt with earlier periods of European thought because central figures in the 18th and 19th centuries themselves referred to, and found inspiration in, such periods. Thirdly, this does not mean, however, that such continuity amounts to an implicit teleology, that the developments which occurred were in any sense inevitable or (from our perspective) desirable. On the contrary, a central theme of this book is that the new value of creativity which arose in the 19th century was possibly incoherent and certainly misleading.

Whether this study makes good its claims is, of course, an entirely different matter. To give an account of so large an issue in so condensed a form raises many obvious difficulties; it inevitably involves a degree of tunnel vision and much selection. Different readers will be conscious of different omissions. But I believe that sufficient detail has been given to a wide enough range of material to provide an account that is both well-grounded and synoptic, combining a worm's eye view with an eagle's overview. The discussion goes no further than the end of the 19th century because by then the essential features of the problem had become evident. Since that time creativity as a value has been taken for granted. The time has now come for it to be taken to pieces.

CHAPTER TWO

Creation myths and virgin birth

I

Throughout Western history there have been two sharply differentiated beliefs about the character of creativity. One of these linked the creative with the morally good. It was embodied in, and mainly transmitted by, Judaeo-Christian theology and neo-Platonic philosophy, and it came to occupy such a dominant position that the very existence of an alternative view has been obscured or ignored. Yet the evidence for this second belief is no less ancient or extensive. Since it was never formulated so coherently, nor adopted at all widely, it never came to constitute an alternative tradition as such; and inasmuch as it was not handed down or consciously invoked it might be thought not to amount to a fully fledged 'tradition'. But having existed over so long a period, and its various elements having been affirmed with such regularity, it should be seen as one — a lost tradition which needs to be recovered.

Just as the Judaeo-Christian belief is first expressed in the mythical opening chapters of the Book of Genesis, so the first evidence of the second view occurs in creation myths.[1] In most of this material we find the business of creation depicted in terms of two activities. The cosmos and subsequent new entities are produced either as a result of the sexual union of two divine creatures or as the result of some struggle or conflict, 'a disjunction which breaks the primordial conjunction'.[2] The sacred marriage is considered to be 'the most diffused mythical theme and also the most ancient';[3] and the belief in conflicts and competitions which 'promote the renovation of life' is 'an extremely archaic scenario that is universally disseminated...[and] holds a privileged place in all types of societies'.[4] The Babylonian creation myth, *Enuma Elish*, is a saga of successive struggles, and in Indo-European mythologies similar conflicts occur, Indra's victory over the dragon Urtra being their prototypical example.[5]

The presence of opposing elements in these myths can be attributed to a number of factors. The basic features of the world and human life consist of oppositions or contrasts — day/night, earth/sky, life/death, hot/cold, male/female, — and their existence has to be explained. Many societies have depended for their survival on their ability to fight; and all religious faiths have to be able to provide a plausible account of the existence of evil. But these factors, fundamental though they are, are not sufficient to explain a central aspect of these stories; for the myths not only describe the coexistence of, or relation between, the diverse elements of the world, they also describe a sequence of events. They recount how our world, defined by time and mortality, is subject to change, how there was an era before our world, and how between these two epochs the creation of new entities occurred. Such creation was an event. This means that the myth could be taken as a model for action; the replication of the original creative event could lead to new creation. Where this occurred, the myth was providing an exemplar for creative activity as such.[6]

The principal elements of these mythical events — sexuality or conflict — are also central features of the mythical characters most often associated with the performance of creative acts, namely, the trickster and the smith. Both these figures were widely regarded as culture heroes; they initiated human civilisation by bringing or stealing fire from the gods, (if not actually inventing fire themselves), and teaching people the working of fire and often agriculture as well. And both were seen as highly ambivalent. The trickster was characterized by his deceitfulness and use of cunning. His sexuality was equivocal or exorbitant, and he delighted in conflict. The Old Norse god Odin, for example, who was called 'Father of man' because it was he who had given human beings life (as well as poetry and magic), at one stage may have changed his sex; and he took pleasure above all in stirring up trouble.[7] (One of the richest sources of material about the trickster occurs in native American myths. There he is depicted as a culture hero who is 'grossly erotic, insatiably hungry, inordinately vain, deceitful and cunning,...a restless wanderer', notable for 'his unsociability, his amorality, his ability to change shape at will'.)[8]

Tricksters and smiths had much in common. The Babylonian smith-god Enki was the embodiment of cunning and at the same time he typified 'active productivity' and was therefore the god of craftsmen.[9] Smiths were involved in mining and in the mastery of fire, both of which were not only dangerous but also ambivalent activities; the first, penetrating into the geological depths, could be taken as a violation of the sacred earth, and fire could be as destructive as creative. As a maker of tools, the smith was a civilising hero, but as a maker of weapons he could be a source of destruction. Like the trickster, smiths tended to be set apart from other creatures. They were often itinerant, in search of work or raw metals, or they lived separately from the rest of the community.[10] In other words, not only did their work in some way violate the natural order, they also did not belong to the social order. Here we have perhaps the most striking analogy between the creative event and the creative character in myths. Both are regarded as essentially disruptive. The making of new life or entities or artefacts only happens through the disturbance of the status quo. This theme is most pronounced in the case of the trickster, for he overtly and deliberately opposes those gods who represent some kind of norm. And a clear connection is seen to exist between this desire for, and delight in, opposition and his inventive skills.[11]

In Greek mythology the characters associated with creativity also displayed these features. Among the Olympian gods, for example, three figures were seen as inventive — Hephaestus, Athene and Hermes. The first two were the patron god and goddess of craftsmen; together, according to Hesiod, they created Pandora, the first woman.[12] As a smith Hephaestus was seen as the inventor of fire and metal-working; on occasion he was credited with the creation of mankind.[13] Athene invented the plough and other useful implements; she helped Jason to build the Argo, Bellerophon to tame his horse, and has been described as 'the force of civilisation'.[14] (She also invented the flute, but threw it away 'in disgust at the ugly look on her face when she was playing it'.)[15] Hermes invented the lyre, the alphabet, numbers and music, as well as being credited with the origin of fire. He was the 'god of boundaries and of the transgression of boundaries'.[16]

In addition to their inventive abilities, these deities shared two characteristics. Firstly, they had an unusually close relationship with human beings. About Hermes, in the *Iliad*, Zeus comments: 'To you beyond all other gods it is dearest to be man's companion';[17] and Athene's concern for heroes, for Achilles, Heracles, and above all, Odysseus, is well known. (Hephaestus is not shown having this kind of involvement, but he, alone of all the gods, has his work compared with that of a human being — Daedalus.)[18] Secondly, all three were renowned for that inventive, resourceful and, if necessary, devious type of intelligence which the Greeks called *metis*, usually translated as cunning.[19] The essential feature of *metis* was that it was only manifest in competition or conflict; as the ability to trick or outwit it was defined largely in terms of whatever opposed it. It was therefore an inherently ambivalent quality. This was especially evident in Hermes, 'the divine trickster, a figure of everchanging colours';[20] it is he who put 'lies and wheedling words of falsehood, and a treacherous nature' into Pandora.[21] Athene was not regarded as ambivalent in this way but she was renowned for two related qualities — her delight in opposition — 'the terrible queen who loves the clash of wars and battles'[22] — and for her daring (*tolma*): 'You are audacious indeed, if truly you dare to lift up your gigantic spear in the face of your father',[23] as indeed she did. While the inventive ability of neither Athene nor Hephaestus was associated with sexuality, their *metis* was as much physical as mental. For it was an animal kind of intelligence: 'it is by drawing on experience from the animal world that *metis* can...become full of all the resources essential to it'.[24]

In addition to these Olympian gods, the Greeks also gave credit for inventions to another mythological group, the heroes. These were outstanding human beings who had lived in the era before historical time; they were honoured by individual cults as well as by athletic competitions. (The warriors of the Homeric epics and the leading figures of most Greek tragedies were heroes of this kind.) They were remembered for their unusual powers, like Heracles for his inexhaustible strength or Tiresias for his prophetic gift, and among them were the heroes who founded cities, established dynasties, and made inventions: Palamedes, inventor of the alphabet and measurement, Daedalus, inventor of images of the gods and living statues, Cadmus, inventor of letters and metallurgy, Phoroneos, inventor of fire, and Tyrrhenos, inventor of the trumpet.[25]

Invariably, the heroes were men apart.[26] They were the archetypal wanderers in the sense that they not only travelled extensively but they crossed all normal boundaries (except that of death).[27] They were often physically mis-shapen, mutilated or deformed,[28] and sometimes regarded as mad or even part-animal.[29] Their appetites were abnormal; their sexuality, for example, could be both extreme (as with Theseus and Heracles)[30] and equivocal: Achilles lived for a while as a girl, Heracles dressed as a woman, Theseus had feminine characteristics.[31] They were masters of trickery and theft;[32] in the case of Autolycus, Odysseus' grandfather, he had learnt this from Hermes himself.[33] This general ambivalence was as central to their nature as those aggressive and daring qualities for which they have always been remembered.

Among the inventors combative qualities were as pronounced as among the warriors. Palamedes and Daedalus, for example, were so intensely competitive about their skills that in each case it led to a death. The rivalry between Palamedes and Odysseus made the latter trick Palamedes into appearing sympathetic to the Trojans, so causing the Greeks to stone him to death.[34] Daedalus was so jealous of his nephew's ability — he had invented the compass and a saw from the spine of a fish — that he killed him;[35] it was because of this murder that he had to leave Athens and go to Crete.

Whatever the heroes did they did to the full. The fact that we can talk of 'fullness' with respect to them, in a way which we cannot with the gods, is due to the fact that for them there was a limit which could give such fullness a meaning. In part this was the obvious limit of mortality. But it was also the fact that being human they had the gods above them. As a result, the pursuit of the fullness which made the heroes great also put them at most risk. For no belief was more fundamental to the Greeks than that the gods were jealous of human greatness; to overstep the invisible limits of what the gods deemed permissible was to be guilty of *hybris*. The striving for excellence could easily become the mark of insolence, and with the heroes this was always the case. Of no one was this more true than the mythological figure who later came to epitomize human inventiveness — Prometheus. He shared a great deal with the other inventive figures, Olympian or heroic. Like these gods he was renowned for his cunning and for his close links with the human race. Like Hermes he was noted for his deceitfulness, like Hephaestus he is associated with fire, like Athene he was distinguished for his daring.[36] Like the heroes he was a creature apart, independent and self-willed.

Two versions of the Prometheus legend have come down to us — one in the poems of Hesiod,[37] and the other in the play (perhaps by Aeschylus) *Prometheus Bound*;[38] the latter is very similar to the version attributed by Plato to the Sophist Protagoras and it may actually have been derived from him.[39] In the first version Hesiod depicts Prometheus as a small-minded trickster whose theft of fire leads to an irrevocable breach between gods and men and is therefore the origin of all human misery. In the second version Prometheus is the heroic benefactor of mankind whose act initiates all human progress. These accounts appear to be diametrically different, and to some extent they are. In *Prometheus Bound,* for example, Zeus' victory over the Titans is only made possible by Prometheus' help, and his reign will only continue if he can learn the secret Prometheus holds about the future. Prometheus not only helps the human race, he actually saved them from destruction; and he not only brought them fire, but also hope, intelligence and the practical arts. Despite these differences, however, the two versions agree on certain facts. Both describe Prometheus as supremely cunning, full of inventive tricks and deceitful skills. Both see his gift of fire as the decisive step in bringing about the current condition of mankind, a condition where humans are able to be (or, as Hesiod would say, have to be) self-reliant. And both see Prometheus' act as done in opposition to Zeus.

This antipathy between Prometheus and Zeus is at the heart of both versions and contains the central insight of the myth. In both, the fire brings a new 'power',[40] which becomes mankind's 'grand resource', enabling them to 'master many crafts'.[41] But this power does not make humans civilized. Prometheus' gift enables people to invent language, architecture, carpentry, agriculture, metallurgy, astronomy, medicine and prophecy; but it does not bring them the ability to live together in peace. By means of it they do not gain either a moral sense or justice.[42] The whole point of the story in Protagoras' version is that humans then had to be given separately 'the qualities of respect for others and a sense of justice, so as to bring order to our cities and create a bond of friendship and union'.[43] And this gift came from Zeus. Unlike the gifts of Prometheus, which were given to specific individuals (so that one person was expert in one skill, another in another) the gift of Zeus was distributed equally; "Distribute justice to all", said Zeus. "Let all have their share. There could never be cities if only a few shared in these virtues, as in the arts"'.[44]

The play *Prometheus Bound* exalts the figure of Prometheus and portrays Zeus in a severely critical light; Hesiod, in his poems, does precisely the opposite, even going so far as to suggest that Prometheus never succeeded in outwitting Zeus. But in their different ways both confirm the version we are given by Protagoras. Because they each show the hostility between the two figures to be fundamental. (This is also how Prometheus is shown in Aristophanes' *The Birds,* as the inveterate champion of man and enemy of the gods.)[45] Prometheus the Titan is not subject to Zeus' Olympian order, and the qualities he represents, of independence, invention, deception and daring, exist in a permanently uneasy relation with the qualities which came to be associated with Zeus — justice, authority and order. Like the heroes Prometheus brings new benefits to humans but, from another point of view, he is an essentially disruptive force. Hesiod, the first Greek writer to exalt Zeus' reign as one of order and justice,[46] saw the Titans in general as insolent and hubristic,[47] and the conflict with Prometheus in this respect could be seen as merely one episode in the mythical war of the gods and the giants (in which the forces of order were always under threat from creatures of turbulent energy).[48]

At the end of *Prometheus Bound*, where Prometheus is depicted as hubristic to the point of madness,[49] he is also like one of the heroes. The most vivid portrayal of the heroic character that has come down to us (apart from the *Iliad*) is that contained in the plays of Sophocles. His heroes are fiercely independent, self-willed, and incapable of compromise or moderation.[50] They stand alone, with an unshakable belief in themselves, acutely conscious of their uniqueness. Their boldness and resolution leads others to regard them as being daring to the point of rashness and stubborn to the point of madness, more like animals in fact than ordinary men or women. These extraordinary and magnificent qualities are the mainspring of the plays' action, and the invariable cause of greater or lesser disaster.

Now we may think, reading or seeing Sophocles' plays, that his heroes are not distinctly creative (though one of them, Oedipus, has been so regarded).[51] But Sophocles undoubtedly saw a connection between the heroic character and inventive ability. The most celebrated lines he wrote, the so-called Ode to Man, address precisely this issue. 'Wonders are many on earth', the chorus begins, 'and the greatest of these is / Is man...He is master of ageless earth...He is lord of all living things...there is nothing beyond his power...Save only death'.[52] By his own resourceful discoveries man has learnt to cross the seas, till the soil and tame animals, to speak and think and live in cities. But, the chorus concludes, this 'wondrous subtlety of man', his inventive skill,[53] is not in itself beneficial. It is, in fact, ambivalent, and 'draws to good or evil ways'. It will only be for the good if it is subordinate to (or compatible with) a 'country's laws and the justice of heaven'. And the chorus condemns the person who has the recklessness, audacity or daring (*tolma*) to live 'in solitary pride (*apolis*)'. The final lines of the chorus, in other words, assert the need to reconcile two attributes, that of invention and that of law, which are not inherently harmonious.[54]

Sophocles was not merely saying, as a character in Euripidies' *Hippolytus* says,[55] or as Aristotle was to write in his *Politics*,[56] that intelligence or cleverness is of no avail unless it is accompanied by moral action. His chorus is speaking specifically about man's inventive ability which they immediately associate with a temperament which is 'daring' and prone to isolation. In making this connection they were following an established model, for heroes were always daring and men apart, and the juxtaposition of invention and daring with divine order was an echo of *Prometheus Bound*.[57] The only significant difference between the accounts of invention in the two plays is that in the chorus of *Antigone* all invention is done by humans, while in *Prometheus Bound* it comes to people from Prometheus. It is possible that it was this new suggestion of human independence, (which we have no reason to suppose was endorsed by Sophocles himself), nevertheless enabled him to formulate the problem more clearly than had hitherto been the case.

We find an even clearer statement in the work of Plato. In the myth about the origin of writing in the *Phaedrus* he depicted an Egyptian god Theuth as the inventor of arithmetic, geometry, astronomy and writing. Theuth came to the king, Ammon, with his inventions, explaining them and praising them. Above all, he praised writing:

> 'Here, O King, is a branch of learning that will make the people of Egypt wiser and improve their memories; my discovery provides a recipe for memory and wisdom'. But the king answered and said, 'O man full of arts, to one it is given to create (*tekein*) the things of art, and to another to judge what measure of harm and of profit they shall have for those that shall employ them'.

Ammon then condemns writing as a bad invention: it will make possible superficial learning, acquired 'by means of external marks' in solitude, rather than true knowledge which is reached by enquiry within, in the company of others.[58]

This myth seems to have been Plato's own invention. But when we are aware that Ammon was the Egyptian Zeus and Theuth the Egyptian Hermes we can see that he was only putting forward explicitly what had been implicit in the mythological stories of Hermes and Prometheus, or in the chorus of *Antigone*. The common Greek view of making, which we find in Aristotle[59] (and also on occasion in Plato)[60] was that value resides in the use or function and is established by the user.[61] In this passage of the *Phaedrus* the maker does not assume that value is determined by the user; on the contrary, he pronounces on the value of his invention himself. He claims to be, like Prometheus or a Sophoclean hero, *autonomos*, a law unto himself. Writing elsewhere about poets, fathers and those who make money, Plato observed that such people 'feel a complacency' about their creations (poems, sons, or wealth) and as a result cannot be trusted as judges of their own work.[62] A clear distinction must be made between making and valuing.

This distinction is also implied in another of Plato's myths, in the *Statesman*. Once the world was under the guidance of God; then all creatures lived in harmony.[63] Not only was there no conflict, there was also no sex — 'no taking of wives and begetting of children' — 'all men rose up anew into life out of the earth', for bodies are elements of disorder, chaos and evil.[64] But this harmony and order came to an end; then people had to fend for themselves in a hostile environment, and conceive and give birth to children 'by their own power'.[65] At this period, in their new time of need, they were given fire by Prometheus and the knowledge of crafts by Hephaestus and Athene.[66] These gifts, in other words, were granted to humans 'at the very time in the cycle when God was supposed to have withdrawn entirely from the world'.[67] Divine order and human creation (associated here with both conflict and sexuality) were as far removed from one another, in the cycles of the life of the world, as it was possible to be.

The most familiar application of this distinction is of course Plato's quarrel with the poets. As makers they were inherently unreliable, often producing works that were untrue or which showed injustice triumphing.[68] The impulse to innovate is itself dangerous.[69] Yet at the same time poets could be informed, authoritative and wise. To explain this disparity, Plato developed his theory of inspiration. The gap between making and valuing could be bridged if a god spoke through a poet. This notion, which was not based on the evidence or claims of poets themselves, was stated most fully in the *Phaedrus* — poetic frenzy being described as one of four kinds of divine madness.[70] But as if to ensure that this did not lead to any misapprehension, when Plato grades human activities in this work, he puts the poet low down (grade six) on the hierarchy of human occupations.[71]

The theory of inspiration answered Plato's needs provided it was accepted that the gods themselves were wise and just. But this was also problematic. For the principal evidence about the gods lay in the writings of the poets and this evidence was, to put it mildly, equivocal. Plato therefore felt it necessary to show in mythical form what he regarded as the truth about the gods, to write a creation myth about 'the grand primal works and deeds'[72] showing that the world was fundamentally and essentially the product of divine goodness. This myth, the *Timaeus,* introduced a creator figure of a kind new to Greek thought, the divine *demiourgos* or craftsman. For Plato this creature did not himself contain the true values; like the traditional Greek artisan (a word which conveys his inferior social status better than 'craftsman') he operated according to an external set of values, the divine Forms, and his work was good because of that. In the *Timaeus* itself, therefore, the distinction between making and valuing was maintained.

The perception of creativity as a problem, evidently widespread in the classical Greek world, can be seen in the Hellenistic period in various accounts of the origin and development of human civilisation. Inasmuch as they answered the question of what happened before historical time, these writings replaced the myths. Many drew on (or agreed with) Hesiod in depicting the life of primitive or natural man as happier and better than that of man once he had become civilized. Like Hesiod too, they linked the inventive capacity with the fall from innocence. The connection is rarely as clear as it is in Hesiod's portrayal of Prometheus but it is nonetheless implicit in the way the two events are described. For the ambition, greed and desire for individual distinction (*philotimia*) which leads to the disruption of the original egalitarian contentment is also a principal characteristic of those who are inventive.[73]

Seneca, for example, takes issue with Posidonius' account of this process when the latter maintains that the first inventors were wise men. Since people originally enjoyed all nature in common, without any competition, how could the developments which ended such a condition be a product of wisdom?[74] The invention of the arts, mechanical tools and agriculture were all identical with greed and the desire to possess everything for oneself.[75] Human invention was therefore the product of cunning (*sagacitas*) not wisdom (*sapientia*);[76] it made use of reason, perhaps, but not 'right reason'.[77] And Seneca juxtaposed the inventor and the moralist in exactly the way Hesiod or Plato might have done: 'how, I ask you, can you consistently admire both Diogenes and Daedalus?'[78] To reconcile the two was inconceivable.

Among the texts which have come down to us, one of the fullest versions of the origin of civilisation is the Epicurean account given by Lucretius in his *On the Nature of Things*. Epicurus was a resolute opponent of Plato. For him there was neither eternal order nor an immortal soul. The visible world is the product of chance, not design, and human reason 'is wholly dependent on the senses';[79] the soul is dependent on the body and therefore, like the body, is mortal. Gods do exist but they have no connection with our lives and are quite indifferent to our fate. Epicurus saw the gods in the same way as Plato, as being blessed, immortal and orderly: 'nothing suggestive of conflict or disquiet is compatible with an immortal or blessed nature'.[80] For this very reason, however, they could have no interest in our disorderly world.

By adopting the philosophers' view of the gods but at the same time refusing to allow that to prevail over his sense of terrestrial and human reality, Epicurus was able to retain the insights of the creation myths. That is to say, he portrayed the world as the product of continual change and conflict, a condition which Lucretius described as 'balanced strife'.[81] An infinite variety of atoms, in ceaseless motion, combine and disperse in a more or less random way. Although there are certain regularities in this process, it follows no design or order. But out of this disorder comes renewal and innovation. Matter in its dynamic interaction with other matter is (in Lucretius' words) 'generative' and 'creative'.[82] Coherent life is not the result of divine ideas being imposed on recalcitrant nature, but, on the contrary, it arises up out of the earth itself. The same process occurs in the formation of worlds, the development of animals, and human invention. In this account Epicurus could be seen as reworking the myth of the battle of the gods and the giants, taking the side of the earth-born giants against the gods in the sky, and opposing his materialism to the idealism of Plato (who in his *Sophist* had given this myth his own philosophical reading).[83]

For Epicurus, human arts and societies arose in various ways — as a result of chance, or trial and error, or from the observation of nature, or by invention. Fire and metal-working were discovered first by chance and then by trial and error;[84] arboriculture and music arose from copying nature.[85] Language developed from spontaneous reactions which were then, as it were, combined (like atoms) to make coherent and mutually comprehensible sounds;[86] in describing this process Lucretius compared early man with children and animals,[87] thus making the greatest possible contrast to the Platonic law- and language-giver. In all cases the practical experience came first and the 'inventiveness' second.[88] 'Necessity is the mother of invention' is a quintessentially Epicurean proverb. This is not to deny human creativity, for there were individuals who were outstandingly gifted — 'pre-eminent in genius (*ingenium*) and strong in mind'.[89] But they in turn were not animated by any principle of order. On the contrary, they were selfish men who became the first kings, appropriating power for themselves, founding cities and building there a citadel 'for their own protection and refuge'.[90]

Epicurus' principal concern was how to attain tranquillity of mind. It is no surprise therefore that in the summary of his views given by Diogenes Laertius he is described as being as opposed to creative activities, like taking part in politics or writing poetry, as he was opposed to falling in love.[91] But in a number of ways his philosophy incorporated elements of, or conditions for, human creativity which were to be of immense subsequent importance.

In the first place, Epicurus asserted the existence of human freedom. Our lives are neither subject to an overarching divine order nor confined by the mechanisms of a deterministic world. Where such a belief in freedom is combined with an emphasis on change, as was the case, there can be a central role for human creation: for the human realm may then be what human beings make of it. Since there is no absolute justice, no 'true' language, no permanent archetype of any kind, the activities of people themselves can be decisive in the formation of their world. Secondly, in pursuing these activities humans are never looking to the heavens for inspiration, nor are they trying to keep their minds pure from contamination by the senses. There is nothing in the heavens to inspire us, we belong on this earth; and our senses are not our enemies but an integral and valuable part of us. Emotions, said Epicurus, are 'no hindrance to wisdom'.[92] In the pursuit of mental tranquillity he did advocate a life of moderate austerity rather than the life of *l'homme moyen sensuel*. But his insistence on the physicality of human existence — we are our bodies and there is no part of us that will survive the death of our bodies — amounted to a rejection of the spiritual as having overriding priority.

In this emphasis on the physical, Epicurus was of course retaining one feature of the mythological writings. The third significant aspect of his philosophy (as far as this subject is concerned) was the retention of another mythological belief: the productive power of disorder and conflict. This theme of the myths had also been important to Heraclitus and Empedocles. For the first 'war is father and king of all', for the second the two 'equal and coeval' opposing forces of Love and Strife brought into being (by combining or separating the four basic elements) the whole visible world.[93] But neither of these philosophies survived in a comprehensive enough form to be influential. The vivid account of Epicurus' ideas given by Lucretius, on the other hand, expressed this mythological belief with remarkable power. This poem, together with the discussion of Epicurean ideas in various other texts, transmitted Epicurus' thought in a coherent and appealing (or threatening) form. His philosophy was not specifically concerned with creativity. But embedded in it were assumptions and beliefs about this attribute (or process) which reflected the view that had been held in the Greek world since the earliest time.[94] In this perspective, creativity was connected with disorder, conflict and physicality, with the daring, the unsociable and the amoral. These were the ingredients of what became the lost tradition.

II

When we turn from creation myths to Judaeo-Christian theology we find a complete contrast. In the former it is very common to find a three-stage sequence: first, primordial chaos or formlessness, then the division or separation of this initial state into different and opposing elements which by their combination or antagonism generate many (if not all) the features of the visible universe, and finally, an ordering of these features. In the Book of Genesis, on the other hand, we have a single process. Nothing existed before God; there was no chaos from which he emerged or which he had to conquer. He divided light from darkness and then created the visible world; and this world was, by virtue of being his creation, at once orderly. Seven times we read: 'And God saw that it was good'. There were no unruly elements until man himself disobeyed God's command. The creative act is wholly unphysical, being conducted purely by speaking. Apart from the sound of a voice all we know of God is that the voice is male;[95] in the words of the Psalmist, 'He spoke, and it was created'.[96] Although at one point man is said to be created in God's image and likeness,[97] this deity refuses to be defined by any specific attribute (except in being male) or even by a name — 'I am who I am'.[98] He is utterly remote and unphysical — 'Yahweh reigns transcendent in the heights'[99] — and he forbade any physical representations of himself which might lead people to suppose otherwise.

The second account of creation in Genesis is less extreme.[100] There the creative act is a physical making, in which Yahweh 'formed' Adam (like a potter) out of the female *adamah* (earth); he then 'breathed' life into him and 'planted' a garden. Over the last hundred years scholars have uncovered a number of passages in the Old Testament which are similar to other Near Eastern creation myths.[101] In this material Yahweh does have to fight the battle against chaos and overcome unruly elements; and he can also be seen to have some of the ambivalent and contradictory qualities we find in the second stage of other myths.

However, these elements are all marginal to the portrait of Yahweh which the Old Testament presents. The first Genesis story of creation is in fact later than the second account, but this first version became the foundation of Jewish teaching about their God. In this teaching there was no place for any ambivalence. The Old Testament is a record of the words and deeds of God and the related behaviour of the Jews. The Covenant between Yahweh and his chosen people is that if they obey his commandments he will enable them to flourish and prosper. As the story of Abraham's sacrifice of Isaac indicates, the obedience has to be total. But this can only be acceptable if Yahweh is omnipotent, because only then can he be certain to perform his side of the Covenant. This is the underlying meaning of Yahweh's 'jealousy'. It is not merely a worshipper's defection that is bad; it is the recognition that other gods exist. How 'wrong' such gods may be is not the danger; it is their existence as possible rivals, in terms of power, that poses the threat. The monotheistic creation provides a guarantee of Yahweh's potency and thus underpins the Covenant in the most formidable and plausible way. (While this monotheism is now seen as not being exclusive, any *de facto* recognition of other gods did not compromise the *de jure* theology which placed Yahweh in a category of his own.)

Yahweh possessed a monopoly of power, and also a monopoly of justice. Yet it could happen that a good and devout person did not flourish in the way which was promised. This problem was confronted in the Book of Job and the solution presented there shows the extent to which Yahweh's creation is just *because* it is his creation. The orthodox explanation for suffering — God is just and no one who is good ever suffers — does not satisfy Job. As his sufferings continue and his refusal to accept this doctrine persists, Yahweh is eventually forced to provide an explanation himself. And he does so by a series of questions which all stress the authority he derives from the fact that he is Creator:

Where were you when I laid the earth's foundations?... Who decided the dimensions of it, do you know?...Who laid its cornerstone when all the stars of morning were singing with joy?... Who pent up the sea behind closed doors?... Has the rain a father? Who begets the dewdrops? What womb brings forth the ice and gives birth to the frost of heaven?... Have you grasped the celestial laws? Could you make their writ run on earth?[102]

The attitude implicit in this passage had previously been expressed in the Book of Isaiah, where a comparison of God and a potter leads to the statement: 'Is the potter no better than the clay? Can something that is made say of its maker "He did not make me?"'[103] In other words, right belongs to the creator by virtue of his creating, and the justice of the world is secured by the fact that God created it. Yahweh is both creator and judge; he embodies a complete identity of creativity and morality.

No such identity occurred in Greek religion — Zeus represented justice, he was not creative[104] — but something similar featured in later Greek thought, taking different forms in Stoicism and neo-Platonism. Stoic philosophy was pantheist, depicting the universe as animated and shaped by an immanent force which was variously described as 'god', 'reason (*logos*)', 'fire', 'breath', or '*demiourgos*'.[105] This source of life, intelligence and order was wholly impersonal, but in human beings it assumed a personal form inasmuch as each of us has the faculty of reason. 'You are a fragment of God', stated Epictetus, 'and have divine power within you'.[106] Our task, therefore, should be to shape our lives according to reason. The creative force of life in general should become the active principle of each individual life, imposing or distilling order, coherence and harmony. A wise man is a 'maker (*artifex*)', wrote Seneca, who works to 'make and form' himself in order to achieve a good life.[107] Although this process was sometimes compared to the work of a sculptor,[108] the end-result was not distinctly individual, (nor was it concerned with aesthetic effect, as we can see from other comparisons like that of a carpenter working on timber or a cobbler on leather).[109] The purpose was moral, and the end-result was a realisation of the universal in the particular. As such, this process was not 'creative' in the sense defined above (p.9), since it introduced nothing distinctly new. But this Stoic association of an animating and forming power with the morally good came to play a part in the emergence of an idealized view of human creativity.

Far more influential, on this issue, was neo-Platonism. While for Plato the *demiourgos* of the *Timaeus* was a maker who worked according to external and pre-existing Forms, his later followers collapsed the distinction between making and valuing. First, the Ideas on which the world was modelled were seen as not being external but present in the mind of the *demiourgos*;[110] then, the cosmology of the *Timaeus* was transformed by Plotinus into a single all-embracing system, with neither pre-existing Forms nor chaotic matter. All reality, visible and invisible, was an emanation from a supreme One, in a vast descending chain of being. The transcendent One, 'perfect because it seeks nothing, has nothing, and needs nothing, overflows, as it were',[111] and this overflowing produced an Other; that

Other is Intellect or Mind (*Nous*), pure, intuitive thought, which also overflowed to produce Soul (*Psyche*), which in turn overflowed to produce the universe, nature and the whole visible world, including man. The more remote any being is from the One the less unity it will have and the less good it will be. At the extreme point the lack of goodness becomes evil, but this evil is in no way a positive or independent force. It is simply the absence of the good.

By making the multiple creatures of the visible world all aspects of an eternal One, Plotinus brought about as complete an identification of creation and order as already existed in Judaism. It is true that the neo-Platonic One was not, strictly speaking, a creator figure and that any emphasis on creativity as such was highly qualified. The emanation of the supreme One was neither willed, nor chosen, nor desired; it was a purely spontaneous overflowing, resulting from the One's inherent abundance. The emanations of the Soul, which produce the visible universe and man, may seem similar to what we would call creation,[112] but for Plotinus any activity directed outwards is less good than contemplation, and any product is inferior to the cause of its existence. The perfect One was seen much more as the goal of our striving than as the origin of all life. But while the emphasis was different from the Creator in Genesis the effect was the same, order being seen not as the end-result but as the very spirit of creation. 'All things when they come to perfection produce', wrote Plotinus.[113]

In Christianity elements of Judaism, Stoicism and neo-Platonism became fused. The Judaic view of creation was explicitly adopted by Paul in the hymn he wrote (or quoted) in his Letter to the Colossians,[114] and Paul also introduced a number of Stoic ideas into the new religion; (Tarsus had been a centre of Stoicism). From the mid-second century, and the writings of Justin Martyr, Christian theologians made increasing use of both Platonic metaphysics and Stoic ethics. The result of this process was a view of the Creator which came to combine the poetic power of the Book of Genesis with the philosophical attractions of Platonism after Plato. The few ambivalences of the Old Testament portrait of God, and certain crucial aspects of the process of creation described in the *Timaeus*, were overlooked in the pursuit of theological consistency. In their arguments against the Gnostics the Christian fathers elaborated a clearer doctrine of creation *ex nihilo* than any that had previously existed, putting forward a view of a Creator who had had no contact with any Other, nor any need of any Other. Unity and spirituality were paramount.

The problem of reconciling this belief with the apparently incompatible doctrine of the Incarnation was met by the idea of the Virgin

Birth. In its first appearance in Christian writings, in the Gospels of Matthew and Luke, the Virgin Birth was seen as the fulfilment of an Old Testament prophecy and it served to establish the continuity of the new religion with Judaism. When Christianity expanded beyond the Jewish community to cover Gentiles as well, this belief ceased to be incidental and became virtually a theological necessity. If in the process of taking on human flesh and blood God had lost his essential unity and purity he would have ceased to have been the Creator. The doctrine of the Virgin Birth preserved him from this danger, and can be seen in this way to have become as integral to the faith as the Incarnation itself. In time, Greek thought came to provide valuable support on this matter, for parthenogenesis was (in effect) a central feature of neo-Platonism. With such impressive philosophical arguments the Virgin Birth of Jesus could be distinguished from alleged virgin births in other religions.[115] In this manner a family event in a remote village of a minor province on the edge of the Roman Empire could be combined with the most far-reaching claims to universality.

III

The contrast between these two traditions — of which the dominant one could be called the tradition of a Creator, and the lost one the tradition of creativity — could be summarized by the following list:

Creator	*Creativity*
Unity	Multiplicity
Stability	Change
Order	Disorder
Harmony	Conflict
Spirituality	Physicality/Sexuality

When presented in this way we can see how closely the first tradition reflects the moral philosophies of Platonism, Stoicism and Christianity. The identity of the creative and the good was indeed the outstanding characteristic of this tradition.

Where such an identity occurred there was always the problem of explaining the existence of evil and injustice. This difficulty, which had been vividly dramatised in the Book of Job, appears constantly in discussions of Stoicism,[116] neo-Platonism and, above all, Christianity. In the Gospel portrait of Jesus the divine goodness had become palpable. How such a good God could have created a world so manifestly deficient in goodness now became even more glaring a difficulty than it had been before. 'Either God wishes to take away the evil from this world and he cannot; or he can and does not wish to; or he neither wishes to nor can; or he both wishes to and can', but does not.[117] From whichever angle the problem was confronted there seemed no way in which it was possible to overcome the fundamental difficulty caused by making the Creator the source also of the Good.

This incoherence reveals how unsatisfactory the tradition of the Creator could be as moral doctrine. But it was equally unsatisfactory as a doctrine of creation; for we also find in this tradition an active hostility to human creativity. In the opening chapters of Genesis, for example, there are four episodes which provoke Yahweh's anger. Three of these can be seen to be related to creativity, and they do so in the terms of the alternative (lost) tradition.

The story of the Fall, for example, has two elements which also occur in pagan myths associated with creation. The first is the link that is made between sexuality and innovation; through sexual experience a decisive development takes place. (For a similar Near Eastern text we have the Babylonian Book of Gilgamesh; there Enkiddu passes from animal ignorance to human knowledge by spending a week with a prostitute.)[118] The second (pagan) mythological feature lies in the resemblance of the serpent to a trickster. He is noted for his subtlety, his ability to deceive and his opposition to the existing order; and what he brings to humans is the gift of civilisation. For it is generally agreed that the knowledge which the tree provides is not narrowly moral, as the translation 'of good and evil' suggests, but is knowledge in general.[119]

Furthermore, the serpent says, and Yahweh repeats, that eating the apple makes the humans 'like Gods'.[120] Now the principle characteristic of God, up to this point in the narrative, is precisely his ability to create. What Yahweh wants to withhold from the humans is not a knowledge of general categories, but a knowledge of specific action. In Rabbinical exegesis this was recognized. According to one classical Rabbinic text, what the serpent said was: 'God ate of this tree and then created the world and therefore he orders you not to eat from it, so that you cannot create other worlds; for everyone hates his fellow-craftsman'.[121]

The second episode that provokes Yahweh's wrath is Cain's murder of Abel. This was provoked by God's preferring Abel's sacrifice to Cain's, an event for which no reason is given and which has been the subject of much bewilderment. We do know, however, that even before the murder

Cain was looked on unfavourably. Now Cain's name can mean 'smith' or 'worker in metal',[122] and his descendants are associated with human invention. Jubal was 'the ancestor of all who play the lyre and the flute', and Tubal-cain was 'the ancestor of all metalworkers, in bronze or iron'.[123] None of these skills was regarded with approval. On the contrary, this was the line from Adam which did not lead to Yahweh's protection. Cain was condemned to be 'a fugitive and a wanderer over the earth',[124] and the list of his descendants ends with the ferocious Song of Lamech. This is immediately followed by the contrasting story of the birth of Seth. He is described as being in Adam's 'likeness, as his image',[125] as being 'the first to invoke the name of Yahweh',[126] and he was the ancestor of Noah and the patriarchs. In him and his descendants lay the path of righteousness; with Cain and his descendants came both invention and immorality.[127]

The list of the patriarchs who descended from Seth ends with Noah and his family. There then occurs the cryptic story of 'the sons of God'. These angelic beings looked on 'the daughters of men, saw they were pleasing, [and] so they married as many as they chose'; they then had children by them, who 'are the heroes of days gone by, the famous men'.[128] As given in these verses, this episode is enigmatic and obscure, although its function is clear because it immediately precedes the story of the Flood. Whatever the episode involves it is undoubtedly an example of that 'wickedness of man' (mentioned in the following sentence) which causes Yahweh to try and destroy human beings altogether.

In the apocryphal Book of Enoch a full account of this episode provides an explanation. Like the story of the Fall it brings together disobedience, sexual experience and new knowledge. The 'sons of God' were angels who desired beautiful women, took them as wives and then 'taught them charms and spells...and the cutting of roots and trees',[129] how 'to make swords...and bracelets and ornaments...and all kinds of coloured dyes. And the world was changed. And there was great impiety and much fornication. And they went astray'.[130] From these angels human beings learnt agriculture, metal-working and writing,[131] 'the eternal secrets which were made in heaven'.[132] It is because of this transmission to humans of the knowledge of creativity that 'the earth and those who dwell upon it will be destroyed'.[133]

The final episode to provoke Yahweh's wrath is the building of the Tower of Babel. Human skill and ambition — 'let us build ourselves a town and a tower with its top reaching heaven. Let us make a name for ourselves'[134] — are punished severely. This episode does not have the close association with creativity evident in the previous three episodes. About this event therefore it is reasonable to suggest that the cause of divine punishment is man's desire to 'assert his independence from God', 'to overstep the limits of his creatureliness'.[135] But to interpret the other episodes, and in particular the Fall itself in these terms is surely wrong. The cause of the Fall is much more specific. What Yahweh displays is the cause of morality and order stamping out that particular form of independence which is endemic to creativity.[136] The Old Testament theology, as set out in Deuteronomy, is based on obedience: 'obedience leads to blessing...disobedience calls forth curse'.[137] Where such a belief prevails there is no place for the quality we always find associated with the tradition of creativity — daring. Obedience and daring are diametrically opposed.

The hostility we see in the Book of Genesis also occurs in neo-Platonism and Christianity. 'The beginning of evil', wrote Plotinus, 'was daring (*tolma*) and coming to birth and the first otherness'.[138] For Augustine, likewise, daring was one of the fatal flaws of human nature.[139] Both Plotinus and Augustine insisted that the Creator was not like a human craftsman,[140] and both were opposed to human creativity. Plotinus rejected Plato's teaching in the *Symposium* that human love can be productive.[141] Augustine went so far as to deny human parents even the ability to create children; all they do is make use of powers which are given by God and depend entirely on God.[142] The existence of the Creator deprives human beings of their own creativity. In other words, Judaic, neo-Platonic and Christian writings reveal the same incompatibility between creativity and morality which was a feature of what has been termed here the tradition of creativity. *Both* traditions show these human attributes to be problematic in relation to one another. Wherever the emphasis falls on order then creativity is a threat, wherever the emphasis falls on creativity then order is an obstacle. The tradition of the Creator in this way can be seen to confirm the central theme of the alternative tradition. Neither the historical triumph of Christianity nor the philosophical triumph of the sons of Plato could in the long run obscure this alternative view.

CHAPTER THREE

The lion, the fox, and celestial harmony

I

In the classical world we can see at least three distinct ideals of human life and behaviour; for the sake of simplicity they could be called the heroic, the civic, and the Stoic. The heroic ideal was one of individual excellence in action, in order to obtain lasting personal fame. The civic ideal was one of public action, to win honour among fellow-citizens and glory for the republic. The Stoic ideal was for individual goodness and contentment, achieved by detachment from worldly affairs and by living in accord with certain ethical values, established by philosophical reasoning. Since this ideal tended to favour a contemplative rather than active life, and the values determining behaviour were regarded as universal and unchanging, it gave little scope for creativity. With the other two ideals, however, the opposite was the case, since both were realized by individuals in action against the unpredictable and unknown.

The heroic ideal, the central theme of the Homeric poems, was to achieve pre-eminence — 'Be always best in battle, and pre-eminent above all others'[1] — winning fame either by brilliant action in combat or (as 'a speaker of words')[2] by brilliant advice in an assembly. In the *Iliad* Achilles and Odysseus provide vivid examples of these two activities; in the *Odyssey* we see further how Odysseus' gifts as a speaker are one aspect of an acute mental agility. In each case, however, outstanding ability was problematic. Achilles' pre-eminence in strength, swiftness and daring (*tharsos* or *tolma*) was generally recognized. But the temperament which made his extraordinary achievements possible also made him personally impossible. The mainspring of the *Iliad* lies precisely in this — his sense of his own superiority and his demand that that should be acknowledged, especially by the commander Agamemnon. His fierce pride could not be contained within a code of *primus inter pares*; he had to be *primus super omnes*. This made him 'a dangerous man'[3] even before the death of Patroclus turned him into the 'inhuman', 'mad', 'savage' creature of Books Twenty, Twenty-One and Twenty-Two.[4] In making his choice for a short, glorious life, rather than a long, contented one, for fame rather than happiness, Achilles demonstrated human greatness in one of its most magnificent forms. But it was obtained only at great cost to others.

Odysseus is in many ways the counterpart and complement to

Achilles, defeating his opponents by quick thinking rather than bold action. Where the epithet for Achilles is 'swift-footed', that for Odysseus is 'inventive' or 'resourceful (*polymechanos*)'.[5] But this attribute can also be seen as somewhat equivocal; for to a great extent it is a matter of cunning (*metis*), deceit and trickery. Odysseus could make 'false things...like true sayings', and excelled all others in his 'cunning' and his 'crafty designs'.[6] He is constantly assisted by Athene, who is 'renowned among all the gods for cunning and craftiness'.[7] On account of his strength and daring Achilles was compared to a lion;[8] Odysseus' cunning was an ability he shared with the fox.[9] Together, the qualities of these two animals epitomised the heroic ideal and they were celebrated as such by Pindar: 'In the stress of fight he is like in soul to the boldness (*tolma*) of wild-roaring lions, / While he is like to a fox in craft (*metis*)'.[10]

The original heroes were isolated or wandering individuals, fighting for their lives; the subject of this poem by Pindar, however, was merely the winner of a chariot-race. With the passing of the age of heroes, and the rise of the city-state, the heroic ideal had to be subordinated to a new set of values, those promoting co-operation. The new kind of shared freedom made possible by the city-state was threatened by the pursuit of individual glory, and the competitive instinct was channelled into non-political activities, like athletics. In the name of the polis Solon castigated all kinds of excess and any ambition directed to private ends.[11]

Nevertheless, while the civic ideal was hostile to the heroic, it also needed it and drew on it. Internally and externally the city-state faced change and uncertainty and so required qualities of imagination and invention, cunning and daring.[12] It is no surprise therefore that among the outstanding politicians of fifth-century Athens were some who had much in common with the Homeric figures, and displayed similarly problematic qualities. Themistocles, for example, possessed remarkable qualities of imagination or foresight; he had, wrote Thucydides, 'a natural genius', and it was 'through force of genius and by rapidity of action [that] this man was supreme at doing precisely the right thing at precisely the right moment'.[13] In addition, he was so versatile and made such use of trickery against both Persians and Spartans, that he won a reputation as a second Odysseus.[14] Accompanying these gifts, however, was an immense ambition, 'no one ever had more ambition (*philotimia*) than Themistocles' . He was therefore, like Achilles, 'a dangerous man',[15] threatening the ever-fragile stability of the city. As a result, less than ten years after the victory he had masterminded at Salamis he was ostracised.

Even more dangerous was the outstanding politician of the final decades of the century — Alcibiades — a man of charismatic charm and undisputed brilliance, superb orator and unrivalled strategist.[16] But he had 'a quality in him that was beyond the normal, [which] showed itself both in the lawlessness of his private life and habits, and in the spirit in which he acted on all occasions. [People] thought that he was aiming at becoming a tyrant'.[17] In Aristophanes' *Frogs* he was referred to as 'a lion in the state'.[18] More than anyone else he was responsible for the disastrous Sicilian expedition; before that had come to an end he had defected to the Spartans, then gone over to the Persians, and then returned to Athens on his own terms Wherever he was he could appear to belong, because 'he could assimilate and adapt himself to the pursuits and the manner of living of others, and submit himself to more startling transformations than a chameleon' . He was in fact 'able to associate with good and bad alike'.[19]

This problem of the way in which great gifts generate their own imperative and go beyond conventional categories also occurs in Thucydides' *History*. In this work the Athenian character is described in terms very similar to those used of Themistocles and Alcibiades. The Athenians were driven by restlessness, ambition, and desire for novelty;[20] their dominant position stemmed from their willingness to take risks, face danger and go to war;[21] from their insight, skill and judgement in assessing situations,[22] and their swiftness and daring in action.[23] But their inability to curb their ambition or restrain their impulse to action led to their undoing. It was by appealing to precisely these qualities that Alcibiades won support for the expedition to Sicily which led to the city's downfall.[24] What had made Athens great came to be an incurable problem.

With the subsequent decline of the city-state and development of philosophy an entirely different problem about political action arose — its inaccessibility to, or inconsistency with, systematic thought. In the name of the latter Plato envisaged a good political order as one which allowed no scope for invention. We can see in his writings the central features of the Stoic ideal take shape: the judgement of all thought and conduct according to timeless and universal norms, the exaltation of unity and harmony, and the subordination of any qualities not compatible with reason. While the heroic ideal was obtained in the conflict of battle, and the civic ideal was fired by the 'beneficial rivalry' of fellow-citizens,[25] the Stoic ideal was one of purely internal struggle, a battle of reason and virtue against instinct and pleasure. From such a perspective, public life became at best a distraction, at worst an arena where opinion masqueraded as knowledge and rhetoricians — 'chameleons...players acting their part in public life'[26] — misled an ever-gullible public.

Since Aristotle did not share Plato's concern for unity and harmony, but saw life essentially as action, he had none of the same hostility to politics, and his writings contain a notable account of the civic ideal. His account of 'practical wisdom' recognised an element of amoral 'cleverness', and a need for the kind of foresight shown by certain animals.[27] His *Rhetoric* likewise dealt with matters of probability and expediency in an entirely uncensorious way. Yet in the final resort Aristotle also gave priority to the life of contemplation, conceiving of his god as a philosopher. This was not only because practical affairs are always changeable and so cannot achieve either the timelessness or self-sufficiency which alone can satisfy reason. It was also because of the inescapably elusive character of politics. 'Politicians seem to [act] by dint of a certain skill and experience rather than of thought; for they are not found either writing or speaking about [their art]...nor are they found to have made statesmen of their own sons or any other of their friends. But it was to be expected that they should if they could'.[28]

The life of action is not susceptible to the kind of description applicable to other activities. Not only is a large part played by 'skill and experience' — imagination, courage or cunning — but a successful action consists in individual decisions and specific acts which have an ad hoc character; they are cumulative but non-sequential. In other words, the decisions and acts do not relate to the end-result either in the way a chain of reasoning leads to a philosophical conclusion, or in the way a work of art may be seen as the realisation of certain intentions or aesthetic principles. In the first place, while the end-result could not have been achieved without the previous acts, other courses of action might have been taken to produce the same result; in the second place, the end-result of the action does not reflect or embody the process by which it was achieved. This makes such action, to use the terminology Aristotle himself employed in his *Poetics*, historical rather than philosophical (see below, p.56).[29]

Fleeting though it is, Aristotle's identification of this problem is of great significance, for it alerts us to the fact that creativity in action will tend to be ignored by philosophers. To discover its character we will need to rely on poets or historians or, in the ancient world, writers on rhetoric. The latter were also prone to a certain degree of idealisation, inventing the myth that orators were the founders of civil society (a role previously claimed by poets),[30] but their works do communicate an awareness of what cannot be incorporated into neat categories of thought. For example, although Isocrates put forward the idealised view that good discourse is the product of a good soul, (a position later taken to the extreme by Quintilian),[31] he was also the author of an important and influential statement of the *disunity* of the agent and the work: 'the roots of literature are bitter, but the fruits are sweet'.[32] The counterpart of this remark was the notion of the orator as actor, an idea which taken up by Cicero in terms which seem like a direct reply to the strictures of Plato (quoted above): 'orators...are the players that act real life' and they should make use of emotions like actors.[33] Since rhetoric in politics and in law was practised in an adversarial manner, there was also a persistent emphasis among such writers on the invigorating effects of rivalry and conflict.[34] This was often described in terms of emulation, but the line between emulation and envy was a thin one,[35] and the final speaker in Tacitus' *Dialogue on orators* depicts eloquence as being inimical to good qualities, like 'probity or modesty', but being instead 'the product of licence...and companion of sedition'.[36]

Romans writing about their own history also commented on the amorality of the drive for novelty or glory. Sallust observed that human beings seemed to be prey to an ineradicable vice in the form of a 'restless and uncontainable impulse which fights for freedom or glory or power over others'.[37] And while Cicero did his utmost to merge the civic ideal with notions of harmony and rational conduct, he also noted that 'it is in the greatest souls and in the most brilliant geniuses that we usually find ambitions for civil and military authority, for power and glory, springing up'. And 'from this...greatness of spirit all too readily spring self-will and an excessive lust for power...The more notable a man is for his greatness of spirit, the more ambitious he is to be the foremost citizen or...sole ruler'.[38]

With the collapse of the republic and the triumph of Augustus the civic ideal became a lost cause. Although historians continued to write accounts of its past triumphs, the rhetoricians retired to the lawcourts and schoolroom, and the stoic ideal came to predominate. In time it merged with the religious values of Christianity. The first significant break away from those values in the early modern period came in Italy in the 12th and 13th centuries. For with the emergence of the Italian city-states, the rediscovery of writings by Aristotle, Cicero and republican historians, and the revival of the study of Roman law, came a new assertion of the civic ideal. In the work of Brunetto Latini we read again the myth of the founding of society by supremely gifted orators[39] and the statement that government by the people is 'far better' than either kingship or aristocracy.[40] This indicated a decisive change. Instead of authority and legitimacy descending from God to a divinely appointed ruler, who then announced laws in conformity with divine (or natural) law, Latini placed authority in the people. In the next generation Marsilio of Padua placed the origin of justice there too.

Marsilio's *Defender of Peace* (1324), which owed much both to his reading of Aristotle and to his knowledge of political life in Padua, amounted to a thorough-going and exclusively secular defence of human action. Seeing that there was no way of settling the endless quarrel of Papacy and Empire, Church and State, unless the terms of the argument were removed from the theological domain, Marsilio insisted that laws obtain their value not as reflections of some higher truth but as the result of the people legislating for themselves. The law which 'each citizen seems to have imposed on himself' is the one which is most likely to be effective, and this will be the case with 'the law which is made through the hearing and command of the entire multitude of the citizens'.[41] When the citizens command, the law takes effect. Throughout his work Marsilio's emphasis is on human agency, on the 'moving', 'acting', 'making', 'productive', or what he calls (following Aristotle) the 'efficient' cause. Whereas the law spoken by kings, being modelled on the law which came from God, was 'given', law in Marsilio's terms is always 'made'.[42] By this insistence on human action, and his rejection of any universal claim of 'right' superior to the republic's law, Marsilio revived the essential features of the classical civic ideal.

In the following century this ideal received eloquent expression from a number of Florentine writers among them Leonardo Bruni, Matteo Palmieri and Leon Battista Alberti. The opportunities for action which had been praised in Greece and Rome were reiterated and acclaimed. 'It is marvellous', declared Bruni in 1428, 'to see how the access to public office, once it is offered to a free people, proves to be in awakening the talents of the citizens. For where men are given the hope of attaining honour in the state, they take courage and raise themselves to a higher plane'.[43] Alberti, likewise, praised the active life of the republic and, in connection with this ideal, drew on Cicero (citing Aristotle) to compare man to 'a happy, mortal god, understanding and acting with reason and virtue'.[44]

But the revival of this notion brought with it an awareness of endemic problems. In his *Defender of Peace* Marsilio quoted Cicero's comments about the uncertain direction of great ambition,[45] and he distinguished between those who discovered or invented and those who should judge, a distinction which recaptured the Greek view that the maker should not himself establish the value of what he had made (p.19).[46] In Florence there were those who saw the opportunity for public office not as a good, but as the principal cause of discord and evil;[47] and Bruni, in his *Histories of the Florentine people*, noted how the introduction of liberty had also opened the door to envy, contention and mistrust.[48] The prevalence of suspicion and deceit in public life was a central element of the attack on the civic ideal voiced by Alberti's elderly uncle in his *On the Family*.[49]

Writers concerned more narrowly with rhetoric likewise drew attention to problematic aspects of human agency. To give just two examples: Petrarch, who struggled with the difficulty of reconciling his secular ambition for fame as a poet with the otherworldly values of Christianity, referred to the 'vileness of origins', the relation that existed between 'foul roots and leafy trees', between 'the foulest dung and abundant crops'.[50] Lorenzo Valla, who made the most thoroughgoing attempt to revive rhetoric as an alternative to (scholastic and Stoic) philosophy, celebrated the benefits of rivalry, seeing invention and excellence as the product of the competition and fight for honour.[51] In his dialogue *On Pleasure* (1431-33), a rehabilitation of the emotions (both using and attacking the ideas of Epicurus) and a polemic for seeing God as essentially active, he also praised the benefits of conflict.[52]

Perhaps the most striking example of the way in which an emphasis on invention and action was accompanied by a sense of ambivalence occurs in Giannozzo Manetti's *On the dignity and excellence of man* (1452/3). Manetti was both an outstanding scholar (translating from the Greek and Hebrew) and a leading citizen in Florence; he gave the funeral oration for Leonardo Bruni and held a variety of official positions.[53] His treatise *On the dignity...* was notable for its assertions of the 'excellent powers' of the human mind, 'as the invention and understanding of many prodigious and great deeds and mechanisms bear witness'.[54] The beauty of the human physique is matched by the subtlety and brilliance of human genius, so that 'after the first initial rough creation of the world everything seems to have been invented, accomplished and completed by us, out of the unique and outstanding sharpness of the human mind. For those things are ours, that is to say, are human, which are perceived as being produced by men'. As evidence Manetti listed human constructions, arts and sciences, ending with the invention of different languages and 'all the mechanical inventions, which the admirable and almost incredible penetration of human (or rather divine) genius — man's outstanding ingenuity and unparalleled acuteness — resolved to construct and make'.[55] He then amplifies this when he comes to describe man's function, for this is essentially to 'govern and administer' by 'understanding and acting'. Man alone has such gifts of *intellectio* and *operatio* and these make him (in Cicero's Aristotelian citation) a 'mortal god'.[56]

Manetti's eulogy reflects the achievements of the Florentine Renaissance. When he writes of the powers of the human mind he makes explicit mention of the works of Brunelleschi and Ghiberti,[57] and when he writes of man's task being to 'govern and administer' he is implicitly drawing on his own experience in the political life of the republic. Although set within an overall Christian framework, his treatise contains a clear recognition of human creativity, the construction of a wholly human realm. For this reason the work has been seen to embody a new vision of man.[58] Yet Manetti (like his republican predecessors) saw this capacity as profoundly equivocal:

> From this so great and sublime dignity and excellence of man, as from the very root (*velut ab ipsa radice*), and not by accident, arise and flow envy, pride, indignation, ambition and the lust for domination, as well as other disturbances of the soul of this kind. For any man who considers himself worthily made, so that he seems to excel and dominate other created things, will not suffer being subordinate in any way to others — which is regarded as the vice of envy — but has an immense desire to stand above everyone else — which is believed to be the vice of pride and ambition. And if it happens by chance that someone is neglected, despised and condemned, he is so indignant that he will pursue those who attack and scorn his abilities as his most bitter and deadly enemies, even to the point of murder. So it is that as I have thought over this again and again, and wished to describe and define man in a new way, I have explained him (not unjustly, I believe) as an animal filled with indignation (*animal indignabundum*).[59]

Unlike much of Manetti's treatise this passage has a distinctly personal flavour, seeming to reflect his own observation or experience. In their origin, at the 'very root', the capacity for excellence and the desire to dominate may be inseparable, and this problem struck him as central to understanding human nature; it leads him to what he sees as a new definition of man. As we have seen, however, such a definition was far from new; it was merely the latest expression of an ancient problem. What more complete example could there be of an 'animal filled with indignation' than Achilles?

The most explicit and provocative treatment of this subject came in the writings of Machiavelli. The many sudden changes which he saw in his adult years, the rise and fall of so many states and men — 'immense alterations of things...beyond any human conception'[60] — had made him intensely aware of the limits to human endeavour. But this instability was not for him a cause of despair. In the first place, he seems to have regarded it as an inescapable fact: while the basic human material is always the same, human affairs are in a state of continual flux. Secondly, impermanence means change, and that brought the opportunity for what was new. The word 'new' was charged with excitement for Machiavelli. Like Bruni or Manetti he believed in success and the fame which came from glorious action, but no fame could be as glorious as that which came from making new. 'No one was ever great in his profession without being inventive (*senza invenzione*)'.[61] This was the subject-matter of *The Prince,* for that work addressed the situation not of all kinds of prince but specifically that of the 'new' prince, the man who acquires a territory and then holds it successfully. Three elements determined success in such an enterprise — the given conditions and turn of events (*Fortuna*), the character of the conquered people (their society and traditions), and the behaviour of the individual prince. Given favourable circumstances and the right material, the opportunity to act could be seized and the greatest glory could follow. The heart of the book is its account of the creative and innovatory powers needed for this task.[62]

In this matter moral considerations should never take priority. 'A man who wants to behave as a good person in every way will (among so many who are not good) come to a bad end. For which reason it is essential that a prince who wishes to keep his position should learn to be able not to be good; he should learn to use goodness, or do without it, as needs be'.[63] Success is an outcome of *prudenzia*, which Machiavelli defined as 'being able to know the character of problems and how to make the best out of the least bad'.[64] It requires sharp insight into present conditions and future possibilities, complete self-reliance and consummate flexibility, 'a mind ready to alter exactly as the winds and variations of fortune demand'.[65] It will be fostered by learning from the example of great men in the past, and by the awareness that people are easily deceived. Virtues as such may or may not be necessary, but the appearance of virtue is essential;[66] the ability to be, like an actor, a master of pretence and disguise (*gran simulatore e dissimulatore*)[67] is therefore vital. These mental qualities must be accompanied by a delight in action, by that combination of courage, energy and resolution known as *virtù*. The prince must be a 'stout-hearted man' who is not cast down by adversity;[68] he must be 'powerful and courageous', 'ferocious and daring'.[69] The ferocity of Cesare Borgia, the impetuosity of Pope Julius II, the ceaseless military campaigns of Ferdinand of Aragon, are held up as worthy examples of men who displayed such *virtù*. Machiavelli's emphasis on *prudenzia* and *virtù* is similar to the abilities of understanding and action, *intellectio* and *operatio,* that had been praised by Alberti or Manetti. But while the combination of these faculties led the latter to follow their classical masters and compare man to a 'mortal god', Machiavelli insists that the model prince should aim not to be half-man and half-god, but should rather take instruction from someone who was 'half-man and half-animal'.[70] The ideal of wisdom is the cunning of the fox and the ideal of action is the courage and strength of the lion. *The Prince*, in other words, envisaged great action in the same terms as the heroic ideal, a fact acknowledged by Machiavelli when, as an example of what he had in mind, he referred to 'Achilles and many other princes of the ancient world'.[71] Creative achievement, in this account, is the product of Protean flexibility, supreme daring and ruthless determination.

The Prince does not only provide an analysis, it also conveys the flavour and pleasure of such achievement. Machiavelli had been close to great men in times of crisis and he had savoured the delights of action himself. He dedicated the book to Lorenzo de' Medici in the hope of enthusing him with this sense, and his final chapter exhorted Lorenzo to take advantage of the present, to drive the foreign armies out of Italy and to create a new state. But it was not to be. The French invaded Italy once more, resistance to them collapsed, and political action in the form described in *The Prince* became, as far as the Italians were concerned, a thing of the past.

Machiavelli came out of the enforced isolation in which he had written *The Prince* (an isolation which pervades the work) and took up the question of why republics flourished or failed. His concern in the *Discourses* (which resulted from this enquiry) was therefore civic rather than heroic *virtù, prudenzia* not as the means to individual success but as what is best for the common good. Yet his enthusiasm for innovation remained. Despite the attention given in the *Discourses* to the historical circumstances and institutional factors which alone could make republican life succeed, Machiavelli refused to admit that times were so different that the past could not be imitated now, by someone 'who wanted to found a new republic'.[72] Such an act of foundation was essentially the work of one person, and the prospect of such an act is the unifying theme of the work. It recurs at the opening of each book and the character of a good foundation is described in Book One. In addition, Machiavelli devoted Book Three to an account of 'how individual men made Rome great',[73] the essential contribution outstanding individuals had made to the republic's survival and success.

This subject brings him up against the problem of reconciling the common good with the impulse to greatness. The republic needs gifted men, and their 'greatness of spirit' is vital to success in war; but to expect them, when the war is over, to return (as they should) to a modest and frugal life, is 'an almost impossible transformation'.[74] Distinguished citizens are essential to the republic's survival, but distinction easily leads to domination.[75] Where opportunities for action are insufficient, outstanding men (like Alcibiades) become indignant at being neglected or seeing others above them, and they start to make trouble or set in motion a disastrous new campaign.[76] Then again, constant change means the continual need for renewal, but (as Machiavelli wrote in reference to his own work) innovation always arouses envy.[77] So he is led to conclude: 'it seems that in the actions of men...the desire to bring something to its perfection always involves some evil mixed with the good. This evil so readily arises with the good that it seems impossible to have one without the other. And this is evident in everything men do'.[78] The impulse to action generates its own imperative; the civic ideal cannot be separated from the heroic, and the relation between them is always uneasy.

Machiavelli's awareness of the problem was especially acute because he had such a comprehensive understanding of what action involved and what benefits it could bring. His enduring interest in warfare and the citizen-militia did not arise simply out of his desire to revive an essential component of republican life, or from his perception of a new need for force in political life. It also sprang from his sense that shared action provides the only solid basis for civic life. Just as his advice to the new prince paid little attention to books and philosophy, but stressed physical activity, or praised warfare because it made the prince's qualities visible (winning allegiance by providing 'firm experience'),[79] so, in more general terms, he stated that 'when there are good arms, good laws will necessarily follow'.[80] What is forged in the heat of war will remain strong in times of peace. In one of his most perceptive comments he wrote that 'the nature of men is such that they feel under obligation as much by the benefits they give as those which they receive'.[81] It is what we *do* that shapes our character and behaviour. Action is not instrumental nor expressive, but formative; it makes us what we can become.

To convey the meaning of this to those who have no direct experience of it is extremely difficult. It is very similar to (indeed, it overlaps with) the problem Aristotle had seen of the elusiveness of politics. The task was made harder by the entirely different view of civic life promoted by Cicero in writings which had had an immense influence on previous Renaissance thought. As the Roman republic was collapsing around him, Cicero had done his utmost to identify the civic life with certain philosophical values. For him the first bonds of society were speech and reason,[82] and it is the continuing predominance of these elements in political life (the rule of morally exemplary orators) which alone can bring that harmony (*concordia*) which will sustain the republic.[83] He asserted that lawgivers like Solon and Lycurgus were superior to men of action like Themistocles and Lysander, just as civil action was superior to military.[84] He drew on Plato to insist that cunning was not wisdom, nor daring courage.[85] Reason must be paramount and the good was incompatible with deception or disguise.[86] If the republic was to survive these values must prevail over the force of the lion and the fraud of the fox.

When in *The Prince* Machiavelli recommended the example of the lion and the fox, he was attacking Cicero and the many Renaissance writers who had followed him. The former's work *On the Republic* had ended with a visionary *Dream of Scipio* in which the moral and political ideas advocated earlier (and in other writings) were assimilated to a quasi-Platonic metaphysic, individual good and participation in a just social order being seen as necessary to realise the divine part of human nature.[87] Unlike most of *On the Republic*, the *Dream of Scipio* was known in the medieval period and the Renaissance, and since it was fully compatible with Christianity, it enjoyed wide popularity.

Machiavelli was resolutely opposed to such a view. His preoccupation with action and innovation derived from an entirely different outlook. In ways which may have owed something to his acquaintance with Epicurean thought, he saw human beings as an integral part of an ever-changing nature, which was both a dynamic force animating the living things of this world, and the totality of such creatures. What we share with other animals has much to teach us, and how we deal with changing circumstances decides whether or not our lives will be successful. The idea that there is any good in trying to detach or abstract ourselves from such conditions is meaningless; on the contrary, it is in the process of grappling with them that we realise our fullest capability.[88] 'Princes become great when they overcome the difficulties and obstacles which are put in their way. So *Fortuna,* most of all when she wishes to make great a new prince...causes enemies to arise and undertake actions against him. She does this in order that he may have opportunity to overcome them and, by means of the ladder which they have offered him, ascend higher'.[89] By the same token, it was not *concordia* which had made the Roman republic great but *disunione;* as warfare against external forces develops *virtù,* so internal conflict had 'made that republic free and powerful'.[90] Machiavelli saw therefore that a supposedly negative emotion like indignation could be not (as Manetti saw it) a regrettable accompaniment to great achievement but rather a principal cause of it. An evil deed, he wrote, can 'have greatness in it or be in some respect bountiful (*generosa*)'.[91]

In trying to communicate to his contemporaries this vision of the active life Machiavelli felt he was a lone voice. It grieved him that Italy seemed 'to have been born to restore to life dead things, as we see in poetry, painting and sculpture' but do not see in warfare,[92] that men imitated classical statues but not the '*virtuosissime* actions' of the men of antiquity.[93] He felt that in the developments which we now most associate with the Renaissance something essential was being lost. He wanted to see the 'imposition of form' on human material,[94] rather than the sculptor's imposition of form on inanimate matter; a true Renaissance would bring the revival of 'actions which are great in themselves,...those concerned with governments and states'.[95] Such greatness for him was essentially connected with innovation, and the political life was the arena of the important kind of creativity. For in playing out the great drama of *fortuna* and *virtù*, we shape not only the public realm but also ourselves.

II

The Renaissance which Machiavelli hoped for did not take place, and the Renaissance which did occur faced its own problems. Claims for a 'rebirth' or 'revival' came to be made with increasing frequency after Petrarch had first referred to the preceding centuries as being 'dark',[96] but the notion of a 'rebirth' presented immediate difficulties. For to describe the period of classical antiquity as a time of greatness, followed by a 'dark age' which was then succeeded by a 'rebirth' of the time of greatness, was to turn upside down the Christian account of history. Similarly, to show an enthusiasm for action, rather than contemplation, and to praise the things of this world, was to adopt an entirely different set of values. The pursuit of fame, or delight in natural beauty, or admiration for the human body, were counter to Christian assumptions that what was 'natural' was sinful.

It is true that the statement in Genesis by God that he had made man 'in our image and likeness', together with a particular reading of the Incarnation, could provide a vindication of these attitudes.[97] There were also Church Fathers like Lactantius, (whose writings had furnished the material for much of Manetti's panegyric), who had drawn from classical sources to incorporate into Christian thought a celebration of human abilities; and the beauty of the natural world had been praised by St Francis. But prevailing Christian doctrine had continued to stress human sinfulness and helplessness. The problem of how that view could be reconciled with the new sense of human potential contributed in the latter part of the 15th century to a crisis of faith. This took dramatic form with Savonarola's sermons on the Apocalypse in 1490, but it had already been anticipated by the way in which the interest in rhetoric, which had dominated the early Renaissance, came to be complemented by a new concern for metaphysics. The most significant and influential work in this respect was that of Marsilio Ficino.

Ficino published the first complete Latin translations of Plato and of the *Enneads* of Plotinus, as well as of other neo-Platonic and Hermetic works; he also wrote his own *Platonic Theology on the Immortality of the Soul* (1474) and a number of commentaries on Plato's dialogues. Although he regarded his own thought as Platonic, (seeing a continuity which stretched from the supposedly ancient Hermes Trismegistus, through Pythagoras and Plato, Plotinus and Proclus, to himself), it was in fact neo-Platonic. While Plato had maintained a strict separation between the realm of the perfect Ideas and our own imperfect world, Plotinus asserted that the whole universe was an emanation of a single Divine Being, in a vast descending hierarchy of creatures, so that even the simplest entity could be seen to contain and reveal some element of the divine. Moreover, this ultimate Being was not defined as a timeless and static source of the good, but rather as a continually active force The whole universe is alive through its dynamic energy and there is a constant movement up and down the chain of creation, as the Divine Being emanates out, and as created beings strive to return to their original spiritual 'homeland'.[98]

Earlier Christian writers, most notably Augustine, had incorporated elements of neo-Platonic philosophy into their theology; Ficino took this process further by giving a new emphasis to two aspects in particular of Plotinus' thought. Firstly, he paid more attention to the element of beauty. For his Christian predecessors the traditional epithets of God were that He was the One, the Good and the True (*Unum, Bonum, Verum*); Ficino stated that the splendour of the One in its first emanation (Intellect or Mind) produced beauty, which was therefore an aspect of all subsequent emanations, and it is this beauty, as much as truth, goodness or the desire for unity, which arouses in us the love which draws us back to the divine.[99] Secondly, drawing on Hermetic sources and earlier commentaries on Plato's *Timaeus*,[100] he emphasised the extent to which the divine part in humans replicated the original Intellect not only in being able to know truth and be good, but also in being creative. Not only does man 'possess in himself images of the divine realities on which he depends', but he also 'possesses the reasons and models of the inferior realities which he in a certain way brings forth'.[101]

In his *Platonic Theology* Ficino unequivocally endorsed human creativity: 'the mind of man is the inventor of an infinite number of different things'.[102] Human beings are 'the inventors of innumerable arts which they practise according to their own free will... Human arts by themselves make whatever nature herself makes, as if we were not servants of nature but her competitors'.[103] He listed the painting of Zeuxis, whose grapes were so lifelike that birds flew to them, Egyptian statues of gods which moved and spoke, inventions of Archimedes and other achievements in antiquity, all of which indicate that 'the power of man is almost like the divine nature'.[104] Humans can provide for themselves far more lavishly than nature provides for the animals, and in so doing give themselves an 'wonderful variety of pleasures'.[105] One example of this is the activity of productive reason (*ratio cogitatrix*) which, 'eager to propagate its own offspring outside itself, manifests its inventive power...in paintings, sculptures and buildings'.[106] By making use of this productive power man transforms the natural world not only for use, but also in adornment. In short, 'he fulfills the role of God'.[107] He does so as a maker, and as a ruler (of himself, his family, and in society), and in his ability to understand and know. So great is the last attribute, that since man has seen how the heavens operate, 'how can it be denied that he possesses almost the same genius (*ingenium*), so to speak, as the Author of the heavens, and that he could in some way make the heavens if he found the instruments and some celestial material?'[108]

This remarkable statement shows how far Ficino went in assimilating his ideas of man to his ideas about God, and vice versa. In similar fashion, he described the human desire to explore, to go beyond all boundaries, as the aspiration to be universal, like God, and the desire for fame as a longing to be eternal.[109] The comparison of God and man was precise and reciprocal. 'In understanding, the mind conceives in itself as many things as God in knowing makes in the world. By speaking it expresses as many things...[and] in making it shapes as many things from the material of the world'. In these respects, 'who could deny that the soul...emulates God and is divine?'[110] In this way Ficino validated the new attitudes and achievements of the Renaissance in terms compatible with Christianity.

Although Plotinus had broken down the separation which for Plato existed between the ideal and the actual, he retained the Platonic dualism of spirit and matter, with the former being characterised in terms of unity and self-sufficiency. The soul was self-moving and the source of movement, and its principal aim was to return to the primordial unity from whence it had come. Although matter for Plotinus was inert and passive (and therefore not actively evil) it was an obstacle, a cause of distraction and error, a prison from which the soul had to escape. The descent of the soul into matter was a fall from unity and purity into multiplicity and obscurity. In this perspective, innovation as such was not necessarily good. 'The beginning of evil', wrote Plotinus, 'was audacity (*tolma*) and coming to birth and the first otherness'.[111] Salvation could only come through release from our individual self to find union with the divine One.

Ficino's desire to vindicate human capacities resulted in a less pronounced emphasis on other-worldliness, but his conception of creativity followed Plotinus very closely. That is to say, insofar as it was an activity of the soul it was an expression of the good, pure and beautiful, and entirely intellectual or spiritual. The creative power in God was itself identical with goodness: he is 'good when he creates',[112] and goodness is the 'fertile power'[113] at work in the world. The process of creation is spiritual both in being active (only the spirit causing action), and because production comes about by realising the forms, the Ideas, already present in the divine Mind. Human beings are able to replicate this process because they have, in their immortal souls, the perfect Ideas which emanate from the Divine. It is by means of 'an intuition of the universal Ideas of things which the world already contains'[114] that an artist proceeds. A beautiful work of art is not an imitation of nature but a realisation of that beauty emanating from God which animates and forms the world, a notion which was subsequently to be expressed by Michelangelo in some of his poems and by Castiglione in the closing pages of *The Courtier*.[115]

The ability to intuit the Ideas is itself dependent on personal goodness and a refinement of the senses: 'let them be purified and they will perceive pure things'.[116] Ficino made a sharp distinction between the desire (*desiderium*) for truth and beauty, which can be obtained by means of seeing and hearing, and lust (*libido*), which was inseparable from the senses of touch, smell and taste.[117] The latter, being inescapably physical and bodily, could only obscure and mislead; Bacchus and Priapus must be sent far away, and there must be no opposition or conflict, because 'there are no contraries in the [divine] mind'.[118] Sight and hearing, on the other hand, could lead us to the disembodied realms both of true beauty, which is 'something incorporeal',[119] and of divine harmony, the music of the planetary spheres. This music, produced by the perfect, orderly movements of the heavens, could only be heard in the inner ear, by those who could abstract themselves from the discord and cacophony of everyday life.[120]

The highest degree of such abstraction occurred in the state of being possessed by divine *furor*. The awareness of 'what we knew before when we existed outside the prison of the body' leads to 'the soul [being] fired by this memory';…by degrees [it] purges itself from contact with the body and its filth and becomes wholly possessed by divine *furor*'.[121] This condition could be one of frenzy or one of trance-like rapture, an experience of being out of the body as much as out of our normal mind, (Ficino's usual synonym for *furor* was *alienatio mentis*).[122] It was 'an illumination of the rational soul', a 'sweet harmony bringing calm', by which 'man is raised above his own nature and ascends into the divine'.[123] As a form of madness it was quite distinct from insanity; it was a putting off of our particular human self, in order to capture once again our universal divine self. In such a state the soul achieves that 'motionless intuition which is beyond the moving understanding and is in accord with the souls above'.[124]

Ficino drew heavily from Plato on this subject and followed him in describing four kinds of *furor* — the prophetic, hieratic, poetic and amatory. The first two were concerned with knowing and willing, the second two with forms of creation or generation. As beauty arouses love, so love desires to propagate itself, 'to generate a form like itself'.[125] Ficino's *De Amore*, his commentary on Plato's *Symposium*, is a rapturous celebration of this aspect of the divine, *Amor* as *Creator omnium*, the 'innate and latent fertility'[126] which exists in everything and inspires all discovery and invention, all propagation of the species and all transmission of knowledge. This love, which is of course distinct from physical or sexual love, is drawn towards unity and permanence in the forms of likeness and harmony. 'Likeness generates love'.[127] Since the world is itself created by a single maker it has an essential likeness in all its parts, linking it together in reciprocal love and so making love 'the eternal knot and copula of the world'.[128] While this has obvious ethical implications, its principal significance is in providing us with means to return to our source, our divine home; (not that these two aspects should be separated, for the practice of virtue is one of the principal ways by which, when not in *furor*, we may return to God).

In poetic *furor* 'the soul receives the echoes of that incomparable music' of the celestial harmony, 'strives wholeheartedly to imitate it' and brings forth 'the most solemn and glorious song'.[129] This song is not like that produced by 'superficial and vulgar musicians', whose sounds give only sensuous pleasures.[130] It is inspired rather by the nine Muses (who were virgins), and who 'were the musical song of the eight spheres [plus] the one great harmony arising from all the others'.[131] Divine poetry of this kind brought together both the musical forms of the heavens themselves (i.e. they used the sacred numbers according to which the universe was created), and the verbal signs which give true knowledge of things. Since poets could have access to that original language used by Adam in Paradise, and employed by Orpheus and other ancient poets, their words could be revelations of true essence and therefore divine.

This conception of poetic *furor*, linked as it was to a comprehensive and accessible metaphysic, made possible a new exaltation of poetry. Earlier in the century the poet had not generally been regarded as being more notable than the orator. Now Poliziano, who was a member of the neo-Platonic circle in Florence, revived the notion that it had not been orators who had first led men to civilisation, but inspired poets. Divine poetry had first 'lit the spark shut away deep in our hearts and reawoken the heavenly seed of Prometheus' fire'; it had brought people together in peace and led them to justice, reason and the power of love.[132] Cristoforo Landino, a close associate of Ficino, likewise insisted that poetry is 'something much more divine that the liberal disciplines'; while the other arts have their origin in 'human excellence', poetry 'originates in the divine *furor*'.[133] In the earliest times 'God wanted his mysteries to be conveyed to everyone by the poets', which had led Aristotle to call poets theologians, and there is 'no small similarity between the poet and the prophet'.[134]

In making these statements neither Poliziano nor Landino did more that renew an ancient tradition. In both Greek and Roman antiquity poets had been regarded as 'divine' because they were believed to possess a superior knowledge or wisdom, a power of insight or foresight.[135] However, in his *Commentary on Dante* (1481) Landino then went on to make an entirely new claim. The Greeks had derived the word 'poet' from *poiein* which, he asserted, 'is halfway between creating, which is what God does when he brings something into being from nothing, and making, which is what men do in any art when they compose something from form and matter. Although the invention of the poet is not all from nothing, it is further from making and comes closer to creating. And God is the supreme poet and the world is his poem'.[136]

For Christian writers the role of the poet had primarily been seen as that of expressing or ornamenting an existing reality. In the early Renaissance this had still been true for Petrarch and Boccaccio; likewise, when Salutati called Dante and Petrarch 'divine' it was because of their outstanding literary achievement.[137] Ficino's Christian neo-Platonism made possible a new idea of the poet as divine, in terms of having the ability actually to 'create'. While Landino's account of this was qualified, fifty years later the qualifications had been dropped: 'because the poet creates, composes and makes his measured conceits almost from nothing, in the manner of other things beyond human comprehension...[so] it seems that his works can accurately be said to be created, composed and made by him'.[138] By the end of the cinquecento this idea of poets as being like God because of their making was beginning to be diffused, occurring in the writings of both Scaliger and Tasso;[139] an analogous comparison of God and visual artists was made by Vasari in the preface to his *Lives of the Painters* (1550).[140]

The fact that this new image of human creativity was derived from Ficino does not mean that he himself would have used these terms, or that he was concerned to promote the status of poets outside a religious context. It is true that in the hierarchy of human activities given in his *Commentary* on the *Phaedrus* he puts the lover, musician and poet in second place, after the philosopher. But he had in mind the divine poetry which is given by God, and merely human poetry is placed on grade seven.[141] In his *De Amore* he wrote of the soul propagating itself not through poetry, but through *scientia,* the teaching of knowledge;[142] and in his *Platonic Theology* his panegyric to human creativity, evidence of the divine powers in man, culminates in the working of miracles.[143] For Ficino everything was subordinate to obtaining that mystical union with God which Plotinus himself was believed to have achieved — 'the whole striving of our soul is to become God'[144] — and, like Plotinus, he regarded any product as being inferior to the cause of its existence.[145]

The impetus which Ficino's writings gave to a more extensive and exalted affirmation of human possibilities did not mean that they promoted human creativity as an independent value. For him the sense of human potential was always grounded in a far greater sense of human dependence on God.[146] (The same could be said of Giovanni Pico della Mirandola's youthful *Oration on the dignity of man,* the opening paragraphs of which have sometimes been read as defining humanity in terms of its 'creative' potential).[147] But in his transmission and development of neo-Platonic thought Ficino put forward a conception of creativity which was to have a lasting appeal. His emphasis on the spiritual and intellectual aspects of the creative process, on detachment from the world, and on a necessary link with aesthetic qualities of beauty and harmony, contributed to an identification of creativity with artistic activity. And his insistence on the interdependence of moral excellence, the intuition of profound truth, and creative power was to be very influential.

III

Eight years before his death in 1499 Ficino published his *Three Books on Life* (*De Vita*). This work, which came to be as widely known as any of his philosophical treatises, presented an entirely different view of human potential. It was an examination of the many ways in which people in general, and intellectuals in particular, are dependent on their physical constitutions and on outside forces, especially the astrological influence of celestial bodies. Instead of celebrating human freedom and achievement, *De Vita* bemoaned the thousand woes and cares that flesh is heir to, with elaborate lists of physical frailties, of malign conjunctions of planets, of diets to follow and conditions to avoid.

Whereas Ficino's neo-Platonic writings had defined intellectual or artistic ability in terms of detachment from everything physical, *De Vita* located it in a specific physical type: 'Priests of the Muses either are from the beginning, or are made by study, into melancholics',[148] that is, people in whom there was a preponderance of black bile. This idea was drawn from a work (attributed to Aristotle) which asked the question: 'why is it that all those who have become eminent in philosophy or politics or poetry or the arts are clearly melancholic?'[149] The answer given was that the melancholy temperament was both more 'variable' than other kinds of temperament — it could rise to greater heights and sink to lower depths — and was less subject to self-control. Without any control strongly melancholic people were liable to be manic-depressive and/or mad, but if their condition was less extreme they could be 'in many respects superior to others either in culture or in the arts or in statesmanship'.[150] 'Those who have a little of this temperament are ordinary, but those who have much of it are unlike the majority of people. For if their melancholy habitus is quite undiluted they are too melancholy; but if it is somewhat tempered they are outstanding'.[151]

Neo-Platonic writers had added an astrological dimension to this theory, associating a melancholy temperament with the influence of Saturn. Ficino took over this astro-physiological conception and assimilated it to his own idea of *furor:* 'divine madness is never incited in anyone else but melancholics'.[152] The result was to obscure the meaning both of the original (pseudo-Aristotelian) theory and of his own previous accounts of *furor.* The aim of the former had been precisely to distinguish the ways in which outstanding individuals, while sharing certain characteristics with highly unstable people, were themselves not mad, because they were able to put their irrationality to positive effect. The purpose of the latter had been to show how insight was achieved through release from any physical dependence, which was also a release from particularity. *De Vita* insisted that only particular individuals of a certain physical type could obtain illumination, those who were highly imaginative, taciturn, withdrawn, ill-tempered and liable to moments of frenzy.

Ficino himself was born under Saturn and suffered from the vexation and depressions which were regarded as the fate of melancholics. But he also drew the benefits of this condition, the fact that 'the soul with an instrument or incitement of this kind...always seeks the centre of all subjects and penetrates to their innermost core'.[153] For him, this meant philosophy, and the epitome of *homo melancholicus* remained the contemplative thinker, later anatomised by Robert Burton and depicted by Milton in *Il Penseroso.* But *De Vita* was equally influential in promoting an image of the poet and artist as eccentric or mad, an image which was to be embodied in the late cinquecento by Tasso.

Such an image was, of course, ancient; but it was not as old as poetry itself. For Homer or Pindar, for example, the poet relied on the Muses but was not possessed by them; his own 'skill' was as important as their 'gift'.[154] In his *Ars poetica* Horace likewise insisted that a poet's skill was as important as his innate *ingenium* and he attacked the idea that poets should be mad.[155] There was an important difference, in other words, between inspiration and possession. Plato had wanted to collapse this distinction, since he could not allow knowledge (which poets did convey) to be associated with the irrational. Aristotle had kept the distinction; it is evident from his remark (in the *Poetics*) that 'poetry requires a man with special gifts of nature and temperament, or else a touch of madness'.[156] Seneca transmitted this observation in a form which became commonplace — 'No great genius has ever existed without a touch of madness' — and then went on to explain why: the mind cannot 'reach any sublime and difficult height [unless] it leaves the common track and becomes wild...and runs away with its rider'.[157]

In this perspective, the poet's madness was akin to, or a part of, that impulse which was otherwise described as daring — Pindar's *tolma,* Horace's *potestas audendi*[158] — or the ambition which Virgil confessed to,[159] or the power and boldness admired by Hellenistic writers, especially the author of *On the Sublime*.[160] It could arise from the intoxication of love — hence the proverb 'Love makes poets of us all'[161] — or the fury of anger — Juvenal's 'Indignation produces poetry'[162] or Horace's 'Anger is a brief *furor*'.[163] All these states can transport a person beyond the usual or conventional and so bring about innovation.

This presupposes that there is space in which such innovation can occur. As well as the impulse there must be freedom for it to be realised. This was sometimes expressed in the form of 'poetic licence', or the 'spirit of playfulness' needed by poets.[164] Alternatively, it was portrayed in the isolation of the poet,[165] either in terms of solitude or of having no fixed place in society — being the equivalent (in the elder Cato's eyes) of a vagrant[166] — or else in terms of being separated from others by a defect, like blindness.[167] In such an area of freedom the poet could go beyond the bounds of whatever was habitual, being removed from the claims of what elsewhere was moral, logical or true. Such a position, however, raised obvious difficulties. 'We know how to tell many lies like truth', said the Muses to Hesiod,[168] and Pindar admitted the same: beauty can 'make the false seem true / Time and again', it can 'trick' us, and 'beguile' us.[169] The very power of 'enchantment' for which poetry was admired by some, was recognised by others as dangerous, perhaps evil.[170] Ambition led to bitter rivalries and the view that poets were endemically troublesome and vindictive, a *genus irritabile*.[171] The desire for individual fame could seem like indifference to everyone else, and the licence which poets claimed could be more than just 'poetic'.

In his *Genealogy of the Gods of the Gentiles* (1375) Boccaccio recorded the hostile opinion that was usually held about poets: they could not be believed, or 'in plain words, they were liars;...they live in the country among woods and mountains, lacking manners and refinement', and what they produce is 'obscure, deceitful and full of obscenity'.[172] Boccaccio had in mind Christian attacks on poetry and the aim of his discussion was to defend literature from such charges, but it is clear that the views he opposed were not peculiar to Christian critics. The writing of poetry (i.e. what we would now call poetic creativity) seems very often to have been associated with qualities which set the poet apart from other people in one way or another, and usually in a manner which moralists found objectionable. With the greater degree of freedom which came with the Renaissance this aspect of poetry received more emphasis. Poliziano, for example, in some verses attacking another writer, used as his main charge the very fact that the man was a poet: he was an atheist (like Lucretius), a sodomite (like Virgil), mad, 'deceitful, unreliable, insolent, stupid, boring and lascivious; and these [characteristics] mark you out as a poet'.[173] A generation later Francesco Berni composed a *Dialogue against the poets* in which we find the same complaints being repeated: poets are irreverent, atheists, and commit every known sin;[174] they are stupid, insincere, vain, untruthful and malicious.[175] This dialogue, like Poliziano's invective, was humourous and quite different from the kind of attack Boccaccio was answering. But it was not light-hearted humour, there was genuine resentment and bitterness, particularly in the repeated charges about poets' *malignità*.

Berni was a contemporary (and lifelong enemy) of Pietro Aretino, and the latter could be seen as an embodiment of the qualities common to these various accounts of poets. He made his reputation by the brilliant lampoons he wrote for different factions in papal politics and by the obscene sonnets he had composed to accompany an equally obscene set of drawings by Giulio Romano. His *Raggionamenti* were unashamedly pornographic. Yet he also wrote works on the humanity of Christ, on the Virgin Mary and a version of some of the Psalms. In similar fashion he changed sides politically, using his pen to flatter and favour whomever he thought would be on the winning side. Francis I of France rewarded him with a gold chain inscribed with the Biblical motto 'His tongue speaketh a lie'.[176] In his own writing he spurned all previous models or fixed principles. His guide was nature, as he perceived her; 'nature gave me the privilege of speaking fully and freely, and I will never be cramped'.[177]

The zest, playfulness and sensuous delight which distinguished Aretino's work might be considered of only minor importance if they had not also been features of the greatest poem of the century, perhaps of the whole Italian Renaissance, Ariosto's *Orlando furioso*. This mock-epic went beyond the bounds of everything which the defenders of poetry had claimed that it could (and should) be. The opening lines were an ironical allusion to the paragon of epics, Virgil's *Aeneid*, and elsewhere Ariosto defied the opening lines of Horace's *Ars poetica*, with its admoniton never to offend plausibility, by inventing outlandish creatures. He not only wrote about a flying horse, the hippogriff, but insisted that 'this horse is not invented but natural'.[178] Where we might expect to find moral exhortation, we have the opposite. Sexual desire, the poet observes, is almost never restrained by reason. When Ruggiero has the opportunity to possesss the beautiful, naked Angelica, he would be 'mad to give up such a prize', even though he is in love with another woman.[179] Ariosto also defends dissimulation:

Although deceit is mostly disapproved,
Seeming to show a mind malevolent,
Many a time it brings, as has been proved,
Advantages that are self-evident.[180]

The sense of detachment and ironical distance, which these lines convey, occurs throughout the poem and goes against another Horatian requirement, that of the unity of the poet and the poem. Ariosto comments on this, both in general — noting the disparity between motives and appearance, the way in which a pious and saintly exterior may hide evil and profane intentions[181] — and with regard to poets. In Canto XXXV, set on the moon, we are told that poems cannot be taken as reliable versions of truth. If poets are well provided for they will flatter their benefactor, however evil he may have been; if Nero had paid attention to keeping writers as friends he would not be called unjust today, and if it had not been for Augustus' liberality Virgil would not have 'blown the trumpet' of his virtue and kindness.[182] Poems, in other words, do not reflect a poet's honesty or integrity, but merely how they have been treated. If the piper is well paid, he will play a good tune. In saying this Ariosto was ridiculing one of the most ancient claims for poetry.

He was also manifesting that boldness and daring which had almost always been seen as a necessary element of innovation. In fact, when we consider the writings of Ariosto and Aretino in the light of earlier remarks about poetic creativity, we see that they display overtly what previously seems to have been implicit. What might appear to be eccentricity or madness could be a high degree of detachment, energy and versatility. 'Someone who does not dare to depart from the rules will never write well', observed Poliziano to a young poet; '[you must learn to] swim without corks...and risk your whole strength'.[183] This advice recalls Machiavelli's admonition *Tentare la fortuna* (which could be translated as 'Take chances', 'Try your luck', 'Put yourself to the test'),[184] and it is no surprise to find Poliziano saying that although human faces most resemble those of apes, he prefers instead (i.e. instead of 'aping', imitating) to have the face of a lion.[185] When Ariosto praises dissimulation, or we consider the multiple stances of Aretino's career as *un gran simulatore e dissimulatore,* we expect to hear one of them recommending the ways of the fox.

IV

The Renaissance had brought a new esteem for poets, first evident in Petrarch being publicly crowned with a laurel wreath in Rome in 1341. The Italian humanists believed that 'where letters cease, darkness covers the land',[186] and the new educational curriculum which they promoted, the *studia humanitatis*, included poetry as one of its five subjects (the others being moral philosophy, history, grammar and rhetoric). For their successors, as for those who came to adopt a neo-Platonic outlook, the brilliant literary achievement of Ariosto posed obvious difficulties, since for the humanists (as for the readers of Ficino) the belief in the value of poetry rested on it having an intrinsic connection with morality. This problem became more acute when the Catholic church, shaken by Protestant revolt, began to reassert its spiritual authority. The Inquisition was revived, an Edict banning heretical books was issued (in 1543, the first Index of Prohibited Books being published in 1559), and the Council of Trent began the first of its three sessions (1545–49) redefining and reaffirming Catholic doctrine.

The guide and inspiration for this reform came from the powerful synthesis of Christian and Aristotelian philosophy that had been constructed by Thomas Aquinas. (When the cardinals and bishops met in conclave in Trent they laid on the altar three works — the Bible, the decrees of the Popes, and Aquinas' *Summa*.) In this context, and in the terms of this Thomist revival, a new evaluation of poetry took shape. Ideas drawn from Horace's *Ars poetica*, which had inspired earlier Renaissance defences of poetry, were now combined with arguments derived from

Aristotle's *Poetics*.[187] Out of the resulting synthesis four main doctrines emerged: first, poetry can be 'philosophical'; second, it can produce a particular moral effect; third, to do this it should obey certain rules; and fourth, poetry is best defined as a kind of imitation.

The *Poetics* discussed tragedy and epic, and Aristotle maintained that poetry in these forms provides a certain kind of understanding. It does not, like history, show events occurring haphazardly but rather as a sequence of interconnected actions, revealing a causal development. This made poetry, in his words, more 'philosophical'; its statements 'are of the nature of universals, whereas those of history are of particulars'.[188] In other words, poetry gives us a distinct and important kind of knowledge. To the Italian critics there was an affinity between this idea and the ancient tradition (recorded by Aristotle)[189] of poets being the first theologians and divinely inspired. It could also be combined with the Horatian (and Ciceronian) notion of decorum; by dealing in universals poetry showed not the incidental characteristics of a person but his or her essential character and those actions appropriate to such a character.

Aristotle's statement that tragedy was beneficial in bringing about a *katharsis* of the emotions was read in terms of a moral benefit.[190] Exactly how this was supposed to occur was a matter of controversy, but since it seemed clear that the idea of *katharsis* was used to counter Plato's attack on poetry, which had primarily been made on moral grounds, Aristotle's defence was perceived as being likewise essentially moral. In addition, the *Poetics* stated that tragedies 'show people who are better than us' with characters who are 'good', and depict a person coming to a bad end 'due to some error (*hamartia*)'.[191] Seen through Horatian eyes this was taken to mean 'due to some moral flaw or weakness'. In these ways *katharsis* and *hamartia* were combined and seen as providing the 'useful' element of Horace's 'useful and pleasing (*utile dulci*)'.[192] Together with previous rhetorical ideas of literature distributing praise and blame, giving examples to follow or wise epithets to digest, these notions aligned poetry closely with the claims of morality.

In his definition of tragedy Aristotle had stated that it was a representation of a single action, occurring 'within a single revolution of the sun', its plot forming 'a unified whole'.[193] Horace had also stressed the need for unity.[194] Out of these statements a number of rules about unity and a classification of genres were formulated, which then assumed canonical status. Poems which infringed these categories, by being romances (like *Orlando Furioso*) or other kinds of hybrid, could not merit the serious consideration given to the established genres, (although an exception was made for lyric poetry).[195]

Finally, poetry was defined in terms of Aristotle's perception of it as 'forms of imitation'. In his eyes humans have a natural instinct for imitation; it was from that instinct that poetry originated, and all art (i.e. all human skill) is 'an imitation of nature'.[196] While the precise meaning of imitation varied, the value of this doctrine was clear. In the first place, it affirmed an external, visible point of reference. Protestants and other heretical groups believed in the priority of an inner truth, as perceived by each individual; for them this inner experience was more important than external forms of religious life and practice. An analogous development had occurred in the increasing emphasis in writings about art on the validity of the artist's imagination. But *fantasia* was, in the eyes of the Catholic Church, an unreliable faculty. In the case of a sincere Christian like Dante it could help illuminate the divine truth, but where no solid foundation or framework existed it could be a 'dangerous power'.[197] The Aristotelian principle of imitation prevented such dangers. It also (secondly) shifted attention away from human invention and the qualities of daring or independence which tended to go with that. So we find the Italian bishop Antonio Minturno, who attended the Council of Trent and wrote two influential arts of poetry, one in Latin (1559) and one in Italian (1563), defining the poet as 'a good man expert in speaking and imitating (*vir bonus dicendi atque imitandi peritus*)'.[198] This definition, incorporating the Aristotelian term within a rhetorical commonplace (*vir bonus dicendi peritus* was the standard Roman definition of the ideal orator) could be seen as an epitome of the new literary orthodoxy.

The importance of this orthodoxy can be judged from the fate of those who transgressed it. The learned and quarrelsome critic Lodovico Castelvetro was not in sympathy with the Catholic Reformation. In 1560 he was accused of translating works by Luther's colleague Melanchthon and condemned by the Inquisition. He fled the country. Ten years later, when his *Poetics* were published in Vienna, they turned out to contain a thorough-going attack on the new criticism in general and Aristotle in particular. The aim of poetry, he maintained, was purely to delight and entertain;[199] if it did anything else, such as purging emotions (which only occurs in certain tragedies), that was incidental.[200] 'The morals do not hold the final place and are accessory to the plot'.[201] The audience's pleasure did not derive from the quality of imitation but the increase in knowledge — especially in coming to know things we did not think could happen — and the pleasure of seeing desires fulfilled.[202] The plot was essentially 'imagined' by the poet,[203] and 'a poet in the true meaning of the word is an inventor'; the extent to which he does invent is the mark of his originality.[204]

We might think that statements like these, written by a known heretic and published in exile, could have been easily ignored. But such a direct attack had to be shown for what it was and the work was immediately put on the Index. Discussion was permissible only within certain limits. As Aristotle's *Politics* came to occupy a dominant position in Italian political thought at this time,[205] so his *Poetics,* interpreted in the above fashion, determined literary debate. A new scholasticism had taken hold. Artists came under pressure to become members of academies as they had once been members of guilds. The nudes of Michelangelo's *Last Judgement* were given clothes. The independent spirit and the naked body were alike condemned as sinful.

Nevertheless, the intellectual energy with which the debates of the late cinquecento were conducted showed how strong was the urge to validate secular literature, in particular the achievement of writers from Petrarch onwards, whose works at their best could rival their classical masters. This validation employed and developed arguments from the ancient world to restore to poetry the status which it had had in antiquity. The attack which the Church Fathers had launched against Greek and Latin poetry had been based mainly on two judgements: what the poets had written about the pagan gods was idolatrous and the human pleasures they had celebrated had been sinful. Ancient poetry, in other words, had been both wrong and immoral. The neo-classical aesthetics which emerged out of the late Renaissance debates in effect met these charges by defending literature as both a useful form of knowledge and as morally beneficial. (Jacopo Mazzini, writing in the 1580s, believed the efficacy of poetry to be so great that in his view 'the *Poetics* is the ninth book of the *Politics*'.)[206] These arguments were seen as so persuasive that what had previously been regarded as the most ambivalent form of poetry, namely, that which was performed in drama, came to occupy a central place in the educational curriculum of the Jesuits, the principal agents of the Catholic Reformation.

In these terms the ancient status of poetry was restored. But that was not all. In his *Life of Pericles,* Plutarch had observed that to admire a work of art does not necessarily mean to admire the person who created it. Seeing the sculptures of Phidias or Polycleitus, or hearing the poems of Anacreon or Archilochus, does not lead us to aspire to be like them, as individuals; 'on the contrary, many times while we delight in the work (*ergon*) we despise the workman (*demiourgos*)'.[207] (Because of his inclusion of poetry in this statement Plutarch was not expressing the low regard held for painting or sculpting because they were manual labour;[208] rather, he was reflecting the make/value distinction which we have seen in Plato and others (p.19).) This judgement had its counterpart in the comments of poets (such as Catullus, Martial, or Ovid)[209] that their writings bore no relation to their own character or behaviour. The neo-classical dogma, however, insisted on a unity of the writer and the work. Drawing on the rhetorical tradition and the *Ars poetica* the critics maintained that morally beneficial literature would be the product of a morally good person. The implication of this was that poetry could be valid not only for its effect (i.e. in aesthetic terms) but also admirable as an activity *per se*. In other words, a moral dimension was attributed to the creative process: a bad person would not produce an (aesthetically) good poem.

In addition, poetic invention was associated with spiritual or intellectual attributes. To ancient notions of poets having suprahuman knowledge (from gods or muses or other inspiration) was now added the Aristotelian notion of poetry as 'philosophical' and the neo-Platonic conception of 'intellectual' beauty, the realisation by the poet or artist of an original or essential 'Idea' (p.46). The wider knowledge or deeper insight of the poet arose out of a mind able to detach itself from the confusion of sense-experience and so have an intuition into the true nature of reality. In this way the writing of good literature was seen as the activity of an intellectually and morally elevated person. Creative cause was of a piece with aesthetic effect.

The Renaissance brought about a revival of the former status of poets and a new esteem for visual artists. It did not lead to an affirmation of human achievement and independence in terms that would make possible the emergence of creativity as a general value. (And it was only when that had occurred, in the middle of the 19th century, that the period came to be seen, in the writings of Michelet and Burckhardt, as being distinctly 'modern' in this respect.) But one of the legacies of the Renaissance discussions of literature and art was to align those activities with a particular view of the creative process. This view was derived from the writings of philosophers and critics. Sometimes it had been endorsed by poets, like Horace in his *Ars poetica* or Michelangelo in his sonnets, but it rarely engaged with the evidence provided by poets. There were many examples in the writings of Horace himself that could be seen as inconsistent with the principles which he himself set out in the *Ars*; but these were not set in the scales against that text. It was of course the case that at this time material about the origins and composition of poetry was comparatively scarce, and the material that was available was often elusive or ambiguous in character. But there was no Machiavelli among the cinquecento critics. As a result, the view of the creative process which came to prevail was one which associated it with the spiritual rather than the material, the intellect rather than the senses, and order rather than its opposite. In other words, it was a view which embodied central features of the tradition of the Creator (p.27).

CHAPTER FOUR

New worlds

I

The first new world was revealed by Columbus. He sailed beyond the limits of what (to Europeans) was known and found something utterly new. But the novelty did not consist only of the massive fact of America. For what slowly came to light called into question, decisively and irreversibly, the wisdom of the ancients and the scriptures of the Church. As a result the voice of the past began to lose its authority.[1] Why should 'a few received authors stand up like Hercules' columns, beyond which there should be no sailing or discovering?' asked Francis Bacon in his *Advancement of Learning* (1605).[2] Columbus, he insisted, had made hope reasonable.[3] Instead of accepting what was known, we should explore the unknown: 'they are ill discoverers that think there is no land, when they can see nothing but sea'.[4]

The second new world followed from the writings of Copernicus. The earth lost its position at the centre of a cosmos in which location corresponded to value. Instead of occupying a fixed place in a visible hierarchy of matter and spirit which stretched from brute soil to pure, starry heavens, our world became one of several planets revolving around the sun in a universe which was infinite in extent and which operated according to laws which, being purely mathematical, were invisible. What is there, up in the skies, no less that what is there, over the seas, transformed the character of what is here, around us.

In both cases the discoveries took people beyond earlier limits and undermined the insistence on limits which had been previously so strong. The classical world had had the motto *non ultra* (No Further), wrote Bacon, but 'these times may justly bear...[the motto] *plus ultra*'.[5] The map of the world began to be filled with new detail; the closed cosmos gave way to an infinite universe. As with space, so with time. The rejection of authority based on the past came to be accompanied by an awareness of ever-increasing possibilities, now and in the future. Writing about scientific knowledge, Pascal observed: 'not only does each individual advance from day to day in the sciences, but mankind as a whole constantly advances in them in proportion as the universe grows older...So that the whole succession of men, through the course of so many centuries, should be seen as the life of a single man who lasts forever and learns continually'.[6]

The past had to be rejected because its description of the world was inaccurate. New accounts were needed. What emerged from this redescription was something which went against common experience: not only did the sun not revolve around the earth, but the natural world was not full of colour. Our immediate perceptions mislead us, what seems obvious is untrue; we should therefore not accept what is given, but be dissatisfied. When Bacon interpreted the Prometheus legend, in *The Wisdom of the Ancients* (1609), he focussed on this need as a key element in the myth. 'They who arraign and accuse nature and the arts, and abound with complainings,...are stimulated perpetually to fresh industry and new discoveries...The preferring of complaints against nature and the arts is a thing well pleasing to the gods, and draws down new alms and bounties from the divine goodness'.[7] This comment also went a step beyond previous limits, for what Bacon applauded was the opposite of classical or Christian moral precepts (praising restraint and the suppression of desire). Instead, dissatisfaction was installed at the heart of human activity, as the motor of innovation. When combined with persistence, analysis and hope, it could lead to new discoveries.[8]

In these developments scientific thinking and technological advance were closely connected. The compass and navigational devices which took Columbus across the Atlantic, like the telescope so important to Galileo, (revealing the moon's surface as not celestially pure but rough and uneven like the earth itself), were human inventions. One reason for the view that the new science was superior to the old lay in its practical application and results; the Greeks were very talkative, observed Bacon, but they were not productive.[9] The endeavours he promoted, on the other hand, aimed at 'the enlarging of the bounds of human empire, to the effecting of all things possible'.[10] Behind these statements lay a decisive shift in the conception of science. The change was not simply one of knowledge being a matter of practice, rather than theory; it was also the fact that the knowledge was obtained by seeing how nature operates, looking not at the end result but at the process by which natural effects are made. (Discoveries, he wrote, 'are like new creations, and imitations of divine works'.)[11] Understanding nature in this way was equivalent to knowing how it was constructed. For Bacon, it is the maker who knows, not (as for Plato or Aristotle) the user or observer, and that is why for him knowledge could be equated with power and why science went hand in hand with technology.[12]

Around the time that the most visionary statement of Bacon's ideas was published (in his *New Atlantis* (1627)), Thomas Mun wrote: 'the people who live by the arts are far more in number than they who are masters of the fruits...We know that our own natural wares do not yield us so much profit as our industry'.[13] In similar vein, Bacon's faith in the benefits of science if it were divided into 'the mine and the furnace...pioneers and smiths...the inquisition of causes and the productions of effects',[14] found literal expression in a work by the mining expert Gabriel Plattes, entitled *A Discovery of Infinite Treasure, Hidden since the World's Beginning, whereunto all men, of what degree soever, are friendly invited to be sharers* (1639).[15] As with the natural world, so also with the human body, the understanding of which was transformed by Harvey's discovery of the circulation of the blood and the heart's function as a pump (described in his *De Motu Cordis* (1628)).

The sense of human advance was at this time mainly confined to science and technology, for in other areas of life the first half of the seventeenth century in northern Europe (where these ideas came to receive most attention) was marked by bitter conflicts and civil wars. To some extent the discoveries (both geographical and astronomical) can be seen to have contributed to these. The first new world had deprived European values of their supposedly universal or absolute status, and the second new world had cut the links between humans and an overarching (meta)physical order. If people were no longer a microcosm of that macrocosm then the rationality of the universe was not, so to speak, binding on them; in Donne's words, all 'coherence' was gone.[16] The proliferation of religious sects, and the intractability of the issues which set them against one another, were in part due to this new situation. The problem of relativism alone could lead to the genial scepticism of Montaigne; the problem of a lack of any 'coherence' at all could open up that vast desert of uncertainty, with its shifting sands and blinding winds, which caused such alarm to Hobbes.

Where limits are not fixed conflict can be avoided, as the Pilgrim Fathers demonstrated. For Hobbes, however, limits always exist in the form of scarce resources, either as material goods — 'the plenty of matter...is a thing limited by nature'[17] — or as social recognition — 'all society...exists for the sake either of advantage or glory,...[but] glorying, like honour, is nothing if everybody has it'.[18] Furthermore, human beings in his view have neither any innate moral sense nor any natural inclination to integrate their individual desires and needs in a shared order. Social conflict is therefore endemic; in this perspective, the English civil war was merely a particular example of a universal problem. To solve it Hobbes introduced into political thought the insights and method of the new science. His account of human nature was an application to people of the approach adopted by Galileo, seeing them as homogeneous bodies in motion, with no intrinsic purpose beyond their own survival. His solution was an application to society of the Baconian view that only the maker has knowledge: 'to men is granted knowledge only of those things whose generation depends upon their judgement'.[19]

Unlike Bacon, Hobbes did not think that we could know nature, since we are not its author. Where we could have true knowledge was in matters of human invention, namely, geometry — 'because we ourselves create the figures' — and politics and ethics — 'because we ourselves create the causes of justice, that is, laws and conventions'.[20] The 'science of natural justice'[21] which he set out in *De Cive* (1642) and *Leviathan* (1651) was a rigorous exposition of the one political order which could provide the social peace that individuals must want for their own survival. The manner in which he conducts his argument conveys both the excitement of a first discovery and the confidence of ideas which can be put into effect, because they relate to human making (where knowledge can be complete and its application effective). Moreover, the very absence of any fixed values or moral principles, which so shocked Hobbes' contemporaries, contributed to this confidence: where so little is given, so much can be made.

At the same time Hobbes' political writings are a sustained attack on human independence and invention. While on one hand he insists on individuals thinking for themselves in order to recognize the futility of past authorities and the accuracy of his own analysis,[22] (and therefore establish for themselves the validity of his ideas), on the other hand he wishes to make all thought subject to the control of an absolute ruler: the sovereign will 'be judge of...opinions and doctrines...and shall examine the doctrine of all books before they be published'.[23] Likewise, *Leviathan* opens with a grandiloquent statement about human invention — 'nature (the art whereby God hath made and governs the world) is by the art of man, as in many other things, so in this also imitated, that it can make an artificial animal...For by art is created that great Leviathan called a Commonwealth or State'.[24] But the agreement which institutes political rule also puts an end to all political activity, except that conducted by the absolute sovereign. In an early work Hobbes compared this act to 'a creation out of nothing by human wit';[25] its effect, however, is to deny all human beings (except one) the further exercise of creative power.

The notion of *creatio ex nihilo* was, of course, associated with the Judaeo-Christian God and in *Leviathan* this connection was explicit: 'the pacts and covenants, by which the parts of this body politic were at first made,...resemble that Fiat, or the "Let us make man", pronounced by God in the Creation'.[26] By the kind of slippage that also occurs in his account of representation (which turns into a medieval concept of authorisation)[27] Hobbes then transfers this act (or, more precisely, all these actions) to the sovereign, who becomes a 'mortal God', like a ruler in ancient times.[28] Since the pact gives him absolute rule, his word becomes law, because justice derives not from any pre-existing right but from having, like God, 'irresistible power'.[29] The conclusive example of this is provided by the Book of Job.[30] In other words, the sovereign is a reincarnation of the Old Testament God,[31] and Hobbes' political theory could be seen as the story of the Creation and Fall in reverse sequence, discontent and strife giving way to an enduring peace and order.

To derive justice from will and power, as expressed in God's commands, was not a new idea. It was a central feature of the voluntarist and nominalist traditions,[32] and Hobbes' ideas on this subject can be seen as similar to those of Pascal. The latter was no less disturbed by the uncertainty of the times, the restlessness of his contemporaries, and the dangers which arose from their claims to self-reliance, independent of God: 'the inclination to the self is the beginning of all disorder'.[33] His solution also was to insist on the absolute position of 'the God of Abraham, Isaac and Jacob'.[34] But there was an element in Hobbes' work which we do not find in Pascal; for the former the range of human making is far more extensive. The experience not only of the new science but also of the republican politics of the middle years of the century (with their belief in a natural 'liberty of inventing')[35] had brought a sense of new possibility, the promise of which Hobbes captures but the consequences of which filled him with dismay. The severity of his response was in part a measure of that very possibility.

Milton experienced a comparable sense of innovation in politics, but with hope rather than fear. He threw himself into the radical cause in the 1640s and worked tirelessly on Cromwell's behalf during the Protectorate. The collapse of the Commonwealth left him isolated and although his opposition to monarchy remained strong his faith in republican politics declined. While in the first edition of his *Defence of the People of England* (1651) he had praised war and commotion in traditional republican terms,[36] in his *Ready and Easy Way to Establish a Free Commonwealth* (1660) he argued against unruly assemblies or elections.[37] By the time he had completed *Paradise Lost* seven years later, not only does his previous hope seem to have evaporated, but he appears to have arrived at a position which bore a surprising resemblance to that of Hobbes.

Paradise Lost asserts the overwhelming importance of obedience to, and dependence on, the absolute rule of God. When these values are observed there is order and unity, 'conformity divine';[38] reason prevails and love is pure. Such is the condition in heaven and was originally that of Paradise. In the characters of Satan and the devils we see the opposing values — disobedience and independence. Satan refused to submit to God's son and 'abide / United as one individual Soul'.[39] Because of his pride he and his associates rebelled against God and broke the unity. They did so because, unlike the good angels, they believed they were 'self-begot [and] self-raised...Our puissance is our own'.[40] On this basis they fought the war in heaven.

In this war (and subsequently) Satan is portrayed as superbly heroic, a creature of 'dauntless courage',[41] for whom strife is an opportunity for 'glory'.[42] His resentment of what he regards as the improper elevation of the Son of God fuels his ambition in ways which inevitably recall Achilles in the *Iliad*. And the latter's behaviour when he finally leaves his tent could well be expressed in Satan's remark: 'Only in destroying I find ease / To my relentless thoughts'.[43] After defeat in battle Satan suggests another way of opposing God, that of winning over the newly created race of humans. This 'bold design'[44] delighted the devils and Satan set off, like a 'great adventurer...[in] search / Of foreign worlds',[45] to accomplish this task. He now exchanged the mantle of Achilles for that of Odysseus. He becomes a 'false dissembler', an 'artificer of fraud', working by 'deceit and lies'.[46] In winning over Eve he is like an actor or an unscrupulous orator.[47] And so doing he is, of course, successful.

Looking back later on what had led to the Fall Adam describes Eve's fatal error as having given in to 'that / Strange desire of wandering', and Eve agrees.[48] They had been told that for them the happiest state was to 'seek / No happier state, and know to know no more'.[49] Again and again, throughout the poem, the prohibition against the new and unknown is repeated.[50] Human 'inventions',[51] and the unchecked imagination[52] are sources of evil; 'be lowly wise:/ Think only what concerns thee and thy being; / Dream not of other worlds'.[53] When nature has lost her natural abundance, after the Fall, people need fire and the instruments of civilisation. But the ideas for these come from God. Adam recognized this: 'Such fire to use, / And what may else be remedy or cure / To evils which our own misdeeds have wrought, / He will instruct us praying'.[54] The sons of Cain, however, did not. They were 'Inventors rare, / Unmindful of their maker, though his Spirit / Taught them, but they his gifts acknowledged none'.[55] Instead of sharing the true belief that human knowledge and ingenuity are gifts of God,[56] they repeated Satan's sin, the heresy of self-begetting. For this reason their homes were 'tents of wickedness'.[57] Human independence and innovation can only lead to the bad.

While much in Milton's poem was traditional, there were also some aspects which were ambiguous or unclear. In the text itself the Fall is shown in a positive light insofar as that state of need which becomes the human condition is also the cause of all subsequent achievement. The poem endorses this idea of the fortunate Fall, the benefits which 'evil shall produce',[58] as clearly as Milton's earlier statement of that view in the *Areopagitica*.[59] Other ambiguities tend to endorse Blake's observation that 'Milton wrote in fetters when he wrote of Angels and God, and at liberty when of Devils and Hell,...because he was a true Poet and of the Devil's party without knowing it'.[60] For Blake this meant that Milton had perceived what he (Blake) regarded as the theological or mythological truth, namely that the Old Testament Creator, embodying reason, had no claim to authority over Satan, who embodied energy and life. For him those myths which portrayed the battle of the sky-gods and the giants as giving victory to the former were wrong; and that error was manifest in the aesthetic power of Milton's writing about Satan.

Shelley had a similar response to the poem — 'nothing can exceed the energy and magnificence of the character of Satan as expressed in *Paradise Lost*'[61] — but for him the truth which this conveyed was not theological but moral and political. In recent years the specifically political aspects of the poem have received much attention. As the story of a failed rebellion it seems plausible that the work should reveal in some way Milton's view of the unsuccessful rebellion to which he himself had been so deeply committed. But exactly what his perspective was is hard to ascertain. To some, his republican hopes remained alive,[62] to others they are subjected to self-criticism,[63] while to others they are portrayed as a stage in a process of gradual human emancipation.[64] For the purposes of this study the most notable feature of Milton's account of Satan is the extent to which he is modelled on (or has parallels with) Prometheus,[65] not only in his defiance of divine authority but also in representing the spirit of innovation. This becomes evident when we see the striking parallels between Milton's poem and another book which was published in 1667, Sprat's *History of the Royal Society*. The way in which the former described sin and wrong-doing is very similar to the way the latter, in his polemical vindication of the Baconian project, portrayed invention and discovery.

Sprat praises change and innovation, 'the hazard of alteration and novelty'.[66] They are the products of a delight in wandering[67] — Eve's fatal error — and boldness: 'nature is...a mistress that soonest yields to the forward and bold'.[68] Both freedom and flexibility — 'never to be limited by constant rules'[69] — are essential. Those who have such characteristics — 'great inventors' — are usually 'violent...fiery, and...impetuous'.[70] The adjective Sprat uses to describe their temperament is 'heroic'.

Invention is an heroic thing...It requires an active, a bold, a nimble, a restless mind: a thousand difficulties must be contemned, with which a mean heart would be broken: much treasure must sometimes be scattered without any return: much violence, and vigour of thoughts must attend it: some irregularities, and excesses must be granted it, that would hardly be pardoned by the severe rules of prudence. All [of] which may persuade us, that a large, and an unbounded mind is likely to be the author of greater productions, than...calm, obscure, and fettered endeavours.[71]

To be 'unbounded' was in *Paradise Lost* the quintessential sin. And as Satan's heroic temperament was revealed in his opposition to God, and conflict was displayed as productive, in a similar fashion Sprat describes warfare and times of 'tempests and thunders in the state' as provoking 'new thought' in men, making them 'active, industrious and inquisitive'.[72] The two writers seem to be describing the same phenomenon, one to praise, the other to condemn.

It became a commonplace in Europe, from the 17th century onwards, to name the decisive inventions which had set this epoch apart from previous times, as the compass, the printing-press, and gunpowder. The latter, however, was for obvious reasons seen as different from the first two and its invention was frequently ascribed to the Devil.[73] Milton was (in his own terms) more consistent. He depicts the devils as inventing gunpowder,[74] but that was not because gunpowder was uniquely bad, but because the inventive impulse itself was bad. We see this not only in his general attitude to novelty and independence but also in particular details, like the way one of the devils, Mulciber, is modelled on Hephaestos,[75] or another, Mammon, makes the claim that 'we can create'.[76] The meaning of obedience is, by contrast, the acceptance of what is God-given.

The new worlds opened up possibilities which had never existed before, the outcome of which it was impossible to foresee. In such circumstances the emphatic positions adopted by Hobbes and Milton were not unusual. Nor were their particular responses in themselves new. The former's assertion of the need for strong political authority was a reworking of a theme that had become common during the previous century, and Milton's rejection of human self-confidence and ambition stood in a long tradition of Christian thought. What makes these instances notable (from our point of view) is the intense engagement, in both *Leviathan* and *Paradise Lost*, with the question of human making and innovation. It is because each writer recognized so clearly and appreciated so fully the capacities and opportunities which were beginning to become available that their refusal of them is so striking. Their writings indicate how difficult it could be to give those capacities independent value.

II

'This is the age wherein all men's souls are in a kind of fermentation, and the spirit of wisdom and learning begins to mount and free itself from those...impediments wherewith it has been so long clogged';[77] 'there is no truth so abstruse, nor so far elevated out of our reach, but man's wit may raise engines to scale and conquer it'.[78] These statements, from the conclusion to Henry Power's *Experimental Philosophy* (1664), display a confidence in human ability which was not theoretical or programmatic (in the manner of Francis Bacon) but based on the achievements of the previous half-century; he refers for example to what had become visible through the microscope (never seen before by human beings) and to discoveries in physics (by Boyle) and medicine (by Harvey).[79] The sense of anticipation which is so striking a feature of this work (as also of Sprat's *History*) was expressed in still more optimistic terms a generation later by Fontenelle. He described the ways in which the solutions to problems of scientific or mathematical enquiry, which appeared to his French contemporaries to be too abstruse or remote to be useful, had already had practical effect. Intellectual advance, now on sure foundations, would lead to the invention of new machines 'to reduce or ease our work', or to 'new and beneficial products for us to use' (and thus 'increase the sum of our wealth'), or enable us to develop new forms of motion so that 'one day we shall be able to fly to the moon'.[80] Between these two declarations by Power and Fontenelle there had occurred the outstanding event in 17th century science — the publication of Newton's *Principia Mathematica* (1687). This work showed that the universe did have a coherence and order (which observations since Copernicus had put in doubt) and was itself a triumphant demonstration of human powers of understanding. As such it gave further impetus to those sailing under the colours of the new science. Previous accounts of the natural world could now be dismissed as being as useless as ancient maps of the earth's surface.

The claim that a new epoch in human history was in the process of arriving was a central issue in the Quarrel of the Ancients and the Moderns, a dispute about the respective merits of each which took place in France and England in the last two decades of the century. Much of the argument was concerned with the literary achievements of classical poets, and the value of the neo-classical aesthetic which had been derived either from their example or from ancient writings about poetry.[81] Insofar as this debate set matters of taste (in poetry) in opposition to matters of knowledge (in science) it was a dialogue of the deaf, but there were also fundamental areas of disagreement. One was the importance of tradition, of authority based on past achievement; another was the view that nature decays, making it impossible for us ever to be more than dwarves on giants' shoulders.[82] On both these issues the moderns (Fontenelle and Perrault in France, William Wotton in England) asserted the priority of the living over the dead and that of the future over the past; nature is not in decline and 'men will never degenerate'.[83]

The claims of the moderns about the human capacity to understand, and exert power over, the natural world were part of a decisive shift which was beginning to occur — a shift in the balance between God's bounty and human endeavour. 'The earth is the Lord's and the fulness thereof', wrote the Psalmist; 'it is He that has made us and not we ourselves'.[84] No longer. As people gradually became conscious of how different they were to the ancients, so they also began to abandon their immemorial sense of dependence on God. Traditional doctrines began to be called into question to an unprecedented extent: the fear of hell began to lose its force, statements attacking the notion of original sin slowly began to increase.[85] The idea of toleration (limited thought it might be) started to win approval; evidence that this was leading to (or a sign of) actual change can be seen from the steady fall in the number of people who felt it necessary to kill others because of disagreement about religious belief. Another indication of this shift can be seen from the way that (in the writings of Pufendorf) the word 'culture' first took on its modern meaning, referring not to the cultivation of what is given but rather to what sets human beings apart from nature, the achievement of that which is distinctly human.[86] What was God-given was beginning to become of less significance than what human beings were making.

'If we will rightly estimate things, as they come to our use, and cast up several expenses about them, what in them is purely owing to nature, and what to labour,' wrote Locke in his *Second Treatise on Government*, 'we shall find that in most of them ninety-nine out of one hundred are wholly to be put on the account of labour'.[87] In his writings different kinds of human making occupied a central place. In his epistemology people come into the world with nothing given, the mind a *tabula rasa;* as a result, they have no choice but to 'think and know for themselves'.[88] We learn from what we experience; from the simple ideas we receive we actively make the complex ideas which come to constitute knowledge. Since everyone's experience is fresh, no true knowledge can be second-hand, and since everyone's experience may be different (and we are each different anyway), then we can only arrive at knowledge in an individual way, each of us making it for him or her self. Likewise, in his political theory, right in property derives from labour, and the basis of obligation in society derives from consenting with others 'to make one body politic under one government'.[89] In his *Essay concerning Human Understanding* Locke himself pointed out the similarity of the kind of making that occurs in our minds and that which takes places in 'the great visible world of things': 'man's power and its way of operation [is] muchwhat the same in the material and intellectual worlds'.[90] In neither, he went on, did men actually make anything new; they only put available materials to use. But elsewhere in the *Essay* he wrote of 'invention', (thinking of an idea 'before it existed'),[91] and in the *Second Treatise* the whole direction of the argument was to attack the illegitimacy of the historically given and to assert the right to institute a new government. A father's authority ends as we come of age and then our fate is (or should be) in our own hands. Indeed, on occasion Locke went so far as to say that our very nature is to a large degree subject to human alteration: 'nine parts out of ten [in human beings] are what they are, good or evil, useful or not, by their education'.[92]

Locke's emphasis on human making did not in any way detract from his belief in the Christian God, 'a Supreme Being, infinite in power, goodness and wisdom, whose workmanship we are, and on whom we depend'.[93] This idea underpins both his philosophical and political writings Yet even though this God was a workman and 'infinitely wise Maker',[94] there is a clear tension in Locke's thought between omnipotent God and semi-independent man. The assurance of a rational, divinely-ordained order is uneasily combined with the empirical realm of human affairs. For many of Locke's contemporaries the insecure character of this combination was only too plain. The *Essay*'s denial of innate ideas, its doubts about substance, real essence and personal identity, made its nominalist and relativist elements seem the main theme. Worse, the primacy it gave to the senses, the limits it set to what we can know, and the suggestion which Locke threw out that God might be able to add the power of thinking to matter,[95] called into question the priority of mind and reason itself. In the words of an English divine, William Sherlock, Locke's suggestions had the effect of depicting mind as 'younger than matter, later than the making of the world, and therefore not the maker of it'.[96]

Although this was not at all Locke's meaning, it points to an important fact about his thought. For him human making was not an image of divine making; he may have owed a debt to Platonism, but on this subject he owed none to neo-Platonism. When God made humans 'in his own image and likeness' this meant for Locke that he gave them reason and therefore made them 'capable of dominion'.[97] It did not mean that he gave them quasi-divine creative powers; for Locke there was a clear distinction between 'creation', 'generation', and 'making'.[98] Nor was human making necessarily the result of superabundant gifts or admirable qualities; in certain respects it was the product of need and discontent. Both were a consequence of the Fall: 'God commanded and [man's] wants forced him to labour'.[99] Labour led to property and that in turn led (with the invention of money) to greed and ambition: 'when private possessions and labour, which now the curse of the earth had made necessary, by degrees made a distinction of conditions, it gave room for covetousness, pride and ambition, which by fashion and example spread the corruption which has so prevailed over mankind'.[100] The moral view was clear: 'God gave the world ...to the use of the industrious and rational...not to the fancy or covetousness of the quarrelsome and contentious'.[101] But we are not only creatures of reason. We have an imagination which is 'always restless', and a will which tends towards 'every extravagant project'.[102] As a result, 'we are seldom at ease', we are beset by 'a constant succession of uneasinesses', not least 'the fantastical uneasiness, (as itch after honour, power or riches, etc), which acquired habits by fashion, example and education have settled in us'.[103] But it is precisely this uneasiness which stimulates us to action and making.

The great business of life, for Locke, was action.[104] We are not only meant to be good but to be vigorous and active; if we were contented we would achieve nothing.[105] The benefits of what humans have done by way of 'arts and inventions, engines and utensils' to improve their lives is obvious, notable, and to be applauded.[106] But these have not come about by simply following rational (or religious) precepts; our duty to labour has become inextricably entangled with the sins of pride and ambition. What lay behind these remarks (apart from the views Locke derived from his Puritan upbringing) was a development which was as significant to him as his association with contemporary scientific thought or his debts to the republican politics of opposition to James II. This development related to human making not in the intellectual or political sphere, but in economics. What Locke was referring to was, in effect, a third new world — that of commerce.

We cannot date the perception of this new world with the historical neatness of the discoveries of Columbus and Copernicus, but in the late 17th century there was a growing awareness that something dramatically new had begun to appear. The decisive experience in this case was the phenomenon of the Dutch Republic, the seven United Provinces of the Netherlands which had succeeded in defeating their Spanish rulers and had then become enormously rich. The distinctive feature about their wealth was that it derived neither from conquest nor from native resources. The population was much greater than indigenous agriculture could support and there was neither natural abundance nor mineral deposits. On the contrary, the Dutch had to reclaim land from the sea and protect it against flooding. The country was, in fact, virtually a *tabula rasa*, 'grown rich', as William Temple wrote in his influential *Observations* (1673), not 'by any natural commodities but by force of industry'.[107]

Temple attributed the wealth of the Dutch principally to their frugal living and hard working, along with their respect for property-rights, their religious toleration (which attracted foreigners), and their political stability. The frugality had 'grown universal by being at first necessary [as a result of the Spanish occupation], but since [become] honourable among them';[108] and it was reinforced, in his view, by a native disposition (the result of the climate) which made them assiduous, obsessive and parsimonious.[109] He thought that if these qualities were lost then Holland's greatness would end, and believed that (as he was writing) this was beginning to occur. The emphasis Temple put on these particular characteristics made the Dutch success seem fragile, which led him to observe: 'it seems to be with trade, as with the sea (its element), that it has a certain pitch, above which it never rises in the highest tides'.[110]

However, Dutch prosperity did not only depend on habits of frugality. Other factors were more important. There was, first, the scale of the activity, literally world-wide, which meant that so great was the volume and variety of goods traded that the market became permanent. There was, second, to support this, an emphasis on freedom as an essential requisite for trade, rather than the previous concern to achieve balance; (this was a matter of practical policy, rather than doctrine). Thirdly, a number of institutional innovations occurred — new kinds of insurance, company organisation, banking and finance — which proved immensely effective. As the market became permanent, so with the joint-stock company the identity of the organisation (in the form of capital) became permanent; individual shares in the company could then change hands and become in themselves a marketable commodity, thus increasing investment. As the market became impersonal so too did banking, credit no longer relying on an individual or family, but on the holders of the bank's stock. Most important of all, in the short term, the Dutch invented a new method of public financing, securing the national debt against future tax-revenue; this both made possible an unprecedented level of public expenditure and made that expenditure a matter of much wider public concern.

None of these facts was restricted to Dutch character or circumstances. All could be applied elsewhere, and in England they were adopted with even more striking results. This was because trade in England did not just mean buying and selling. It was rather, as Nicholas Barbon wrote in his *Discourse of Trade* (1690), both 'the making and the selling',[111] or as Defoe wrote in his *Plan of English Commerce* (1729) 'manufacture' as well as 'commerce', 'labouring' as well as 'dealing'.[112] The two were mutually stimulating, and both were assisted by the new kinds of finance. The result was that while the Dutch had depended mostly on their imports in order to re-export, the English trade was 'raised wholly within itself'.[113] Defoe qualified this comment, since the British (as they now were) were not in fact self-sufficient, but the point he was making was important: the British had substantial native industries which not only provided goods to export but which were themselves stimulated by the expansion of trade. The result was that Defoe did not think of trade as a tide which ebbed and flowed within limits; rather, it was like an incoming tide overcoming obstacles in its way. In fact the image of the tide was less suitable for trade than that of 'an unbounded ocean', and it called for the 'enterprising genius' and 'adventuring spirit' of former times, in order 'to raise new worlds of commerce'.[114] Expansion overseas would also be a stimulus to activity at home. 'Trade encourages manufacture, prompts invention, employs people, increases labour, and pays wages';[115] 'as the industry of mankind is set to work, their hopes and views are raised, and their ambition fired; the view and prospect of gain inspires the world with the keenest vigour, [and] puts new life into their souls'.[116]

The overall result was that economic activity was seen less and less as something needing to be regulated in order to achieve a balance, as suggested for example in Misselden's *The Circle of Commerce* (1623). Rather, it was dynamic, expanding, and oriented towards the future. As restrictive regulations from above were harmful, so dependence on the past was fatal; the man of landed wealth, Sir Roger de Coverley, had to give way to the man of moveable wealth, Sir Andrew Freeport.[117] For (as Defoe was fond of writing) 'an estate's a pond, but a trade is a spring,...an inexhausted current, which not only fills the pond and keeps it full, but is continually running over, and fills all the lower ponds and places about it'.[118]

This third new world, therefore, was also one which (like the earlier new worlds in geography and astronomy) went beyond previous limits, which broke down existing frameworks and introduced new possibilities along with new difficulties. The possibilities were those of Defoe's 'unbounded ocean'; the difficulties were those itemized by Locke — the central place which 'covetousness, pride and ambition' seemed to occupy in these economic conditions. 'Trade', wrote Davenant in 1696, 'without doubt, is in its nature a pernicious thing;…it gives rise to fraud and avarice, and extinguishes virtue and simplicity of manners'.[119]

The moral problems which came to be seen as integral to commercial activity were (in many respects) both novel and unwelcome. So too was another feature of this new world, that which Locke referred to as 'constant uneasiness'. This was a result of the high degree of uncertainty which accompanied ever-increasing competition. The world of human affairs had, of course, long been seen as one of 'mutability', both unstable and unpredictable.[120] But that view had been contained within an overarching framework of permanence. With commerce, instability was not merely to be expected — any 'unbounded ocean' would have its treacherous currents and hidden reefs — but rather, it was necessary. Prosperity depended on continual change, according not to plans but to fashion. 'Fashion…is the great promoter of trade…It is [its] spirit and life;…it makes a circulation and gives a value, by turns, to all sorts of commodities [and so] keeps the great body of trade in motion'.[121] In such a world nothing was fixed, and no value was intrinsic. There is no 'real worth or excellency in things', wrote Mandeville, and 'in morals there is no greater certainty'.[122] In other words, all values were evanescent.

Everyone lived under the threat of new competition, with the result that anyone who did not 'turn his talents to account…will undoubtedly be left behind…The richest men in a trading nation have no security against poverty'.[123] But that very pressure, though unavoidable, could also be beneficial. Considering the problems caused by cheap imports from India Henry Martyn observed (in 1701) that that trade, instead of being a threat, was 'very likely to be the cause of the invention of arts, and mills, and engines, [and so] save the labour of hands in other manufactures. Such things are successively invented to do a great deal of work with little labour or hands; they are the effects of necessity and emulation'.[124] As a result, he continued, 'every man must still be inventing himself, or still be advancing to further perfection upon the invention of other men'.[125] As increased scientific understanding and developments in technology were making more invention *possible,* so the conditions of commerce began to make more invention and innovative action *necessary.* What such action and invention actually involved therefore became a matter of central concern.

CHAPTER FIVE

Action and imagination

I

In the ancient world the fall of man, his departure from a Golden Age, was attributed to invention, ambition and greed. As soon as people were not content to accept what nature provided, and the cry went up 'Enough of acorns!', the Golden Age came to an end. The bonds which tied human beings to nature were broken; a separation began which could never be repaired. In the metaphysics and theology which subsequently came to dominate European thought a new kind of bonding was constructed (with transcendent Forms or the Logos or God), while the separation between man and nature was magnified, in a dualism of the flesh and the spirit. Not surprisingly, the myth of an original unity remained potent.

In the early 18th century, social and economic change began to raise new questions about order or stability in human affairs. To make people understand what this change involved Mandeville took up the traditional idea of the Golden Age (in his expanded edition of *The Fable of the Bees* (1723)). He described it as a time of innocence and 'true happiness',[1] when people found their needs met by nature, and were content with that.[2] They lived peacefully and poorly, in small societies,[3] with a frugality which was acceptable because both knowledge and desires were limited.[4] There were no books, no money, no trade, no foreign contact of any kind.[5] It was a static world in which (as among illiterates, or 'poor silly country people') there was fellow-feeling and generosity.[6] At that time people had been temperate, honest, healthy, docile and sincere.[7]

Mandeville used this idea in order to draw attention to the situation now, in 'industrious, wealthy and powerful' countries.[8] For here everything is the reverse of the Golden Age. Instead of peaceful calm there is instability;[9] instead of happiness and innocence, there is restlessness and discontent;[10] instead of frugality there is a 'thirst after gain',[11] and instead of generosity there is rivalry, envy and deceit.[12] But as a result of all these bad qualities, there are also wealth and power, 'the most elegant comforts of life', arts and sciences, variety and abundance.[13]

Mandeville called his work a 'satire',[14] and perhaps its most satirical aspect was his picture of the Golden Age. In his account there never was any natural goodness in man,[15] nor generosity or restraint. People were governed by their passions, essentially individualist — 'every individual is a little world by itself'[16] — selfish, headstrong and cunning.[17] Nature operated according to fixed laws and therefore had a 'stability', but that was 'nowhere to be met with in things of human contrivance';[18] 'mankind are naturally fickle, and delight in change and variety'.[19] For that reason, 'the invention of money [was] more skilfully adapted to the whole bent of our nature, than any other human contrivance'.[20] In other words, the Golden Age was a delusion, and the present, instead of being a lapse into corruption, should be seen rather as revealing most clearly what we are, the time when our innate qualities have become most clearly manifest.

There never was an original unity, either among people or within any single person. Contradiction is endemic.[21] Just as our 'vital spirits and life itself' are not beautiful or noble but 'small trifling films and little pipes',[22] so, in general, outward appearances do not correspond to inner motives. 'A beautiful superstructure may be raised upon a rotten and despicable foundation';[23] a clear and beautiful stream may derive from a mean and muddy spring.[24] The immediate polemical aim of the *Fable* was to demonstrate how mean and muddy were the springs of human action, to drag 'the lurking fiend from his darkest recesses into a glaring light'.[25] The fiend was pride, vanity or, as Mandeville also called it 'self-liking' — 'the natural faculty by which every mortal...over-values and imagines better things of himself'.[26] The 'prodigious force and exorbitant power' of our need for approval and distinction[27] forms the basis for the idea of honour, and this, in conjunction with the corresponding fear of shame, is the mainspring of human behaviour in society. Being ever alert to the opinion other people may have of us, and ever envious of praise given to anyone else, we are always restless and in state of 'uneasiness' or discontent.[28] This picture of human society as a 'continual striving to outdo one another'[29] has obvious affinities with that of Hobbes, but Mandeville's view was less brittle and more sinuous. And the principal reason for that difference lay in the fact that, as he saw it, the existence of vanity and rivalry was not a threat to society. On the contrary, in the new world of commerce, it was its lifeblood.

If a Golden Age had ever existed there would have been no need to leave it. But the condition of man was never one of tranquillity and contentment; both the initial situation in which humans lived and the character of human nature itself drove people to alter their original situation. The first was imperfect and the second was vicious; that is to say, the first left much to be desired and the second then *imagined* much more to be desired. Our physical nakedness, for example, left us exposed to the weather and injury; so we invented clothing. Then our 'boundless pride'[30] made us want to look better than we actually did look. People delight 'to imagine that they appear what they would be', 'they hug themselves in their disguise';[31] and this appearance or disguise is, because of our natural envy, assessed in comparison with others. This leads to a continual process of change and need for invention. It is this 'that sets the poor to work, adds spurs to industry and encourages the skilful artificer to search after further improvements', thus making a continual *'plus ultra* for the ingenious'.[32] In this way it was possible to see how 'vice nursed ingenuity'; for it is our wants and imperfections which are 'the seeds of all arts, industry and labour'.[33]

Mandeville described two kinds of invention. The first, which he applied to the invention of politics, was a matter of trial and error; not due to 'the excellency of man's genius, and the depths of his penetration', but the 'experience of many generations'.[34] The second, which he related to individual activities, either economic or artistic, was a product of discontent, envy and ambition. Inventive people are those who are most driven by these passions. It is their individual need, and their particular 'active, stirring' temperament which leads them to try the unknown. To suppose that innovation comes about by *a priori* reasoning is an error. Rather, it is animated by 'the lurking fiend', and is a matter more of touch than of thought.[35]

These two kinds of invention could be seen as manifestations of a single theory, the most important aspects of which were the dominant roles played by necessity and by trial and error. It was, in other words, a fundamentally Epicurean theory and was one of several Epicurean elements in Mandeville's work, most notably his conjectural history of the development of human society and his view of human psychology. The writings of Gassendi in the middle of the 17th century had stimulated a revival of interest in Epicurus' thought, and Mandeville acknowledged a debt to the Frenchman.[36] In his *Free Thoughts on Religion* (1720) he also endorsed Epicurus' objections to the idea of Providence,[37] and in Part Two of the *Fable* he expounded the view of nature as a self-regulating process of generation and destruction, indifferent to human well-being.[38] (We may also note that one of his earliest publications, *Typhon* (1704), was an incomplete mock epic about the war of the gods and the giants, mocking the gods and applauding the giants.)[39] Furthermore, it is possible to see what has been regarded as Mandeville's most significant conceptual innovation – the law of unintended consequences[40] — as the result of his applying to human society the Epicurean view of the cosmos. Just as the coherence we see in the starry heavens was (for Epicurus) the result not of the activity of a supremely powerful intelligence, but rather a temporary order produced by the fortuitous combination of randomly moving atoms, so, similarly, the peaceful and productive interaction of human beings in commercial society is not the outcome of consciously harmonious intentions but the result of what occurs when thousands of individuals pursue their particular goals, driven by insecurity and pride.[41]

The central theme of the *Fable* — the radical disparity between agency and outcome: 'private vices, public benefits'[42] — was part of a broader disagreement with the dominant traditions of Christian thought. Mandeville made this clear by taking issue with the ideas of the third Earl of Shaftesbury. Where the latter asserted the existence of permanent values, Mandeville asserted relativism, the precarious instability of the *pulchrum* and *honestum*.[43] We are not motivated by generosity or fellow-feeling, Shaftesbury's 'participation' (p.138), but by our 'bad and hateful qualities', and, far from being any kind of spiritual creature, man is an animal.[44] (Mandeville always stressed the role of physicality and sexuality in human life, and wrote severely against human cruelty to other animals.)[45] At the same time, humans are obviously different from other animals, but that is less because of reason than because of 'pride'; this had first made people aware of their difference from other animals, and then led to this difference becoming so immense.[46] Above all, perhaps, Mandeville wished to stress the impotence of unity: we are contradictory creatures and always in conflict, but therein lies the source of our achievement. Similarly, what looks good may originate in the bad; there is no necessary unity in a human product, in the sense of something which looks beautiful being the result of a beautiful idea. It is an error to suppose that a design visible in an end-product had originally been present in the impulses or motives which had led to its production,[47] the error I call the ergonic fallacy (p.9). In general, therefore, Mandeville claimed that 'those who can enlarge their view, and will give themselves the leisure of gazing on the prospect of concatenated events, may, in a hundred places, see good spring up and pullulate from evil as naturally as chicken do from eggs'.[48] To understand commercial society it is necessary to recognize that 'evil in this world...is the grand principle',[49] for that is the driving force in human life.

Mandeville wrote in a provocative manner, but the immense impact of *The Fable of the Bees* (from 1723 onwards) was due not to the way he caused offence but to the accuracy of his analysis. For some people rivalry and competition could be categorized under the heading of 'emulation', which had long had an honourable place in the book of virtues. But emulation had always been problematic, since it was merely the sunny side of that quality which had envy as its shady side.[50] And the difficulties which arose with commerce were not confined to envy alone. 'Custom has driven us beyond the limits of our morals in many things, which trade makes necessary and which we cannot now avoid', wrote Defoe; 'it is impossible for tradesmen to be Christians;...[for] all the ordinary communication of life is now full of lying'.[51] 'In the language of trade', he observed elsewhere, 'our vices are our virtues, and our extravagances as necessary as our essentials'.[52] Such conditions seemed morally bewildering, falling outside habitual values and beliefs.

The fact was that the vast changes being brought about by the new worlds of science and commerce demanded a new way of thinking. In the generation following Mandeville and Defoe this was what Hume set out to provide. He took over three features of the new science: the picture of nature as consisting of atomic units coming together in certain ways; the Baconian-Newtonian insistence on experiment, on making observation and experience decisive; and (thirdly) the drastic separation between human beings and nature which was embodied in the distinction of primary and secondary qualities or in the exclusion of final causes. The natural world in itself is not as we as humans see it; we endow it with certain features, like colours, but they are only in our minds, our receiving sensory apparatus. Nature itself is colourless. Similarly, we have purposes and intentions, but nature has none. In Hume's famous phrase, 'is' does not imply 'ought'.[53] For the purposes of this study it was this third aspect which was most significant. By making the separation of humanity from the natural world fundamental, Hume put to one side the model of order and permanence to which Newton had given new life. To take seriously the methodological assumptions of the new science meant recognising the limits of what was regarded as its greatest achievement. Instead, the 'science of man' which Hume wanted to construct must be derived entirely from the human realm: 'we must therefore glean up our experiments in this science from a cautious observation of human life and take them as they appear in the common course of the world, by men's behaviour in company, in affairs, and in their pleasures'.[54]

This meant taking account of the new world of commerce, in which Hume was briefly employed and for which he had the greatest respect. ('It is an ancient prejudice industriously propagated by the dunces of all countries: that a man of genius is unfit for business'.)[55] To take commerce seriously, (that is, to think of it more as a norm than an aberration), was one factor which gave new life to ancient arguments for scepticism. On contemporary as well as philosophical grounds Hume attacked assumptions about permanence or inherent rationality, and showed how the world could be seen as wholly contingent: 'all beings in the universe, considered in themselves, appear entirely loose and independent of each other'.[56] In his *Treatise on Human Nature* (1739-40) he shifted the basis of mental activity from reason to the imagination,[57] but his insistence that 'whatever we can imagine is possible', that 'what is [now], may not be [tomorrow]',[58] derived its force less from philosophical analysis than from the fact that such indeed was our experience in 'the common course of the world', above all in the new world of commerce. What in the *Treatise* is set out as a general principle, in the *Essays* is related to social (and especially economic) experience. In his essay 'Of Commerce' (1752), for example, Hume wrote: 'when a man deliberates concerning his conduct in any particular affair, and forms schemes in politics, trade, economy or any business in life, he never ought to draw his arguments too fine, or connect too long a chain of reasoning, and produce an event different from what he expected'.[59]

In this essay Hume went on to distinguish between particular affairs and general subjects in a way that would allow him to make general statements about so changeable a matter as commerce; and the problem he faced there was comparable to the problem of making a science out of the contingent. Hume never tired of pointing out the instability of our world and the unsteadiness of our thought; nor the fact that moral principles and speculative opinions were 'in a continual flux and revolution', and that the uniformity and regularity of the universe was in utter contrast to 'the various and contrary events of human life'.[60] He needed to do this in order to clear away all traces of rationalism and notions of essence or substance. Only when that was done was it possible to see humans as naturally equipped for, and adapted to, this unstable and changeable life. A science of man (in the sense of knowledge based on evident regularities) was possible because human beings did operate in a regular manner. There are 'permanent, irresistible and universal' principles in our minds which 'are the foundation of all our thoughts and actions'.[61] While there are severe limits to what we can know about ultimate truths — what or why nature 'really' is — we can observe precise and regular characteristics about human nature. In this way we can be saved from extreme scepticism and have a foundation for ideas of morality and justice. For this reason the instability of our lives need not alarm us.

Inside or alongside this minimal case Hume had another attitude to instability which, instead of being defensive and erecting barriers against it, positively welcomed it. 'There is no craving or demand of the human mind more constant and insatiable than that for exercise and employment'.[62] A static, unchanging world would be tedious and insipid. The chief ingredients of human happiness are action and pleasure, and above all pleasure in action, in whatever stimulates 'that quick march of the spirits which takes a man from himself, and chiefly gives satisfaction'.[63] Such stimulation is not provided by the predictable or the known; accordingly, 'the mind...naturally seeks after foreign objects, which may produce a lively sensation, and agitate the spirits. On the appearance of such an object...the blood flows with a new tide, the heart is elevated; and the whole man acquires a vigour'.[64] Whether a man is occupied in philosophy or hunting, his pleasure 'consists in the action of the mind and body; the motion, the attention, the difficulty, and the uncertainty'.[65]

Hume was here articulating one of the great themes of the 18th century — man is born for action. From Steele and Defoe to James Thomson and Edward Young, from Voltaire's attack on Pascal to Diderot's *Encyclopédie,* or the ringing declaration of Goethe's Faust — 'In the beginning was the deed (*Im Anfang war die Tat*)'[66] — this theme recurs. It was one aspect of that belief which was common to all the diverse writers and thinkers who have come to be associated with the Enlightenment, namely, the belief in human potential and (as a corollary) the need for freedom in which it could be realized. For Hume, the uncertainty of the human realm was more than matched by the ability to make use of opportunities: 'mankind is an inventive species'.[67] In many areas such opportunity was still denied; but the expansion of commerce (and all that that involved) had opened up a vast new field of action. Hume recognized the significance of this: 'in times when industry and the arts flourish, men are kept in perpetual occupation, and enjoy, as their reward, the occupation itself, as well as those pleasures which are the fruit of their labour'.[68] In other words, so great could be the pleasure in action that it could be satisfying as such, 'the occupation itself', irrespective of a particular end-result.

This point, which had earlier been made by Mandeville, was developed by Adam Ferguson. In the chapter 'Of Happiness' in his *Essay on the History of Civil Society* (1767) he drew on Hume and gave particular emphasis to this idea. Man's 'activity is of more importance than the very pleasure he seeks'; happiness 'arises more from the pursuit, than from the attainment of any end whatsoever'.[69] Unlike Hume, Ferguson was hostile to commercial society, so his recognition of the satisfactions it could give is even more notable. 'Why may not the man whose object is money', he asked, 'be understood to lead a life of amusement and pleasure, not only more than that of the spendthrift, but even as much as the virtuoso, the scholar, the man of taste?'[70] In this perspective, to see the accumulation of wealth simply as bad was to suffer from long-sightedness, to be able to see only the distant goal and unaware that much more (and much that could be admirable) might be involved.

Essential to Hume's theory of action (as to that of Ferguson) was the pleasure to be derived from difficulty: it is 'a quality very observable in human nature, that any opposition, which does not entirely discourage and intimidate us, has rather a contrary effect, and inspires us with a more than ordinary grandeur and magnanimity. In collecting our force to overcome the opposition, we invigorate the soul, and give it an elevation with which otherwise it would never have been acquainted. Compliance, by rendering our strength useless, makes us insensible of it; but opposition awakens and employs it'.[71] To face and overcome the difficult and unknown demanded not only energy but also invention. Opposition was valuable because it was productive. Just as individuals are aroused by 'foreign objects', so economic activity in a nation is enlivened by rivalry with foreigners.

> A commerce with strangers...rouses men from their indolence; and, presenting the gayer and more opulent part of the nation with objects of luxury which they never before dreamed of, raises in them a desire of a more splendid way of life than what their ancestors enjoyed. And at the same time, the few merchants who possess the secret of this importation and exportation, make great profits and, becoming rivals in wealth of the ancient nobility, tempt other adventurers to become their rivals in commerce. Imitation soon diffuses all those arts, while domestic manufacturers emulate the foreign in their improvements, and work up every home commodity to the utmost perfection of which it is susceptible.[72]

Hume was here describing what historically had been occurring in Britain. At the same time, he was attempting to put forward general rules about the character of commerce, the benefits which arose from challenge and opposition. These benefits were, obviously and evidently, those of material improvement. But there was also another, more profound, kind of benefit, in terms of self-development. The human need for 'exercise and employment' did not only stem from a desire for variety, interest and pleasure. It was also the principal means to become and reveal who you were. Since the notion of an essence was to Hume nonsensical, and we can only determine what an entity is by the way in which it is seen to work, so the distinction between 'a *power* and the *exercise* of it is entirely frivolous...Neither [a] man nor any other being ought ever to be thought possessed of any ability, unless it be exerted or put in action'.[73] The need for constant action in commercial society (due to the evanescence of value) could therefore be enriching in terms of individual personality, as much as in measurable wealth.

Hume's emphasis on the benefits of commerce was part of his polemic against Mandeville's theme of the dynamic force of 'evil'. He regarded this view as an exaggeration, for human motives are mixed: 'ambition, avarice, self-love, vanity, friendship, generosity, public spirit; these passions, mixed in various degrees, and distributed throughout society, have been...and still are the sources of all the actions and enterprize, which have ever been observed among mankind'.[74] More generally, Hume wanted to shift the focus of attention from motives (on which Mandeville had concentrated) to consequences. While not denying that commerce, like all human activities, was open to abuse he argued that the good should be assessed not by individuals' intentions but in terms of benefit and utility. In his *Political Discourses* (1752) he set out a number of arguments on this basis. As well as the fact of economic growth, and the advantages which came with that,[75] commerce had brought more social freedom, in terms of individual independence,[76] and more political freedom, as had become evident in Britain.[77] Furthermore, with the growth of towns and cities had come an increase in sociability, toleration, intellectual exchange and cultural activity,[78] so that 'industry, knowledge and humanity' could be seen as being 'linked together by an indissoluble chain'.[79] Hume provided extensive historical and comparative evidence to make his case, and this was one reason these essays were so influential.

While these writings undermined the force of Mandeville's sardonic criticism (as well as the objections of other critics of commerce), Hume nevertheless continued to have much in common with Mandeville. The latter's hostility to Shaftesbury was paralleled by Hume's distaste for all forms of Platonism. Writing about the benefits of opposition he observed: 'opposition awakens and employs [our strength]. This is also true in the inverse. Opposition not only enlarges the soul; but the soul, when full of courage and magnanimity, in a manner seeks opposition'.[80] It was a commonplace of Christian neo-Platonism, familiar to Hume's readers from the poems of Mallet or Thomson or Young, that the love of God and union with God 'enlarges' the soul.[81] Hume asserted that the reverse was true, not love but opposition, not union but conflict 'enlarges' the soul. In similar vein he attacked the idea of supernatural inspiration,[82] and insisted that 'everything useful to the life of man arises from the ground'.[83] Necessity, he asserted, is 'the great spur to industry and invention',[84] and government had arisen not out any clear idea about justice or order but rather out of a gradual process of trial and error.[85]

In an early letter Hume observed that 'there are different ways of examining the mind as well as the body. One may consider it either as an anatomist or as a painter; either to discover its most secret springs and principles or to describe the grace and beauty of its actions. I imagine it impossible to conjoin these two views'.[86] This statement echoes similar remarks by Mandeville on foundation and superstructure (p.76), or agent and outcome (p.78) and like them was an attack on the ergonic fallacy. Hume argued against this error in ways which were both more precise and more far-reaching. In his precise analysis in the *Treatise* he called into question the extent to which it was possible to establish any exact connection between cause and effect. (There could never be a logical entailment; we can only have working assumptions based on previous experience.)[87] Then, in his *Enquiry concerning human understanding* (1748) and his *Dialogues concerning natural religion* (published posthumously, 1779), he challenged the most common form of the fallacy, namely the argument from design.

Newton's success in demonstrating the mathematical regularity of the movements of all the known planets and their satellites had given compelling new life to this ancient belief. In the Queries to his *Optics* (1706-8), and the General Scholium he added to the 1713 edition of the *Principia*, Newton himself insisted that 'this most beautiful system' could only have come about from 'an intelligent and powerful Being', 'eternal, infinite, absolutely perfect',[88] and this view came to be held not only by Christians but also by deists, the main opponents of organized religion in 18th century Europe. Hume, who regarded the idea of design as 'the chief or sole argument for a divine existence',[89] attacked it on a number of grounds — the limits of human knowledge, the error of attributing greater qualities to a cause than are evident in its effects, the difficulty of deducing a totality from a single part, the implausibility of assuming that order and constancy are more fundamental than their opposites, and the problem of evil. In both the *Enquiry* and the *Dialogues* he drew on earlier disagreements between Stoics and Epicureans. While the former had maintained that order in a work must reflect the 'project and forethought of a workman',[90] the latter had pointed out that that order could be the result of a long process of trial and error.[91] While for the Stoics the first principle must be intelligent and rational, for Epicureans such an assumption was impossible to verify, for (in Hume's words) 'in all cases which we have ever seen, ideas are copied from real objects and are ectypal, not archetypal';[92] that is (to paraphrase), they echo, they do not activate. In the *Enquiry* the arguments against design are put into the mouth of a sceptical friend who speaks as 'Epicurus', and in the *Dialogues* the discussion of the problem of evil includes a statement that 'Epicurus' old questions are yet unanswered';[93] all the evidence we have supports not the idea of a benign Creator but rather the (Epicurean) notion of 'a blind nature, impregnated by a great vivifying principle'.[94]

Despite this apparent endorsement of Epicurean thought it does not follow (given the ambiguities of the dialogue-form) that Hume himself was an atheist. The *Dialogues* are modelled on Cicero's *De natura deorum* and Philo, the character in Hume's work who is the principal mouthpiece for his attack on the argument from design, corresponds more to Cotta, the sceptic in Cicero's dialogue, than to Velleius, the Epicurean.[95] But Philo does put forward some Epicurean views which are not refuted by the other speakers, and from the perspective of this study we can see why that could be the case. The new world of commerce had brought new problems and instabilities but also new freedoms and possibilities. Hume took the measure of both. In his eyes the difficulties themselves could be rewarding and opposition could be productive; it is what we lack that generates our own capacities. Seeing things in this way meant realising the cogency not only of previous scepticism but also of certain ancient ideas about that human attribute which these new conditions were making ever more important, namely, the capacity to innovate or create.

II

Britain's commercial prosperity turned it into a European power on a new scale, first evident in its success in financing the unprecedentedly expensive wars against Louis XIV. As a result the reasons for that success became as much a matter of interest for Frenchmen as the causes of Dutch achievement in the previous century had been for Englishmen. In its politics, philosophy and economics, Britain presented an alternative to the situation in France and the analysis of that alternative came to have a major impact on French thought.

Both Voltaire and Montesquieu spent time in Britain and their accounts of this country, in the *Lettres philosophiques* (1734) and *De l'Esprit des lois* (1748), were widely read. Both saw commerce as contributing to peace and toleration, as well as to wealth, and an important factor in establishing the political liberty which was so conspicuously lacking in France. And both also realized that to accept commerce also meant accepting Mandeville's paradox and rejecting certain ethical norms or unitary ways of thinking. Voltaire made this clear in his attack on Pascal at the end of his *Lettres philosophiques*, and in his celebration of luxury in *Le Mondain* (1736). The passions are necessary to man, they are the animating force of that action for which we were born; what Pascal called 'contradictions' are essential components of human nature, and it is luxury, not austerity, which makes people happy.[96]

Montesquieu saw commerce in the modern world as connected with restlessness and a certain indifference to morality. Where it prevails, he wrote, 'people trade in all human actions and all moral virtues; the smallest things, normally a matter of humanity, are done or given for money'.[97] While on one hand commerce brings about a sense of fair dealing, on the other hand it puts self-interest before any concern for others. In England this predominance of self-interest was especially noticeable,[98] and there it was combined with turbulent activity. In part, Montequieu saw this as a result of the restless, anxious and impatient character of the English people.[99] (This character, which was due to the climate, kept their political life in a state of agitation and instability and had therefore been a vital element in preserving liberty.) But it was also a product of luxury, which fostered the desire for distinction, generated a continual spiral of fantasies, needs and desires, and disrupted previous conditions in which there had been a 'harmony between needs and the means [of gratifying them]'.[100] Montesquieu closed his chapter on the English with the observation that their poets displayed more energy than elegance, more the 'original roughness of invention' than any delicacy of taste,[101] a comment close to Voltaire's judgement on Shakespeare — 'a genius full of energy and invention, of the natural and the sublime, [but] without the slightest spark of good taste'.[102] For both men the English lacked certain qualities; but they also possessed other qualities which the French could not afford to be without.

The cause of commerce came to be promoted vigorously in France, but it faced powerful opposition, both institutional and moral. Mandeville's observation that 'trade is one thing, religion is another' was adopted by Melon in his *Essai politique sur le commerce* (1734),[103] and articles in the *Encyclopédie* (1751-65) stressed the benefits of self-interest and competition.[104] While de Jaucourt, writing about 'Emulation' and 'Envie', made the traditional distinction of seeing the first as virtuous and productive and the second as disorderly and sterile,[105] other articles gave a positive role to envy, for providing the essential stimulus to 'genius and talent'.[106] It was not envy which was harmful, wrote Saint-Lambert, but greed. Yet he conceded that economic advance brought social disruption and needed to be balanced by measures which would promote an *esprit de communauté*.[107]

To those in favour of commerce the evanescence of value was an inescapable fact: 'a nation loses its trade unawares if it does not do all it can to sustain it'.[108] Given the 'continual variation' in which we live, arrangements established in the past must not be allowed to prevail over current thinking.[109] On the contrary, the greatest possible freedom of trade should be permitted, for only that can bring the flexibility necessary to meet ever new conditions. 'Give men freedom (*laissez-les faire*): that is the one great principle'.[110] But to others, this advice seemed disastrous; it was to compound the uncertainty, to launch out into an ocean of fantasy and caprice, to encourage moral corruption and social disorder. To the opponents of commerce freedom would bring not abundance but licence, not prosperity but anarchy.

The most vigorously argued solution to these problems was the economic doctrine of the physiocrats — Quesnay, Mirabeau, Le Mercier de la Rivière and others. They saw commerce as playing a vital role but being, nevertheless, unproductive; the only real economic surplus came from the land. Free trade was beneficial but if manufacturing was favoured at the expense of agriculture then it was harmful. The basis of this view was a penetrating analysis of economic life as a circulation of production and consumption, and a belief that this analysis was scientific in its objectivity and rigour and therefore corresponded to natural law. There were constant and unchanging laws of economics and we should look on the agricultural cycle in the same way that we look on the movements of the heavens, as the evidence of God's design in creation. The physiocrats believed that by using their reason, the 'natural light' given us by God, they had discovered the 'natural order' of economic life.[111] If investment was shifted from commerce to agriculture, and the barriers to agricultural development were lifted, national prosperity would follow.

For a number of years the physiocrats were successful in winning adherents to their cause and part of their success can be seen to derive from the doctrine's powerful metaphysical underpinning. It rested on an assumption of the priority of the natural over the artificial, regularity over transience. Luxury and commerce might provide riches, but their 'fleeting and ever-changing' character, and the 'disorder' they brought with them,[112] meant that they could not be taken to reflect the laws of creation. These laws were those of order and harmony; to suppose otherwise would be tantamount to believing in an Epicurean cosmology.[113] For the physiocrats harmony alone was productive. This doctrine, in other words, could be regarded as a statement in economic terms of the tradition of the Creator, and some of the assurance with which the physiocrats asserted their ideas could be seen to come from the power of this tradition and its appeal to the French monarchy. For the physiocrats were advocating the kind of *dirigiste* policy which had been conducted in the previous century and which went so well with the monarchy's absolutist claims, (themselves underpinned by divine right). These aspects of their doctrine became evident in the 1760s when they suggested that the ideal form of government would be in effect a theocracy and that their doctrine should be implemented by 'legal despotism'.[114] The original legal despot, we may recall, was the Old Testament Creator.

The most successful attack on the physiocrats, and the most comprehensive account of the new commercial world in general, came with the publication of Adam Smith's *The Wealth of Nations* (1776). Smith's analysis of the interaction in a free market of the products of the division of labour, the flow of capital, and the effects of technical change, showed how an economy could function in an orderly yet progressively expanding way. Provided that the government performed certain public tasks (defence, justice, education, communications) and did all it could to realize 'the system of natural liberty'[115] (i.e. neither restraining nor giving preference to any individuals or groups), then prosperity would follow. The animating force in this economy was the natural tendency of individuals to pursue their own interest, conceived not only as economic self-interest for material improvement, but as the desire for recognition and social goods generally. This drive was both stimulated and checked by competition, to everyone's mutual advantage. Although the complete realisation of such a system was regarded by Smith as utopian,[116] there was in his view sufficient evidence to demonstrate its validity; and such was the insight and scope of his analysis that this came in time to be generally accepted.

Smith's first major work, *The Theory of Moral Sentiments* (1759), had dealt with the psychological roots and social dimension of morality, and had stressed two values in particular — a Stoic self-command and a Christian good neighbourliness: 'to restrain our selfish, and to indulge our benevolent affections, constitutes the perfection of human nature'. Achieving such a combination makes possible a 'harmony of sentiments and passions'.[117] This is the first statement in Smith's work of an abiding preoccupation: the incorporation of ethics within a wider concern for harmony and order. Smith even went so far as to suggest that the desire for social reform may stem less from the practical end-result than from a 'love of system...the beauty of order', the ways in which the political machine can be made 'to move with more harmony and ease'.[118] A similar emphasis on detachment was central to his account of the development of moral awareness, which arises out our self-reflection, the process whereby 'we suppose ourselves the spectators of our own behaviour'.[119] We consider our intentions and actions through the eyes of a 'fair and impartial spectator',[120] and it is the judgement of this 'man within the breast'[121] which sets the standards we should live by. While we all have a natural instinct for justice (in our sense of 'sympathy'), the development of moral notions depends on our attention to this person within, and the virtue of self-command will only arise in circumstances where it needs to be exercised.[122]

In *The Wealth of Nations* these ideas of self-command and the conditions favourable to it are embodied in the virtues of frugality and competition. The former had been already singled out in *The Theory of Moral Sentiments,* along with regularity, industry and attention, as a prime instance of self-command.[123] In the later book it is praised not merely as a social virtue — 'every frugal man [is] a public benefactor'[124] — but as one of the main causes of England's 'natural progress towards wealth',[125] since frugality enabled capital accumulation and was synonymous with the kind of reliable conduct favourable to trade. The benefits of competition are complementary. On the one hand, 'where competition is free, the rivalship of competitors, who are all endeavouring to jostle one another out of employment, obliges every man to endeavour to execute his work with a certain degree of exactness'; on the other hand, 'rivalship and emulation render excellency an object of ambition, and frequently occasion the very greatest exertions'.[126] Where things are static or subject to constraint, and such opportunities do not exist, people become indolent (as is the case with landowners)[127] or dull and uninventive, (as happens to labourers whose work is 'confined to a few very simple operations' and who know only 'the uniformity of [a] stationary life').[128] The fact that increasing division of labour, the greatest contributory factor to economic advance, is in this way liable to make many of the population 'as stupid and ignorant…as possible'[129] meant that Smith's view of the future of commercial society was not complacent.

His principal disenchantment, however, did not lie here, but in his opinion of 'projectors' and merchants. Although he recognized an element of good speculation involved in a projector establishing a new manufacture,[130] or the benefits which a merchant, as a 'bold…undertaker', may sometimes bring,[131] he is more often contemptuous of 'prodigals and projectors',[132] and merchants are castigated for their 'mean rapacity' and 'impertinent jealousy',[133] their tendency 'to deceive and even oppress the public'.[134] With their 'exclusive corporation spirit' they are like 'an overgrown standing army'.[135] In addition, they are always associated with instability. The fact that their capital 'seems to have no fixed or necessary residence anywhere, but may wander about from place to place, according as it can either buy cheap or sell dear',[136] means that they are never rooted anywhere, nor have any sense of being 'necessarily attached to any particular country'.[137] Since this economic system is characterized by the fact that everyone lives by exchanging and therefore 'becomes in some measure a merchant',[138] Smith's almost unrelieved hostility to merchants is remarkable.

Part of his animus can be seen to spring from the fact that his principal opponents (in writing *The Wealth of Nations*) were the supporters of 'the mercantile system', those who favoured government regulations to promote their sectional interest at the expense of the public as a whole. In addition, merchants were in a position which made it easy for them to transgress the two virtues of frugality and competition, either by their 'mean rapacity', taking too much profit, or by their 'monopolising spirit', trying to suppress competition.[139] Yet while this may explain Smith's hostility, it seems insufficient to account for the absence of any recognition for positive qualities of invention and resourcefulness. While competition is seen as fostering 'excellency'[140] *The Wealth of Nations* seems to have a limited view of what that excellence involves.

In *The Theory of Moral Sentiments* (especially in the additions Smith made to its sixth edition (1790)), one reason for this limitation is apparent. Emulation may be indistinguishable from ambition[141] and ambition leads to strife and injustice. 'With what impatience does the man of spirit and ambition... look around for some great opportunity to distinguish himself? ....He even looks forward with satisfaction to the prospect of foreign war, or civil dissension'.[142] 'The candidates for fortune', likewise, 'too frequently abandon the paths of virtue'; 'the foulness of the steps' and baseness of 'the means' by which they achieve their distinction may involve not only 'fraud and falsehood, the...arts of intrigue and cabal', but resorting to 'the most enormous crimes'.[143] Individuals 'whom no difficulty can discourage, no danger appal, and who are at all times ready for the most daring and desperate enterprises,...at the same time seem to be hardened against all sense either of justice or humanity'.[144] Presumption and self-admiration have marked the characters of most of those who have achieved great success in the world, and 'success...covers frequently the great injustice of their enterprises'.[145]

By the time Smith was writing, the moral dilemmas posed by the demands of commercial society were a commonplace, and the ambivalent character of the drive for distinction had long been recognized. But his account allows almost no place for dilemmas or ambivalence. The occasional remarks about stormy skies, or the 'ennobling hazards' of war,[146] relate only to the moral improvements they may bring; greatness does not feature. The reason for this lay in Smith's overriding desire for regularity, order and tranquillity, for that is incompatible with novelty, risk, and going off 'in quest of new enterprises and adventures'.[147] He made this clear in a contrast he drew between 'two different roads' leading to the universal aim of winning respect from our fellows. One is 'the acquisition of wealth and greatness', the other is 'the study of wisdom and the practice of virtues'. The former may be 'more gaudy and glittering in its colouring', 'forcing itself upon the notice of every wandering eye', but the latter is 'more correct and exquisitely beautiful'.[148]

This choice between the superficial and the serious was traditional, but in at least one way it had new meaning for Smith. It was not a choice between the transient and the permanent, because permanence no longer existed. All value is evanescent, and in his early essay on *The History of Astronomy* he had gone so far as to suggest that all truth is provisional: 'nature...seems to abound with events which appear solitary and incoherent with all that go before them', it is a 'chaos of jarring and discordant appearances'.[149] The task of philosophy, faced with this situation, is to find connections, to 'invent' and 'create' systems of thought which could bring coherence. Such systems are like machines: 'a machine is a little system, created to perform, as well as to connect together, in reality those different movements and effects which the artist has occasion for. A system is an imaginary machine invented to connect together in the fancy those different movements and effects which are already in reality performed'.[150] In this perspective all philosophical systems are no more than 'mere inventions of the imagination',[151] but they alone can bring to the mind 'tranquillity and composure', 'harmony and order'.[152] While Hume had set philosophy to work to dismantle a permanence which, in his view, people erroneously took for granted, Smith used philosophy to construct some regularity as a defence against an everyday threat of chaos.

When he wrote *The Theory of Moral Sentiments* Smith had another defence, namely, his belief in a providential God; the idea of a 'fatherless world' was too dreadful to contemplate.[153] By the time he came to publish *The Wealth of Nations* he may no longer have held this view but he evidently subscribed to some kind of natural religion, the existence of certain rationally operating and providential laws of nature whose workings were evident in human societies and the course of human history, an 'invisible hand'[154] which reconciled self-interest and social interest. Yet this belief also led to problems. In a much stronger form it was held by the physiocrats, but their confidence in the theory meant they were unable to accept the actual course of European history. It was inconceivable to them that the extreme instability of commercial society could be compatible with any divinely established design. Smith disagreed; it was possible to see the undisputed material benefits brought by commerce as consistent with rational order, if the notion of unintended consequences was accepted, and if the predominant values of commercial society were seen in terms of frugality and competition. But both these components of Smith's own theory were precarious. The idea of unintended consequences was so loose and imprecise that it could equally well be seen (as it had been by Mandeville, and perhaps also by Hume) as purely a matter of Epicurean *isonomia,* an equilibrium which was entirely fortuitous. In other words, it could function in a way which embodied no providential design (and might conceivably not even be beneficial to human beings).[155] Competition was open to abuse, for reasons which Smith himself had indicated: pressure or greed pushes people beyond the bounds of justice. And frugality on its own was never enough to meet the continual new demands made by changing conditions, for these required imagination and invention. Yet the main bearers of these qualities, the principal agents of the innovations which were essential to sustain value, were the projectors and merchants about whom Smith was so scathing.

There was in fact a fundamental contradiction in Smith's thought. He wanted to vindicate commercial society as being compatible with his deepest aspirations to justice, harmony and order, but he could only do that by seeing it as a system or structure, and not as a field of action. His ethical concerns could be preserved if the economic process was envisaged in quasi-scientific terms. But when faced with the contingencies of action his scientific detachment faltered, as we see from his comments about merchants or his similarly contemptuous remarks about 'that insidious and crafty animal, vulgarly called a statesman or politician'.[156] People went into politics, he stated, solely for reasons of self-importance, and little insight could be expected of them, since their 'councils are directed by the momentary fluctuations of affairs'.[157] Smith had little sense of the pleasures of action, and showed a persistent hostility to those most visibly active. Invention was praised in a philosopher or scientist and, in the economic world, in an artisan or 'makers of machines'.[158] Otherwise, it was largely ignored. The result was that his great achievement, in providing a comprehensive account of the free market economy, was obtained at the cost of ignoring the kind of agency which made that economy flourish.

III

During the course of the 18th century in Britain, the verb 'to create' came to be applied increasingly to commercial activity, in one aspect or another. Henry Martyn (in 1701) argued that the East India trade was 'creating a greater plenty of money';[159] John Cary (in 1719) observed that 'cheapness creates expense' (i.e. expenditure);[160] Defoe (in 1729) wrote of the opportunity offered by newly-colonized countries to 'create a new commerce'.[161] A new dimension to economic activity was expressed in terms of 'creating' new wants or needs (i.e. creating demand),[162] which led to the development of advertising and the modern concept of fashion. In this context a contributor to *The London Tradesman* (in 1747) stated that someone working in fashion need 'a fruitful fancy, to invent new whims...[and] a quick invention for new patterns...to create trade', (for this reason a tradesman had to be 'a perfect Proteus, change shapes as often as the moon, and still find something new').[163] A poem published in 1755, which celebrated the joint achievement of technological innovation (a steam-pump to facilitate coal-mining) and economic advance, ended with the couplet: 'These are the glories of the mine! / Creative commerce, these are thine!'[164] Adam Smith referred to 'creating' a new market, new capital, new funds, new produce and new demand.[165] Yet neither he nor anyone else at this time applied the word 'creative' to a merchant or 'projector' or 'undertaker' (the names used in the 18th century to describe what later came to be called an entrepreneur).[166]

James Steuart, in his *Inquiry into the Principles of Political Economy* (1767), recognized the importance of 'ingenuity' in the activity of manufacturers, but only saw instances of creative achievement in the measures of such figures as Colbert, Law and Robert Walpole, whom he called men of 'genius', 'creators of new ideas'.[167] Smith himself had restricted invention almost entirely to the individual workman, thinking up a new way to ease his specific task, and after his death his biographer Dugald Stewart took issue with him on this subject. Economic growth depended as much on 'the progressive improvement of machinery' as it did on hard work, as much on 'ingenuity' as on 'industry'.[168] But it was the employer rather than the workers who had most reason to be inventive, for new machines could deprive the latter of their livelihood. The employer, on the other hand, could see obvious advantages, the awareness of which 'can excite the efforts of inventive genius'; and in this context there had been examples of 'astonishing exertions of human ingenuity', showing 'the comprehensive skill of the undertaker'.[169]

Writing at the start of a new century, Stewart's greater emphasis on invention could be seen as due (at least in part) to the continuing expansion of the manufacturing sector, for new processes and occupations were 'enlarging our prospect of the boundless field which will never be exhausted by human industry'.[170] For Smith on the other hand the most important sector of the economy (both in aggregate and in productive possibility) was agriculture. 'The land constitutes by far the greatest, the most important, and the most durable part of the wealth of every extensive country',[171] and 'no equal quantity of productive labour employed in manufactures can ever occasion so great a reproduction' as that involved in agriculture.[172] Of course, there was scope here for human invention, in improving fertility and crops breeds. Referring to human power over nature in this respect, Buffon wrote in his *Époques de la nature* (1779) that 'man has, so to speak, created secondary species which he can propagate and multiply at will'.[173] But Smith played down any such emphasis, stating that generally agriculture did 'not so much increase...[as] direct the fertility of nature', regulating rather than animating it.[174] For him the natural was always more than just a resource; it had exemplary and normative status. In a summary of his early lectures he was reported as stating that 'in the course of her operations in human affairs...[nature] requires no more than to let her alone and give her fair play in the pursuit of her ends, that she may establish her own designs'.[175]

Nature, for Smith, was orderly; mutability occurred within an overall regularity. Human society, likewise, was meant to be harmonious, with individual self-interest contributing to a general concord of interests. When this belief, fundamental to all Smith's writings, was combined with the systematic character of his analysis, the effect was to take attention away from commerce as a field of action. When Smith wrote that 'man was made for action'[176] his focus was on individual moral achievement and this moral concern could not be reconciled with the unwelcome qualities which brought about innovation. It was precisely 'the man of spirit and ambition' or the 'candidates for fortune', about whom he was so scathing (p.90), who were likely to introduce new techniques and ideas into the economy. This was clearly recognized by Bentham in his *Defence of Usury* (1787), when he defended projectors against Smith's criticisms. 'A prudent man', he wrote, 'will not meddle with projects at all'.[177] It is precisely the 'adventurous spirits' who 'strike out in any new channel, and more especially into any channel of invention'.[178] Projects require 'courage' and 'singularity' and, on occasion, 'the rare endowment of genius';[179] they are brought about by those unusual individuals 'with whom the womb of futurity is still pregnant'.[180]

To see future possibilities and then attempt to realize them involves more than invention, in the terms used by Smith or Stewart. A new machine can have a decisive impact on a productive process, but it is obviously only one element in the life of a business. To start a new venture, or move an existing business in a new direction, requires different qualities of insight, ambition and flair. These are developed, become evident, and are vindicated in the activities which alone make such a venture possible, namely, convincing other people of a project's viability (to raise capital), keeping employees motivated (to ensure efficiency), persuading buyers of the value of what is offered (to win sales), anticipating change and seeing new opportunities (to keep ahead of rivals). An article in the *Journal de Commerce*, published in Paris in 1759, gave an indication of these qualities. The successful man of trade or business, it stated, must have 'the same kind of genius as the Lockes and the Newtons' in their range and subtlety of thought, and then 'go beyond that…[and] employ the genius of the Richelieus, Cromwells, Colberts' in a knowledge of the varieties of human character and an insight into people's behaviour;[181] he also needs 'courage' and 'genius'.[182]

This article was part of a campaign in France in the 1750s arguing the case for free trade and at one point in its enthusiasm for this cause it appears to overstate its case. For the exemplary merchant, it claims, in learning how to deal with unpredictable events, will 'create systems'.[183] In a loose way this might be true but in a strict sense it was not, because the uncertainties and variables were such that no systematic method could be adequate (as Hume had indicated, p.80). Success in such a world did indeed require intellectual abilities of calculation and perception (the analyst and strategist) but also other more elusive qualities of adaptability, cunning and daring (the chameleon, the fox and the lion). Above all, there was the central role now played by that traditionally ambivalent faculty, the imagination. The financial developments which were integral to commercial expansion (the extension of credit, the trading of stocks, and so forth) depended on confidence in the future, which could only be imagined.[184] And the progress of trade itself was often seen as depending on an ever-new awareness of 'imaginary' wants;[185] as the 'whims' and 'fantasies' of the rich generate new demands, so (in Cantillon's account) others must 'imagine' and invent ways of satisfying them.[186] It is not surprising, therefore, that we find the imagination itself (if it were not under the control of reason) being described as 'an adventurous but vain projector'.[187]

To recognize commerce as a new field of action, needing the qualities of a Richelieu or a Cromwell, was to face the problem which Aristotle had seen in his account of politics: political action was a matter more of 'a certain skill and experience, rather than of thought', and it was therefore not susceptible to a philosophical analysis (p.34). It is possible, however, that at least some understanding of commercial action could have been obtained from looking to the past, and specifically at the one historical instance of a previous society which had also been endemically unstable and where survival had also depended on individuals' action and enterprise. This was the ancient city republic. The most comprehensive account of those conditions — Machiavelli's *Discourses* — contained many of the features which came to be seen as characteristic of commercial society: the sense of insecurity and restlessness, the need to adapt to changing circumstances, the constant pressure for renewal, and the way in which individuals in competition can be productive and effective.[188] Algernon Sidney's praise of free republics as 'nurseries of great and able men'[189] was paralleled by Mandeville's picture of commercial society as the 'nursery of sciences and industry'.[190]

In France the physiocrats did associate commercial society with republics, where 'everything was based on continual action,...altering according to different circumstances'. For them, however, the comparison was entirely negative; the example of England, which Quesnay described as a 'universal republic of traders', demonstrated a high degree of instability as well as undesirable levelling tendencies.[191] In England itself no such connection was made; on the contrary, there republican ideas became an important part of the opposition to commerce. This drew on a particular form of republican thought — more Venetian than Roman — which focussed on structure and balance, rather than action and conflict. In his *Oceana* (1656) Harrington had adapted these ideas to English circumstances, and they became influential in political debate in the early 18th century.[192] In part this was because Harrington gave special importance to landed wealth (the aristocracy and gentry whose political and economic status was threatened by new financial and commercial forces); in part because republican thought had always attacked the rise of luxury as corrupting and fatal to a country's survival; and in part because republicans were confident about occupying the moral high ground, since their ethos was one of 'public virtue'.[193] Commerce, by contrast, was neither public-spirited nor Christian, being animated (in Berkeley's words) by 'an atheistical narrow spirit, centring all our cares upon private interest, and contracting all our hopes within the enjoyment of this present life'.[194]

In Scotland, where attitudes to both commerce and politics were different, the Roman (or Machiavellian) form of republicanism continued to be influential, not least because of a recurring debate about the need for Scotland to have its own militia. One of the main protagonists on this issue was Adam Ferguson, who had himself seen active service with the Black Watch (even if only as a chaplain). In his writings we find an invigorating sense of the value of action, of the benefits of difficulty and struggle, and of the human capacity to innovate. Man 'is destined...to invent and contrive;...[he] is never sated with novelty'.[195] It is 'difficulty [which] tries and sharpens the wits of man, [and] in the contest of human abilities invention is continually at work'.[196] This includes activity in the pursuit of wealth.[197] Struggle and competition are therefore not to be regretted, for 'mankind not only find in their condition the sources of variance and dissension; [but] they appear to have in their minds the seeds of animosity, and to embrace the occasions of mutual opposition, with alacrity and pleasure'.[198] 'The most animating occasions of human life are calls to danger and hardship', as we see from the lives of 'the able, the brave and the ardent';[199] and Ferguson gives as examples those who choose a career as a soldier, a mariner, or 'a politician, whose sport is the conduct of parties and factions, and who, rather than be idle, will do the business of men and of nations, for whom he has not the slightest regard'.[200] For such people the activity itself, the opportunity 'to make continued exertions of capacity and resolution',[201] is more important than the end-result. In his last work, the *Principles of Moral and Political Science* (1792), Ferguson applied this perception to commerce: 'the object of commerce is wealth', but that end 'is not to [a person] of so much value as the pursuit in which it engages him, or the means he is led to employ, in the conduct of that pursuit'.[202]

At this point we seem to be on the verge of a vindication of commerce as action. But it was not possible for Ferguson to take that step. Moral considerations weighed heavier than the implications of his insight. Not only was he committed to the republican preoccupation with the common good, shared action, all that was epitomized in the phrase 'public virtue', (and all of which were undermined by the isolation and narrow interests which came with commercial society);[203] but he also had a Stoic regard for self-improvement, to be 'in some measure the artificer of [your] own nature'.[204] When he wrote positively of 'the pursuit' and 'the means' involved in commerce he had in mind the morally enhancing qualities of 'industry, sobriety and frugality' and 'the study of justice…and good order, in the conduct of life'.[205]

The moral problems generated by commerce could not be absorbed within a theory of action derived from the republican tradition. But there was another literature of action which was available, that of greatness and the heroic, the Machiavelli not of the *Discourses* but *The Prince*. This was, of course, no solution to the moral problem, but it could bring appreciation of the inventive qualities of the action. Mandeville, who was to give a thoroughly Machiavellian portrait of Cromwell in his *Enquiry into the Origin of Honour* (1732),[206] brought this perspective to economic activity in *The Fable*. He describes 'the active stirring man, [who] is easily reconciled to the bustle of the world', as someone who will be unscrupulous when necessary and give the 'appearance of honesty' as much as possible;[207] such a 'man of action [with] an enterprising temper' will also need 'a great deal of good fortune as well as cunning'.[208] The disparity between agency and outcome — 'there are evil qualities which make great talents'[209] — had also been a theme of a number of French moralists (on whom Mandeville had drawn) and it was eloquently expressed by Pope in his *Essay on Man* (1732-34): 'There, in the rich, the honoured, famed and great, / See the false scale of happiness complete! /.../ Mark by what wretched steps their glory grows, / From dirt and sea-weed as proud Venice rose; / In each how guilt and greatness equal ran, / And all that raised the Hero, sunk the Man'.[210] A more extended example of this contrast at this time was Fielding's *The Life of Mr Jonathan Wild the Great* (1743), a portrayal of Walpole in the character of a notorious criminal. The avowed aim of the novel was to show how goodness and greatness were incompatible.[211] Wild is restless, ambitious, deceitful and unscrupulous;[212] but he is also cunning, bold, imaginative and inventive,[213] knowing how 'to play with the passions of men, to set them at variance with each other, and to work his own purposes out of those jealousies and apprehensions which he was wonderfully ready at creating'.[214]

In writing this novel Fielding presented his hero in mock-heroic terms, and his readers would have understood his aim because his target, as the leading politician of the day, was a public figure and highly visible. Politics and warfare were activities which gave occasion for creative action, not only because they engaged with unpredictable circumstances, requiring inventive and other outstanding abilities, but also because they affected large numbers of people. Both in the process (arguing for a policy or course of action, winning support, maintaining loyalty, seeing opportunities, taking decisions), and in the end-result such actions were matters of intense public concern. In other words, they were (or could be) of obvious *significance*. In the case of politics they were also, with the spread of print-culture, becoming increasingly visible.

Neither of these features tended to be the case with commercial activity. Given the evanescence of value the need for innovation was constantly present (even though, of course, most actors in the economic world, as in the political world, were not innovative in a significant way);[215] and success could only come with the ability to win backing (in the process) and by meeting needs which were recognized by others (in the end-result). If a new venture could, like a new policy or poem, 'resonate' or 'strike a chord' in this way it could likewise be significant. But commerce did not deal with matters of shared public concern, it met particular needs; and the benefits of a successful enterprise were usually measured in terms of an individual's private wealth. While in politics or war unscrupulous means could sometimes be justified by an eventual outcome, because that was for the public benefit, no such perspective was likely to apply to commerce.

In addition, the activity which generated new economic life was rarely, if at all, visible. During their tour of the Hebrides Boswell asked Johnson 'What is the reason we are angry at a trader's having opulence?';

to which the latter replied, 'Why, sir, the reason is…we *see* no qualities in trade that should entitle a man to superiority'.[216] In the context of everyday experience, Johnson was right; but just as most knowledge of political or military action came indirectly (from histories and biographies), so now new kinds of printed material were becoming available which could convey a sense of economic action: there was a rapid expansion of journalism and the new literary form of the novel.

The best-known example of such a work was *Robinson Crusoe* (1718). On one level Defoe's book is a retelling of the story of the Prodigal Son, set within a benignly Providential framework.[217] On another level it is a narrative in which imagination, combined with courage, industry and intelligence, is duly rewarded. It is Robinson's 'rambling thoughts' and 'wandering inclinations' which lead him to reject his father's praise for 'moderation [and] quietness'; only exceptional people, the latter insisted, 'went abroad upon adventures, to rise by enterprise'.[218] But Robinson will be such a person. His head is 'full of projects'[219] and he prefers to follow his 'fancy' rather than his 'reason'.[220] When shipwrecked he has to learn to support himself the hard way, and he gains a degree of wisdom in recognising the contentment which comes with accepting limits. But that does not change his basic character, because (as he observes at the end of the novel) he 'was inured to a wandering life'.[221]

Few writers conveyed the flavour of the new world of commerce with the immediacy and frankness of Defoe. Reading him we are constantly struck by the energy and resourcefulness of his characters, and the way he combines admiration for an 'enterprising genius' or an 'adventuring temper'[222] with a recognition of the moral dilemmas that were involved — 'whenever we break our confederacy with Satan, we are certainly ruined and undone'.[223] *Robinson Crusoe* was an instant and lasting success, but its popularity was not due to its attention to the qualities discussed here. For Defoe's contemporaries it was rather the Providential framework and the (related) insistence on the moral value of hard work which made the novel a companion volume to *Pilgrim's Progress*. As a result Defoe's grasp of the imaginative and inventive dimensions to action in commercial society seems to have gone largely unrecognized. It was also the case that both the forms in which Defoe was writing — journalism and prose fiction — had low status. Only in exceptional cases (like *The Spectator*) was journalism reprinted, and only with the novels of Richardson and Fielding, which began appearing in the decade after Defoe's death, did this new kind of fiction begin to become respectable. In the process novels began to suffer from one of the limits of respectability, namely, a reluctance to get their hands dirty. So the character of this newly important kind of action continued to go unrecognized.

IV

The word 'create' did not always have positive connotations in 18th century Britain. In his defence of his books *Joseph Andrews* (1742) and *Tom Jones* (1749) Fielding insisted that these narratives were not 'romances or...modern novel[s]',[224] but each was (as its full title claimed) a 'history', that is, an 'imitation of nature', 'copied from the book of nature'.[225] Authors of romances, by contrast, 'record persons who never were, or will be, and facts which never did, nor possibly can, happen; [their] heroes are of their own creation', the product of invention 'understood [as] a creative faculty'.[226] The words 'creation' and 'creative' here had the sense of fantasy or deception, a meaning similar to that sometimes used by Shakespeare (although for him the deception tended to be a form of delusion or self-deception).[227] Such 'foolish novels and monstrous romances'[228] might captivate or amuse but they could not teach anything of value. Fielding's own books, on the other hand, were the result of 'invention' in the original meaning of the word, namely, 'discovery or finding out;...a quick and sagacious penetration into the true essence' of people and events.[229] The principal reason for this distinction was his desire to validate his own fiction within the terms of neo-classical aesthetics,[230] and so apply to a form of writing which lay outside existing conventions the most eminent and respectable criteria.

At the same time, however, Fielding did not hesitate to claim that he was 'the founder of a new province of writing',[231] opening 'a new vein of knowledge',[232] and he could therefore call *Tom Jones* 'a great creation of our own'.[233] One reason for this became clear several chapters later when he asserted, 'I absolutely claim a property in what I write', and then went on to attack plagiarists and 'unjust dealing in the poetical trade'.[234] These comments relate to a new factor which was beginning to complicate the relationship between writers and commerce — the introduction of copyright.

The first Copyright Act, passed in 1710, was mainly concerned with securing the rights of booksellers, but it also gave legal recognition to an author's right of property in his or her work, something which had been claimed earlier but only then received formal legal status. The precise nature of this right was not immediately clear. Copyright (a word which became current from the 1730s) was a claim to property in a text, not in a material object, and disputes arose over how ownership could exist in something immaterial, what distinguished literary works from other types of invention (already recognized in law about patents), and whether ownership should be perpetual.

On the first of these issues a strong case was made for authors having a common law right based on the right to the fruits of one's own labour. This was claimed by Addison and Steele at the time of the passage of the 1710 Act,[235] and was subsequently supported by two of the outstanding legal figures in the country, Lord Mansfield and William Blackstone. The common law right had been developed by Locke into an influential theory of property rights in general and it was in these Lockeian terms that we find the most succint definition of the case for literary property: 'labour gives a man a natural right of property in that which he produces; literary compositions are the effect of labour; authors have therefore a natural right of property in their works'.[236]

The next question which arose was whether literary property was any different from rights in patents. The latter were in effect a form of privilege, giving exclusive rights to an inventor for a limited term.[237] The supporters of copyright, however, wanted it to be an unequivocal right of ownership which (like all other kinds of property) was a right in perpetuity. The basis for this claim (first set out by William Warburton in 1747) was the ancient distinction between the liberal and mechanical arts. Although both an invention and a literary work were products of the mind, the former was often an outcome of manual activity and it was ineffective without material embodiment; in other words, it was not wholly mental. The distinguishing feature of a literary work, by contrast, was its specific 'doctrine', the ideas or themes 'peculiar' to that individual text, which did not depend on the material form in which they were conveyed.[238] Another distinct aspect claimed for literary works was that the labour involved in producing them was itself unusual. Right to property might be derived from labour, or else from occupancy, but an author did something more, 'for, in some case, he may be said to create, [rather] than to discover or plant his land'.[239] Dr. Johnson likewise described an author's claim to copyright as 'a metaphysical right, as it were, of creation'.[240]

The arguments against perpetual copyright, which carried the day in the definitive House of Lords judgement in 1774, were based on that key feature of a flourishing commerce — competition. To allow authors rights in perpetuity would discourage publishers from new ventures and so deprive 'the commonwealth of letters...of all the benefits arising from that great source of improvement, the emulation of various artisans'.[241] It would put the interests of a few writers above the wider public interest. In literature, therefore, as 'in every kind of commerce, and in every art, there ought to be competition. Without this, industry will not prosper; and any monopoly or restraint must nourish tyrants, to oppress the country, and to annihilate ingenuity'.[242]

The establishing of copyright, in conjunction with other changes (such as the end of censorship and the growth of an ever-larger reading public), made possible a new kind of life for writers who otherwise (unless they wrote for the theatre) had been reliant on patronage. The pioneer of this new situation was Pope, who grandly described himself as being 'above a patron'[243] and was the first writer to make more money than his publisher;[244] the self-conscious standard-bearer was Dr Johnson, who defined a patron in his *Dictionary* as 'commonly a wretch who supports with insolence, and is paid with flattery'.[245] With copyright came the possibility of an independent life and new opportunities for those (notably, women) who had previously been denied the chance of a career as a writer.

At the same time, however, market conditions exacerbated an old problem, one which was as ancient as poetry itself — that high degree of envy and rivalry which made poets, in Horace's famous phrase, a *genus irritabile*.[246] In the 18th century this characteristic of writers was widely recognized. We find it discussed by Mandeville or Adam Smith as well as by poets and writers themselves.[247] The republic of letters, observed Oliver Goldsmith, was a very unsuitable term to use of a situation in which 'every member...is desirous of governing, and none willing to obey; each [writer] looks to his fellow as a rival...They calumniate, they injure, they despise, they ridicule each other...They are divided into almost as many factions as there are men; and their jarring constitution, instead of being styled a republic of letters, should be entitled an anarchy of literature'.[248] From this perspective, for writers to become active members of commercial society could be seen as more or less a continuation of business as usual.

Some writers, Goldsmith among them, saw the new condition in a positive light;[249] others viewed it with alarm. On one hand, it led to an increasing number of writers clamouring for attention; on the other hand, literary success could now be measured in economic terms, something which had never happened before and which clashed with previous criteria of what determined 'good' writing. 'Wit and money have always been at war, and always treated one another with reciprocal contempt' wrote James Ralph;[250] even now, to become a 'writer by trade' was to be 'branded as a mercenary'.[251] Success in market terms could bring independence and recognition, but what kind of recognition was that, or (more precisely) recognition by whom? Pope declared war on this issue — essentially one of

an individual criterion of quality versus an external measure of quantity —
in *The Dunciad* (1728/1749). This poem, surely the most magnificently
savage attack on fellow-writers ever published, depicts with imperious and
withering contempt the world of minor talents trying to make a living by
the pen. They inhabit a realm of anarchy, darkness and chaos,[252] where
dullness and the 'uncreating word' reign supreme,[253] where true genius is
hated and self-interest predominates.[254] Grub Street is the antithesis of true
merit or goodness and Pope associates the hacks with a familiar roll-call of
villains (Lucretius and Mandeville among them).[255] The poem contrasts
their base, formless, petty, ephemeral and vicious practices with the values
of his own literary circle, which are taken to embody all that is noble,
orderly, universal, timeless and moral.

Johnson said of Pope that 'it would be hard to find a man so well
entitled to notice by his wit that ever delighted so much in talking of his
money',[256] and in some respects *The Dunciad* can be seen as revealing as
much a conflict within Pope as one between him and other authors.[257] But
his animus against the hacks is also fuelled by an insecurity common to
writers, if they are ambitious and have 'the immense desire for fame';[258]
because fame, by definition, is always in short supply. The busy number of
aspiring writers using more immediate (i.e. less sophisticated) forms, was
seen by Pope as a threat, and that undoubtedly contributed to the range and
venom of his attack. By depicting his would-be rivals in grossly physical
terms, and by making his epic a kind of inverted *Paradise Lost*, Pope aimed
to portray as sharp as possible a contrast between the material and the
spiritual, between the coarse life of trade and the elevated world of poetry.
Although his treatment of his enemies (in the poem) was as savage as
Apollo's handling of poets who competed against him (blinding Thamyris,
flaying Marsyas, and killing Linus), he implied a self-image which
contained elements only of the idealized Apollo, the model of wisdom,
harmony, and prophetic insight.[259]

We find similar distinctions being made by Johnson and Edward
Young. The former set his own work apart from that of 'drudges of the pen,
the manufacturers of literature, who have set up for authors',[260] (and
Boswell wrote of him pointedly as 'a man whose *profession* was
literature').[261] Young attacked 'the wretched unanimity...of ordinary
writers' and 'invaders of the press' relying on imitation,[262] which he
described as 'a sort of manufacture, wrought up by those mechanics art and
labour, out of pre-existent materials not their own'.[263] In other words, both
men followed Warburton (in the copyright debate) in using the traditional
taxonomy of the liberal and the mechanical arts to give their own work
superior status. In addition, they distinguished a good writer from a bad by

the extent to which the former was creative. For Johnson the writers who were superior to the 'drudges' were those who 'produce, or endeavour to produce, new ideas'.[264] Young restricted 'the noble title of author' to 'one who thinks and composes' in an original manner, that is, someone who 'is born of himself, is his own progenitor'.[265]

In these ways the activity of certain writers was set apart from, and depicted as superior to, the economic world in which they existed and from which they now could benefit. This had the twofold effect of obscuring the ambivalent aspects of poetic creativity and of denying the element of creative action in commerce. The qualitative judgement, which discriminated between a few writers of merit and a crowd of 'hacks' or 'drudges', was not applied to the economic realm; instead, routine and uniformity were assumed to prevail there. The imaginative and innovative abilities, which the free market gave opportunity for and stimulated, went unrecognized or were seen as wholly inferior to their counterparts in literature.

In 1712 *The Spectator* had devoted an issue to the 'art of growing rich'. After describing the benefits of thrift, diligence and 'method in business' (a matter of being regular and orderly), the writer added that 'beside these ordinary forms of growing rich, it must be allowed that there is room for genius [in business]…We daily see methods put in practice by hungry and ingenious men, which demonstrate the power of invention in particular…Trade and commerce might doubtless be still varied a thousand ways, out of which would arise such branches as have not yet been touched'.[266] Such 'hungry and ingenious' men, it concluded, would not go about things in a cautious or methodical way, 'it being almost impossible that the mind should be intent upon trifles, while it is at the same time forming some great design. I may therefore compare these men to a great poet who, as Longinus says, while he is full of the most magnificent ideas is not always at leisure to mind the little…niceties of his art'.[267] A similar point was made by Defoe when he observed that 'there are some latitudes, like poetical licences in other cases, which a tradesman is and must be allowed'.[268] Likewise, a comment made by Young with regard to literature — 'all eminence and distinction lies out of the beaten road; excursion and deviation are necessary to find it'[269] — had its counterpart in a statement by Bentham on projectors — they need 'courage' and 'singularity' in 'stepping aside from the beaten paths'.[270]

The common features of these statements are one reason why individuals who have been successful in literary endeavours and in free market conditions have often been outsiders. (Examples in literature then were Defoe, Pope or Johnson, and in commerce were Antwerp Calvinists,

French Huguenots or English Dissenters, as well as most of the heroes of Defoe's fictions.)[271] An outsider will have a distinct perspective (seeing matters differently from others) and a greater need (because of insecure status) to make a name or a place in the world. Talent and invention, sharpened by need and given opportunity to flourish, can bring distinction in several kinds of activity. This had been (or became) recognized in literature or politics; it was rarely applied to commerce.

The new insecurity of writers in commercial society, and the ambiguities of a success which could be measured in economic terms, made it important for them to deny any common ground between an author and an entrepreneur. The superior status of the former could be maintained by a number of powerful arguments, based on the tradition of the Creator, or on the poetics which connected literary excellence with moral value, or on the hierarchy of the liberal and mechanical arts, in which the liberal arts exercised freedom and aspired to the spiritual, while the mechanical arts were subject to circumstance and confined to the material. In this way an awareness of some of the qualities which were distinct to literature were preserved and heightened, while an understanding of other aspects (in particular the subject of this study, the character of creativity) was effectively obscured. There was nothing new in defenders of literary value showing disdain for material concerns;[272] but new conditions gave this antipathy a new sharpness.

This contrast was reinforced in the closing decades of the century when, as far as commerce was concerned, the skies began to cloud over. To the ethical ambiguities which had been generally recognized were now added grave social problems. In Britain developments in both agriculture and manufacturing began to cause widespread social disruption. The increased productivity which was possible with larger units in farming meant the introduction of enclosures. With the end of the open-field system came also the end of many small communities; peasants became landless labourers and villages were deserted.[273] Increasing division of labour in new kinds of manufacturing brought deadening routines, and the pace of change which excited some caused hardship and dismay to many others.[274]

The expansion of trade overseas had equally, or more, severe repercussions. The abuses of power by the East India Company, highlighted by the proceedings to impeach Warren Hastings, were made prominent by the ostentatious wealth of nabobs returning to Britain.[275] They were evidence of James Steuart's observation that when 'the former simplicity' of the inhabitants of a foreign country had been eradicated (by stimulating a 'taste for superfluity'), 'then they are surely in the fetters of the traders'.[276] This comment had literal as well as metaphorical truth, in the grim facts of slavery and the slave-trade. 'The majority of European nations are soiled by [these atrocities]', stated Diderot, and he defied anyone to justify the way in which European prosperity had been achieved by the mistreatment of other peoples.[277] To be sure, there was no necessary connection between commerce and slavery, as can be seen from the many supporters of the former — from Addison to Paine — who were opponents of the latter. But it had become evident that the commercial spirit could release not only astonishing energies but also terrible cruelties. These seemed to be fuelled not by an ancient lust for power (*libido dominandi*) but a new ruthless greed to possess (*cupiditas habendi*), stemming from that combination of fear and hope — endemic instability and vast possibility — which now prevailed. When these aspects of economic life were taken into account it was obvious that no common characteristics would be perceived between the animating features of high culture and those of low commerce.

CHAPTER SIX

Genius

I

From the writings of Mandeville, Hume and many others we can see how in the first half of the 18th century there was a sense of the past ceasing to provide guidance and of instability becoming pervasive. A new dimension of possibility seemed to be coming into being, which brought a new sense of potential but which also clashed with moral norms. To be aware of this perspective enables us to understand why the new aesthetic categories of the sublime, originality, and genius arose in this period. For these ideas reflected, expressed and helped to define the experience of this new world.

The Hellenistic treatise on the sublime (attributed since the medieval period to Longinus) began to arouse interest after Boileau had translated it into French in 1674. The work was a handbook of rhetoric, about how to write in order to produce a particular effect of force or power (*ekplexis*) and rapture (*ekstasis*).[1] While the treatise points out the gains that may result from not slavishly following rules, its emphasis is continually on the element of judgement, skill and calculation in literary composition, the need for the 'curb' as well as the 'spur'.[2] For Boileau there was no essential disparity between Longinus' aims and the neo-classical precepts he expounded in his *Ars poétique*. Over the subsequent decades, however, British writers dismantled this rhetorical framework and discussion of the sublime became the exploration of a (conceptually) new aesthetic experience.

As described by Addison, Hume, William Smith, Akenside and Baillie, the principal features of the sublime were novelty, vastness or limitlessness, energy or power, and moral or emotional confusion.[3] The sublime gloried in what was unexpected and obscure, in the energy that carried you beyond the limited and known, in the pleasure to be derived from danger or fear, and in whatever could convey a dynamic sense of power. Unlike the neo-classical notion of beauty, which because of its attention to harmony and proportion could easily be assimilated with the morally good, the sublime seemed entirely amoral. 'The sublime and virtue are quite different things', wrote Baillie in 1747.[4] While 'beauty and [decorum] of character' spring from 'a just order of affections, where no one desire...breaks the harmony of the passions', a 'sublime' emotion, like the 'desire of fame, honours or empire, often creates the greatest tumult in the affections, and the greatest mischief to mankind'.[5]

For the young Burke, whose *Philosophical Enquiry into...the Sublime and Beautiful* was published in 1757, the two aesthetic categories were 'opposite and contradictory'.[6] Beauty was the quality which arouses love; it 'inspires us with sentiments of tenderness and affection', and is therefore 'a social quality', based on what is aesthetically pleasing.[7] The sublime, by contrast, is 'founded upon pain'.[8] It is aroused by terror, danger, the dark and unknown,[9] the infinite and the unexpected,[10] different manifestations of power,[11] and 'the noise of vast cataracts, raging storms, thunder or artillery'.[12] 'No pleasure from a positive cause belongs to it'.[13] Yet the fear or pain give us delight if we experience them without actually being in danger, i.e. at a safe (aesthetic) distance. Since the threat as such involves our self-preservation it affects us intensely,[14] but because we are in reality secure the result is excitement and stimulation.[15] While beauty relaxes and draws us towards others, the sublime invigorates and throws us back on our self. In so doing it gives us a sense of 'inward greatness', and is therefore associated with the heroic.[16] In this respect, the sublime is the mental equivalent of that stimulation which ambition provides in everyday life, and which is the motor of change. If we did no more than imitate our fellow-humans, Burke observes, we would never break out of 'an eternal circle'; it is because of our ambition and desire to be different that 'improvement' comes about.[17]

As the sublime, going beyond the limits of both the moral and the known, can be seen to relate to a new sense of power, so originality was connected with an awareness that the past was no longer a model; in other words, value is evanescent. Young's *Conjectures on Original Composition* (1759) recognized this fact: 'it is with thoughts as it is with words,...they may grow old and die'. There is therefore a need for novelty: 'thoughts, when become too common,...lose their currency; and we should send new metal to the mint, that is, new meaning to the press'.[18] In such a world, what is given or inherited will not retain its value: 'those that are born rich, by neglecting the cultivation and produce of their own possessions...may be beggared at last';[19] (compare these statements to similar observations above, pp.74 and 80). Originals, on the other hand, 'extend the republic of letters, and add a province to its dominion...the pen of an original writer...out of a barren waste calls a blooming spring'.[20] Such figures are distinguished by their self-reliance — 'there is a mine in man, which must be deeply dug'[21] — and by their concern not for existing rules or laws, but for what is new. In the attainment of originality Young stressed the importance of ambition, emulation and rivalry; in Athens 'men of genius [had] struck fire against each other; and kindled, by conflict, into glories'.[22]

He opposed 'wretched unanimity' and praised those who could surprise their readers, bringing 'news from a foreign land'.[23] Writers should aspire to 'individuality' (a word then coming into use),[24] which could be achieved by those who did not imitate or rely on others, but had confidence in themselves: 'dive deep into thy bosom...[and] let thy genius rise...as the sun from chaos'.[25]

Dr Johnson dismissed Young's *Conjectures* itself as being quite unoriginal — the essay contained nothing but 'very common maxims'[26] — and to some extent that was true. As a classical scholar Johnson was aware of the claims which poets (from Pindar onwards) had made for their work being new, and from the early years of the 18th century the word 'original' had been used as a term of praise. Pope had enthused about what Shakespeare had achieved, and Addison had criticized Milton for what he lacked, in these terms.[27] Young himself in an essay on lyric poetry (published over thirty years before) had written that 'in every work of genius something of an original spirit should be...attempted...Originals only have true life'.[28] In all these cases 'original' was opposed to 'imitation', where the latter referred less to the imitation of nature than that of previous authors who were set up as models other writers should try to emulate. Young contrasted the situation in the liberal arts with that of the mechanical arts. The latter were 'in perpetual progress and increase', because with them 'men are ever endeavouring to go beyond their predecessors'; as a result, their achievements 'resemble rivers which, from a small fountain-head, are [now] spreading ever wider and wider as they run'.[29] In literature, on the other hand, writers were so intimidated by the past, and so ready to follow their predecessors, that the condition of literature (and the liberal arts) resembled pyramids, 'broad at the bottom but lessen[ing] exceedingly as they rise'.[30]

Young's essay was fired by a sense of potential: who knows 'the possible dimensions of the mind of man'?[31] The ancients and the moderns should no longer be 'considered as masters and pupils, but as hard-matched rivals for renown'.[32] And this ambition was underpinned by a moral confidence derived in part from his Protestant belief in the value of self-reliance, thinking and working for yourself, and in part from the quasi-Stoic ethics given new cogency earlier in the century by Shaftesbury (p.137). But there was also a reason why writers were now faced with a new need to be original, namely, the introduction of copyright. The ability to show title in a literary work, the basis for any grounds for payment, rested on that work being a new product by a particular individual, its having a distinct (i.e. original) identity. In his *Commentaries on the Laws of England* (1765–69), Blackstone defined this in terms of 'the sentiment and the language; the same conceptions, clothed in the same words, must necessarily be the same composition'.[33] A similar description was made by one of the participants in the 1774 debate: 'a literary work really original, like the human face, will always have some singularities, some lines, some features, to characterize it, and to fix and establish its identity'.[34] As literature became a form of commerce writers had a new reason to display their uniqueness; for their own survival, in material terms, they needed to be in some way original. Their habitual envy and rivalry now became economic competition, and borrowing or imitation (of another writer) or plagiarism ceased to be merely issues of reputation; they could be matters of legal dispute.

In Young's *Conjectures* moral, aesthetic and economic considerations are interwoven seamlessly and often unclearly. He observed that the author whose works are 'the native growth of [his] own mind' will find that 'his works will stand distinguished; his the sole property in them; which property alone can confer the noble title of an author'.[35] When we read such a statement we cannot be sure whether the emphasis is primarily moral or legal or economic, because the different criteria overlap and often use the same language. The debate about originality was not merely one aspect of the gradually emerging sense of aesthetic value *per se*; but neither, on the other hand, was it a sign of economic self-interest masquerading as an issue of taste. The moral, aesthetic, legal and economic categories were not synonymous; nor can the first two aspects be collapsed into the last two.[36] Individuality was as much an ethical concern as an economic one, and the individual integrity of the poet could be seen to be confirmed as much by the neglect of the world as by its applause (the theme of Gray's *Elegy in a Country Churchyard* (1751)). The new conditions reinforced old difficulties, introduced new problems, and brought new opportunities. Almost all these aspects — the good and the bad — were related to the new degree of independence which writers were gradually coming to have, as the Enlightenment commonplace 'Dare to think for yourself' began to give way to the Romantic commonplace 'Dare to write for yourself'.

II

For Young, as for his contemporaries, originality was a property of genius, a term derived from the two Latin words *genius* and *ingenium*. The former had referred in antiquity to a non-human spirit which was associated either with energy and fertility, or with personal destiny (good and bad), or (when assimilated with the Greek *daemon*) with messages from the gods. *Ingenium* referred to innate character and especially to intellectual distinction.[37] The emergence of the modern idea of genius drew on all these associations — individuality, insight, outstanding ability and, in particular, fertility. 'True genius', wrote Robert Wolsley in 1685, 'like the *anima mundi* [in] which some of the ancients believed, will enter into the hardest and driest thing, enrich the most barren soil, and inform the meanest and most uncomely matter;...the formings of his plastic heat and...operations of his vivifying power... can,...as Horace says of Homer,...fetch light out of smoke, roses out of dunghills, and give a kind of life to the inanimate'.[38] For Wolsley this power still had a divine origin; for William Temple, writing five years later, it was a purely human attribute, which when it occurred in poets made them 'creators'.[39] From this time on the association of genius with human (which then meant male) 'creative' ability gradually began to become standard.[40]

The process whereby this capacity became naturalized was, however, not at all straightforward; because genius was dependent on the imagination, and this faculty was regarded as inherently equivocal or unstable. Since it relied on the senses it was often taken to be in league with them in a perpetual conspiracy against reason. Puritan writers were fond of quoting Genesis 8, 21, which (in the Authorized Version) read 'the imagination of man's heart is evil from his youth';[41] and Samuel Parker wrote of it 'climbing up into the bed of reason...[to] defile it by unchaste and illegitimate embraces, [and] instead of real conceptions and notices of things, impregnate the mind with...subventaneous phantasms'.[42] (In this image the genders of the two parties are unclear; generally speaking, reason or judgement was seen as male and imagination as female; in addition, women were regarded as being particularly susceptible, both mentally and physically, to the bad effects of imagination.)[43] It was seen as being both powerful — like gunpowder — and wayward — like a Proteus or chameleon,[44] or the 'wild and roaming' children 'of some giant race'.[45]

The classical commonplace of *ingenium* needing *ars,* or of the 'spur' needing a 'curb',[46] came to be applied to this problem in terms of genius needing art (or industry, or taste) and imagination (or wit, or fancy) needing judgement. 'Imagination in a poet is a faculty so wild and lawless that like a high-ranging spaniel it must have clogs tied to it, lest it outrun the judgement.'[47] At the same time, Homer and Virgil came to be characterized by each having a predominance of one of these two attributes; the former was gifted with genius, force, a 'strong, vast and boundless imagination', the latter with nobility, wisdom, order and judgement.[48]

In the early part of the 18th century a number of developments began to make it possible for the imagination to be seen in a new light: natural feelings came to be validated, the senses were seen (by Locke) as contributing valuably to perception, and emphasis was put on the limits of reason (by Hume).[49] In addition, imagination had a central role in new forms of finance and commerce (p.80). Addison's series of articles in *The Spectator* on 'The Pleasures of the Imagination' (1712) were an indication of this change. As this occurred, Homer's star rose and that of Virgil began to decline. The moral excellence of the Roman, which for over a thousand years had led the *Aeneid* to be regarded as the finest poem of antiquity, no longer counted as much as the sublime greatness of the Greek. The 'spirit and fire' of Homer's work conveyed an energy which was captivating; 'what he writes is of the most animated nature imaginable,' observed Pope, 'everything moves, everything lives, and is put in action'.[50] The abundance of his powers of invention made him 'like the Nile, pour[ing] out his riches with a boundless overflow', and his poems were like 'a wild paradise'.[51] That 'wild' could now be a term of approval was a sign of a notable shift in perception, pointing towards not just an esteem for the imagination but an acceptance of the (supposedly) bad company which it had always been seen as keeping.[52]

In his *Enquiry into the Life and Writings of Homer* (1735) Thomas Blackwell set out to describe the 'natural causes' which had produced the poet, in terms not of psychology or literary practice but rather of geographical, political and social circumstances. Homer was, of course, remarkable for his imagination — 'it is this that distinguishes the real poet'[53] — but the question Blackwell raised was what had formed his imagination. And the answer he gave was a characterisation of external conditions which was remarkably similar to the account which had previously been given to the imagination's inner workings. Freedom and absence of restraint — 'in Greece...nature was obstructed in none of her operations; and no rule or prescription gave a check to rapture and enthusiasm';[54] a wandering life — 'much travelling', for poets and 'strollers' are 'men of the quickest and truest feelings';[55] absence of education and of book-learning — 'the less of it the better';[56] unstable, often turbulent times — 'it was when Greece was ill-settled, when violence prevailed in many places, amidst the confusion of wandering tribes, that Homer produced his immortal poem';[57] and a language in its primitive condition, which meant that it was then 'expressive...of the highest passions...full of metaphor...of the boldest, daring and most natural kind'.[58]

The freedom Blackwell depicted might have been that of a curious and carefree child; (and in this respect, there is an interesting similarity between Locke's account of a child's mentality and later descriptions of the imagination).[59] But the energy was associated with strife, turbulence and disorder. On both these points his characterisation had much in common with Vico's account in *La scienza nuova* of poetry as the natural expression of a primitive mentality, which 'felt and imagined' as children do.[60] Such an imagination was intensely physical, drawing its strength from the body, and quite amoral. First nature, wrote Vico, which was 'poetic or creative *(poetica o sia creatrice)*', was also 'all fierce and cruel'.[61]

An equally physical, though less violent, imagination was celebrated by Joseph Warton in his *Ode to Fancy* (1746). This poem appeared in a volume which attacked the prevailing taste for 'didactic poetry and essays on moral subjects' and proclaimed 'invention and imagination to be the chief functions of a poet'.[62] Warton depicted Fancy in alluring terms, with 'loose-flowing hair...and bosom bare', and placed her in remote spots 'where nature seems to sit alone'; she could be found where there was laughter, or melancholy, or 'tumult and destruction', or sensual love.[63] In his *Essay on the Writings and Genius of Pope,* ten years later, Warton criticized Pope for being too rational: 'a clear head and acute understanding are not sufficient, alone, to make a poet;...the most solid observations on human life, expressed with the utmost elegance and brevity are morality, not poetry;...[only] a creative and glowing imagination can stamp a writer with this exalted and very uncommon character'.[64] 'True genius seldom resides in a cold, phlegmatic constitution. The same temperament and...sensibility that makes a poet, or a painter, will be apt to make a man a lover or a debauchee'.[65] And he concluded his *Essay* by asking whether 'that philosophical...and systematical spirit so much in vogue...by consulting only reason, has not diminished and destroyed sentiment, and made our poets write from the head rather than the heart?'[66]

What we see in each of these writings by Blackwell, Vico and Warton is an attack on reason in the name of imagination. The traditional opposition between the two faculties was developed in a way that would vindicate the claims of the latter. For Vico, this was part of his critique of Cartesian philosophy; for Blackwell it was in order to give a naturalistic account of Homer; for Warton it was to re-invigorate British poetry. But the approach was the same, stressing the qualities that arose from the untamed imagination, and adopting a historical perspective to make the case. For underlying each of these texts was the primitivist view that, as Dr. Johnson put it, 'the early writers are in possession of nature...[and] excel in strength and invention', while later writers have 'elegance and refinement'.[67] In the early years of the century discussion of genius had emphasized the need for art, judgement and taste; from the mid-century a new view began to emerge of reason stifling the powers of invention. Accompanying this development was a move away from neo-classical values of beauty and decorum, and the classical view of art as imitation, towards a new demand for emotional effects — 'the sublime and the pathetic are the two chief nerves of all genuine poetry'[68] — and a concern for individual expression. We can see both aspects of this change as being related to the general shift away from what was God-given (permanent in kind and superior to any human artefact) towards purely human powers of making.

The kind of primitivism on which Blackwell and Vico drew was that portrayed by Lucretius in his *De rerum natura*. This showed early humans as responding to physical needs and driven by instinctive desires in a world which was not benign, since there were many things these creatures lacked; but that lack stimulated their inventiveness. Because this account did not present these first humans as noble savages, (i.e. as morally admirable and/or intellectually gifted, living in an Arcadian peace), it matched the opposition between imagination and reason, passion and refinement, poetry and morality, which was central to these views of genius.

The attack on the neo-classical aesthetic went hand in hand with a re-evaluation of earlier writings — medieval romances, Spenser and Shakespeare — and the discovery of a distinctly northern primitivism — the mythology of the Scandinavians and Celts. To the long-standing view that political liberty in northern Europe had originally sprung from 'Gothic government' (handed down from the German tribes admired by Tacitus), was now added the belief that the original Germans, Scandinavians and Celts had possessed a rich poetic talent. In his *Progress of Poesy* Thomas Gray wrote of the 'influence of poetic genius over the remotest and most uncivilized nations',[69] and he gave an example of this in his widely-read *The Bard* (1757). Supposedly direct evidence of Celtic genius was then conveniently supplied by the publication of an ancient epic *Fingal* (1762) by Ossian. In his *Critical Dissertation on the Poems of Ossian* (1763) Hugh Blair praised their 'vehemence and fire, which are the soul of poetry', and were a product of primitive society: 'that state, in which human nature shoots wild and free, though unfit for other improvements, certainly encourages the high exertions of fancy and passion'.[70] Ossian excelled, above all, in the sublime, which dwells 'amidst the rude scenes of nature, amidst rocks and torrents and whirlwinds and battles...It is the thunder and lightning of genius'. In short, Ossian possessed 'the voice of nature'.[71] In William Duff's *Essay on Original Genius* (1767) we find the same association of poetic genius with the wild, vehement and irregular,[72] with youth or an early stage of society (where contact with nature was direct and fresh, unmediated by learning or rules or traditions),[73] and with a pagan, pre-Christian mythology: 'though the heathen theology must be confessed to be the disgrace and degradation of human reason, yet it must also be acknowledged to be a remarkable proof of the creative power of human imagination'.[74]

There were many similarities to these views of genius in French discussions of the subject from the middle years of the century. The word *génie*, like 'genius' in English, combined the meaning of *ingenium* (as natural gifts and character)[75] and *genius* (as an animating force and ability to 'create').[76] As the latter it had previously been seen, like in Britain, as needing to be balanced by taste or judgement; this had been the view, for example, of Dubos in his influential *Réflexions critiques sur la poésie et sur la peinture* (1719), and it continued to be that of Voltaire.[77] But in the next generation a growing number of voices started to argue against the need for balance or regulation. We see this in the writings of La Mettrie, or Turgot, or Toussaint,[78] and it was a central theme of the article '*Génie*' which appeared in Volume VII of the *Encyclopédie* (1757). This described the activity of genius in the fine arts, philosophy, and politics. In all three areas the genius was the person who went beyond the rules, or method, or laws, in order to create works or perform actions which were powerful, sublime, great, decisive, penetrating. The genius 'imagines more than he has seen; he produces more than he discovers'. But this ability did not make for being a good citizen.[79]

Although this article came to be attributed to (and its authorship was claimed by) Saint-Lambert, it is generally agreed that it owed much to Diderot,[80] and it was in Diderot's writings that we find the fullest treatment of these themes. In his *Discours sur la poésie dramatique* (1758) he asked 'What does a poet need?', and answered: 'Poetry wants something tremendous, barbaric and wild (*énorme, barbare, sauvage*). It is when the fury of civil war or fanaticism puts swords in men's hands, and blood flows in great waves on the ground, that the laurels of Apollo are shaken and become green...They fade away in times of peace and leisure'.[81] Unlike the British writers, however, Diderot did not confine himself to literary issues, or rely so heavily on a primitivist framework. He had an interest in theatre and in aesthetic matters generally, but they were only aspects of his wider belief that he was living in an era of decisive change, which demanded new ways of thinking. One of the main purposes of the *Encyclopédie*, of which he was principal editor, was to make people aware of such change, especially the benefits of scientific and technological advance. The project which Francis Bacon had initiated was now bearing fruit, and the result was an invigorating confidence in human potential: 'today philosophy advances with giant strides'.[82] The philosophy in question was the empirical thinking of Locke — the view that we have no innate ideas, all knowledge coming to us via the senses — and the scientific method of Bacon and Newton — the insistence that truth is established by evidence, that the hypotheses of reason must be confirmed by the observation of facts. These both promoted a critical and open-minded way of thinking and in the hands of Diderot Newtonian certainties were soon called into doubt.

The achievements of the new science had been based on a view of the natural world in which matter was regarded as being inert, both its movement and the laws according to which it moved being given to it by God. For Newton the beauty and regularity of the heavens above and the laws of physics on earth could only be the work of an intelligent designer and maker. In the early part of the 18th century a similar beauty and order had become apparent in the discoveries of biologists working for the first time with microscopes, so that in its smallest particular (as well as its grandest dimension) nature seemed to operate according to fixed and harmonious laws. But then observations began to undermine this view. Discoveries in geology led to theories that the earth was much older and had had a far more uneven history than that recorded in the Bible; researches in biology and physiology brought suggestions that matter did not obtain its movement or form from any external source but was self-animating and self-organising.

Diderot saw how these ideas could call into question arguments for the existence of God. It is true, he wrote in his *Lettre sur les aveugles* (1749), that the universe looks beautiful and coherent now; but we have no evidence that it has always been so. The visible order might be only 'momentary', 'a fleeting symmetry'. It could have been the result of aeons of ceaseless activity, 'irregular agitations' in which self-animating elements came together in a random process of trial and error to form worlds and creatures.[83] In formulating this view Diderot drew heavily on Lucretius and he adopted the Epicurean belief that, since nothing is permanent, the forces which have produced our earth are even now working for its dissolution. Nature is in a state of constant flux, 'a universal copulation' which is endlessly fertile, producing 'an infinite multitude of phenemona',[84] but also destructive and therefore in simultaneous decay.

The perceptions about instability and change which had occurred earlier in the century in British writings about social and economic conditions were here developed by Diderot at a metaphysical level. For him, as for Hume, mathematics or geometry could no longer serve as models for enquiry; philosophy and science had to take account of more tangible realities, and non-rational factors. Foremost among these for

Diderot were researches in biology and physiology. Not the observation of the starry heavens, but the examination of animal bodies was the way to the truth: 'only someone who has practised medicine a long time can write about metaphysics'.[85] Contemporary findings about the properties of matter and attributes of living organisms seemed to confirm his insights. There was an inherent energy animating the universe and present in each one of us, a point he demonstrated in *Le Rêve de d'Alembert* when the rapturous excitement with which the dreaming d'Alembert enthuses over the fertility of nature is followed by him ejaculating in his sleep.[86]

As nature is productive, so are humans; not only in procreating, but also by invention and, above all, genius. The genius was the person who 'creates',[87] and the capacity to do this derived from being more closely in touch with nature than other people: 'there is no intermediary between genius and nature'.[88] In his *Entretiens sur le Fils Naturel* (1757) Diderot portrayed such a figure in the character of Dorval. In 'a wild and solitary spot', either where nature has calm beauty — by the shore of a lake, in meadows of flowers, beside a running stream — or where she evokes a sublime fear — among dark woods, isolated caves, mountain waterfalls — the poet is gripped by 'enthusiasm'. His imagination is stirred, passions aroused, and his whole body feels vividly alive, first trembling, then seized by an intense fire 'which makes him gasp, burns him up, and destroys him'.[89] The experience, in other words, is close to sexual ecstasy. The next *Entretien* shows Dorval in a comparable state of possession but this time in the midst of a storm, a strong wind blowing and lightning flashes piercing the darkness.[90] What both images conveyed was the link between genius and a certain kind of nature. The second image was, of course, the same as that described soon after by Blair or Duff, it was an 'Ossianism *avant la lettre*'.[91] What made Diderot's treatment so significant was the way he then related these states to individual experience and physiology, for it was as important for him to take the divine or supernatural out of genius as to take God out of the universe. The primitivist approach was in effect one way of doing this, but Diderot wanted something more definite, not a vaguely historical but a precisely naturalistic explanation.

The results of this enquiry were never presented in a systematic manner or a single work, but from his scattered comments we can see two different conceptions of genius. The first, evident in writings in the 1750s and 1760s, was that the ability to grasp and convey a new truth derived partly from greater *sensibilité,* the way in which a genius is more affected by experiences than other people,[92] and partly from a particular mental aptitude which Diderot described as a flair (*pressentiment*) for seeing remote connections,[93] or from an extraordinary passivity. The latter (which he called *distraction* and which was like Keats' 'negative capability')[94] enabled the genius to present things as they were, actually or essentially. This unusual sensory apparatus and mental capacity was combined with a susceptibility to being carried away in 'enthusiasm' or, as Diderot sometimes called it, *aliénation*.[95] The insights of genius occurred in moments of dream or delirium or vacancy or enthusiasm, which was one reason why genius had been seen as close to madness.[96] The ancient perception was not inaccurate if it was understood as describing an acute abnormality. For just as nature's progress is neither peaceful nor orderly, so genius operates in an aberrant and irregular manner. It 'always presupposes some disorder in the machine', which is why geniuses could be described as 'kinds of monsters'.[97]

While the wisdom of a philosopher comes from a harmony in the mind, a man (never, in these texts, a woman) of genius is dominated by a single ability. In this respect, being limited in this way, good for only one thing, he is more like an animal than a properly developed human being. This meant that he was not only a physiological monster, but also a social monster, a 'solitary, wild, untamable' creature who was driven by the 'tyrannical impulse' of his extraordinary gifts.[98] The energy displayed by genius was associated by Diderot not only with sexuality or tempests, it was also seen as the same energy which could inspire great crimes.[99] Not only could violence and evil be aesthetically pleasing, something implicitly recognized in discussions of the sublime,[100] they could also be productive. An artist's morality was diametrically opposed to normal morality, for his imperative was always to take things to the extreme;[101] it was no accident, therefore, that France's greatest playwright, Racine, had also been a thoroughly bad man.[102]

The disturbing consequences of this view form one of the central themes of Diderot's masterpiece, *Le Neveu de Rameau*, which portrays an encounter between himself and the nephew of the great composer. The latter is also a musician, but unlike his uncle he has never achieved any success. Despite his acute *sensibilité* and fine aesthetic sense, his own compositions are mediocre and he is bitter at his lack of genius. Yet the nephew is a genius of a kind, for his extraordinary character — cynical, caustic and inventive — 'provokes the truth' in a way that only genius can do,[103] and his astonishing versatility as a performer is recognized by everyone who witnesses it. These gifts are accompanied by complete unscrupulousness and an overt hostility to moral norms of any kind.[104] To be true to his own character, which also means being true to 'the accents...of nature' and the 'animal cry of passion',[105] is to be indifferent to any claims of goodness. It is an unwelcome fact that all greatness exacts a terrible cost: a great man is like a magnificent tree, 'its top reaches up into the clouds and its branches spread out into the distance', but 'it stunts the trees around it and stifles the plants beneath it'.[106]

In his later works Diderot adopted a different view of genius; he saw it less as a result of an identity or fusion with nature and more as an ability to be detached. But this was no return to a neo-classical concern for reason or judgement; for in the fullest expression of this view, his *Paradoxe sur le comédien,* he compared the genius to an actor, a figure which had been persistently attacked by moralists from Solon onwards, largely because of the lack of any stable personality, any fixed principle, but also because of the sexuality of the theatre and the vanity of display. The actor in the *Paradoxe* is not at the mercy of his *sensibilité* (like Rameau's nephew),[107] but is a creature of *sang-froid*,[108] always in control. He has an 'equal aptitude for all kinds of characters and roles', wearing different masks,[109] deceiving us, the audience, into thinking he was the character he was playing but being himself none of them. Who really was he? 'Everyone and no one'.[110]

The great performances of the actress Clairon were the result not of self-expression, but rather of self-denial; in playing her roles she was not herself but 'another (*double*)'.[111] It is not the performer who acts 'but the spirit of another person'.[112] The evidence for this view lay in what Diderot had observed or read about actors and from his own personal experience. It had been by impersonation or *dédoublement* that his most remarkable works had been achieved.[113] In the disguise afforded by another character, or in dialogue form, his own imagination had taken its boldest flights. The implications of this conception of genius were as disturbing as those of Diderot's first view. If what we read of a writer is like what we see of Clairon onstage, giving no indication of what she herself thinks or feels, then there can be no necessary connection between the character of the maker and that of the work. Just as Diderot at the outset of his career had attacked the metaphysical argument for design, so in his final years he called into question the notion of the integrity of the writer. In the same way that (to use an ancient argument against design) the intention of a giver cannot be deduced from the character of a gift,[114] so a writer whose words move us with moral passion may himself not be in the least moral. And Diderot indicated the error of what I have called the ergonic fallacy: 'we cannot be sure of the purity of [a writer's] morals from the wisdom of the writing; it can happen that someone who is morally worthless writes and speaks as copiously about virtue as someone who is [wholly] virtuous'.[115]

The idea of a disunity between writer and work was no more new than that of the distinctive attributes of genius being an amoral energy (like that of a lion) or chameleon versatility (like that of a fox). But wherever the world is perceived as being shaped by human actions and subject to continual change the ambivalent and dangerous aspects of these attributes pose a threat. As Diderot grew older the course of change in France seemed to be blocked and he himself lost some of his confidence in human potential. But while this may have made the issue less acute it did little to ease the difficult questions about genius, which he had had the honesty to depict and the unhappiness not to be able to resolve.

III

Behind much of Diderot's writing on genius stood the figure of Rousseau. The two men had been close friends from the time they were both struggling to make a living in Paris (in the early 1740s) until their acrimonious quarrel (in the late 1750s). It was on the way to visit Diderot, then in prison because of the publication of his *Lettre sur les aveugles,* that Rousseau had had his visionary insight into the natural goodness of man and the corrupting effect of social institutions. This *illumination* had been provoked by a question for a prize essay on whether advances in the arts and sciences had been morally beneficial, and Rousseau's answer, later published as his *Discours sur les sciences et les arts* (1751), had been emphatically negative: cultural and intellectual progress was invariably a sign of moral decline.

Many of the reasons Rousseau gave for this view were derived from traditional philosophical, religious or republican opposition to the arts, based on their frivolity, superficiality or connection with luxury. But at the heart of his *Discours* was a perception of selfish ambition as the driving force behind literary activity. Writers want fame and applause and they will do anything to gain it; their *fureur de se distinguer* makes them indifferent to virtue; in their scale of priorities the good is always subordinate to the new, and their lives are dominated by searching for any novelty which could win attention and make them stand out.[116] Hence the bitter rivalries of poets and the malicious back-biting of literary life.

This perception was based on Rousseau's own experience. He had come to Paris to make his name, as a musician and a writer, and after many setbacks his opera *Les Muses galantes* came near to having a success. A private performance of some extracts so impressed the Duc de Richelieu that he wanted the opera to be staged at Versailles. But then the great Rameau heard some of the score and he attacked it vehemently; 'I have never seen so many cabals and hostilities', wrote Rousseau to a friend. As a result of this criticism the project was dropped. But that was not the end of the matter; because Rousseau then discovered that this hostility, and the anger in him which it aroused, stimulated his own work.[117] Hatred could bring inspiration, competition and ill-will could be productive; what was morally bad was artistically fruitful. Hence the theme of the first *Discours*.

The publication of this work made Rousseau's reputation and led to a lively controversy in which he defended his viewpoint and became aware of its inadequacies. In particular, he was led to see how this kind of selfishness was not distinct to the arts but was one aspect of a much wider problem. Writers were not alone in being dominated by the *fureur de se distinguer*, in craving applause, and in ignoring their inner being (*être*) for a purely external show (*paraître*). For these were also the characteristics of commercial society, as it had been described by Mandeville and Montesquieu. This similarity between literary invention and economic productivity enabled Rousseau to move from his personal experience to the brilliantly original and influential social theory set out in his *Discours sur l'inégalité* (1755), an account of how an originally good (or, more precisely, innocent) human nature had been altered over the centuries as the result of adverse circumstances.[118]

Although the body of this *Discours* portrayed the development of society in almost wholly negative terms, it was preceded by a Dedication to the Republic of Geneva, where Rousseau had spent his childhood and a citizen of which he proudly announced himself to be. This praised the Swiss city-republic as a model of good social arrangements and the way in which shared values and activities prevented any need for excessive self-assertion. Rousseau described his father as exemplary in this respect: 'he was not *distingué* among his fellow-citizens; he only was what they all are'.[119] The same vision of a harmonious social order, where the affirmation of the common ethos is a constant source of pleasure, inspired the political theory of the *Contrat social* (1762). Where republican institutions provide regular occasions for shared happiness, then 'there is less need to look for happiness in individual concerns',[120] and so private interests will not develop or expand to the degree that provokes malign competition and hostility. In other words, to lead a good life means not needing or aspiring to be creative.

Such conditions could only exist before commerce had arisen; accordingly, as Rousseau recognized, the *Contrat social* could have little relevance to the situation in France. He was therefore led to devise other solutions to the problem of how to be moral in the contemporary world. One solution — lyrically described in *La Nouvelle Héloïse* (1761) — was a family community living self-sufficiently in the countryside, beyond the range of pernicious cities and malevolent institutions. The other — the subject of *Emile* (1762) — was a quasi-Stoic independence which might be achieved by an upbringing which gave protection from bad social influences and set limits to the self. This independence was underpinned by a belief in God; the beauty of the natural world and the voice of individual conscience suggest to us that a benevolent God exists, and this can give us confidence that we were intended to be moral and that, whatever may happen in this life, the pursuit of the good will in the end be justified.

Neither of these proposals was effective for Rousseau himself. Fleeing from France to avoid arrest he wandered from country to country, winning and losing friends, subject to hostility and suffering from paranoia. A fixed life in a small community was never a viable option, and the prospect of justice in an afterlife was not enough to reconcile him to the misunderstanding which always came his way. He devoted himself increasingly to the study of plants, to a contact with an unspoilt reality which could vindicate his belief in nature; but this could not satisfy his need for human recognition, a justification in the eyes not of God but of the world. He could only achieve that by means of his writings, and so he spent his final years engaged in the composition of one autobiographical work after another, the *Confessions, Dialogues* and *Rêveries.*

On the opening page of the *Confessions* Rousseau announced that his aim was to show 'a man in all the truth of nature'.[121] By telling the story of his life he would demonstrate how mistaken were the reports of his dishonesty or malice, and how good his natural inclinations and intentions had been. If he had ever acted badly, that had been the result of adverse circumstances. In this respect his own life was presented as an example of his social theory, innocent nature being preserved or distorted by the good or bad influences to which it was subject. But his account was far richer and more evocative that this might suggest. It became an extensive self-examination, a record of personal feelings and exploration of inner life which was unprecedented in its depth and frankness. And while the first humans in the *Discours sur l'inegalité* were portrayed as having scarcely any distinct personality (with a sense of themselves but otherwise little beyond their immediate, elementary needs), the character depicted in the *Confessions* had an acutely self-conscious awareness of himself as a unique individual: 'I am not made like anyone else I have seen. I dare to suppose that I am not made like anyone else who exists. If I am no better, at least I am different'.[122]

This difference was manifest in a number of ways. One was an extreme variety and volatility of mood and emotion: 'there are times when I am so unlike myself that I could be taken as having another, completely opposite character'.[123] This condition was sometimes the product of his own ardent, impulsive temperament, and sometimes the effect of weakness, a passivity and susceptibility which meant that he took on the character of his surroundings. It was combined with an innate resistance to all constraint, to whatever would inhibit the free play of his feelings. He enjoyed the idleness of 'a child who is in continual movement, doing nothing...I love beginning a hundred things and finishing none of them...in everything following only the whim of the moment'.[124] This was why he had liked walking and 'the itinerant life',[125] and hated all kinds of dependence. If he was constrained he wandered in his mind; thanks to his vivid imagination he could enter 'a land of fantasy'.[126] The strength of this imagination had often caused him suffering, since its tendency to exaggerate made everything bad seem terrible. But it had also provided consolation for what he had lacked or been denied. More than that, it was his ability to see beyond existing conditions, by means of his imagination, which had been the mainspring of his achievement.

Rousseau did not publish the *Confessions* in his lifetime; they were meant to set the record straight after his death. When they did appear — Part One in 1782, Part Two in 1789 — they made as great an impact as any of his previous books, and to a certain extent achieved their aim of presenting the author's innocence. But the book did more than exonerate Jean-Jacques the man; it became a model for a new kind of self-realization, by means of being a writer.

In his first *Discours* Rousseau had attacked writers not only for their self-interest and amoral ambition, but also for their complicity with the existing social order, their deference to those in power and to current conventions. Nowadays, he wrote, there is a 'hideous conformity' in behaviour, as if everyone had been formed in the same mould; each person follows convention and 'never his own genius; no one any longer dares to show himself as he is'.[127] The *Confessions,* by contrast, were written precisely out of this latter impulse, showing how Rousseau had followed his own nature and daring to tell the truth exactly as it had been. The first thing he points out about his character is its uniqueness; far from being cast in the same mould as anyone else, he had been formed by nature in a mould which had then been destroyed.[128] This work was therefore a self-portrait of the writer as original genius, and as such it revealed a character with many affinities with what had been described by Young or Blackwell or Diderot. Like Young's original writer he had ignored previous models, (his work he claimed was without precedent);[129] he had taken many an 'excursion and deviation' (p.105) been true to his own character and relied on his own 'strong…[and] boundless imagination' (p.111). Like Blackwell's Homer he had led a wandering life, with little organized education, and in (personally) unstable conditions (p.112). Like Diderot's *génie* he had been subject to *délire* and the tyrannical impulse of his *sensibilité,* yet also known that passive kind of free association which the former termed *distraction* (p.118). He was as volatile as Rameau's nephew, and had the same combination of a child's playfulness and an adult's sensuality.[130] He saw himself as a 'species of creature apart', with 'a bizarre, singular mixture' of qualities,[131] in other words, like a 'kind of monster' (p.118). And he found his greatest pleasure in being alone, in a 'wild' place where he could feel that there was 'no intermediary between [himself] and nature' (p.117).[132] There his imagination could invent new worlds.

While Rousseau did not welcome conflict, or see that as productive in the way that Hume, Diderot (or Voltaire)[133] did, his own writing had taken shape from a comprehensive opposition to existing conditions and individuals. And while he denounced the *fureur de se distinguer* of other writers, his own autobiographical project was stamped with a defiant sense of his own superiority. In an unpublished note he wrote: 'I would prefer to be forgotten by the whole human race than regarded as someone ordinary'.[134] This confidence in himself and in his own view of the world was inextricably bound up with his alienation from it. Having tried and failed to achieve a reputation within existing conventions (his pre-*illumination* writings), he had then discovered his own powers by attacking all such conventions. And his conviction of the worthlessness of present society was an essential element in his own sense of personal integrity. In this respect he needed to be attacked by his contemporaries to have his integrity confirmed.

But Rousseau had not only been attacked because of his ideas, and his alienation was not only a result of the failure of other people's generosity or perception. His position outside, on the margins of, society had also been one which he had chosen. He could not tolerate constraint or dependence, and had always acted to secure his own freedom. His success in doing that, in basing himself outside his contemporary world, had enabled him to diagnose that world without making compromises. But that very independence, fundamental to his own achievement, had been obtained at terrible cost to others: he had taken the five children he fathered to the Foundlings' Hospital, where the mortality rate was even higher than it would have been in the poor household he shared with the children's mother. This practice was not uncommon in 18th century Paris, but that could not excuse the abandonment of all the children. (While at the outset, prior to his *illumination,* he might have been under the sway of malign social pressures, the last child had been given away after he had conducted his 'personal reform',[135] rejecting the offer of a royal pension, taking up music-copying to secure his independence, and so bringing his life into conformity with his own principles.) Such behaviour may have been what Diderot had in mind when he wrote of greatness as a magnificent tree which stunts and stifles everything about it (p.119). The revelation of this terrible fact (in a pamphlet written by Voltaire) had been one of the reasons why Rousseau undertook his self-justification in the *Confessions*; to some extent the whole work is a protestation of innocence. None of the arguments he adopts to explain the treatment of the children is convincing but such is the fullness of his description of himself that up to a point we can understand his actions, but for psychological (rather than historical or sociological) reasons. Because what Rousseau shows is not just how this statue had feet of clay, but the essential interdependence of its head of gold with those feet of clay: without the latter there would have been no greatness.

In describing his own mind Rousseau wrote that 'it is a very odd fact that my imagination never manifests itself more agreeably than when I am in the least agreeable situation; and, on the other hand, when all around me is cheerful it is least so...My mind is incapable of making [immediate reality] beautiful; it wants to create [another reality]...If I wish to depict spring I must be in winter; if I want to describe a beautiful landscape I must be shut in by walls;...if I were ever to be put into the Bastille, there I would compose the picture of freedom'.[136] This observation shows the psychological process by which his masterpieces came to be written. They were the result of an overwhelming need to escape adverse conditions; in other words, the negative experience was the seedbed of the positive achievement. A clear example of this was *La Nouvelle Héloïse*, the work which had the widest readership during his own lifetime. In Rousseau's own account it had been dissatisfaction with his life which had thrown him 'into the land of fantasies...an ideal world which my creative imagination had soon peopled with creatures close to my heart'.[137] Moreover, he had not depicted this world in a third-person narrative; it had been vividly brought to life in the letters exchanged by the principal characters. That is to say, Rousseau had enacted the drama, he had done exactly what he had condemned about actors in his *Lettre à d'Alembert*; he had not been himself but had performed a role.[138]

In his *Essay concerning human understanding* Locke had discussed what makes us will or choose an action. He had initially thought that we act in order to improve things, for the sake of 'the greater good in view'; but he had then changed his mind. The determining factor is, rather, an 'uneasiness a man is at present under,...an uneasiness in the want of an absent good...As much as we desire any absent good, so much are we in pain for it'.[139] Unhappiness, or dissatisfaction, is what spurs us on. This notion came to be widely adopted in the 18th century, human beings being seen as prey to an inherent restlessness or uneasiness (*inquiétude*). Sometimes it was envisaged (by Diderot) as a property of all life-forms,[140] at other times (by James Harris) as a purely human sense of what is missing.[141] In this respect it seemed to reflect what Hume had described in terms of uncertainty — 'moral principles, [like]...speculative principles of any kind,...are in continual flux and revolution'[142] — and his more general perception of the evanescence of value — 'Whatever is, may not be' (p.80). But this uneasiness was also seen as central to innovation, invention, and the cause of liberty (in reference, for example, to Peter the Great remaking Russia, or scientific discoveries, or the rise of political freedom in Britain).[143] In these contexts it was a positive search for an alternative, an expression of that growing belief in human potential which would come to generate the sense that 'Whatever is, need not be'.

Rousseau's writings (product of his own 'restless imagination'),[144] made a major contribution to this sense of alternative possibilities. The central theme of his *Discours sur l'inégalité* was that present conditions are not evidence of intrinsic human failings, for human nature could have undergone drastic alteration over time, and we can therefore see the existing order of things as neither inevitable nor unchangeable. As he grew older, however, Rousseau's focus became ever narrower and the title of his *Confessions* invited comparison with St. Augustine's autobiography. The pivotal moment in the latter's life had been his conversion in the garden in Turin. Before then he had suffered continual dissatisfaction, a sense of alienation which he described in terms of feeling 'restless (*inquietus*)'.[145] With his conversion, and his sense of total dependence on God, that problem had been ended. For Rousseau, by contrast, the pivotal moment of his life, his *illumination,* had only increased his alienation. Not only had it confirmed his dissatisfaction with almost all existing societies, it also led to that success as a writer which had brought fame, hostility and vilification, a life that became (until his final two years) ever more restless.

In the very last years of his life, however, Rousseau appears to have arrived at a still point, free from *inquiétude*. This was not by surrendering his soul to God, like Augustine, but by becoming wholly self-sufficient in himself, 'like God'.[146] In his *Rêveries* he gave an account of how he could become completely absorbed in the *sentiment de l'existence*, the experience of sheer pleasure in life, in being alive. He described this condition as being like God because the attainment of self-sufficiency in harmony with nature was a kind of perfection, a perfection which he realized and conveyed in his own magically evocative prose. In this way he indicated how aesthetic achievement itself could come to have a redemptive function, and transform the pain from which it had emerged into a new kind of consolation.

IV

For the frontispiece of his First Discourse Rousseau chose an engraving of Prometheus warning a Satyr of the dangers of the fire which he had brought to earth.[147] This encounter between Prometheus and the Satyr was recorded in a short essay by Plutarch entitled 'How to profit from your enemies', and this essay may have provided Rousseau with one of the central themes of his subsequent work — *le remède du mal même*: 'let us strive to draw from the evil itself the remedy which should cure it', putting right the damage caused by bad social arrangements by making good social arrangements.[148] For Rousseau personally the remedy turned out to be not social change but withdrawal from society altogether. The Prometheus whom he identified with, as the citizen of Geneva warning his fellow-men of danger, became the Prometheus described by Diderot in the *Encyclopédie,* who was not just a symbol of 'the daring genius of the human race' but also, when chained to the rock, 'an emblem of solitude and profound meditation'.[149] In his isolation Rousseau did find a cure, and it was through *le mal même*: the very attribute which set him apart from other people, namely, his gifts as a writer, became the medium for his own relation to the world.

What for Rousseau was the final stage of a troubled career was for Goethe a confident point of departure. In his early twenties he came to see that everyone arrives at a stage when you must rely on your own resources, and he decided to establish his own independence on what had proved most consistent in his life up till then — his creative ability (*mein produktives Talent*). 'As I thought about this natural gift and realized that it was entirely my own, immune to external influence either good or bad, I wanted to base my whole mental existence upon it'. This notion then took shape as a play about Prometheus, not as the fire-bringer but as the creator of human beings. On his own the Titan had 'peopled a world from his workshop. I was convinced that something of significance can only be produced when a person isolates himself. My own works which had won so much applause were children of solitude'.[150]

The dramatic fragment which resulted from this conviction asserts more powerfully than anything previously written what might be called a right of creativity, that is, a right to action which is wholly autonomous in the sense that it cannot be judged by any existing criteria but only by those values which that action or work itself brings into being. (This problem was to be discussed by Kant as an aspect of originality[151] and by Wordsworth in terms of a poet 'creating that taste by which a truly original poet' can be appreciated.)[152] Prometheus' hostility to the Olympian gods is a rejection of dependence on, or connection with, any external framework or forces: 'I share nothing with them, and what I have they cannot take from me'.[153] They have a right to what is theirs, and he a right to what is his. But what exactly is his? his brother Epimetheus asks. 'The area covered by what I have produced', is the answer.[154] In the second act Prometheus teaches the first humans this labour theory of value and in the poem which Goethe extracted from and developed out of the play he abuses the gods for their reliance on others, in terms of the vapours from sacrifices made to them or the breath of prayers spoken to them.[155] Everything he had achieved, by contrast, he had done for himself.

To adopt a position of such complete independence is, as Epimetheus points out, to be condemned to solitude; it means never having the pleasure of feeling 'an inner wholeness' which was shared with others.[156] Prometheus knows that and accepts it, because he has a superior pleasure, which we see once he is left on his own. Then he delights in the world of his own creations, the (as yet lifeless) figures of human beings which he has made:

> Hier meine Welt, mein All!
> Hier fühl' ich mich.
> Hier alle meine Wünsche
> In körperlichen Gestalten.
> Meinen Geist so tausendfach
> Geteilt und ganz, in meinen teuern Kindern.

> ('Here is my world, my universe! / Here I experience myself. / Here all my wishes are realized in bodily forms; / My own spirit, a thousandfold / Dispersed and whole, in my beloved children'.)[157]

In these compact and ecstatic lines Goethe describes the same feeling expressed by Byron in *Childe Harold's Pilgrimage*: 'To create! And in creating / Live a being more intense'.[158] It is a combination of self-intensity and self-expression, of personal powers fully realized and *Geist* made wholly visible. The individual experience is so complete that it obtains its own validity: what more could be needed?

At this point Minerva (Athene) enters. She had been Prometheus' inspiration, in the literal sense of having breathed into him what he had then developed as his own capacities. The recognition of this external element in his own past leads him to acknowledge that his work had not always been pleasurable. At times it had been 'a self-chosen servitude', a burden imposed on himself by his own powers. But he had carried out such labour because in his eyes her approval meant that his works would attain lasting value.[159] In this way, his achievements went beyond self-assertion. Recognising this, Minerva declares that he has become worthy of freedom, and because she sees that the humans made by Prometheus have a similar capacity for freedom she agrees to breathe life into them. In the second act of the fragment we see Prometheus beginning to teach these first humans about their freedom, for, as he proclaims defiantly, humans are formed 'in my image', a phrase with deliberate Biblical resonance. Their destiny is neither to be like the gods, nor to live in fear of any gods, but rather to experience life to the full — 'suffering, weeping, having delight and pleasure' — and so achieve their independence as he had done.[160] The most complete realisation of such life, we are led to believe, is in being creative, and the essential impulse of the play is to vindicate creativity as self-justifying autonomy.

In other writings of these years Goethe portrayed different aspects of this theme: the bliss of exuberant inspiration, in *Mailied,* or the pain of its absence (and delight its return will bring) in *Kunstlers Abendlied,* elemental power and defiant strength in *Wanderers Sturmlied,* the haunting meditation on solitude, destiny and revelation of *Harzreise im Winter.* All these poems convey a rapturous identification of a poet with the physical world, the pulse of living nature as the heartbeat of poetic invention. The sap in a plant, the bud opening into blossom, the rush of torrents, the turbulence of storms, all invigorate the writer, and seem to illustrate Goethe's conviction that whatever is productive has its own validity, or (as he wrote in one of his last poems) 'whatever is fruitful, that alone is true'.[161]

On their own these poems could not be taken as evidence of creativity being amoral; that would be the ergonic fallacy. But with Goethe, for the first time, we have independent, contemporaneous evidence of the poet's feelings, attitudes and beliefs. In letters to friends he described himself as surrendering to the fullness of each moment,[162] encompassing 'God and Satan, Hell and Heaven',[163] being in a state of continual oscillation,[164] knowing all joys and pains,[165] 'ever striving and working...struggling and playing', following his impulse indifferent to the opinions or judgements of other people.[166] And further evidence is provided by a short text, written under Goethe's guidance in 1781, which describes what nature meant to him at this time:

> Nature! We are surrounded by her and embraced by her...Unrequested and unexpected she gathers us up into the round of her dance and carries us away, until we are exhausted and fall from her arms. / She creates ever new forms...All is new and yet always old. / We live within her and are foreign to her...We continually work on her and yet have no power over her. / She seems to direct everything to individuality and she cares nothing for individuals. She is always building and destroying, and her workshop is inaccessible. / She lives in innocent children...She is the only artist.../ She acts a play; whether she is aware of that, we do not know.../ There is eternal life, movement and becoming in her and yet she never moves forward...She has no notion of permanence and has put her curse on whatever stands still./ ...She encloses man in darkness and spurs him on eternally to the light.../ She gives needs, because she loves movement.../ Her crown is love; only through love do we come near her. She sets distances between all creatures and all want to be entangled with one another.../ ...She knows neither past nor future. The present is her eternity.[167]

The identification of nature and writer, which seems evident in the poems, also informs this fragment; what is described as physical reality also incorporates human nature, more precisely creative human nature. However, while such feelings may bring forth superb poetry the literary triumph was not a triumph in life, for the poems were as much an escape from reality as a reflection of it. In a famous passage Goethe once wrote of his works as being 'fragments of a great confession', but immediately before this comment he described the process of writing as being a way of coming to terms with experience, of finding a point of repose and coherence in what otherwise tended to be chaotic movement, (as had been the case with *Werther*).[168] This is what he meant when he referred to his poetry's 'healing powers'.[169] In an early letter he compared himself to a chameleon[170] and in the late 1790s, in perhaps the frankest account he ever gave of himself, he described his nature as being both extremely changeable, susceptible to every outside pressure, and yet restlessly driven on from within to write, even though that drive in turn, being active rather than reflective, worked in ways contrary to what he might intend. These elements of susceptibility and restlessness were in themselves as much a liability as a blessing.[171] The problems which they caused become evident as soon as we move away from Prometheus in his isolation or the poet as *Wanderer*, and move into a social setting.

The two works which made Goethe's reputation, *Götz von Berlichingen* (1773) and *Werther* (1774), deal with this issue. Götz is driven on by a powerful, energetic restlessness, and Werther is volatile and susceptible; both are isolated figures with a passionate belief in themselves. But that belief brings them into a conflict with society which destroys them. In Götz's case his defiant determination to assert his independence arouses forces which, for their own survival, are compelled to get rid of him. In Werther's case, his acute sense of an uncorrupt world of innocence and beauty, feeling closer to children than to most adults, sets him at such odds with existing reality that he loses touch altogether. If he were able to construct an alternative world (as Goethe himself could do in his writing), he might have survived. As it is, he becomes more and more isolated, convinced of his insight into a superior truth — 'the light becomes brighter beside the grave'[172] — but so absorbed in his own feelings that suicide becomes his only solution.

The Faust story addresses the same problem, for the combination of self-obsession and restlessness which characterizes Faust also leads to destruction. Goethe's earliest version, the *Urfaust*, contains no explicit pact with the devil. We see Faust alone, tormented by his dissatisfaction with learning, summoning up (and being rejected by) the Erdgeist; then together with Mephistopheles working trivial magic; then, most extensively, pursuing Gretchen (with help from Mephistopheles), falling in love with her, and abandoning her. The simple happiness which she offers cannot satisfy him. His desire 'to know the inmost essence of the world',[173] not through books but in experience, means he has a hunger for novelty and so must pass through every door the devil opens to him. Nature 'gives needs, because she loves movement'. Faust has to keep moving, and his determination to be true to that impulse, at whatever cost, destroys Gretchen.

All these works, dealing with German characters in German settings, in a manner which owed little to foreign models, were part of the *Sturm und Drang*, the movement of rebellion against the predominance of French culture and neo-classical aesthetics. For Goethe and such contemporaries as Lenz, Merck, Klinger and Bürger, literary and social conventions were seen as an intolerable restraint; neither should stand in the way of the direct expression of personal feeling. Instead of obeying rules writers should follow or manifest their 'genius', and for this reason the 1770s became known as the *Genieperiode*. However, this term was more critical than admiring, used more with reference to examples of excess or of grandiose claims than to any notable achievements. Herder, who played a decisive role in encouraging the movement, soon disassociated himself from the cult of genius (see p.163), and Goethe, by his move to Weimar (in 1775), effectively did the same. Taking this step, he later observed, had been a way of moving on to a 'higher stage of cultivation (*Bildung*)'.[174]

In the following years Goethe developed means of dealing with those elements of his own personality which his early works had shown to be both exhilarating yet destructive. He came to adopt a quasi-Spinozist philosophy of nature, in which nature's presence was no less pervasive but her movement more regular, a continual transformation according to laws of polarity and intensification. In collaboration with Schiller he developed a view of art which reasserted classical values of beauty and order, and opposed the subjective intensities of what he later called 'unhealthy' Romanticism.[175] The problem of the extreme susceptibility which afflicted Werther was treated with detachment in *Tasso* and then, in the Wilhelm Meister novels, comprehensively put in its place, as a mere stage on the way to adulthood. He distanced himself from Prometheus in *Ilmenau* and portrayed the character as critically inadequate in *Pandora*. The *Urfaust* was expanded and given a framework which set evil within a benign theodicy. The lines spoken by the dying Faust, 'Life and freedom are only earnt by the person / Who has to conquer them every day',[176] could be taken as a statement of Goethe's own lifework in achieving self-mastery, in reaching the serenity which he prized so highly in his last years.

But impressive though they were, the works of Goethe's maturity did not solve the problem which had earlier preoccupied him. They might cast it in a new light, or remove it into the middle distance, but they did not eradicate it, as his continuing preoccupation with Faust showed. The Lord might announce, in the Prologue 'Man errs, so long as he strives',[177] and in Part Two Faust may be saved because he comes to devote his activity to good works. But that activity still involves the destruction of innocent people (Philemon and Baucis), which scarcely seems a matter of simply 'erring'. Goethe hoped that his stay in Weimar would end the conflict between his poetic character and reality. In fact, it merely put that conflict in abeyance as he moved in different company and took on new responsibilities. The principal reason for his escape to Italy was 'to renew his poetic productivity',[178] and such a renewal did occur, not only because of the stimulus of Mediterranean light and flora and Italian collections of art, but also because he was free from social constraints. He recaptured some of his youthful isolation and, as subsequent comments on his egotism and remoteness testify, that remained with him.[179]

In addition Goethe made contact again with physical reality, in the form of sex. His release from social conventions or demands was accompanied by 'the joys of true, naked love',[180] recorded in his *Römische Elegien* and sustained on his return from Italy by his life with Christiane Vulpius. Nature for him had always included sexuality, and in a poem like *Kenner und Künstler* he had made an explicit link between the creative and the sexual act.[181] The connection between them did not lie simply in the nature of the impulse or the energy; it was also the fact that in sex, as in creation, we experience the process of nature — 'eternal, living activity'[182] — in a form which is both intensely personal and yet also impersonal.

It was this impersonality which saved Goethe from the problems caused by his susceptibility and self-obsession. He once observed that he would often have thought himself mad if he had not taken such an interest in the natural world,[183] because in nature he believed he saw forces at work which also operated in him but for which therefore he had only limited responsibility. In this perspective we can understand the chilling remark he made to Benjamin Constant, 'When I am involved in something that really concerns me, I do not care about the consequences'.[184] The fact was that while humans are (or aim to be) moral, nature is not. She creates and she destroys, and both are parts, systole and diastole, of her inexorable rhythm. Good and evil are equally necessary to form a whole and the two are connected in the most intricate way, as in the final stanza of *Harzreise im Winter* where the figure of the poet incorporates both Christ and Satan.[185] In *Dichtung und Wahrheit* Goethe wrote that while a work of art may have moral effects, as far as the artist is concerned moral aims are not merely irrelevant but a hindrance.[186] It is contradiction, not goodness, which makes us productive,[187] and to be true to nature means, above all, to be productive. 'The true life is the eternal innocence of action'.[188] The incompatibilities which arose from such an attitude were summed up by Goethe in his maxim: 'Exploring nature we are pantheists, being inventive we are polytheists, being moral we are monotheists'.[189]

Although some of these views could be supported by a reading of Spinoza, there was much that could not. Herder was able to adapt Spinoza to new circumstances, the Enlightenment emphasis on movement and change, by effectively substituting for the timeless truths of geometry the dynamic forces of biology; this did not conflict with Spinoza's idea of greater perfection being achieved by means of mental and moral improvement. But such a course was not open to Goethe. Indeed, his scathing comments about Herder's ideal of *Humanität*, (which he saw as leading to a world in which everyone was someone else's nurse),[190] indicate how opposed he was to any measure which would lessen the opposition between the creative and the moral at the expense of the former.

As a result Goethe was faced with a profoundly disturbing problem, to which he seems to have given considerable attention in his final years. He published nothing about it but conveyed his views in conversation to Eckermann and in the last book of his autobiography. There he described what he called 'the daemonic (*das Dämonische*)', the 'productive power' evident in individuals who had been outstandingly creative either in action — Luther, Peter the Great, Frederick the Great, Napoleon — or in the arts — Raphael, Shakespeare, Mozart, Byron.[191] He had discovered in nature, he believed, something which only revealed itself in contradictions and therefore could not be grasped in a single concept, even less in a single word. It was not divine, because it seemed without reason; not human, because it had no understanding; not devilish, because it brought good results; not angelic, because it often delighted in pain. It resembled chance, because it displayed no consequence; it was similar to Providence, since it suggested connections. It could pass through everything which limits us. It seemed to have arbitrary power over elements of our existence which we regard as bound by necessity; it contracted time and expanded space. It seemed to have pleasure in the impossible and it pushed away the possible with contempt.[192] 'While expressing itself most remarkably in animals, [the daemonic] is most wonderfully connected with human beings, and forms a power which if not antagonistic to the moral order is so at odds with it that one could be taken for the warp and the other for the woof...The daemonic appears at its most alarming when it predominates in a single person. In the course of my life I have been able to observe this, partly close-up and partly at a distance. Such individuals are not always the most distinguished either by intellect or talent, and can rarely be recommended for the goodness of their heart. But they convey an immense energy, and have an unbelievable power over all creatures, even over the elements. Who can say how far such effects may extend? All the moral powers together can do nothing against them'.[193]

Goethe's own experience of this element was not confined to himself, nor was it limited to writers or artists. He had seen it at work in the Duke of Weimar, with his 'unlimited powers of action and unrest',[194] and in Napoleon, whom he met in 1808. The productive power which marked the daemonic, as it characterized the genius, had nothing to do with the kind of activity a person undertook; it is the same whatever the 'business, art or occupation', expressing itself 'in an energy that is entirely positive'.[195] When Goethe had met Napoleon the latter had taken issue with tragedies which had shown characters at the mercy of fate. 'What do we want nowadays with fate?' asked the Emperor; 'Politics is our fate'.[196] Humans makes their own world; that is the reality now. Exhilarating to contemplate, but not always easy to endure. Napoleon ended his life on St. Helena, chained to the rock like Prometheus. To Goethe, who saw Napoleon as a Promethean figure,[197] this could have come as no surprise.

CHAPTER SEVEN

Intuition and judgement

I

The Reverend Edward Young, author of *Night Thoughts* and the *Conjectures on Original Composition,* was visiting friends in Hammersmith when a 'violent storm of rain and wind' broke out. To his host's amazement Young went into the garden. When he came back inside he was asked why he had gone out, seeing that it was such 'a dreadful night'. 'No, Sir', replied Young, 'It is a very fine night. The Lord is abroad'.[1] Stormy heavens, as much as starry heavens could proclaim the glory of God.

While for Hume or Diderot the experience of the sublime was linked to the realisation of human power, by way of stimulation or release, for Addison or Young it was evidence of the divine. In the Hellenistic treatise itself sublimity in literature had been described as raising us up 'towards the spiritual greatness of God', and the human longing to go beyond natural limits had been related to our sense of 'splendour, grandeur and beauty' [i.e. the divine].[2] In his influential *Sacred Theory of the Earth* (1690) Thomas Burnet stated that the vast and frightening aspects of nature (oceans and mountains), being the result of God's wrath at the time of the Flood, could make us think in awe of his greatness.[3] So it came about that as the beauty and order of creation could be taken as signs of the intelligence and wisdom of the Lord, the sublimity of storms or high mountains could be taken to show his power. In this perspective, whatever went beyond the orderly was not necessarily an aberration; it could be a step towards the infinite divine.

That nature could be seen in this way, the wild perceived as aesthetically pleasing, was a sign of that entirely new relation between human beings and the natural world, that ending of dependence, which began to come about in the late 17th and early 18th centuries. To see dark woods not as the haunt of malevolent spirits but a place to experience an invigorating shudder (or a delightful frisson) indicated a historically unprecedented degree of security, of human power over the natural. (This changed relation was evident in a new interest in animals — they were seen as intelligent and adopted as pets — as well as in the 'animal' part of humans, the emotions.)[4] But when emphasis on the human dimension was accompanied by ever more naturalistic accounts of human nature, there was an immediate reaction. The conflict which developed over this issue came to be of decisive significance in shaping attitudes to, and beliefs about, human attributes, in particular that with which this study is concerned.

In England the first round of what was in effect a modern version of the battle between the gods and the giants (p.17) came in response to the writings of Hobbes. His account of human beings as material entities, driven by self-interest and entirely selfish, lacking any moral ideas beyond their own interest (i.e. regarding as good whatever was in their interest),[5] provoked a reaction which was furious not only in its opposition but also in its vehemence. All the furies that Anglican (and other) divines could summon up were unleashed against him. Among his opponents probably the most influential were a group of philosophers who came to be known as the Cambridge Platonists — Benjamin Whichcote, John Smith, Henry More, Ralph Cudworth. Their writings owed their appeal to the way they took a position against both Hobbes and his Puritan critics, attacking the former's egoism and materialism and the latter's insistence on original sin, while drawing on arguments which owed nothing to the Scholasticism that Hobbes had opposed. For them the universe was, in the words of Cudworth's magnum opus, a 'true intellectual system'. It was orderly and coherent (not random or indifferent), animated by spirit or mind (not matter), but at the same time it was not 'fallen' or sinful; (in this respect they were as much neo-Platonic as Platonist).[6] Newton, in his own opposition to Descartes, drew on these ideas; and his subsequent demonstration of this order being realized in physical laws — the visible universe being, in his words, the 'sensorium' of God[7] — transformed a quasi-mystical notion into natural fact. In effect, his work led to 'the deification of space and the glorification of nature'.[8]

The next round of the conflict was initiated by the publication of Locke's *Essay concerning Human Understanding* (1690). This work began as an attack on innate ideas but it seemed to end in reducing morality to opinion or fashion and human beings to a level barely distinguishable from animals, the mind itself initially no more than an 'empty cabinet'[9] and all knowledge coming from what was experienced through the senses. Worst of all, despite Locke's statements about our dependence on God and 'the candle of the Lord' being in our minds,[10] he seemed to deny any fixed identity or essential self. His insistence that 'nothing...[is] essential' to humans[11] and that personal identity is only a matter of consciousness,[12] opened the door to a new kind of chaos (later demonstrated, parodied and celebrated in *Tristram Shandy*).

The writer in England who engaged with this problem most effectively was Locke's former pupil the third earl of Shaftesbury.

Knowing and respecting his tutor Shaftesbury was aware that Locke was a sincere Christian, but he stated nevertheless that the *Essay* 'struck at all fundamentals [and] threw all order and virtue out of the world', because he had 'made the very ideas of these...unnatural, and without foundation in our minds'.[13] In response Shaftesbury set out to show how these ideas were indeed an integral part of, and had a commanding role in, our human nature. To do this he drew on arguments used by the Cambridge Platonists (his first publication was an edition of Whichcote's sermons), and also on ancient Stoic thought. To counter a doctrine about an insubstantial self he turned to those writers (principally Epictetus and Marcus Aurelius) whose philosophy had been focussed on strengthening the individual self. The Stoics maintained that life should be lived 'according to nature', by which they meant both 'universal nature' (or 'the world-nature') and a person's 'own nature',[14] the two being interlinked and intrinsically good (see p.25). A life that would be both moral and fulfilled would be one in which you nurtured your own natural talent (*ingenium*) and discarded or rejected whatever was foreign (*alienum*).[15] There was a persistent emphasis in Stoic writing on the need for self-reliance and self-sufficiency, independence from what is external; (this derived from two fundamentally Platonic notions — the good as self-sufficient and the soul as self-moving).[16] The sources of truth and goodness are within, in that part of us (our mind or reason) which partakes of the universal Mind or Reason.

The revival of Stoic thought in the Renaissance reintroduced the notion that people should develop and be true to their own *ingenium* and this was what Polonius meant when he admonished Laertes 'To thine own self be true'. That these words were referring to his son's 'best self' is evident from the words with which he continued: 'And it must follow, as the night the day, / Thou canst not then be false to any man'.[17] Individual integrity was synonymous with moral behaviour since the true and the good (as perceived by reason) were one and the same. (The good self, for Stoics, was your 'own' in that you alone had access to it, and were responsible for it; but it only became your 'own' when you made it so, and the result was not a singularity but part of a (or rather, the) universality.)

The need to turn away from 'the irregular fancy of the world'[18] and nurture 'this self of mine', my 'real self',[19] my 'better self', or 'genuine, true and natural self',[20] is one of the central themes of Shaftesbury's writings. His insistence is evidence not only of his own ethical concerns, but also of his part in contemporary discussions about the individual self. The emphasis on self-reliance, common to Protestants and manifest in a statement like Locke's 'men must think and know for themselves',[21] had also been a feature of the thought of two of Shaftesbury's other *bêtes noires*

— Descartes and Hobbes. His account of the true self was intended to show that it was neither sinful (the Puritan view), nor material (Hobbes), nor the product of circumstances (Locke), nor isolated (Descartes). On the contrary, it was inherently good, spiritual, self-animating, and part of a wider whole.

Shaftesbury's confidence in this belief rested on this last aspect, the existence of an all-encompassing order, proportion and harmony, in which we feel we belong. At the social level we feel an integral part of a wider group as a result of our 'natural affection', our satisfaction and happiness in 'community and participation'.[22] On a metaphysical level our feeling of belonging stems from our aesthetic sense of the beauty, order and perfection of the universe.[23] This beauty is more than a delight in the visible world, for the latter reveals a supreme intelligence beyond it: 'the beautiful...[is] in the art and design,...the form or forming power,...the effect of mind. [Because it] is mind alone which forms'.[24] This was Shaftesbury's synthesis of the Stoics' 'universal nature' and the neo-Platonic equivalent with its additional emphasis on beauty.

The fullest expression of these ideas occurs in *The Moralists* (1709), a series of dialogues set in a beautiful landscape, which culminate with a rapturous panegyric to creative nature — 'Mighty genius! sole animating and inspiring power'.[25] The form of the work and the rural setting are similar to Diderot's *Entretiens sur le fils naturel,* but the characterisation of genius is utterly different. (Diderot was familiar with Shaftesbury's text and was surely rewriting this scene in his own work.) While Dorval's ecstasy is associated with tempestuous energy or sexual rapture, that of Shaftesbury's character Theocles is a 'sensible kind of madness', 'serene, soft and harmonious',[26] and the nature he addresses is chaste, peaceful and innocent.[27] 'Inspired with harmony of thoughts',[28] he sings of nature's order, the beauty of creation. His own 'genius', the 'genius of the place', and the 'sovereign genius'[29] are as one in their affirmation of nature's primordial unity and its fusion of the beautiful with the good.

What is true of 'fruitful and exuberant nature',[30] also applies to human powers of creation. A true poet will not be moved by selfish motives or particular beauties, but by harmony, proportion and the morally correct.[31] He will not be enticed by the superficial or purely physical, and 'design merely after bodies', but rather 'study the graces and perfections of minds',[32] 'the inward form and structure of his fellow-creature'.[33] This means going beyond immediate sense-impressions or the products of 'fancy'; the imagination must be 'brought under subjection'[34] and purely instinctive 'genius' must be tamed by 'art'.[35] A writer who achieves that, 'who truly and in a just sense deserves the name of poet', will be 'a second maker: a just Prometheus, under Jove. Like that sovereign artist or universal plastic nature, he forms a whole, coherent and proportioned in itself, with due subjection and subordinacy of constituent parts'.[36] 'Though villains may have strong tones and natural capacities of action, [it] is impossible that true judgement and ingenuity should reside where harmony and honesty have no being'.[37] The true poet, in a word, is the 'moral artist who can thus imitate the Creator'.[38]

The concept of a 'just' Prometheus, who was 'under' Jove, was (mythologically speaking) a contradiction in terms; for Prometheus to be obedient, rather than defiantly opposed, to Zeus/Jove was to empty the myth of its content. What Shaftesbury was proposing was some kind of ideal poet, who embodied the qualities he thought necessary for good poetry, above all, order and harmony. Only such a person, animated by the universal 'forming power', could convey the features of that ideal world in which we should all aspire to participate. This idea was taken up by younger writers, like Akenside, for example, when he described the poet as exercising 'Promethean art' with an 'energy divine', to reveal a 'lucid order'.[39] Here the creative act is assimilated to the morally good and the aesthetically beautiful, as it had been by Ficino, and from this perspective we can see how Shaftesbury had in effect reformulated, for the 18th century, the tradition of the Creator.

In the actual, material world the forms of order and harmony are obscured and it is therefore no surprise that Shaftesbury's praise of the 'moral artist' was accompanied by denunciations of mechanistic science and empirical philosophy. He poured scorn on those 'mountebanks', 'modern Prometheuses',[40] who had 'a strange fancy to be creators', wanting 'to know the knack or secret by which nature does all...[to] solve all her phenomena...see all her designs and...account for all her operations'.[41] In the same vein he deplored an obsession with 'interest, policy,...trade [and] power', and attacked 'merchant-adventurers in the letter-trade'.[42] In his *Soliloquy* (1610), a work of advice to an author, he insisted on the harm caused by any reliance on external factors, whether it was the favour of the great, or the applause of critics, or the 'irregular fancy of the world'.[43] Instead the author should cultivate 'independency'.[44]

This demand for the writer to be detached from ordinary, workaday lives had its counterpart in his concepts of the beautiful and the good as non-instrumental, valuable in themselves, for their own sake. Our attitudes to them, in other words, should be like our love of God, one of 'disinterestedness'.[45] In the course of the century this idea was to be developed into the new concept of a distinctly aesthetic experience, but Shaftesbury's own concerns were principally ethical. The artist he wished to promote was the 'self-improving artist', who 'builds in a different matter from that of stone or marble; and having righter models in his eye, becomes in truth the architect of his own life and fortune'.[46] (Here he was drawing on ancient analogies of an individual 'making' or 'forming' a true self like a sculptor, (p.25)). Individuals who did that would realize most fully their 'own' and 'true' selves.

Another word Shaftesbury used, as a synonym for 'own', 'native', 'genuine', 'natural' or 'true', was 'original'. 'They are mean spirits who love to copy merely. Nothing is agreeable or natural but what is original'.[47] Writing of the ancient Athenians, for example, he described them as 'original' because they were 'self-formed, wrought out of nature, and drawn from the necessary operation and course of things, working as it were of their own accord and proper inclination'.[48] It is this (Stoic) notion of originality which appeared later in Young's *Conjectures on Original Composition* (1759) as a doctrine of literary parthenogenesis. In Young's words, writers should develop their own 'mental individuality',[49] and rely on 'the native growth of [their] own mind',[50] for 'nothing original can rise...in any other sun' except from 'the beams of our own genius';[51] 'an original...rises spontaneously from the vital root of genius; it grows, it is not made';[52] in short, 'an original author is born of himself, is his own progenitor'.[53]

Young was not the first to apply this idea to literature. There had been a prolonged debate in the Renaissance about literary imitation — the issue was a central theme in Erasmus' *Ciceronianus* (1528)[54] — but it gained new significance in the 18th century. For Erasmus it was not a matter of self-legislation (against which he voiced the traditional opposition) but rather of allowing the written work to reveal individual character. For Young the original genius did legislate for himself: 'genius can set us right in composition, without the rules of the learned; as conscience sets us right in life, without the laws of the land'.[55] In this remark we can see a fusion of Stoic notions of true *ingenium* with Protestant ideas of the validity of the individual self which was to be very influential. Originality, in this perspective, was an affirmation of moral integrity.

A further consequence of Shaftesbury's belief in the good character of original, unspoilt nature, (which we also find in other 18th century writers and which was epitomized in Cowper's line 'God made the country, man made the town'),[56] was that it gave a moral dimension to primitivist thought. To a certain degree this had often been the case. Blackwell had claimed that in Homer's time people had had 'natural and simple manners', (while now we are surrounded by 'more refined but double characters'),[57] so that Homer's age had not only been more productive of genius, it was also more honest. For Blackwell, however, as for Blair or Duff, this kind of integrity was found amidst turbulence, in an unstable pagan world. For Robert Lowth, on the other hand, there was a superior example of primitive writing which was spared 'all the wantonnesss of fiction' indulged in by the Greeks;[58] namely, the sacred poetry of the Hebrews contained in the Old Testament. Lowth's aesthetic preferences, especially for the sublime, were similar to those of Blackwell or Blair. But he saw them as the product of a life which was 'simple, regular and natural',[59] where the 'fancy was restrained...by the tenets of their religion',[60] and where 'almost every point of conduct was connected either directly or indirectly with their religion'.[61] Such a way of life, being unspoilt, gave more immediate access to the divine and hence to a feeling for the sublime; for 'nothing in nature...can be so conducive to the sublime as those conceptions which are suggested by the contemplation of the greatest of all beings'.[62] The only violence in this case was that extreme agitation experienced by the poets and prophets in their moments of inspiration or vision.[63] In these terms, Lowth set out a primitivism which reaffirmed a divine component in genius.

In his *Essay on Genius* (sketched in 1758, published in 1774), Alexander Gerard also opposed the kind of primitivism adopted by Blackwell. He did not make use of religious counter examples but analysed genius in terms of its mental operations, following the method used by Hume. For Gerard it was imagination's 'creative power' which was the source of invention and therefore the distinguishing mark of genius.[64] On its own, however, imagination could be 'a false fertility' and 'a confused chaos',[65] producing nothing better than the 'disorder and incoherence' of Ariosto or Spenser.[66] Imagination had an essentially unprincipled 'flexibility' and 'pliancy',[67] and was a 'faculty so wild in its own nature that it must be accustomed to the discipline of reason'.[68] In his view, therefore, judgement 'must constantly attend it, and correct it and regulate its suggestions'.[69] Unless this happened, ensuring that a work was 'organized into one whole',[70] nothing worthwhile would be achieved. 'Genius implies regularity',[71] in the pursuit either of truth (which was genius in science) or of beauty (genius in the arts).[72]

On an entirely different basis from Shaftesbury or Lowth, therefore, Gerard made an equally strong association between genius and aesthetic or ethical values of regularity, unity and order. For all these writers the creative attribute was seen as linked to a more general coherence in nature and was fostered by achieving a particular integrity or balance. This idea was shared by Young when he related genius to conscience or wrote that 'virtue assists genius;...the writer will be more able when better is the man'.[73] There were elements in Young's treatise which were not easily reconciled with this view, in particular the attention he gave to ambition, rivalry, and 'deviation';[74] and at certain points he revealed an awareness of this difficulty. There was a danger that a 'too great indulgence of genius' may pose a threat to the man, as distinct from the writer.[75] 'Originals are not here recommended', he warned, 'but under the strong guard of my first rule — know thyself'.[76] At such points we catch a glimpse of the tensions which, for Diderot or Rousseau or Goethe, lay at the heart of creative achievement. For Young, however, as for Shaftesbury or Gerard, such tensions were perceived as counter-productive and the future literary achievement which he was encouraging could only be built on a firm moral foundation.

II

In British and French writings the qualities of energy and invention shown by a genius were usually connected with the imagination. Given the empirical assumptions on which such discussions were based this meant that a significant role was played by physical or sensual factors and external circumstances. What an imagination produced depended on the nature of an individual body, in a specific social and historical situation. In Germany, by contrast, genius was often associated with intuition, the power which had earlier been regarded as an attribute of angels, and which 'the spirits of just men [when] made perfect shall have in a future state'.[77] This capacity, which Shakespeare and Milton called 'apprehension',[78] made possible a direct perception of the truth, unclouded by the senses and unaffected by historical contingency.

The immediate source of this notion of genius was the philosophy of Leibniz. The Leibnizian monad was endowed with qualities of both energy and invention; the first was a manifestation of its inner active force, and the second was a product of its rationality. The highest kind of created monad was spirit — 'the rational soul' — which is an 'image of the divinity'; as such, 'the spirit does not only have a perception of the works of God, but is even capable of producing on a smaller scale something which resembles them'.[79] For this reason it could be called 'a little divinity in its own realm'.[80] In this perspective, the more spiritual a person may be, the more ability he or she will have to be productive. Leibniz owed an obvious debt to neo-Platonism in formulating this view, but he made important changes to this tradition. Instead of making the monads recipients of a generally available spiritual force he saw that force as inherent in the monad itself. Furthermore, each monad was unique, and its degree of perfection was assessed by the extent to which its action was independent. The more influence there was from outside, the more imperfect it was. The consequence of such a belief was that someone distinguished by both self-sufficiency and uniqueness (two qualities which came to be, by definition, those of genius), and who was active in a field where both self-sufficiency and uniqueness could be most fully achieved (i.e. the making of imaginary worlds), would be perceived as attaining one of the highest forms of human existence.

Leibniz stressed the wisdom and beauty of God, rather than his power, and the overall harmony of the universe (the recognition of which took away the significance of what might otherwise seem evil). These aesthetic qualities were an integral part of his metaphysics. Given the immense influence of his philosophy on 18th century German thought, it is therefore not surprising that when aesthetics came to be discussed independently from metaphysics, these same qualities remained paramount. In Baumgarten's writings we see the first indications of a distinct concept of genius; it was characterized by qualities of harmony, proportion and order,[81] and these became regular features of German treatments of the subject. Mendelssohn, for example, wrote that 'genius requires a perfection of all the powers of the soul, and a harmony among them, aiming at a single goal'.[82] Sulzer made the same point.[83] What the genius then achieved, asserted Resewitz, was 'intuitive knowledge';[84] he could see beyond the contingent to the essential heart of things. In similar vein Lessing, in his *Hamburgische Dramaturgie,* depicted genius not as copying the actual world but making a possible world, one with qualities of wholeness, harmony and evident purpose. In this way he imitated the activity of 'the highest genius' (i.e. God).[85]

The Enlightenment values of Mendelssohn, Sulzer or Lessing were strongly opposed in the 1770s by the young writers of the *Sturm und Drang.* For them, individual feeling was more important than universal reason or accepted conventions, whether literary or social, and the person who displayed such individuality was the genius. Yet although the *Sturm und Drang* was synonymous with extravagant expressions of disorder, these writers' conception of genius was in many respects the same as that evident in earlier German accounts, in particular the identification of genius with the divine Creator. In *Von deutscher Art und Kunst* (1773), the collection of essays which came to be seen as initiating the movement, Herder praised Shakespeare for his ability to realize those aesthetic qualities of unity and wholeness which reveal his similarity to 'a world-soul'.[86] Goethe's admiration for Erwin von Steinbach (in the same work) took similar form,[87] and writing about Falconet around this time he saw him likewise as possessing intuition, which was the product of an inner harmony.[88] Where these writers differed from their predecessors was in seeing this harmony more in terms of emotional integrity than of quasi-rational equilibrium.

This view owed much to Pietist religious thought, with its emphasis on subjective experience, the need to attend to 'the heart' rather than 'the head', and its belief in a quasi-pantheistic universe. The element of disorder in *Sturm und Drang* texts (as, for example, in Herder's comments on Ossian)[89] should be seen in this perspective; it was part of an attempt to throw off artifice in order to recapture an original energy and truth. Behind Herder stood his mentor Hamann, and in the work of the latter elements of a secular notion of genius (as, for example, in being sensual, or childlike, or intellectually naive)[90] were regarded as ways by which we can come closer to the divine. For Hamann, God's being was expressed above all in language; he was creative by means of the Word. Since man was formed in God's image, the human ability to use language was also potentially creative. The paradigm of such activity was Adam's naming of the animals. By his intuitive ability to perceive their essential nature and then express that in a word Adam had displayed the human likeness to the divine.[91] Such notions could easily be linked to ideas about genius.

A notable feature of German Protestantism was the separation it made between the sphere of personal belief and that of political life. This division, deriving from Luther's doctrine of the two kingdoms, had its counterpart in the radical dualism of Leibniz's philosophy, where the realm of the spirit and necessary truths was completely distinct from that of the material world and contingent truths; the two were never in contact but coincided according to pre-established harmony. When Lessing wrote about freedom in Frederick the Great's Berlin, stating that anything could be said there against religion, but almost nothing about politics,[92] he was commenting on the effects of the Lutheran division. When he observed in one of his theological essays that there is an unbridgeable 'broad, ugly ditch' set between religion and history,[93] he was reflecting the Leibnizian separation. Wherever these two kinds of dualism prevailed, the identification of genius with the spiritual inevitably set it apart from politics and history. This is what happened in the writings of Kant.

At the centre of Kant's philosophy was a firm belief in the value of human making. The first *Critique* rests on the assumption that only insofar as our minds make knowledge out of raw experience can that knowledge be sound. The second *Critique* insists that moral good derives from making independent choices, free of any external support. Kant refused to allow value to anything that is given; we must think for ourselves and act for ourselves. To the extent that people do that they can be said to be mature, to have come of age; and the *Aufklärung* in which he was living was (in his opinion) a time when this was taking place.[94] In the same year that Kant made this observation (1784) he wrote a short essay on history, addressing the question of whether history has any inherent purpose. His answer was positive: it did indeed seem that man was meant 'to bring forth everything out of himself...entirely as his own work' and that, as if following some 'guiding thread', humanity as moving towards greater freedom.[95] However, this process was not straightforward, because the motor of development both in individuals and in society, was antagonism, competition, ambition and vanity. Morally, human beings want peace and harmony; but their natural drives lead them to conflict and discord.[96] Yet — and this is the clue to understanding history — it is only by means of the latter that the former is achieved.

There was one kind of human making, however, which did not spring from conflict or disorder. That was art. When Kant described genius in his *Critique of Judgement* he drew heavily on previous German accounts which characterized it in terms of a harmony of the faculties. When we judge something to be beautiful, it is the result of a spontaneous accord (*Einstimmung, Zusammenstimmung, Harmonie*) between imagination and understanding in our minds;[97] and beauty in a work of art has been created by someone whose productive powers are in a similar balance (*Proportion*) or accord (*Stimmung*).[98] Furthermore, the 'creative' imagination of a genius does not operate in an empirical manner, but according to the principles of reason (*Vernunft*).[99] In these respects a genius is someone exceptional, a favoured child of nature.[100] Unlike in history, where nature wills discord, in the production of art nature wills concord.

Kant needed to see the making of beauty in this way because the aesthetic experience of the beautiful and sublime came to occupy a pivotal role in his thought, reconciling the two realms of nature and morality. In his *Critique of Pure Reason* he had accepted Hume's attack on previous metaphysics as having been no more than speculative, but he rejected the sceptical elements in Hume's thought which threatened a scientific knowledge of nature. In setting out the limits of what we can know, and showing how secure our knowledge is within those limits, he provided a philosophical basis for Newtonian science. The physical world can be understood as being fully coherent; it operates according to mechanistic laws of cause and effect, and insofar as we are physical creatures we are also necessarily subject to these laws. As moral beings, however, we have freewill, and to exercise this freedom is to realize our humanity. Unlike our understanding, which depends on what we experience (the external circumstances in which we find ourselves), our will can be completely independent. The *Critique of Practical Reason* was devoted to this subject and gave a lucid picture of the moral life as the achievement of complete autonomy, choosing the right and the good according to essential principles (of reason) and free from contingent causes or particular interests. The restriction of metaphysics led to an elevation of ethics, the assertion that the world exists so that human beings can be good. In having moral freedom we are unique, and the proper exercise of this freedom, 'the value which man alone can give himself',[101] should be the main purpose of our lives.

This exalted view immediately faced two problems: first, the world did not seem to exist for the sake of good people, and, second, to be good in Kant's terms meant rejecting a large part of normal experience — feelings, loyalties, or benefits — since any of these could compromise the pure exercise of the will. He met the first of these problems in part by suggesting grounds for believing in God and the immortality of the soul, and in part by his view of history as gradually progressive. With the second of these problems, however, he seemed to face insuperable difficulties. The elevation of our status to being the final purpose of creation was only obtained by means of severe isolation, both from the world and from other human beings. In the kingdom of ends we will all be together without conflict or injustice, but we will only reach that state by repressing our feelings of togetherness. The moral realm owes its pre-eminence precisely to the fact that it is no part of nature; freedom exists insofar as it is distinct from the natural. Only if we can pass through the fire and the water and be untouched by both will we be truly virtuous.

For Kant, as for Mozart in *Die Zauberflöte,* the key to this problem was beauty. Tamino survives the ordeals of fire and water by means of the beautiful music of his magic flute; Kant bridges the 'vast gulf'[102] between nature and morality, necessity and freedom, by analysing aesthetic experience. When we see nature as beautiful that is a result of the harmony which such nature arouses in the faculties of our minds; this gives us a sense that despite our detachment (as free agents) from the natural world, we nevertheless belong in it; 'the object seems as it were predetermined for our power of judgement'.[103] A similar sense of conformity can arise from the way in which our 'productive and spontaneous' imagination[104] can bring forth images which coincide with those presented by beautiful natural objects. A third instance of beauty is that aroused by a work of art created by a genius. Since the latter functions in a largely instinctive way, he can be regarded as a natural power (*die Natur im Subjekte*),[105] and the beauty which he creates therefore provides a comparable sense of belonging.

Analysing beauty reveals how our cognitive apparatus seems intended not merely to know nature but to take a wholly 'disinterested' pleasure in contemplating her.[106] Analysing the experience of the sublime provides a different kind of reassurance. By expanding our imagination the sublime makes us aware of mental powers independent from, and superior to, nature. In this respect it puts us in touch with a spiritual dimension and so gives rise to a feeling which conforms with our moral vocation.[107] In these different ways, aesthetic experience overcomes the dualism resulting from the first two *Critiques* and provides a decisive link between nature and human beings.

Another connection is provided by our examination of teleology, the idea that nature has purpose or is the result of design. The developments in biology which made such an impression on Diderot led Kant to see that a mechanical view of nature was inadequate to explain organic life. The apparent ability of plants to organize themselves, and the interdependence between the parts and the whole evident in their development (presupposing some knowledge in the parts of a final goal), was only intelligible if they did have some inherent purpose. While the limits of our knowledge are such that we cannot establish as scientific fact that nature has purpose (any more than we can prove the existence of God), nevertheless we can only make sense of the world by adopting the notion of it having a 'moral cause' or 'author'.[108] We can look at it *as if* it had been designed, the result of purposeful action, in the same way as we do with a human artefact.

To see directly into nature would only be possible if we had intuition (in the traditional sense, which Kant called 'intellectual intuition').[109] This is beyond our capacity; even the genius is not explicitly credited with such power by Kant. But he comes close to such a position in his discussion of the 'aesthetic ideas' produced by genius, in which a harmony of form is combined with a rich cognitive content, beyond the limits of conceptual understanding.[110] Parallel to this elevation of the genius for what he conveys to us in thought is the close affinity Kant sees between him and the moral individual. The mental powers aroused by the sublime are similar to the disposition associated with reason's role in ethical thought,[111] and an interest in beauty promotes moral feeling.[112] Furthermore, the attributes of beauty are like ethical rules in being disinterested, universal, and independent of sensual charm In such terms Kant emphasized the ways in which the aesthetic relates to the moral, concluding with the statement that beauty is a symbol of, or analogous to, the good.[113]

In his earlier comments on genius Kant had shared the same view as other German writers who had drawn on Leibniz or been influenced by Shaftesbury.[114] Despite its immense sophistication the third *Critique* adopted the same position. One reason for this was a similarity of purpose. Like Leibniz and Shaftesbury attacking Locke, (or Spalding combating La Mettrie, or Wieland against Diderot), so Kant in his opposition to Hume was defending the existence of a certain permanence, coherence and order. Empirical philosophy inevitably led (in his view) to relativism, scepticism, materialism and atheism; the aim of his critical philosophy was to resist that. The analyses of how we know, and how we can be good, and how we judge beauty, reveal a coherence in our minds that is not physiological (which would differ from person to person) but essential (and therefore universal), and it points us towards a spiritual reality which we cannot prove but nevertheless cannot doubt.

Where Leibniz had maintained that philosophy can establish an innate coherence in the universe, Kant insisted that the limits of our knowledge mean that our sense of coherence must be based solely on the operations of our minds. This change of perspective (which he called his Copernican revolution)[115] might seem an admission of human insignificance, a diminishing of man's place in creation as drastic as that which Copernicus himself had effected. In fact it was the opposite: an incorporation into human beings of attributes which had previously been seen as aspects of the divine. For Stoics or Christians to be good meant acting according to notions which conformed to the Logos or the teachings of Jesus; for Kant such notions must be constructed by an individual alone. For Newton, the explanation of space and time was that they were forms of God's awareness of objects; Kant saw space and time as forms of human perception. Again and again he insisted that knowledge and value derives not from what is given, but from what is made.[116]

As we have seen, however, there were for Kant radically different kinds of making. For humans beings, either generally in history or individually in society, development only occurs through struggle, conflict and suffering, and there is an unavoidable disparity between the process and the result. In the making of art, however, the opposite is the case; there the work reflects its maker. Although his own philosophical analysis had led Kant to show the argument for design to be invalid, in the *Critique of Judgement* it crept back into the picture, principally in the hypothetical possibility he grants it in his discussion of teleology, but also in miniature (as it were) in his account of genius. The contrast between these different (historical or artistic) kinds of making was, of course, a repetition of the same dualism which had informed the thought of Leibniz. In this respect, as in his concept of genius (and his use of the ergonic fallacy), Kant was not saying anything new.

Kant's account of aesthetic judgement, on the other hand, did break new ground. The third *Critique* was immensely influential in establishing, effectively, the philosophy of art, soon known as 'aesthetics'.[117] (This would have surprised Kant himself since his main concern was less the experience of art than the human response to the beauty of nature.) His analysis of what is involved when we judge something to be beautiful focussed on three aspects of the experience: the formal properties of the image (i.e. its shape rather than its colour),[118] the perception of its coherence (which he called 'purposefulness without purpose',[119] meaning that it is neither directed at anything nor arbitrary), and the way our pleasure is disinterested (a delight in the image for its own sake).[120] The beauty of nature is its own reward, and an aesthetic appreciation of it has intrinsic value. Kant calls such an attitude 'contemplative'.[121] The aesthetic experience, which includes that of the sublime as well as the beautiful, could in this way take on a religious or metaphysical dimension.

What Kant derived principally from the experience of nature his younger readers applied solely to the experience of art, by which they meant what had come to be called the 'fine arts' (*beaux arts, schöne Künste*) — poetry, painting, sculpture, music and architecture.[122] In the hands of Schiller, Schelling and their associates it was the creation and appreciation of works of art in these fields which became charged with significance. For Schiller, the aesthetic experience of art became the key to human development, the means to achieve a harmony within ourselves and so overcome the dualism which Kant had not only accepted but insisted upon. Such an integration of our mental and emotional faculties could then enable us to live together in the freedom which was our birthright. The forces which had led to the French Revolution were irresistible, but only a 'complete revolution in [our] whole way of feeling' could make those aspirations a reality.[123] 'Taste alone brings harmony into society, because it fosters harmony in the individual';[124] 'the aesthetic disposition (*Stimmung*)' contains everything valuable, it is the heart of our humanity.[125] For these reasons Schiller regarded an aesthetic education as the key to future human progress.[126]

For Schelling the separations which art could overcome were philosophical rather than personal. Once we start to think we are confronted by a number of oppositions — subjective and objective, conscious and unconscious, freedom and necessity — which thought seems unable to reconcile. In art, however, he believed that they could be transcended. Philosophy sets out from a subjective position — 'I think' —

and is haunted by the fear that whatever it may achieve may not go beyond a first person perspective, that what it regards as objective truth may only be a subjective delusion. For Descartes this problem had been solved by God; for Schelling it was solved by art. A work of art which embodies an aesthetic intuition, conveying to the observer an immediate and complete experience of reality, has independent and objective validity.[127] Schelling called this a 'revelation'.[128] In his writings the priority of nature over art was reversed. For him the beauty of nature was only a contingent beauty, while art could attain an aesthetic perfection which then enabled us to pass judgement on nature.[129] The humanly-made had supplanted the God-given, or rather, one kind of human achievement had been elevated to a level previously reserved for the divine.

In the decade following the publication of the *Critique of Judgement*, German romantic writers (such as Novalis and the Schlegel brothers) began to endow art with a new kind of spiritual significance.[130] 'Art galleries ought to be temples', wrote one of their contemporaries, for the proper attitude to 'the masterpieces of art [is] to employ them…for the salvation of our soul'.[131] Works of art had of course previously had a role in religious life; music, poetry and the visual arts had all been used to accompany, dramatize or illustrate sacred texts. What was new was that the spiritual meaning now lay in the work of art *per se*. A poem by Goethe, a quartet by Beethoven, a painting by Caspar David Friedrich, could each by itself provide a spiritual experience. This development led to a new hierarchy among the fine arts, (with music coming to occupy the highest place), and it also had implications for attitudes to human creativity. Schelling made these explicit. The ancient criterion for judging works of art — as imitations of nature (actual or ideal) — was no longer applicable. It should be replaced (he suggested) by the extent to which a work displayed 'the creative life in it, its power to be what it is'.[132] An excellent work of art therefore is one 'which shows us the true power of creation'.[133] Given the significance which Schelling gave to art, this remark was effectively making the capacity for artistic creation the highest human attribute. Such an attitude was of course only possible because of the specific view he held about the character of such creation.

In the year of Kant's death (1804) a German poet wrote a couplet which was turned into a proverb: '*Wo man singt, da lässt dich ruhig nieder; / Böse Menschen haben keine Lieder* (Where you hear singing you can settle down in peace; evil people do not have any songs)'.[134] Around the same time a Methodist minister in Britain, the Reverend Rowland Hill, confessed that he 'did not see any reason why the devil should have all the good tunes'.[135] (A similar perplexity was evident in Kant's observation that 'there is little or nothing at all to say about the good angels'.) [136] For neither the poet nor the Methodist could evil and beauty co-exist. This view had ancient antecedents, but at this time it was beginning to assume new significance, firstly because of the importance now being given to the aesthetic, and secondly because of the assumption of an identity between the creative and the aesthetic. When Kant wrote, in his *Anthropology*, of the 'beautiful soul' as being both 'originally creative [and] heavenly (*urschöpferisch [und]...überirdisch*)' [137] he might have been quoting Plotinus; but in the terms which he himself had insisted on he could only be referring to human beings in the present world. The problem was that he had not overcome 'the vast gulf' between nature and morality, necessity and freedom; he had merely relocated it, between matter-of-fact reality and a new kind of spiritual realm.

III

When Aristotle had referred to Homer as 'divine' it was not for being creative, since with a few exceptions the Greek gods were not creative. Rather, it was because of the insight, focus and coherence of his vision, and its range — like the gods he could see everything. [138] At times, in the ancient world, this gift was associated with prophetic vision, the poet as seer; [139] on occasions it was seen as disruptive, Cato the elder attacking poets as vagrants. [140] In all cases the insight was regarded as an outcome of the poet being alone, on the edge of society, and this detachment was integral to the range or depth of the insight. In the 18th century this had been exemplified in the life of Rousseau; his very alienation was a source of his strength as a writer, as well as a factor in his subsequent influence.

In 1779 Christian Garve, reflecting on Ferguson's comments about the increasing atomisation of society and the spread of the division of labour ('thinking itself, in this age of separations, may become a peculiar craft'), [141] suggested that the modern writer was inevitably 'a wanderer', [142] with no place in the public world. But, he added, this did not mean that the writer was marginal. The fact that isolation had become general, a common social fact, meant that there was now a greater need for plays or novels, to provide human company and supply in fiction what we have lost in reality. [143] In particular, writers could reveal to us a previously unknown inner world of thought and emotion. [144] What had been lost in social belonging could be replaced by depth of feeling, the route which Rousseau himself had taken in his passage from the *Contrat social* to *La Nouvelle Héloïse* and then to the *Confessions*.

Garve's analysis was based on the loss of that public role which had originally been epitomized in the legend of Amphion, the poet not as seer but as legislator.[145] While this contrast between ancient and modern times was experienced as a loss by some writers (like Thomas Gray in Britain)[146] to others no such problem occurred. In France, for example, the view of the poet as legislator took on new life. Trained in, or armed with, neo-classical arguments for the moral value of theatre (derived from that fusion of Aristotelian and rhetorical poetics which had been constructed in *cinquecento* Italy (p.54)), playwrights like Voltaire or Diderot asserted the importance of the stage to society as a whole. In his *Siècle de Louis XIV* (1751) Voltaire wrote of Corneille and Racine as having 'taught the nation to think, to feel and to express itself';[147] his own plays aimed to do the same for his contemporaries. In circumstances where the circulation of ideas was severely restricted, with vigilant censorship and no free press, theatre could perform an important social function. Diderot envisaged it as an alternative to the church,[148] and Louis-Sebastian Mercier regarded the playwright as a 'legislator' and 'public orator'.[149]

In many ways these French writers were doing no more than repeat points which had been made earlier in Britain and were to be adopted subsequently in Germany. But the situation in France gave this conception of the writer's social role sharper definition and wider application, referring not just to poets or playwrights but to writers in general. The inflexibility of the French monarchy, the rigid hierarchy of French society, and the pervasively oppressive influence of the Church, aroused mounting antagonism, and it was writers who gave voice to this. Voltaire's views were not confined to the stage; increasingly he used his pen to attack superstition, arguing for toleration and campaigning against specific cases of injustice. The aim of the *Encyclopédie*, wrote Diderot in 1755, was 'to change the general way of thinking',[150] to draw attention to anachronisms or abuses and indicate possible improvements. Twenty years later, Malesherbes claimed that the *gens de lettres* were 'in the midst of a dispersed people what the orators of Athens and Rome were in the midst of the assembled people', and that literature and philosophy were once more providing 'legislators for nations'.[151]

One subject treated at length in the *Encyclopédie* was the history of philosophy. This was not out of purely antiquarian interest; it was also a way of indicating the power of ideas, for 'philosophers have been the creators of opinions (*les philosophes...ont été créateurs d'opinions*)'.[152] This statement might seem to us unremarkable but at the time each of the nouns in this sentence was assuming a new significance. The notion of a *philosophe* expanded to apply to intellectuals in general,[153] the emphasis on their work as creation was (like the value of originality for writers) an indication that they were not discovering or articulating a pre-existing truth but making new truths, and the word 'opinion', in the form of 'public opinion', was beginning to take on a positive new meaning.[154]

The social and economic changes which occurred during the century brought into existence an independent and educated middle-class. In coffee-houses and salons, clubs, academies and societies, as well as in literary periodicals, moral weeklies and newspapers, people exchanged ideas, extended their knowledge and formed their own views. Such activity was valued for its own sake, in terms of personal development, but it was also important politically. It became less and less acceptable that matters of policy should be decided by traditional elites or by traditionally secret procedures. In Britain, new kinds of extra-parliamentary activity became habitual, the publication of parliamentary debates was allowed (from 1772), and the need for a free press was generally acknowledged: 'the liberty of the press is indeed essential to the nation of a free state'.[155] Out of these various developments arose a new element in political life — public opinion. In Germany, conditions were much more restricted but the need for public criticism and the value of disseminating opinion were equally accepted. When Kant wrote that Enlightenment is brought about by the 'public use of reason',[156] or that 'the freedom of the pen is the sole safeguard of the rights of the people',[157] he was stating a view which was coming to be increasingly common.

In France there was no free press and (unlike in Germany) the educated elite had only limited access to the official business of government or administration. But there was much pamphleteering, a thriving market in forbidden books, and some uncensored newspapers did circulate. Above all, there was confidence in the status of the writer as legislator, the person who did not merely express opinion but create it. 'The man in power commands, [but] the men of intellect govern, because in the long run they form public opinion, [and] sooner or later this will master or overthrow every kind of despotism'.[158] These words (by Duclos in 1767) were followed by a growing number of statements about the political role of the writer: 'men of letters will become patriots and scholars will become citizens' (Chastellux, 1772),[159] 'every writer of genius is born a magistrate of his country' (Diderot, 1774),[160] the *philosophe* aspires 'to the sublime function of statesman and legislator' (Robinet, 1776).[161] A vivid example of this occurred in 1776 when Tom Paine published his *Common Sense,* for this short work had a decisive effect in crystallising American opposition to

British rule and in transforming colonial resistance into a self-proclaimed revolution. When the French Revolution itself broke out it was as if the word had become flesh, for there was an explosion in publishing and innumerable writers active in politics.

For the purpose of this study the significance of these developments is twofold. In the first place, this conception of the writer or artist (for the two were regarded in the same light) validated a form of creative activity for its public, social effect.[162] The process of creation, or the character of the creator, was irrelevant. What the writer had was a power of judgement and a special responsibility to use that: 'every writer is born an advocate of humanity; for providence gave him talent only so that he could benefit society...He is the natural organ of public justice'.[163] While the conception of genius discussed in the previous sections of this chapter was based on the creative insight being valid because it issued from some intrinsic harmony or goodness, this alternative view gave credit to a creative figure for his or her position as judge, someone who, because set apart from the everyday, could see more clearly and assess more truly. The two conceptions were, of course, not incompatible, and were often found together. But they were distinct, and the latter had the advantage of being less exclusive and more obviously secular.

In the second place, this view of the writer met a clear and pressing need. The magnificent eruption and tragic course of the French Revolution was inspired by two guiding beliefs. Both were expressed in terms of right, but one was drawn from the idea of justice, while the other was derived from a right as maker (the labour theory of value). When Sièyes attacked the aristocracy in his *Qu'est-ce que le tiers état?* (1789), his case rested on these grounds: the nobility's legal privileges and exemptions from tax were manifestly unjust, and in addition they were at fault for consuming most of the national product 'without contributing anything to generate it'.[164] What could be more bizarre than such a situation, 'where it is honorable to consume but demeaning to produce'?[165] The Third Estate, on the other hand, stood for a just order, (being the most numerous part of society and therefore the one best placed to represent the nation), and being also the principal agents of that 'general [economic] movement' which made the nation flourish.[166] It was their activity in commerce and manufacture which had brought new wealth and 'created, so to speak, a multitude of new [social] classes' in such a way that previous political arrangements were now inappropriate.[167] The time had come to change the constitution, and in discussing this subject Sièyes revealed the extent to which his view of a right as maker was related to a confidence in human making. The Third Estate must not act in 'a spirit of imitation', as for example, by copying the

English model;[168] 'if we lack a constitution, we must make one'.[169] In his view there was no reason why 'the science of social organisation' or 'the social art', like other arts, should not produce 'creations' superior to any seen in the past.[170]

For Sièyes, revolution meant the act of making a new, just constitution. For others this was not enough, they wanted a rebirth of republican politics, the political as a field of action which was itself creative, realising otherwise undiscovered qualities in each citizen. Revolutions, wrote Paine in his *Rights of Man* (1791–2), bring forth such a dazzling array of gifted individuals that they seem to 'create genius and talents'. But in fact 'those events do no more than bring them forward', because they 'excite [into] action' capacities which were previously dormant.[171] A republican government is one where such opportunity and stimulation are always present. To Robespierre, 'the aim of every political association' was twofold: 'the maintenance of the natural and imprescriptible rights of man', and 'the development of all his faculties'.[172] For a brief period the dream of such a government seemed about to become reality. But this did not happen, and within ten years of the fall of the Bastille France was under a new autocratic rule. The possibility of reviving republican politics in the vast and increasingly complex nation-states of the modern world became remote and from this time the republican model of action was seen by many as anachronistic, a distinctly 'ancient' form of liberty.[173]

There were others, however, for whom the example of the Revolution remained an inspiration and one reason for that — apart from the obvious claims of justice and demands for freedom — was the evidence it provided of the power of ideas. The astonishing changes which took place from the summer of 1789 onwards had been proposed, debated, contested, reformulated, challenged and argued over in innumerable articles, pamphlets and writings of every conceivable kind. Furthermore, the Revolution did not only provide an example of the power of ideas, it also generated a new need for them. The main shock of its impact, still vivid to us in the pages of Burke or de Maistre, stemmed from the revelation that political institutions were fragile, and the social order unstable, in a new kind of way: the sanctions of tradition, precedent, or divine authority no longer applied. Notions of permanence or of immemorial custom may always have been illusory, but now they were emphatically a thing of the past; evanescence was inescapable. In such circumstances — where the claims for some form of democracy had become compelling but opportunities were restricted, where the force of ideas was recognized and the need for them was paramount (to establish meanings, for order or continuity or change) — a public role for the writer was assured. So the initial failure of the Third Estate stimulated the development of the Fourth Estate, and every writer of genius could feel in the exercise of his or her ability the source of a new authority.

CHAPTER EIGHT

Progress

I

The clearest indication of the general change which occurred in Europe between the late 17th century and the end of the 18th century is the new meaning which came to be given to the word 'progress'. Before the 18th century it most commonly referred to a journey, a course travelled or pursued; as the opposite of regress it could also mean an advance, a movement forwards, but that did not necessarily imply a qualitative development. Gray's poem *The Progress of Poesy* (1757), for instance, which described the stages by which literary excellence had passed from ancient Greece to modern Britain, did not assume that the latter was superior to the former. In his *Dictionary* Johnson's first two meanings of the word are '1. Course, progression, passage...2. Advancement, motion forward' ('Advancement' he defined as 'Act of coming forward'). The third meaning was 'Intellectual improvement, advancement in knowledge', and it was this sense which was gradually expanded to apply to notions of material, social and moral improvement.[1] These kinds of development came to be seen as both general and cumulative, so that not only was the present superior to the past, but the future would be better than the situation now.

'The human species', wrote Joseph Priestley in 1771, 'is capable of unbounded improvement'. The principle evidence of 'this progress of the species towards perfection' lay in that scientific and technological advance to which he himself was making important contributions. 'Human powers will, in fact, be enlarged; nature...will be more at our command; men will make their situation in this world abundantly more easy and comfortable; they will probably prolong their existence in it, and will grow daily more happy, each in himself, and more able (and, I believe, more disposed) to communicate happiness to others. Thus whatever was the beginning of this world, the end will be glorious and paradisiacal, beyond what our imaginations can now conceive'.[2] A few years later a French writer saw similar progress in political terms; the victory of popular sovereignty, achieved in the American Revolution, heralded the imminent arrival of the third and final stage of history 'when nature and equality will reclaim their rights'.[3] In his *Education of the Human Race* (1780), Lessing saw a comparable third age about to dawn in terms of spiritual progress: 'it will come, it will certainly come, the time of perfecting, when man...will do good [simply] because it is good'.[4]

The notion of a future third age, when goodness and justice would prevail, was Christian, and it was one of several Christian doctrines which were linked with ideas about progress. Priestley's assertion that the end would be 'paradisiacal' had obvious millenial overtones, and the title of Lessing's short work referred to the belief in the progressive religious education of the human race which had been proposed by a number of Christian writers (Clement, Origen, Tertullian); the fact that humans had been created in God's image and likeness meant that they could and should strive for 'assimilation' with the divine.[5] Both doctrines (millenial and assimilationist) had been employed in late 17th century England — the former by Thomas Burnet, the latter by Henry More — as advances in scientific understanding began to be taken as evidence of God's word being realized on earth.[6] For Priestley there was not only scientific evidence but also new developments in technology, the practical work of men like James Watt or Matthew Boulton with whom he was closely associated. The significance of these innovations was becoming generally evident, as Boulton observed to Boswell when the latter visited his iron-works in 1776: 'I sell, Sir, what all the world desires to have — Power'.[7] The Baconian ambition of 'the effecting of all things possible' was slowly being realized, perhaps most strikingly displayed with the first human ascent into the air, Montgolfier's balloon flight in 1783.

While to Priestley these advances were confirmation that Christianity was (in the words of a contemporary) 'in its nature progressive towards a state of greater perfection',[8] for others the opposite was the case: the spread of science was connected with the decline of religion. Those who associated religion with darkness and obscurantism saw science and reason as bringing ever more enlightenment. The end of blind faith and ignorant superstition would bring future happiness for all. The most complete statement of progress in these terms was Condorcet's *Sketch of a Historical Picture of the Progress of the Human Mind* (written in 1793), which depicted history as a continuous development — 'never moving backwards'[9] — towards an ever greater possession of truth, light and happiness. On the basis of increasing certainty about the laws of physical nature, Condorcet saw a future eradication of errors in morality and politics.[10] Science and education would lead the way; universal language and more extensive knowledge of social behaviour would bring about the fulfillment of that unlimited 'perfectibility' of which human beings were capable.[11] A clear view of the future would show it to be 'an elysium, created by reason and adorned by the purest pleasures which arise from a love of humanity'.[12] What reason 'created' was seen as unproblematic, because scientific discoveries had an impersonal validity. The truths they expressed had objective status and were regarded as universal. A new truth took its place within an existing network of similar truths, and the greater the number and the wider the application of such truths (it was assumed) the fewer discordant elements or warring parties there were likely to be. This was the hope and promise which Condorcet articulated.

While Newtonian science was regarded as having established truths which were universal and timeless, empirical philosophy had undermined ideas of universality and atemporality. The element of time, of the gradual growth of knowledge and experience, became central to ideas of personality and contributed to another notion of progress, one which could be brought about by education. In *Some Thoughts concerning Education* (1693) Locke had written that 'of all the men we meet with, nine parts out of ten are what they are, good or evil, useful or not, by their education';[13] in the second paragraph of the work he expressed a belief that 'the minds of children [are] as easily turned this way or that as water itself'.[14] Not only was the mind at birth empty, but it was also open to all impressions; it was (to use the word employed in the 18th century) 'pliable'.[15] The implication of these remarks was that if bad character was a result of bad kinds of teaching and upbringing, then a reformed education could produce better people. These ideas were developed by a number of writers of whom the most influential came to be David Hartley, particularly after his *Observations on Man...*(1749) was published in an accessible form (in 1775) by Priestley. Hartley gave a detailed description of the stages of the mind's growth, by means of the association of ideas and the respective effect of pleasurable and painful sensations; as our experience widens so too do our 'intellectual affections', in a sequence which moves from sensation to imagination, to ambition and self-interest, then to sympathy, theopathy (the love of God) and the moral sense.[16] Hartley depicted the mind as basically passive — the child learning by 'mechanical tendencies' — and without freewill — the will being no more than 'that desire or aversion which is strongest';[17] accordingly, 'the moral sense is generated necessarily and mechanically'.[18] But while he argued for 'philosophical necessity' Hartley allowed for freewill 'in the popular and practical sense',[19] and as a devout Christian he insisted that we are each responsible for our actions. For him the happiness to which we are drawn is moral and spiritual and the overall purpose of his work was religious. As a result his belief that 'children may be formed and moulded as we please'[20] came to be put into practice, especially by Dissenters with their strong interest in education. The effect was to promote an idea of improvement which came about through a new kind of human making — 'there is not a virtue or vice that belongs to humanity which we do not make ourselves'[21] — and this was central to ideas about progress formulated by Priestley or Price or Godwin (and in the next century by Robert Owen).

The empirical notion of the growth of individual knowledge came to be applied to history in the writings of Turgot (around 1750) which have been seen as the first clearly secular declarations of progress. In a discourse given at the Sorbonne, and then in an essay *On Universal History* written soon after, he stated that taken as a whole 'the human race is continually moving, though slowly, by good and evil, calm and unrest in turn, towards greater perfection'.[22] Although his views have been seen as quasi-providential, they owed nothing to Christianity, because the arguments on which they were based were purely philosophical and historical. The most important features of human beings, in Turgot's account, are, firstly, their 'active freedom' and 'always restless' curiosity,[23] and, secondly, their capacity to learn by experience, by trial and error. The wider the range of experience which they encounter, the more they will learn. Where there is an emphasis on limits, tradition or routine (of the kind which had occurred in ancient Sparta or Confucian China), development would not occur.[24] 'It is not error which stands in the way of the advance of truth, it is not wars and revolutions which hold back improvements in government, it is...everything which fosters inaction'.[25] If reason and justice had always prevailed human beings would never have developed beyond a restricted and modest condition (*la médiocrité*). But since people had mostly acted out of the 'tumultuous and dangerous passions' so, in the same way that 'violent fermentation is necessary to the making of good wine', there had been a gradual, uneven but nevertheless continual 'movement towards perfection'.[26]

While empirical philosophy explained how progress was possible, the fact that it had actually occurred, and the belief that it would continue, rested mainly on historical evidence. Turgot described how humanity had developed through different epochs, characterized principally (though not exclusively) by their economic arrangements. More or less simultaneously in his writings and those of Adam Smith there appeared what has become known as the four-stage theory: human societies were seen as having passed through a sequence of economic epochs — from hunting to pasturage to agriculture to commerce — with each stage bringing more complexity and greater prosperity.[27] Turgot's economic writings (in the *Encyclopédie* and elsewhere) showed how closely linked were his belief in progress and his appreciation of commercial society. Since all change in his eyes was beneficial, the evanescence of value was not alarming but (as long as it was accompanied by freedom) a continual stimulus to innovation. He saw the same process taking place in economics as that which occurred with individual growth — improvement by means of trial and error: 'to lay down regulations against possible abuses is to sacrifice the whole progress of industry for the sake of a chimerical perfection; it is to restrict the imaginations of artisans to the narrow limits of normal practice...[and] prevent them from taking new initiatives'.[28] Advances come about through openness and the willingness to take risks; not to take an unknown route for fear of breaking your legs, he wrote, puts you in the same condition as someone who already has broken legs, for without activity your limbs become useless.[29] Where freedom prevailed, therefore, knowledge and prosperity would both grow.

However, while the growth of knowledge, whether conceived in terms of science or of education, could be seen as relatively straightforward, the increase of prosperity could not; because that was connected with self-interest and competition. The issues which Mandeville had raised so provocatively continued to be troubling. In time, the arguments of Hume or Turgot or Adam Smith came to be widely adopted, but prior to this it was mainly religious beliefs which provided a framework within which commerce could be reconciled with conscience. Prominent among these beliefs were the doctrine of the Fortunate Fall and the idea of Providence. Just as it was Adam's Fall which had brought Christ to earth, so 'sin is more fruitful than innocence', or (in Milton's words) 'assuredly we bring not innocence into the world, we bring impurity much rather; [but] that which purifies us is trial, and trial is by what is contrary'.[30] This Christian adaptation of the ancient notion of conflict being productive, and of striving and struggle having a positive value, was common in Protestant communities. It could be applied to individual action, as the means by which human talents and abilities were stimulated, and as such was central to the account of progress given by Kant (among others). It was also used to defend the idea of Providence. If we recognize the extent to which human knowledge is limited then we can accept that what appears to us evil may from an overall perspective be good, (in Pope's words 'All partial evil [is] universal good').[31] This was not a new suggestion but it was especially appropriate to the new circumstances, corresponding as it did to one of the arguments Hume had used to refute Mandeville, namely, that our judgement of what is good should be based not on individual motives but on general results.[32]

The strongest reasons for seeing commerce as progressive were the visible signs of increasing prosperity and the historical sense that the modern world had taken a decisive step forward from earlier forms of society. The combination of greater wealth and new kinds of liberty gave

rise to what (from the 1760s) came to be called 'civilization'. This word
was used to describe a social condition in which individual freedom was
protected by the rule of law and an advanced level of prosperity allowed for
more sociability, humanity and the cultivation of the arts.[33] In the General
Observations with which he concluded Volume Three of his *Decline and
Fall of the Roman Empire* (published in 1781), Gibbon considered whether
Europe might one day decline as Rome had done. His answer was negative.
The geographical area inhabited by 'independent barbarism' was much
reduced and modern weapons gave Europeans security against any future
invasion; the political systems of Europe were less liable to that form of
military despotism which had proved fatal to Rome; and the technological
inventions and skills which had brought material improvement were so
widely diffused that a relapse into primitivism was inconceivable.[34]
(Another factor, implicit in Gibbon's account, was the absence of that
'species of tyranny' which had been formed out of Platonic philosophy and
Christian religion, a conjunction of metaphysics and superstition which had
stamped out earlier toleration.)[35] As a result of these differences, Gibbon
was able to end his volume with the confident statement that 'every age of
the world has increased and still increases the real wealth, the happiness,
the knowledge, and perhaps the virtue, of the human race'.[36]

Condorcet regarded 'the supreme faculty of human intelligence' to
be the 'talent of invention', and the word he used for that was 'genius'.[37]
Since he associated it almost entirely with scientific discovery this faculty
presented no problems for him. However, when genius was envisaged in
the way that Blackwell or Diderot or Goethe saw it, then the very idea of
progress was put into doubt. If powers of significant innovation were
intrinsically connected with the irregular, amoral or disorderly, there could
be no automatic assumption that the new would be beneficial; alternatively,
if the results were benign then why would further innovation occur? In
France, the first of these perceptions contributed to Rousseau's hostility to
ideas about general improvement. In Germany it became a central
preoccupation for Herder. His writings were permeated by a sense of
development and change, for he saw human beings as 'always on the move,
restless and dissatisfied'; 'the essence of our life is...always to be moving
forward (*Progression*)'.[38] But the capacity to invent is far from
straightforward. 'It is in the dark area of our soul', he wrote in 1764, that
the spark of invention lies.[39] The origin of most human productions is not
in distinct purposes or a single cause, but in chance and irregularity; the
process resembles 'an Epicurean cosmogony'.[40] Religion and poetry, for
example, did not arise out of calm, reasonable, philosophical insight but
from 'raw events', fear and need, the haphazard and the anomalous.[41] This

belief was based on Herder's own insight into genius, on his extensive reading (of Lucretius, Bacon, Blackwell, Hume and Diderot, among others), and on his acute sense of a changing world. In his dissatisfaction, his huge appetite for learning, and his desire for the new, he was sometimes taken as the model for Goethe's Faust; whether or not that was so there were clear similarities between Goethe's early poems and plays and that elemental energy which Herder celebrated in his essays on Ossian and Shakespeare. At the same time, as a friend of Hamann and former pupil of Kant, Herder believed that these amoral aspects of creativity could be incorporated within a divine plan. When he praised Shakespeare (in *Von deutscher Art und Kunst*) it was not only because of his 'divine power' but also for his 'divine grasp', the ability to make a whole out of apparently random parts. In other words, he was like the Creator not only by virtue of his energy and invention, but also because he revealed an inner coherence in the action of his plays, making them seem like the workings of Providence.[42]

There was nevertheless an uneasy tension between these two attributes — a naturalistic view of creativity and an aesthetic demand for unity. This became evident the following year in Herder's first important writing about history, the pamphlet *Auch eine Philosophie der Geschichte* (1773). Continuing the *Sturm und Drang* campaign against neo-classical conventions and what was seen as Enlightenment rationalism, Herder attacked the idea that more philosophy would make the world better, (and its corollary, that previously unenlightened times had been worse). One of his principal targets was the *Geschichte der Menschheit* (1764) by Isaak Iselin, which described human history as a sequence of three stages in each of which one human faculty had been predominant. The first age had been that of pure sensation (like infancy); the second age (from the time of agriculture up to the present) had been that of the imagination; and the third future age, now dawning, would see reason in command, bringing 'light and clarity into the soul' and a harmony of the faculties.[43] In other words, progress for Iselin (as later for Kant) consisted in the increasing mastery of nature by reason, and the spread of universal values.[44] Insofar as the Enlightenment was bringing philosophy to the fore, the third age was at hand.

Herder's violent hostility to this attitude gave the impression that he was as scornful as Rousseau of his contemporaries' self-confidence; (since Iselin's work itself had been written to rebut Rousseau, this reaction was not surprising). But Herder's reasons for disagreement were his own. While he shared Rousseau's concern for the emotions rather than the intellect (the 'heart' rather than the 'head'),[45] he did not see history as being a more or less continual deterioration. On the contrary, all such comparisons between historical periods was misleading; each age and nation must be judged on its own terms, for their differences were in themselves valuable.[46] Furthermore, Iselin (and others like him) were mistaken to suppose that an extension of reason or philosophy would be progressive. More 'light' means less 'life',[47] and the sources of action and invention are not in ideas or books. The bonds which unite society are not forged in the mind;[48] nor is reason creative. It is, rather, the very lack of knowledge that produces innovation; it is the struggle against needs, the wrestling with error and evil, that leads to improvement;[49] it is out of chance and chaos that new creations emerge.[50]

Herder's acute sense of distinctness, of history as an ever-changing kaleidoscope in which 'no two moments are the same',[51] drew on what has been called the principle of plenitude, the idea that the creation must include all possible forms of life.[52] But his enthusiasm seemed so comprehensive that it verged on being indiscriminate. 'The wheel of all ills must complete its course',[53] he wrote, and such was the pressure of variety that he was in continual danger of losing touch with the counterweight of unity. At one point he identified together 'chance, fate and divinity';[54] at another he admitted that he was unable to hear any overall harmony;[55] an image of 'the whole' as 'a sea of surging waves' led him to exclaim 'How powerfully they roar! But to what end?'[56]

The problem was aggravated by an emphasis on struggle and conflict as generating the energy which brings change. To celebrate difference is not necessarily also to applaud the energy which brings it into being, but in Herder's case the two were closely linked. The stronger his attack on Iselin's elevation of reason and harmony, the more he was led to stress the physical and the disorderly, and the more tenuous became the evidence of benevolent purposes. The difficulty had already surfaced in his essay on Shakespeare, for despite Herder's assertions of aesthetic unity, the playwright's vitality seemed somehow connected with that 'pagan philosophy of fate and the stars',[57] which dominated a play like *King Lear*: 'As flies to wanton boys are we to the gods. / They kill us for their sport'.[58] Creative energy did not necessarily entail human improvement.

Over the following decade Herder moved steadily away from this problem. When the individualistic implications of his view of genius were developed as Goethe did in his *Prometheus* or as other young writers did more openly and extravagantly, he attacked them sharply. Prometheus was justly punished, he observed; 'happy the person whom nature protects from such aspiration to genius'.[59] His feeling for energy and change became subsumed within a regular, rule-governed process, Leibnizian variety incorporated within a Spinozist philosophy of unity. When he next came to write about history, in his magisterial *Ideen zur Philosophie der Geschichte der Menschheit* (1784–91), all wild elements of naturalism had been tamed. Before he dealt with specific earthly times and places he gave an account of the heavenly origin of powers of organisation and preservation which pervade the universe. Since these are then shown to apply to history as much as to nature, the former reveals the divine as much as the latter. Human beings are made in the image of God and by their 'God-imitating reason'[60] they can find in history the connections that reveal the divine plan. Creative power (another aspect of the divine in humans) is associated with order and preservation.[61] Conflict and struggle remain central to development, but they are contained within a benevolent framework, Epicurean strife becoming Hippocratic balance or mathematical regularity. Competition and destruction have a necessary role to play in bringing about the continuous metamorphosis of life, but that process is now less a celebration of energy than a movement towards a better condition: 'every destruction is a transition to a higher life'.[62] The contradictory aspects of history arise out of the ineradicably contradictory character of human beings, and that is merely one aspect of their unique place in creation as the link between nature and history, the physical and the spiritual, the given and the achieved, the present and the future.

'We are not really human beings, we *become* so, day be day'.[63] The delight in becoming which the *Ideen* convey has few of the ambiguities of Herder's early pamphlet. Instead, there is a quiet conviction of man's spiritual destiny. The body is only an instrument for the inner, spiritual person, and the most important conflict which people face is that which develops this aspect of their nature, which Herder calls *Humanität*.[64] This is one further image of the divine in humans, and history is an account of its progressive development. As the physical world emerged from confusion to become orderly, so too will the historical world.[65] Instead of the earlier emphasis on the dark and irrational — 'soil, sap and power'[66] — the *Ideen* stress the active power of light, 'the instructor of creation'.[67] Warfare and tyranny will (and already do) give way to 'the more beautiful and calmer spirit' of industry, agriculture, commerce and science;[68] the spread of reason brings wealth by trade rather than conquest, and human ability turns poisons into medicines.[69] A balance and harmony of co-operating forces can develop in society, with a 'necessary antagonism' bringing progress;[70] for both good and bad drives promote the will of Providence.[71] Behind the storms of history, no less than the storms of nature, a benign God is active.

In writing the *Ideen* Herder made use of (and also contributed to) a notion of individual development which was taking shape at this time and which was to become influential in Germany. This was the concept of *Bildung*. In 1781 the naturalist Blumenbach had used the word (as *Bildungstrieb*) to describe the self-organising power inherent in all forms of life; in the hands of Herder and others it came to be applied to a specifically human process of individual growth. The primary meaning of the noun *Bild* is 'image' or 'picture', and that of the verb *bilden* is to 'form' or 'shape'. *Bildung* came to be used to describe a process of self-formation according to a person's own inner *Bild*. By this was meant what Stoics had called your 'own' nature (which Shaftesbury sometimes called 'inner form'), or that potentially divine part of us which results from our being created in God's own 'image (*Bild*) and likeness'.[72] The text in Genesis which recorded this was a favourite of Pietist theologians, who described spiritual regeneration as the death of a corrupt self and the birth of a new self in the image of God. Herder drew on this Pietist language when he wrote that 'we all bear within us an idea of what we should be and are not; the dross we discard, the form to which we should aspire, we all know'.[73] Elsewhere, he described the process as becoming aware of 'the contours of the statue...deep in the marble', and then bringing that to light.[74] This was the metaphor which had been used by Epictetus, Plotinus, and Renaissance writers such as Michelangelo and Edmund Spenser.[75]

Unlike the educational ideas of Hartley, in which development was shaped by external factors, *Bildung* was a process of growth from within, according to inner forces. We each have an inner, active, original self which should be both the foundation and the agent of our own development. Since it exists initially as mere potential only the individual can know what it is, in what directions it should go, and what forms it should take, in order to realize itself truthfully and fully. Its growth was compared to the natural process by which a seed develops into a fully mature form, (which it why it was called 'organic' in contrast to 'mechanical'), except that for human beings, of course, there are critical issues of choice and responsibility. 'We *become* [human]' (p.165) by our own action and development. In itself, *Bildung* did not imply progress generally. Since it was, and could only be, an individual process, it could be seen as no more than a variation on the Stoic themes evident in Adam Smith or Ferguson. The former wrote (in 1790) that 'the wise and virtuous man...endeavours...to assimilate his own character to [the] archetype of perfection' in his mind, and in so doing 'imitates the work of a divine artist';[76] the latter observed (in 1792) that man 'is in some measure the artificer of his own nature', 'he is entrusted to himself, as the clay is entrusted to the hands of the potter [so that] he may be formed by himself';[77] but neither of them was integrating his ethical concern within a progressive philosophy of history. That that was the case for Herder was a reflection of the greater emphasis on specifically spiritual development in German thought at this time, the belief that history was informed by a spiritual principle.[78]

The confidence in progress which is so striking a feature of the *Ideen* did not depend only on this spiritual element, because it was a confidence which was present as much in Britain and France as in Germany. It is often said that the Enlightenment was synonymous with a belief in progress, but that was not the case; in the first two-thirds of the 18th century statements of progress (in the modern sense) of the word are rare. Hume or Voltaire or Diderot argued for, and believed in the possibility of, improvement in various fields, but they did not think that the future would bring uninterrupted advance. Only in the 1770s and 1780s do we find that idea being articulated ever more frequently, as in the writers referred to above — Priestley (1771), Lessing (1780), Gibbon (1781), Kant (1784), Herder (1784–91), and Condorcet (1793). Many factors contributed to these statements of confidence, of which perhaps the most important was continuing scientific, technological and economic advance. (Writing about agriculture, in 1779, Buffon observed that 'man has, so to speak, [now] created secondary species which he can propagate and increase at will', and not long after this Humphrey Davy stated that 'science has bestowed on [man] powers which may be almost called creative'.)[79] There was also a belief in the power of ideas themselves, in conditions of increasing literacy and an expanding print-culture, and an underlying faith (which had been shared by earlier Enlightenment writers) in humanity itself, the belief that human impulses are fundamentally benign. Furthermore, the American Revolution (in 1776) had a major impact in Europe. It introduced, in Paine's words, 'a new era of politics…[and] a new method of thinking', because it had broken with all precedent, demonstrated that 'we have it in our power to begin the world over again', and given rise to the view (expressed by Price in 1785) that 'the progress must continue'.[80]

It seems to be the case that in the 1780s a belief in continuing human advance reached a critical mass, so to speak, and gave rise to what became the modern idea of progress.[81] This was then given decisive impetus by the events which occurred in France from the summer of 1789 onwards, for these shattered all previous assumptions about the limits of what was possible. Venerable traditions and institutions, time-honoured precedents, formalities and restrictions were swept away in a matter of months; what had seemed like a vast and immovable edifice resisting change disintegrated almost as suddenly as an ancient mummy being exposed to fresh air. For those who, like Herder and Condorcet, had (in their respective states) opposed the *ancien régime*, this transformation was especially significant, and this experience more than any other inspired the last books of Herder's *Ideen* and the writing of Condorcet's *Esquisse*. Not even the alarming turn of events which led to the latter writing this last work while in hiding from arrest (and execution) could undermine this new confidence in the future.

Among those who came of age at this time the sense of possibility was even more striking. In France the young threw themselves into action and debate about what that future should be. In Britain and Germany young writers (romantic and radical) were seized with equal enthusiasm, still evident in the texts of the young Wordsworth and Coleridge, in the visions of Blake, the impatience of Fichte, the calm assurance of Schiller. It was in the 1790s also that we find what may be the first statements that human beings should be creative *per se*. In 1792 Humboldt wrote that all human activities do (or should) relate to two needs or abilities — 'to enquire and to create (*forschen und schaffen*)'.[82] In 1795 Coleridge stated in a lecture that 'to develop the powers of the Creator is our proper employment — and to imitate creativeness by combination our most exalted and self-satisfying delight'.[83] The two men were living in different conditions and addressing different issues; Humboldt published his remarks in an intellectual periodical in Berlin, Coleridge (then influenced by Hartley and not yet captivated by German ideas) was at a public meeting attacking the slave-trade in Bristol. But the similarities between them are striking, and they give an indication of the widespread and profound character of the developments which were taking place.

II

One of the most striking differences between the discussions of progress in the 1770s and 1780s and those made subsequently was the absence in the former of any emphasis on literary or artistic activity. The same difference can also be seen in Utopian projects composed before or after these years; earlier accounts did not depict a future state of happiness (as Fourier was to do in his *Théorie des quatre mouvements* (1808)) as one where there would be a vast number of brilliant new poets.[84] On the contrary, during most of the 18th century it was just as common to read statements about the current or future decline of poetry as about its improvement. This was due in part to the recognition that in literature, unlike in science, there could not be cumulative development, and in part to the belief that the imagination flourished most in the early stages of a society's existence, the view that Blackwell had explored most fully and which Johnson expressed succintly — 'genius decays as judgement increases'.[85] Only from the 1790s do we start to find assertions that it is by means of the production or experience of art that humanity will progress. Schiller's *On the Aesthetic Education of Man* was one example of this, another was in the writings of Blake — 'nations are destroyed or flourish in proportion as their poetry, painting and music are destroyed or flourish', for 'art is the tree of life'.[86]

A further example of this new attitude was a brief outline for a future philosophy written around 1796 by Schelling, Hölderlin, or Hegel. The basis of this programme was a self which was 'creative spirit' and absolutely free.[87] This self, (absolute, but embodied in certain human beings), will reshape the understanding of the physical world and the practical conditions of the human world in accord with ideas of freedom, reason, humanity, and by means of 'an aesthetic philosophy'.[88] For it is the idea of beauty which unites the truth with goodness, and it is only by means of sensual embodiment that philosophy can speak to everyone. The result would be a new kind of religion — a 'mythology of reason'.[89] This would combine 'monotheism of reason and the heart' with 'polytheism of the imagination and art', and bring about universal freedom and equality, 'eternal unity' and the 'equal development of all [human] powers'.[90] Aesthetically informed philosophical reason (or philosophically informed aesthetic reason) was here expected to produce that elysium which Condorcet hoped would be achieved by scientific reason.

In their subsequent writings Schelling and Hölderlin developed different aspects of this programme but Hegel abandoned it. For him, as for the others, the ideal of a good society had been the classical Greek city-state. There, individual and community were seen as having existed in harmony, with freedom realized and the state itself visibly 'a product of [each citizen's] own energies';[91] there, the arts had flourished and all aspects of life — political, cultural, personal — had been infused with a vivid sense of religion. In their attempt to retain parts of this ideal Schelling and Hölderlin were led to discard the political for the sake of the aesthetic and/or mythological. Hegel, however, came to see that this ideal had to be comprehensively refashioned for the modern world. This meant taking account of the actual changes occurring at the time and therefore relating philosophy and religion to politics and economics. As a private tutor in Berne he took a keen interest in Swiss politics and when back in Germany translated a book on this subject (his first publication). He also wrote a pamphlet about reforms in his native Württemburg, and worked on ideas for a new German constitution. All these projects were marked by a high degree of realism, a concern for specific conditions and a sense of necessary change.

In reflecting on the contemporary situation he came to the view that the experience of revolution and the 'actions of individual men of greatness',[92] no less than innovations in literature, had revealed possibilities which Germany could not ignore. The old social and political order was inadequate to these new circumstances; its rigid, hierarchical form, which inhibited movement and regulated everything from above, stifled vitality.[93] New structures were needed. These would not result from new ways of thinking but must be introduced by a charismatic leader — a society in rapid political decline 'can only be saved by a genius' — who would combine creative insight with decisive (and, if necessary, violent) powers of action, like Machiavelli's Prince.[94] Such a person could establish a modern, centralized state which would overcome the current fragmentation of Germany and generate a new sense of common identity.

Hegel was equally sensitive to economic change. He read Hume, Adam Smith and James Steuart, and recognized in commercial society an essential component of modern freedom. The claims for universal personal liberty, which were one of the driving forces of the French Revolution, had their counterpart in (and to some extent could be seen as the product of) economic ideas of property and contract. The fact that individuals could only enjoy the fruits of their labour by virtue of mutual recognition (of each other's property) and general exchange, fostered an idea of freedom which was both individual and universal.[95] Economic activity could also promote personal development. In its simplest form work is the application of human thought and energy to the natural world, in order to produce something. It is through this encounter with matter that individuals discover otherwise unknown qualities in themselves, some of which will be made explicit in the process and others which may be embodied in an end-product In this way, labour can be seen as 'externalising [one]self';[96] Hegel later described it as 'formative action' and a 'moment of emancipation'.[97] This personal dimension is at one and the same time encouraged and stifled by modern conditions. On one hand continual innovations (on the part of producers) and the ever-new desire for individual distinction (on the part of consumers) give rise to constant change, in which everyone has to be active. On the other hand, greater division of labour leads to less and less individual forms of work and to a general loss of control. The result is increasing impersonality and the economy as a whole lurching 'in a blind and elemental way...like a wild animal'.[98]

Despite his awareness of these aspects of economic life Hegel did not turn against commercial society, any more than the grim events in France under the Jacobins led him to condemn the French Revolution. On the contrary, he saw both as irrevocable historical realities which had to be understood, and this could only be achieved by paying the closest attention to what they involved. Indeed, his mature philosophy was in certain respects as much an elaboration of themes first addressed in his early reflections on politics and economics as it was a development of his early essays on religion. In the former he explored ideas about the inexorable pressure for change, the inevitably antagonistic character of the new, the need to assess actions in terms of results rather than motives, the desire to move from particularity to generality, and the way this may occur without any conscious intention. While his overall purpose was to construct a philosophical system which was also a new theology, he never lost touch with these hard historical realities; and his ability to break down the dualisms of Leibniz or Kant, and weld together the philosophical and the historical, was one reason for his work's immense influence.

'We have to think pure change', 'the evanescent itself must...be regarded as essential'.[99] These statements, in *The Phenomenology of Spirit* (*Geist*) (1807), describe Hegel's central idea, also expressed in the title of the work: the changing forms of human thought in history embody the gradual unfolding of *Geist,* by which Hegel meant both spiritual reality and the human mind. In his account we have no access to any spiritual reality outside our minds and the evolving consciousness of humanity. But the slow and tortuous development of this reality has not been a result of individual choices or intentions; it has been the outcome of *Geist*'s own need to come to self-knowledge. Since minds only exist in living human beings all knowledge is historically determined and nothing can be known prior to experience. 'The history of *Geist* is its deed (*Tat*), for it only is what it does'.[100] (Like Macbeth, the *Geist* could have said: 'Strange things I have in head, that will to hand, / Which must be acted, ere they may be scanned'.)[101] Such action is only informative if it engages with what is different and unknown; hence the central place of hard work (*Arbeit*), struggle, opposition and conflict in the process of development.

The Phenomenology celebrates the present — 'ours is a birth-time and a period of transition to a new era'[102] — and claims to provide the first true science or knowledge.[103] It is suffused by a sense of movement which is also progress. *Geist* is both an original energy, 'the truth...as subject' (i.e. agent),[104] and eventual complete understanding, which comes from knowing all that there is to be known, 'the absolute as result'.[105] This end-state, in which nothing is foreign, brings a sense of being at home in the world, and therefore the reassurance that life is purposeful and good. In order to reach such a state each mind must work through (and so make its own) the evolution of knowledge. We each have to travel through the stages of *Geist*'s development, narrated in this work as a sequence of states of mind which is simultaneously a history of European thought. The work is therefore at one and the same time a kind of philosophical primer, a spiritual autobiography, a secular history, an account of the education of the human race, and the sketch of a new theology.[106]

Hegel's text is notorious for its allusiveness and obscurities, but the central theme of *The Phenomenology* is not hard to grasp and it is one which relates directly to the subject of this study. Because the work put forward what was in effect a new concept of Creation. It is sometimes argued that Hegel's philosophy owed much to neo-Platonism and there is some truth in that claim.[107] But it can also be misleading, because on the fundamental issue of why the universe exists Hegel thought differently. For him there was no original wholeness and perfection which out of its abundance had overflowed to produce human beings and the natural world. What characterized the primordial 'single vitality',[108] as he called it, was (apart from its innate energy) the fact that it was conscious. But this consciousness was empty, since there was nothing else for it to be aware of and also, therefore, nothing by means of which it could know itself. It was accordingly out of an acute sense of *need* that the Creation had occurred. Only by creating an external, natural world could God manifest himself and move from consciousness to self-consciousness. To achieve this aim, however, the world could not be a simple reflection of God; rather, it had to be something different (which is why the created world is 'the Other' of God).[109] Only the engagement with what is different enables God, the Absolute, *Geist*, to know itself. This meant that not only was the Creation, or the ongoing process of 'eternal creating',[110] the outcome of need, it also involved opposition and conflict. (This view of Creation led to a new perspective on the ancient quarrel of the gods and the giants; this was, for Hegel, a 'struggle of the spiritual and the natural', in which the Olympians only attained their 'spiritual individuality' *by means of* their conflict with the Titans, i.e. the conflict was necessary to the gods.)[111]

At the outset God is spiritual, unitary and (potentially) harmonious. But he only comes to realize that harmony by a process of 'dialectical movement'[112] in which dissatisfaction and need leads to opposition which is then engaged and transcended. In *The Phenomenology* Hegel uses a range of terms to describe this process; some are neutral, impersonal and innocent (emergence, unfolding, movement, becoming, development), others are active and transitive (activity, labour, formation, self-determining, producing) and these tend to involve unrest, effort and pain.

While the initial impulse to knowledge and understanding is self-generated, actual achievement involves struggle with the 'mighty power of the negative'.[113] In terms of continual enrichment, Hegel's account was a song of praise; but since that process also meant isolation and conflict, it was more a lament, which is why he described the evolution as 'a way of despair'.[114] On one hand, he insisted on action and making as inherently valuable; on the other, he saw the urge to innovate as a product of alienation, an awareness of difference and particularity, of not being 'at home in the world',[115] and the need to overcome that. Not every engagement with the negative is creative, but there is no creativity which does not involve the negative.

Hegel's later lectures on history gave another account of the development of *Geist,* less in terms of knowledge than of freedom, and they reveal more clearly his double-sided attitude to the creative process. In *The Phenomenology* the growth of knowledge is shown to follow a consistent pattern with a quasi-logical necessity, and its conclusion is to establish a new 'science'.[116] Insofar as this comes across as the unfolding of pre-existing truths, by untangling difficulties and resolving uncertainties, the work reads as much like an account of revelation as one of creation. But in the lectures of history the human record is shown as far more unpredictable, allowing for unexpected actions and decisive new insights. While as active subject *Geist* is 'creative reason',[117] and as reflective outcome ('consciousness')[118] it shows history to have had purposeful direction, the means by which this has been accomplished are neither reasonable nor clear-headed. On the contrary, history has been a catalogue of violence, crimes and wars. For only human action moves history forward and such action is driven by individual passions, energies and desires, which provoke endless conflicts as they create ever-new historical forms.[119]

The most visible examples of the character of this process occur in those 'world-historical individuals',[120] like Alexander or Caesar or Napoleon, whose individual lives had had a decisive influence on their times. These men were not happy, but restless and obsessed; they were not generous-minded, but strove to satisfy themselves; and in so doing they were utterly unscrupulous. But they should not be condemned for that, since they could not have done otherwise. Hegel's conception of creative action in history had affinities with that of Machiavelli, but he drew on other sources as well. His observation that 'a great man must demolish much and tread on many innocent flowers'[121] is reminiscent of the discussion of genius in *Le Neveu de Rameau* (p.118), (which he had read in Goethe's translation); so also is his statement that while 'at times we are drawn to something by beauty...at other times we are attracted by the energy by which even vice can become significant'.[122] This is the case with world-historical individuals or an event like the French Revolution, the violence of which did not prevent it from being 'a glorious mental dawn'.[123]

Reconciliation in history comes not with philosophy but with the political state, that human arrangement by which individuals are gathered together in a whole to which they feel they belong. In the state freedom was combined with law, the individual with the universal.[124] Hegel suggested that the modern state, in the form of his preferred example (a reformed Prussian monarchy), could be likened to a developed form of ancient Athens, with the citizens being united in a political community and obeying laws which were not imposed from outside but corresponded to conscious choices.[125] The fact that the proposed reforms in Prussia were not put into effect meant that this comparison became implausible, to say the least; and his statement implying that the present situation was rational (and therefore essentially good)[126] then gave the impression that he was satisfied with the status quo and, in political terms, was reactionary. This was not the case. But Hegel was opposed to certain innovations.

Some areas of modern life were in a state of continual and necessary flux; one such was economic activity. Hegel saw this as deeply problematic. The commercial world in his account was a 'battleground', a realm of egoism, division and discontent.[127] As such it was productive, (and could be seen as creative).[128] But it was also highly unstable and one of the major functions of the political realm was to control that instability, mainly by providing institutions which brought individuals together but also by its responsibility for those activities (like war) which could generate a sense of common interest and belonging. Given the paramount need for this harmonising and integrating role of political institutions Hegel wished to prevent certain changes in politics. He opposed any tendency to see constitutions as something made, created by their subjects like a work of art,[129] and he argued against any extensions of democracy. Unlike ancient democracy, which existed within the framework of a shared religion and without the problem of commerce, modern democracy would mean more fragmentation. If the state itself became a battleground there would be nowhere left where reconciliation could occur in contemporary society, in actual history.

Hegel could only vindicate progress by this element of political conservatism. His philosophy of history was, he claimed, a theodicy of a new kind, because it did not so much justify the existence of evil as show how it was essential to development, and to the fulfillment of our spiritual life.[130] Evil is not a worm in the bud but the grit in the oyster, which alone can produce the pearl of knowledge and wisdom. Only by means of the negative (in all its forms) do we pass from the belief or hope that there is an overall purpose to a clear, conscious awareness of that, as a matter of demonstration and argument. And the final term of the demonstration is the evidence that the negative is always transcended, that there is a resolution of a superior kind, judged by the highest principles of reason. If Hegel's version of the past was no more than a winners' history it could obviously not qualify as a theodicy. Similarly, if the present gave no signs of resolution to contemporary struggles, then no secure conclusion could be reached. The jury would still be out. Only the existence of a reasonable degree of social harmony could give us confidence that in history, as in philosophy, the evanescent is indeed the essential.

The good outcome for Hegel was accordingly not in being creative, but in achieving intellectual coherence and a sense of belonging. When he wrote that 'the original calling of man [is] to be an image of God' he was referring to God as the One, the True and the Good.[131] The negative (as means or medium or middle term or moment) is always subordinated to that higher condition of knowledge to which it contributes. For it is in the calm groves of philosophy, within a balanced political order, that all manner of things can be well; there alone is wholeness. Nature is always inferior to *Geist*. At times Hegel saw this as a commonplace (as, among German philosophers, it was); at other times he regarded it as a harsh and unwelcome truth, akin to the bitter wisdom of Greek tragedy (learning comes through suffering) or to Protestant despair at the human lot, the evolution of *Geist* being a series of stations of the Cross.[132]

But the misery was also grandeur; the extremes met. Hegel's persistent aim was to do justice to both. He took the measure of earlier insights into the character of the creative attribute, whether it was describing (in *The Phenomenology*) the protean resourcefulness of *Geist* as subject, assuming ever-new forms like a chameleon, or (in the lectures on history) portraying the amoral 'cunning' of reason,[133] and the productive force of restlessness, aggression and self-assertion. But because he recognized these qualities, he was also aware of their limits. The way of genius (*Genialität*), he observed, does not lead to community (*Gemeinsamkeit*).[134] Living through a time of immense change, Hegel had good reason to assert the need for limitations. The element of conservatism in his thought was not a nostalgia for something which was on the point of vanishing. Rather, it was a product of his acute insight into the modern world then emerging, one which — given his view of the process of development and what that can involve — he had cause both to celebrate and to fear.

III

Hegel's opposition to the extension of the franchise was the subject of one of his last writings, the essay *On the English Reform Bill* (1831). In his view the proposed changes to the British constitution would be more harmful than beneficial. But he saw the Bill as more than an ill-judged political measure; it was also an example of the inadequacies of British thought in general. The opposition which Leibniz had mounted against Locke, or Kant against Hume, had also been evident in Hegel's own preference for the economic writings of James Steuart over those of Adam Smith and his support for the Humboldt-Hardenberg reform programme in Prussia rather than the changes which later occurred in Britain. In all these instances the demands of, and necessity for, coherence and integration overcame what was otherwise seen as atomistic and contingent.

The contrast between these two ways of thought also came to be formulated as one between the organic and the mechanical, or the internal and the external. This was especially clear in new ideas about education. Whereas Hartley (drawing on Locke and Hume) had seen individual development as being shaped by external circumstances, in Germany an opposite view had arisen — the concept of *Bildung* — which stressed personal evolution according to inner forces (p.166). This concept was central to Hegel's thought. For him the *Geist* was 'self-forming (*sich bildende*)', going through stages of its own development (*Bildungsstufen*), in order to achieve a truth which accorded with its own 'native form'.[135] *The Phenomenology* was 'a history of the *Bildung* of consciousness'; it was a process of 'testing everything oneself and…producing everything for oneself and only taking one's own act for the true'.[136] The activity was self-animating and self-confirming, both generated by the self and validated by it. Hegel's overall aim was to show the ways in which history could be seen to embody this process, the apparent chaos of human development over time understood as a coherent *Bildung*.

However, the histories which Hegel wrote were not only accounts of the education of the human race; because the effect of applying this notion on a large scale was to reveal history as embodying an inner purpose. Since this purpose was synonymous with 'divine wisdom' the result was that world history could be seen as a theodicy.[137] Hegel's theology was in many ways unorthodox but by providing a strong, new version of Providence which was also a story of progress it was accessible and influential. The significance of this (for our purposes here) was that neither his account of the broad range of creative activity, nor his recognition of the problematic aspects of the creative process, had much evident impact. The disorderly, combative, amoral elements were subsumed within the overall development of a reason which was orderly, moral and divine, and was therefore taken to be essentially conservative in outlook.[138] Furthermore, since Hegel's 'creative reason (*schöpferische Vernunft*)'[139] emanated from (and was animated by) God the Creator (*der Schöpfer*) his writings seemed compatible with the notion of creativity derived from the Judaeo-Christian tradition.

During Hegel's lifetime the new idea of progress brought into existence a new meaning to the word 'history'. It was no longer seen as being determined by certain unavoidable limits (such as repeating cycles of growth, maturity and decline), or as providing some guide to the future (like a museum of exemplary or cautionary actions), because what lies ahead is open to ever-new possibilities and human action alone determines their outcome. The balance between nature and artifice had moved decisively to emphasize the latter. When Burke wrote that 'man's prerogative is to be in a great degree a creature of his own making'[140] he was in one sense expressing a traditional idea (about freewill and the place of humanity among other forms of life). But the observation also had a more topical meaning, inspired by the French Revolution, of both the fragility of human achievements and the possibilities of change; and it was in this context that people began to see history for the first time as something 'makeable'.[141] This view had been implicit in Napoleon's criticism of the role that had been given in Greek drama to fate (p.134), and the point was made explicitly a few years later by an associate of the Emperor: 'a state like ours...is a creation in which – as in the creation of the universe — everything present is just raw material in the hands of the creator, by whom it is transformed into existence'.[142]

While this statement made use of the Biblical archetype it referred to it only as a matter of power and the confidence which it displayed could be equally expressed in anti-religious terms. This was the case with a number of Romantic writings, most notably perhaps Shelley's *Prometheus Unbound*, which rewrote the ancient myth to portray Zeus as a tyrannical Old Testament God who is overthrown by Prometheus; the inveterate enemy of lawful authority became the bringer of freedom to humanity. All these examples were of course underpinned by the belief in progress and this, in turn, was a necessary precondition for the emergence in the course of the nineteenth century of the new value. The sense of history as something 'made' was on its own not enough to give creativity the recognition and status which it was to receive. There also had to be the confidence that this history would bring continuing improvement, that what was new would also be better, a sense (as Wordsworth put it) of 'the sweet air of futurity'.[143] This confidence now existed. So while scientific and technological advances had made a new degree of human independence *possible*, and commerce had made continual innovation *necessary*, the new idea of progress now made both independence and innovation *desirable*.

CHAPTER NINE

'The true function of man'

I

In March 1834 a new word entered the English language — 'industrialism'. It appeared in the serialization of a novel by Thomas Carlyle entitled *Sartor Resartus,* and was used to describe a new kind of society being brought into being by the invention and proliferation of the steam-engine.[1] As Carlyle was writing manufacturing output was constantly increasing and railways had begun to spread rapidly across Great Britain. In his sonnet 'Steamboats, Viaducts and Railways' (1833) even Wordsworth had expressed his admiration at these developments: 'In spite of all that beauty may disown / In your harsh features, Nature doth embrace / Her lawful offspring in Man's art'.[2] A few years later the phrase 'Industrial Revolution' was coined to describe the immensity of the changes which had taken place — social upheaval, urbanization, technological development, economic advance — on a scale that was as unprecedented (and as unexpected) as the political transformations of the French Revolution.[3]

Although these changes can be seen to have been underway in the last third of the 18th century, it was only around this time that a full awareness of them took shape. The Napoleonic Wars and then the post-war crises brought about by demobilization, poor harvests and heavy taxes, as well as the gradual pace of change itself, prevented a broad perspective on what was occurring. There were certainly voices raised against enclosure, or towns as 'haunts of wretchedness',[4] or factories where children worked in cruel conditions, 'senseless member[s] of a vast machine', subject to the 'inward chains' of a new form of servitude.[5] But only gradually did these come to be seen as parts of a new socio-economic system — Carlyle's 'industrialism' — in which the principle agent of economic growth was manufacturing, in factories powered by new forms of energy, with machines constructed by new methods, manned by workers disciplined in new ways, who lived in towns of a new kind. The steam-engine, described by Andrew Ure as 'the controller-general and mainspring of British industry',[6] was not merely a vivid display of human power over nature; both its energy and the material of its construction were derived from new sources — coal and iron — which indicated a new distance from nature. Previously, machines had been made mostly out of wood and the energy to power them had been derived mainly from water or wood (in the form of charcoal). The new developments saw a move from organic to inorganic (mineral) raw materials, in a manner no one had envisaged.[7] For Adam Smith agricultural surplus had been essential in making possible the growth of manufactures;[8] these new developments set manufacturing free from such dependence.

The productive activity of the new factories was not subject to seasonal variations and work in them became more routine, because of the competitive advantage afforded by increasing specialization and mechanization. It seemed that individual skills were becoming superfluous and Frances Jeffrey lamented that the 'age of original genius' was over.[9] The work-force itself consisted of the cheapest labour available, which meant a high proportion of children (who were also easier to discipline). As for the poor, the traditional sense of obligation to provide charity for them was cut off at the root by Malthus' arguments that the existing measures of poor relief 'create the poor which they maintain', because they undermined individuals' own initiative (i.e. making them 'become dependent').[10] The Poor Law Amendment Act (passed in 1834, in line with these ideas) was seen by its advocates as a necessarily harsh improvement on the previous law; by many others it was regarded as cruel and inhumane.

These immense changes could be understood, and their negative corollaries accepted, because of two equally new systems of thought: the moral and social philosophy of utilitarianism and the economic philosophy which came to be called Political Economy. The first attacked all notions of good and bad based either on tradition or on natural law and natural rights. Human feelings and behaviour were assessed as forms of the pursuit of pleasure and the avoidance of pain, and moral value was located in terms of results, based only on what could evidently be compared by being measured. The good, in Bentham's view, could be calculated by seeing how many elements of happiness could be attained by any particular social measure, adding up the units in terms of individual pleasures. The method had a salutary effect on legal reform, leading to a steady reduction in the number of offences liable for capital punishment. But in relation to economics it tended to exclude all criteria except those relating to outcomes. Whatever increased production was likely to count more than the human costs simply because the former could more easily be quantified.

Political Economy, as expounded in numerous treatises (most influentially those by Ricardo (1817) and James Mill (1821)), was a new science, setting out what were regarded as universal laws of production, distribution, and exchange. It drew heavily on Adam Smith in its belief that economic freedom promoted wealth, and its view that individuals' self-interest, within an open, competitive, free market, would lead to mutually beneficial results. But it excluded significant aspects of Smith's work to focus on those features of economic life that could be quantified, in neutral terms, and thus make possible the formulation of precise and universal laws. Among the doctrines which resulted were those that not only taxes but also wages must be kept as low as possible, to accumulate capital and to mitigate the problem of declining rates of profit.[11] Low wages, in other words, were not more or less desirable; they were a necessary component of a system which, if allowed to function properly, could be immensely productive. The systematic character of Political Economy, its clear principles and strong logic, and the reliance (which it shared with utilitarianism) on a view of human beings as rational, self-interested individuals, gave it polemical strength. It needed that, because it was by no means clear initially that its claims were true; until the 1850s the negative effects of the Industrial Revolution were to many more obvious than the good.

In 1829, five years before the term industrialism was coined, Robert Southey, then Poet Laureate, published *Sir Thomas More: or Colloquies on the Progress and Prospects of Society,* a series of conversations between the author (under the fictional name of Montesimos) and the ghost of Thomas More. The latter wishes to compare the crisis which he had lived through, the Reformation, with 'this age of revolutions'.[12] One matter which alarms him is the decline of religion, and the separation of religion and state.[13] Another is the 'loss of kindly feelings and ennobling attachments' which had been a feature of feudal society, since there everyone had had a fixed place;[14] now, by contrast, countless numbers were 'subsisting by chance or by prey, living in filth, mischief and wretchedness'.[15] But the main focus of his attack is the manufacturing system: 'society has...its climacterics...This is one of its grand climacterics. A new principle...a *novum organum* has been introduced...the most powerful that has ever yet been wielded by man...Steam'. This, he adds, 'will govern the world'.[16] More's indictment is uncompromising. 'There are calamities for people worse than extermination',[17] and this is one: 'a system which in its direct consequences debases all who are engaged in it...An expense of human misery and degradation' which was without precedent.[18] People who had been born free were 'in an actual state of servitude';[19] 'everything which is connected with manufactures presents...features of unqualified deformity', producing 'physical and moral deformity'.[20]

Southey's book was a comprehensive attack on 'what are called liberal opinions',[21] and it was answered (in 1830) by a rising star of 'liberal' politics, Thomas Macaulay, then in the process of being elected to Parliament. Macaulay had made his name as a journalist and excelled in writing single-topic essays for the reviews which provided the arena of intellectual debate in 19th century Britain. (The previous year he had taken apart James Mill's *Essay on Government* with merciless panache.) His reply to Southey was alternately sarcastic — 'everybody is to tolerate him, and he is to tolerate nobody'[22] — florid — Sir Thomas More was 'like a bilious old nabob at a watering-place'[23] — and crushing: Southey had not researched, let alone produced, a single fact.[24] Had he troubled to do so he would have learnt that in manufacturing districts there was less poverty than in agricultural areas and that since the introduction of manufacture life-expectancy in general had increased, in part because of medical advances and in part because people were better fed, housed, and clothed.[25] The former was due to the progress of science, the latter to 'that increase of national wealth which the manufacturing system has produced'.[26] Macaulay did not deny that 'the present moment is one of great distress',[27] but that had to be seen in perspective. Compared with the situation fifty or one hundred years before, there could be no question that the country was richer, and would continue to become more so: 'a single breaker may recede, but the tide is evidently coming in'.[28]

Macaulay's confidence was based on scientific advance since the acceptance of Baconian principles (i.e. science concerned with practical results rather than speculative truths),[29] and what he termed the 'natural progress of society'.[30] By the latter he meant both the evidence of the historical record and 'the natural tendency of society to improvement', which stems from the 'constant effort of every man to better himself'.[31] In the closing pages of his essay on Southey's *Colloquies* he described this progress: 'we see in almost every part of the annals of mankind how the industry of individuals, struggling up against wars, taxes, famines, conflagrations, mischievous prohibitions, and more mischievous protections, creates faster than governments can squander and repairs whatever invaders can destroy. We see the wealth of nations increasing, and all the arts of life approaching nearer and nearer to perfection'.[32]

'The industry of individuals...creates...' These words epitomize Macaulay's argument, the reason for his confidence, conveyed here with youthful enthusiasm. His belief in progress was not in the least religious, nor was it conjectural. It rested on a long historical perspective which saw how developments since the 17th century had led to human beings achieving independence, that is to say, living in a world of their own making. The industrial revolution was the culmination of changes which, in Macaulay's view, had been set in motion by Bacon's *Novum Organum*, and as a result of which the relationship between man and nature had altered, fundamentally and irrevocably. Old proverbs — 'God sends the meat, the devil sends the cooks' — began to fall into disuse. Before the end of the century May Day would cease to be a thanksgiving for the earth's fertility and become a celebration of human labour. It was no longer God but 'the industry of individuals [which]...creates'.

As we have seen, developments in commerce over the previous hundred and fifty years had brought about an awareness of human ability to make wealth: firstly, because the evanescence of value generated a constant need for innovation, and secondly, because people then learnt to stimulate this need by 'creating' demand.[33] But only in the early 19th century do we find the phrase 'creation of wealth' coming into general usage, and that change was related to the new 'inventions', 'ingenious engines', 'the wondrous works of still more wondrous man'[34] which human beings 'created', and which then did in turn themselves 'create'. 'Engine of Watt! unrivalled is thy sway. / Compared with thine, what is the tyrant's power? / His might destroys, while thine creates and saves'.[35] Not only therefore could Wordsworth write in 1814 of this 'inventive age',[36] but three years later Owen could describe it as 'this era of creation'.[37]

When Macaulay wrote of the industry of individuals he did not specify anyone in particular, but the question of which individuals did create, apart from the actual inventors, became a matter of bitter dispute. From the 1820s battle lines on this issue were drawn between capital and labour. Since there was a general perception that people were entitled to the fruits of their labour — 'He who sows shall reap'[38] — and since value came to be seen, by political economists, as deriving from the amount of labour embodied in a product, a strong case could be made that 'labour is the true source of all wealth'.[39] Capital had no independent claim since capital itself, wrote Thomas Hodgskin in 1825, 'is the creation of labour and of skill'.[40] William Thompson, two years later, agreed; it was 'the industrious classes' who were 'the creators' of capital.[41] What gave strength to this position was not simply the ethical dimension (although, given the grotesque inequalities, that had obvious force); it was also the sense of new possibilities. Owen had been among the first to realize that machine-production could for the first time in human history bring an end to the problem of scarcity, and in 1825 one of his supporters wrote that human beings now had the power 'to produce the comforts of life in a sufficient quantity, nay in quantities four-fold sufficient, to supply the wants of every member of the community...We have the desire for wealth [and] we have the power to create it'. And it was the 'working classes', the 'productive members of society', who did in fact 'create it'.[42]

In *The Philosophy of Manufactures* (1835) Andrew Ure saw matters otherwise. This comprehensive survey of how the new factory system operated emphasized the role of the inventors and capitalists. The latter were those who not only provided capital but also organized the new factories. Ure's model was Arkwright — 'a man of a Napoleon[ic] nerve and ambition' — because not only did he invent the machinery but he also established the necessary 'factory discipline'.[43] Ure defined a factory as 'a vast automaton...acting in uninterrupted concert for the production of a common object'.[44] That is to say, alongside the new kinds of machinery there was also a 'new system of labour', and only someone able to establish and maintain that would realize the 'unbounded prospects of wealth'.[45] For Ure it was the capitalist who 'animates [the] otherwise torpid talents of operatives',[46] and the inventors and capitalists together were 'the inventive head and the sustaining heart' of the national economy, the decisive agents of 'creative industry'.[47]

Ure was aware of Southey's attack on the new factories and working conditions and regarded it important enough to reply to. But he made no response to another attack which had appeared in the same year as the *Colloquies*, Carlyle's 'Signs of the Times'. This essay was more substantial in its criticism and less evasive in its outlook; that is to say, it did not lapse into the plangent nostalgia which marked Southey's text. On the contrary, Carlyle was conscious of new possibilities at hand and saw the very discontent and unrest of the present time as a sign of promise, since it is precisely by grappling with problems that we move forward.[48] What dismayed him were the excessively narrow moral and philosophical principles underpinning industrialism. Utilitarianism and Political Economy reduced all activity to mechanical calculation, self-interest, profit and loss. They made no allowance for imagination, or virtue, or even free will; human beings were regarded principally as the creatures of circumstances, devoid of almost any qualities that were not physical or material. But there is, Carlyle insisted, 'the science of dynamics' as well as one of mechanics, and we are not so much the creature and product of mechanism as its 'creator and producer'.[49] These ideas were subsequently developed to become the central theme of *Sartor Resartus,* the work that established his reputation.

The title of this novel, which literally translated means 'The Tailor Re-Clothed', refers to a 'Philosophy of Clothes' which has been developed by an obscure German philosopher Teufelsdröckh and expounded by him in a treatise entitled *Die Kleider: Ihr Werden und Wirken* (*Clothes, their Origin and Influence*). The novel provides an account of this work and an intellectual biography of its author. It describes his education in a time of scepticism and atheism, his despair at that, and then his sudden realization that there is more than mechanism, pleasure, and profit and loss, because we have a soul, a spiritual centre, which is free and active and part of a greater living force. This spiritual reality pervades our world, because nature is 'the living visible garment of God'.[50] The visible is a clothing of the invisible, and man therefore could be described as 'a spirit... [who] wears clothes'.[51] If we assume that what we perceive through our senses, and what we can measure or count, is all that there is, then we will remain stunted and dissatisfied. Once we realize that we are part of the 'great vital system of immensity' life will assume meaning and radiance.[52]

The heart of the novel lies in Teufelsdröckh's spiritual crisis, his movement from utter despair to defiant affirmation. The latter occurs when he asserts his distinct individuality: 'my whole ME stood up in native God-created majesty'.[53] He says No to 'savage animalism', and declares that 'Inventive Spiritualism is all'.[54] This crisis is a mystical experience; we are not given reasons for its resolution. On the contrary, we have been prepared not to expect any, by assertions of the limits of thought.[55] But we understand it because of the way the first part of the novel had prepared us for it, and the rest of the book repeats its two central points: first, everything and everyone is interconnected,[56] and second, everything has an innate force and everyone has a 'self-perfecting vitality'.[57] The first means that self-interest and self-centredness are wrong; the second means that to realize ourselves we must be active, or, more precisely, creative.

Despite its extraordinary style — dense, allusive, alternately archaic and rhapsodic — Sartor Resartus is a work of striking immediacy and power. It resounds like the organ accompaniment to a Victorian hymn, and the wind that blows through its diapasons is a Victorian confidence: 'the golden age...is before us'.[58] We have the 'promise of new Fortunate Isles',[59] because what lies within us, within each of us, is an 'active power', a 'creative instinct'.[60] 'Be no longer a chaos, but a world...Produce! Produce!';[61] 'mankind [is] the image that reflects and creates nature, without which nature were not'.[62]

Both the Calvinist belief in the value of work (on which Carlyle was raised), and the more general Protestant view of the spiritual being realized in struggle with the material, contributed to these assertions. But they are driven by an energy, and convey a sense of power, which would have been inconceivable before that time. That is to say, while they could have been imagined, they could not have been proclaimed with such conviction. (That this conviction articulated a view that was shared was made evident by the book's immediate success.) In other words, both the energy and power owed much to the very industrialism which Carlyle was attacking. At times Carlyle himself made this connection. In Chartism (1839) he praised Watt and Arkwright and declared that Manchester was not hideous: 'a precious substance, beautiful as magical dreams, and yet no dream but a reality, lies hidden in that noisome wrappage'.[63] In Past and Present (1843) he claimed that 'even cotton-spinning is noble';[64] he praised 'the inventive genius of England' and labour as the 'truest emblem...of God the World-Worker'.[65] He declared that 'a Captain of Industry' could be a member of 'the genuine aristocracy of the universe'.[66] But he did not take the step of actually calling capitalists or manufacturers 'creative'.

Where he failed, others followed. In Charles Kingsley's *Yeast* (1851), for example, the central character Lancelot rejects his brother's decision to become a Roman Catholic and embraces instead 'English civilization': 'Give me the political economist, the sanitary reformer, the engineer,...the spinning-jenny and the railroad...To me [they] are signs that.. there is a mighty spirit working among us,...the Ordering and Creating God'.[67] But the industrialist in the novel, Lord Minchampstead, is not seen as in any way 'creative'. The same omission occurred in the writings of Samuel Smiles, who despite owing much to Carlyle was anxious in his *Self-Help* (1858) to portray the exemplary figures of the industrial revolution — Watt, Boulton, Arkwright, Stephenson — as ordinary, rather than extrordinary. Their achievements were the result of energy, application, perseverance and will. Genius had had little or nothing to do with it,[68] and the term 'creator' only applied to makers of works of art.[69] Even an inventor, he insisted in his *Industrial Biography* (1863) was 'not a creator', that word only applied to 'the poet'.[70]

There were a number of reasons for this. While in many quarters commerce had by the late 18th century become accepted as beneficial and respectable, so that Southey could praise it as 'humanizing, civilizing, liberalising',[71] manufacturing industry was seen as anything but benign. The social disruption, with brutal working conditions and squalid living conditions, and the inhumanity of political economists' acceptance of these, (as well as their emphasis on self-interest and competition), were both morally offensive. Fictional accounts of manufacturers and factory owners in these years usually portrayed them as harsh, mean and narrow-minded, and John Stuart Mill, in essays published in 1836 and 1840, presented a similar view. Almost the only outlet for individual energy, in the 'high state of civilization' which now existed, was 'the narrow sphere of [an] individual's money-getting pursuits'.[72] This was 'more or less a mechanical routine', an 'irksome drudgery', with 'nothing agreeable ...except the ultimate end', and it had the effect of making people both 'selfish and cowardly'.[73]

The inadequacies of this view can be seen from the report of a House of Commons Select Committee dealing with the Woollen Industry. This argued the case for factories (against domestic manufacture) precisely because of the scope they gave to invention, flexibility and innovation. The owner of a factory, having greater capital resources and more workmen at his disposal, 'may make experiments, hazard speculation, invent shorter or better modes of performing old processes, may introduce new articles, and improve and perfect old ones, thus giving range to his taste and fancy, and thereby alone enabling our manufacturers to stand the competition with their commercial rivals'.[74] In short, he could use his imagination and, given the evanescence of value, he must. He would only succeed if he did.

Although this report dealt with the new industrial factories, it was written in 1806 and so its tone was closer to 18th century discussions of commerce; the iron had not yet entered the soul. In particular, it conveys a sense of individual action per se. As we have seen, this was an aspect of economic life which had received limited attention from Adam Smith, (something for which Bentham and Stewart had criticized him). But Smith's work had nevertheless retained a human dimension, evident in his treatment of merchants and his consideration for labourers. The development of Political Economy in the 19th century effectively excluded this dimension, and this exclusion became one of its strengths. Political Economy claimed to be a science, setting out laws of universal validity; these laws in turn depended on reducing the personal element to a common denominator of self-interest. Once this reduction was conceded the structure seemed watertight. Given the assumption (since Newton) that the fewer the components of a scientific theory the more cogent it was (the principle of parsimony), the simplicity of the doctrine helped it to ride out the storms of criticism which assailed it.

Carlyle was one of the most forceful and influential critics, but when we read his writings we have a constant sense of his running as much with the hares as with the hounds. He welcomed the fact of evanescence, continual change. To rely on what is inherited or given was, in his view, bad. We all ought to exert ourselves and we all have the capacity to address new conditions: everyone 'discovers...invents and devises somewhat of his own'.[75] Anyone who works, 'whatsoever be his work,...bodies forth the form of things unseen; a small poet every worker is'.[76] Furthermore, Carlyle constantly stressed the benefits of struggle and conflict: 'man is created for fighting; in conflict the perishable part...flies off into dust' and the imperishable aspect appears.[77] Given these views we would expect his admiration for captains of industry to include a recognition of their being 'creative'. Were they not heroes, whom he described as 'leaders...and in a wide sense creators'?[78] Were they not contemporary equivalents of that combination of the 'Captain and Fighter' — with 'wild lion-heart daring' — and 'the poet', such as he saw in the mythological Odinn, in Mirabeau, or in Napoleon's early career?[79]

They were not. (It was left to others in less polarized circumstances, such as Friedrich List, to take a broader and more positive view.)[80] Carlyle could not see economic competition as a life-enhancing conflict, and the phrase 'Captains of Industry' for him meant above all a revived feudal nobility. Such figures would form the apex of a new 'chivalry of work';[81] they would restore social cohesion, in part by applying their 'inventive genius...[to] contrive...fairer distribution of the produce',[82] and in part by their moral example, their life being as much 'a stern pilgrimage' as 'a battle and a march'.[83] For these reasons they would command obedience, gratitude and loyalty — 'submissive admiration for the truly great'.[84]

On the subject of work and productive action Carlyle brings us to the edge of seeing why the word 'creative' took on new significance in Britain in this period. But in his view of society and political action he reverses direction and leads us back to the middle ages. While it seems that in our economic life we are to use all available opportunities to fulfil our potential as self-animating agents, in the sphere of politics we are to take off our boots, sit on our hands and obey the orders of a new aristocracy. Democracy in Carlyle's view was nothing more than 'a regulated method of rebellion and abrogation',[85] and he regarded the programme of the Chartists as essentially a cry for help. Their programme could be reduced to four words: 'Guide me, Govern me'.[86] In one respect this should not surprise us. Far from being alone in holding such ideas he was in tune almost as much with liberals like Macaulay as with a Tory like Southey. At this stage in his life (in the 1840s) his position was not extreme. But given his emphasis on action it is difficult for us not to be puzzled by the vehemence with which his calls for work and production were accompanied by attacks on movements like Chartism as 'social pestilences'.[87] The explanation lies in Carlyle's sources. He had been able to adopt a critical perspective on the world around him because he had found an Archimedean point outside it, in the form of German Idealism. Developed from Kant's criticism of empirical philosophy, the thought of Fichte and Schelling provided ideas and arguments which could be used as effectively against utilitarianism, political economy, and democracy as Kant's initial attack on empiricism (and the atheism and fatalism which were seen as its unavoidable consequences).

Carlyle's first publications had been devoted to German culture, most notably his biography of Schiller and his translation of Goethe's *Wilhelm Meister*, and it was his essay on 'The State of German Literature' (1827) which first brought him wide recognition. But while he owed much to these writers, his greatest debt here was to Fichte. Unlike most of his fellow philosophers, Fichte had produced a series of popular works aimed at making his ideas accessible to the general public. From these texts, Carlyle derived the central elements of the Philosophy of Clothes which he expounded in *Sartor Resartus*: there is a spiritual realm, a 'divine Idea', pervading the visible universe, which in each age takes on a 'new form'.[88] This divine Idea is essentially active and creative and we realize this Idea in our lives, not by thinking or knowing but by doing, by leading a moral life and so making a better world.

Fichte regarded Kant as having exhausted the field of theoretical philosophy in his first *Critique*; the task now was to complete the practical philosophy which Kant had outlined in his second *Critique*. In our free will we are in touch with ultimate reality; on this certainty, and the corresponding priority of the moral will, Fichte constructed his own system. In his *Anthropology* Kant had written that the distinctive feature of a human being was to have 'a [moral] character which he himself creates (*schafft*)';[89] in many respects Fichte's thought could be seen as a brilliant elaboration of that view. He perceived conscious rational life as the manifestation of an Absolute Ego, and the human world as the field in which it (*das absolute Ich*) can realize its moral potential, which is also synonymous with its creative potential. In effect, Fichte developed the principal features of Kant's ethical thought (the stress on self-reliance and the value of struggle to bring about the triumph of spirit over matter) and transformed Kant's (atemporal) transcendental ego into a force active in history. Furthermore, inspired by the revolutionary events from 1789 onwards Fichte wrote with a new sense of urgency. This was subsequently to lead him to adopt an authoritarian stance completely at odds with the Kantian inheritance. The problem for Fichte was that if some people have a perception (in his terms 'an intellectual intuition')[90] of the divine Idea then they have a duty to impose that on others, (a Platonic solution to a quasi-Platonic problem). He therefore came to exalt the power of heroes, world-historical leaders, and religious or intellectual authorities.

Once we are aware of this background to Carlyle's ideas we can understand his infectious confidence and the connection between his calls both for action and for authoritarianism. As Fichte had endorsed the intellectual leader, so Carlyle's Hero as 'Man of Letters' was 'our most important modern person...the soul of all'.[91] From this perspective it also becomes clear why Carlyle could not exalt economic activity. A central feature of the philosophy on which he drew was that the creative must also be the moral, and who could justify 'The Condition of England' morally in the 1830s and 1840s?

II

When Samuel Smiles wrote that an inventor was not 'a creator like a poet' he was expressing a commonplace. Since the Renaissance claims had been made for poets having 'creative' powers; (the first English writer to use this term had been George Puttenham in his *Art of English Poesie* (1589)).[92] In 18th century discussions of literature the imagination came to be regarded as the faculty which 'creates', the genius was seen as the person with exceptional imaginative (or intuitive) ability, and the outstanding poet was the quintessential genius. The word 'create' in this context had the most exalted associations and these were not lost when the word itself began to be applied more extensively in the second half of the 18th century.

In addition, poetry itself had a place in a wider framework of value which gave it special status — the neoclassical aesthetic which had been constructed in *cinquecento* Italy and then adopted throughout Europe, (the first full account in English being Ben Jonson's *Timber* (1640)). The most contested form of poetry was drama, because stage performance involved levels of feeling (in particular, sexual) which the private or public reading of dramatic works either did not arouse or which were less amenable to official control. An active and popular theatre therefore tended to lead to vigorous arguments in defence of poetry. In the 18th century, the terms of this defence also came to be used to vindicate the new literary form of the novel, and journals and periodicals likewise made claims for a role as moral critic or guardian, fulfilling a public responsibility.

The poems which Wordsworth and Coleridge published in *Lyrical Ballads* (1798) broke sharply with existing literary conventions but the Preface which Wordsworth added in 1800 used the traditional criteria of value. The poet, wrote Wordsworth, was 'a man speaking to men', concerned 'to produce or enlarge' the sensibility of his readers, to evoke a pleasure which will increase their knowledge of, and sympathy for, their fellows.[93] In the Preface and Supplementary Essay which he included with his *Poems* (published in 1815), we find the same claim made for the fine arts in general and poetry in particular; they are capable of 'the widening of the sphere of human sensibility, for the delight, honour and benefit of human nature'.[94] It was on this basis also that Southey, in his *Colloquies*, put forward 'the humanizing effects of literature', its role as an indirect source of moral good,[95] as one possible counter to the effects of industrialization. In this general perspective we can see how poetry's ancient place among the liberal arts could enable it to claim that it was 'creative' in a way that was denied to the mechanical (now all-too-mechanical) arts.

In one significant respect, however, Wordsworth's 1815 essay did move beyond previous attitudes. In 1800 he had written of 'the mind of man' as 'the mirror of the fairest and most interesting properties of nature'; in 1815 he wrote that the imagination did not make 'a faithful copy' of nature, because the mind 'shapes and *creates*,... proceeding from, and governed by, a sublime consciousness of the soul in her mighty and almost divine powers'.[96] This statement may seem to be no more than a reiteration of Renaissance (and later) neo-Platonic views, and to a large extent that is true; but in the context of Wordsworth's poetry and that of the time, the remark had new implications. Despite the quasi-Platonic themes that recur in his writings — especially in poems like *Tintern Abbey* and the Immortality Ode — Wordsworth's focus was resolutely human. His experience of the natural world does not lead him to believe in a better world elsewhere, but rather in the possibility of paradise here, in the 'simple produce of a common day'.[97] Natural beauty evokes a sense of 'the moral properties and scope of things'; and nature teaches a 'lesson deep of love', drawing us close to this life among our fellows.[98] (This is why his writings could have such a profound impact on someone like John Stuart Mill who was contemptuous of all kinds of Platonism.) The feelings which Wordsworth experienced and conveyed were intense affirmations of the here and now.

In the previous century Young had stated that 'our senses...half-create the wondrous world they see' and Thomson had referred to 'the mind's creative eye', but by that they meant no more than the automatic physical process by which (as Newton had shown) our sensory apparatus produces colour.[99] Wordsworth's claim was of a different order, endowing the poet's imagination with a power of insight and transformation — 'a plastic power...a forming hand'[100] — which produced a new reality. Insofar as this was not only a power *of* nature, but a power *over* nature, it could be seen as a higher form of what Wordsworth observed in new world of manufacturing. For as well as being dismayed by many of its results the poet also rejoiced 'to see / An intellectual mastery exercised / O'er the blind elements', 'the force of those gigantic powers', products of the 'thinking mind', bringing forth 'a new and unforeseen creation';[101] such activity gave rise to 'the animating hope' that one day all people would meet their needs'.[102] In other words, it might bring about an affirmation of the here and now which would benefit more than just a select few.

The publication of Wordsworth's *Poems*, with their theoretical Preface and Essay, provoked Coleridge into writing his own treatise on the nature and aim of poetry, the *Biographia Literaria* (1817). In their twenties the two men had been close, but they had grown apart and then quarrelled. As Wordsworth's reputation had risen Coleridge had become increasingly insecure; he struggled through bouts of depression and intermittent periods of writing, increasingly aware of being seen as having 'dreamt away [his] life to no purpose'.[103] *Biographia Literaria* was an attempt to rescue his situation; in part it was an assessment of his former friend's achievement, in part a manifesto for a new view of poetry.

In his youth Coleridge had been powerfully affected by Hartley and Godwin; he saw their empirical philosophy as the means to a more just and happier society. If what we think and feel is shaped by the circumstances of our upbringing, then a more favourable — sensitive, humane, moral —

upbringing could produce better human beings. This was the plan set out by Godwin on the basis of Hartley's psychology. Coleridge adopted it so enthusiastically that (in 1794) he was regarded as a Jacobin. Three years later, when he became friends with Wordsworth, he had abandoned these ideas and immersed himself instead in German philosophy. He spent almost two years in Germany and was strongly influenced by Kant and Schelling. In Britain their ideas were almost entirely unknown (and where known, mostly distorted),[104] which increased Coleridge's sense of isolation and played a part in making the structure of *Biographia Literaria* so convoluted and its style so opaque.

The publication of this work was, nevertheless, a significant event, because (in conjunction with the lecture 'On Poesy or Art' which he gave the following year) Coleridge here presented in English a new view of poetry; (readers of German would have been aware of his debts to German thought).[105] Instead of poetry being an imitation of nature (as in neo-classical aesthetics), or an expression of the individual poet's mind or feelings (as in Romantic aesthetics), or the realization of certain forms (as in Kantian aesthetics), it was a synthesis of all these. It did not copy 'nature (*natura naturata*)' but it imitated 'the *Naturgeist*', 'the essence, the *natura naturans*', 'the indwelling power' in nature;[106] more precisely, it embodied this power. The poet's imagination was part of a universal force, and as such it was also a shaping power, producing works according to forms (or rules) which it generated itself.[107]

In his poetry, Coleridge observed, Wordsworth had shown himself to be 'an original poetic genius'; he had united 'deep feeling with profound thought', 'the tone [and] atmosphere' of the visible — 'as fresh as if it had then sprung forth at the first creative fiat' — with 'the depth and height of the ideal world'.[108] But in his prose writings about poetry he had limited the imagination to poetic art, not seeing it as universal in its scope; and he had given too much credit to the passive aspect of the imagination, 'fancy'. For Coleridge, this was to lapse back into 'the despotism of outward impressions', the Hartleian empirical psychology which made us the product of external, 'wholly...alien', forces.[109] Consideration of this issue in the *Biographia* led him then to recapitulate Leibniz's attack on Locke and initiate a discussion of Kant, Fichte and Schelling which was (and is) bewildering for anyone unfamiliar with their philosophies. What was at issue for him, exactly as for Carlyle a few years later, was the existence of a spiritual realm, accessible to us, which validated our intimations of a meaning in life beyond the daily routine of work, self-interest, and calculation. For Carlyle the evidence of a spiritual power lay in independent moral action; our creative capacity is a moral capacity. For Coleridge, a true creation must also have an aesthetic dimension; the creative is the beautiful as well as the good, and is supremely manifest in poetry and art. He was here aligning himself with the neo-Platonic tradition, as he acknowledged in the *Biographia,* but the exalted status he gave to poetry, and his attitude to nature, made his position something new.

Coleridge's difference from this tradition is evident in the pivotal role which he gave to the imagination. It is true that he was prone to assimilate imagination and intuition which (in the form of 'apprehension' or 'intuitive reason' or (in Kantian terminology) 'intellectual intuition') had a recognized place in earlier and later neo-Platonic philosophy; and in doing this he was able to draw on a number of German writers who had aimed to distance imagination from any purely empirical associations. But while intuition was a perception of truth 'without a medium'[110] (which we could call 'pure knowledge'), imagination could grasp reality in its fullness (which we might call 'complete experience'). Intuition, in other words, was confined to the spiritual, in Coleridge's terms 'the ideal', while imagination revealed the ideal in the real. By his 'synthetic and magical power [of] imagination' the poet 'brings the whole soul of man into activity' and achieves a 'balance or reconciliation of opposite and discordant qualities'.[111] In works of art a genius makes 'the external internal, the internal external, nature thought and thought nature'.[112]

In statements of this kind we see how complete was the identity of the creative and the aesthetic for Coleridge, and the exalted position which art therefore assumed for him (as it had for a number of Kant's successors). The latter had related the qualities of formal beauty and harmony which we see in nature to the same qualities in the genius who produces a beautiful work of art. But for him our experience of nature was the decisive factor, and the character of art and genius secondary, because the beauty which nature evoked in our minds linked us to the natural world (the God-given) and could therefore give us a sense that we belonged here. For Coleridge, on the other hand, art, the humanly made, was the decisive factor. The creative powers in human beings, which themselves generated aesthetic norms, enabled us to bridge the gap between human beings and nature. In this respect art (rather than the aesthetic sense of nature) was the 'mediatress between, and reconciler of, nature and man'.[113] Furthermore, both the creation and experience of art took us beyond nature to an awareness of the ideal (which for Kant only came about in morality). Genius acted from 'the feeling that body is but a striving to become mind', and in poetry 'all its materials are from the mind and all its products are for the mind'.[114]

Coleridge announced in the *Biographia* that he would discuss his ideas more fully in a future work, to be called *The Productive Logos Human and Divine.* As its title suggests, this was to be more a work of philosophy or theology than aesthetics, and in this respect the *Biographia* was no more than an introduction, a bridge between his previous writings on literature and his future work on philosophy. But in another sense this distinction is false, because for Coleridge there was nothing beyond aesthetics; or rather, everything depended on aesthetics, if that failed then everything failed. For him, the existence of God could not be derived from external factors, as in the arguments from first cause or design; it must be based on an internal awareness.[115] We are conscious of possessing a self which is free and has the power to realize itself. It is 'by the act of constructing itself' that this self actually becomes self;[116] and only by this process — by the way our creative power harmonizes with both our moral intuitions and our aesthetic sense — that it also comes to perceive that that power is benign.[117] Along these lines 'we proceed from the self, in order to lose and find all self in God'.[118] Only the existence of beautiful, spiritually-enhancing works of art could prevent this argument from being circular. Their objective reality, available to all, can indicate that these claims were not subjective but could be true. (Hence Schelling's conclusion that a work of art overcomes the division — between thought and existence — with which philosophy begins (p.149)). It is in this sense that everything, for Coleridge, depended on aesthetics.

It was in this context also that, in the next generation, Art came to acquire a capital A, like a silhouette of two hands in prayer. For Ruskin or Wagner, for example, art had redemptive power; it could save us from those developments which had alarmed Carlyle — the fear of atheism, materialism, mass politics — and which were of increasing concern to Coleridge. At this time in his life, however, the latter had reason for anxiety about more personal and specific issues: the former was doubt about his own poetic talent, the latter lay in changing conditions for, and perceptions of, poets in general. The decline of patronage and introduction of copyright did not benefit poets as it had writers of prose. While an ever-growing number of novelists earned a living from their pen, only a very small number of poets did. (And there was also an ancient tradition that poets should not be concerned about money anyway.)[119] This problem contributed to that image — made famous by Gray's *Elegy* — of the poet as a marginal figure. For accompanying the new socio-economic predicament there was also a growing sense of poets as outsiders intellectually. With the first (economic) kind of marginality the extreme term was destitution, with the second (intellectual) kind it was madness. It was during Coleridge's lifetime that the ancient issue of genius and madness (p.51) came to attract serious attention.[120] (The prime example of an intrinsic connection between the two was Blake; for him madness was something to be welcomed rather than avoided, because it opened the mind to truths which were otherwise concealed or repressed.) Finally, there was an ethical dimension. While Coleridge insisted that a good poet was always also a good person morally,[121] the most prominent poet of the time was Byron – a writer of outstanding ability who was widely perceived as 'bad and dangerous to know'.[122] Macaulay, commenting after his death on his immense influence, wrote that Byron had 'created in the minds of many of [his] enthusiasts a pernicious and absurd association between intellectual power and moral depravity'.[123] This was precisely the opposite of what Coleridge asserted.

Biographia Literaria was not a work which either did or could have a major influence. But Coleridge's subsequent prose writings, especially his *Aids to Reflection* (1825) and *On the Constitution of the Church and State* (1830), came to be widely read. These works dealt not with literature but with religion, arguing for its importance as 'a counter-charm to the sorcery of wealth'.[124] Coleridge attacked the prevailing emphasis on utility, the measurement of everything in terms of 'marketable value' and, above all, the treatment of people as 'things'.[125] Only a sense of God and a reassertion of the 'divine image in the soul'[126] could rescue his contemporaries from what he saw as a drastic imbalance of the practical over the spiritual. This concern led him to suggest an institutional counterweight to the two dominant powers in the state — the landed interest and the commercial/ manufacturing/professional interest — namely, a national church in the form of a national 'clerisy'. This would not be a purely ecclesiastical body but would consist of 'the learned of all denominations', 'all the...liberal arts and sciences', as well as theology.[127] Its concern would be the spiritual well-being of the nation. In a time when instrumental reason prevailed there was an urgent need for a consideration of 'the ultimate ends'; 'not without celestial observations can even terrestrial charts be accurately constructed'.[128] This was the problem which the clerisy would tackle, mainly by their role in education. Their method would not be to transmit information, in the manner of 'tract societies,...mechanics' institutions,...[and] lecture-bazaars under the absurd name of universities'; all of these were 'marked with the same asterisk of spuriousness' (by providing 'empirical specifics' which only fed the disease).[129] Rather, the clerisy would be concerned with individuals as persons, helping them to think for themselves and to develop their personalities in a fully rounded way, to realize 'the potential divinity in every man'.[130]

When Coleridge wrote this work it must have seemed that it was no more likely that these ideas would win approval than that his aesthetic-philosophical ideas would be understood. But this was not to be the case. The problem he was addressing came to be recognized by the younger generation, and the German ideas which informed his overall position came to be appreciated (as a result, in part, of Carlyle's writings). In 1840 John

Stuart Mill claimed that 'every Englishman of the present day is...either a Benthamite or a Coleridgian'.[131] (What he omitted to add was that he himself was the one exception to this, since he was both.) Mill regarded Coleridge on the subject of political economy to be an 'arrant driveller',[132] and had no time at all for his idealist metaphysics; (he also regarded the philosopher as superior to the artist, the 'conceptive genius [being]...a higher faculty than the creative').[133] On these matters Bentham was more reliable. However, what the latter lacked, and Coleridge provided, was a concern for 'the culture of the inward man', a sense of 'spiritual perfection as an end',[134] all the things which Mill himself had been deprived of in his own upbringing — 'imagination', 'poetical culture', the 'cultivation of feeling', and a sense of freewill'.[135] We are not merely the creatures of circumstances but 'have real power over the formation of our character'.[136]

In Victorian society Mill saw these qualities under serious threat: in the first place, from the success of Bentham and his father in promoting an emphasis on facts and utility, and in the second place from a new pressure to conform. The combined effects of increasing urbanization — in 1851 the town-dwelling proportion of the population exceeded the rural for the first time — and what was seen as homogenization — of work, and ways of living and thinking — was a 'growing insignificance of individuals in comparison with the mass'.[137] Mill viewed this development with alarm and addressed the issue frequently. His most extensive discussion, the essay *On Liberty* (1859), set out a number of arguments as to why individuals should be protected from pressures to conform. Among them was the idea that (as the title of the central chapter announced) 'individuality [is] one of the elements of well-being'.[138]

While most of Mill's case for personal freedom was based on the social benefits it could bring, at the heart of this chapter was a view of a life being good insofar as it was distinctly individual. In part, this was no more than the Victorian commonplace on the need for moral autonomy, but inspired by his reading of what he termed the 'Germano-Coleridgian school'[139] Mill advocated a richer notion of individuality. The ideal to which he aimed was 'the highest and harmonious development of [an individual's] powers to a complete and consistent whole'.[140] Individual potential and attributes had intrinsic worth, because a human being was not a machine but rather 'a tree, which requires to grow and develop itself on all sides, according to the tendency of the inward forces which make it a living thing'.[141] Mill praised not only 'pagan self-asertion' (in opposition to Puritan self-denial) but also the realization of an 'originality' which would have aesthetic value and could be 'a noble and beautiful object of contemplation'.[142] This aim was shared by Matthew Arnold, whose *Culture and Anarchy* (1869) set out a programme for achieving a comparable ideal.

Much of Arnold's thought (e.g. on the importance of religion, or the role of the state) was completely at odds with that of Mill, but he felt the same alarm at the narrow conformity of much of Victorian society and a similar concern to promote a richer model of individual development, one which would realize 'all sides of our humanity'.[143] If widely adopted this could benefit not only individuals but lead to a more harmonious society as well.[144] For Arnold the way in which this could be achieved was by 'culture'.

By this word he meant the nurturing of a person's mind and character — 'an inward operation' of 'spiritual growth'[145] — i.e. culture in its original sense of cultivating our distinctly human capacities, *cultura animi*. But this was enriched by the new emphasis on aesthetic sensibility, which in Arnold's view could be developed by contact and engagement with 'the best which has been thought and said in the world', meaning predominantly, but not exclusively, great works of literature, i.e. culture in the sense it came to assume as 'high culture'.[146] Arnold's usage owed much to the German concepts of *Bildung* and *Kultur*. During the course of the nineteenth century the latter became identified with what was natural, organic, internal, spiritual and ethical (especially in the world of the intellect and the arts), in contrast to *Zivilisation*, which came to be associated with the artificial, mechanical, external, material and instrumental (as evident in the worlds of politics and economics). In his *Church and State* Coleridge had made the comparison as follows: 'civilization is itself but a mixed good, if not far more a corrupting influence...where [it] is not grounded in *cultivation*, in the harmonious development of those qualities and faculties that characterize our *humanity*. We must be men in order to be citizens'.[147] This was precisely Arnold's belief.

Culture and Anarchy was subtitled 'An Essay in Political and Social Criticism' and the work was a sustained attack on most of the values and achievements central to English pride and Victorian self-confidence. The degree of individual liberty, then more extensive in Britain than elsewhere in Europe, resulted (in Arnold's view) in an 'anarchical...worship of freedom' and indifference to what was best for the population as a whole.[148] There was an unshakable belief in the virtues of 'energy, self-reliance, and capital', and in the importance of 'free trade, unrestricted competition, and the making of large industrial fortunes';[149] as for English public life, that was a 'banquet of clap-trap'.[150] The increase in overall prosperity, which had made Britain the wealthiest country in the world, had been obtained by a narrowly practical approach to everything, overvaluing 'doing' at the expense of 'knowing'.[151] The concern for moral rectitude, most evident in Dissenting communities but characteristic of middle-class society as a whole, had instilled in people a habit of obedience, a sense of sinfulness, and a 'strictness of conscience' which shut out any 'spontaneity of consciousness'.[152] The effect had been to deny them any awareness of that 'aerial ease, clearness and radiancy', that 'sweetness and light' (i.e. beauty and truth) which had been for Arnold the hallmark of classical Greece.[153] Only contact with those Hellenic values could lift people out of their 'ordinary' or 'everyday' selves, in which they were 'separate, personal [and] at war', and enable them to realize instead their 'best self', by which we can all be 'united, impersonal, [and] at harmony'.[154]

A few years before he published this work Arnold had sketched out these ideas in an essay on 'The Function of Criticism at the Present Time' (1864). This had attacked the practical spirit of the time and had praised literary criticism for its power to correct that, if it were undertaken in a free and disinterested manner. In the opening section of this essay Arnold made a notable statement of what he took to be a representative view: 'it is undeniable that the exercise of a creative power, that a free creative activity, is the true function of man; it is proved to be so by man's finding in it his true happiness'. The most obvious example 'of exercising this free creative activity...[is in] producing great works of literature and art'. But, he continued, it was possible to be creative in other ways, namely by being active 'in well-doing', and even 'in criticising'.[155]

In an essay on Heine, the previous year, Arnold had written about 'the modern spirit', which he saw Heine as having exemplified and which he himself admired. This 'modern spirit', the 'new wine of the eighteenth and nineteenth centuries', was the rejection of custom, routine and prescription. It was the sense that the 'immense [inherited] system of institutions, established facts, accredited dogmas, customs, [and] rules...by no means corresponds exactly to the wants of [people's] actual life'. This was because people felt that 'this system is not of their own creation'.[156] Heine's greatness had been to show them that it ought to be. We might imagine that Arnold was referring here, in some way or to some degree, to the quintessentially modern 'creations' of political emancipation and industrial production, but he was not. While he does discuss Heine's opposition to the lack of liberty in Germany the main aim of the essay is rather to praise his attack on 'Philistinism', narrow-minded attitudes and ignorance of ideas.[157]

For Arnold the word 'creative' (in his statement about 'the true function of man') meant a combination of the aesthetic and the moral. This is what constituted the merit of a great work of literature, and this was the focus of 'criticism' and 'culture'. As we can see from his repeated invocations of 'beauty and wisdom', 'grace and serenity', or 'sweetness and light',[158] Arnold's thought was informed by the same conviction which lay at the heart of Coleridge's writings: a belief in the priority of the spiritual, and in access to that by means of aesthetic experience. Arnold's spirituality may have taken a more Hellenic than Christian form, but as his admiration for Curtius' *History of Greece* made plain, his Greeks were monotheists at heart, proto-Christians under the skin.[159] Like Coleridge Arnold saw the union of the beautiful and the good as synonymous with (or the necessary condition for) the creative; it was 'when the whole of society is in fullest measure permeated by thought, [and] sensible to beauty', that there occur 'the flowering times for literature and art and all the creative power of genius'.[160] Given its spiritual origin and function creative power for Arnold was inevitably confined to artistic and/or moral activities.

The assertion that 'the true function of man [lies] in exercising a creative power' marks a point at which we can see creativity being recognized as a value; but the terms in which Arnold defines the creative owed nothing to the modern world in which this value had arisen. On the contrary, the creative was something which Arnold saw as being able to save us from almost everything which made modern life disagreeable, by which he meant a large part of what actually made it 'modern'. Throughout *Culture and Anarchy* he juxtaposed the 'ordinary selves' of people active in their everyday lives with the 'best self' to which they should aspire, and which 'culture' could make available to them. The antithesis of these two kinds of self was Stoic, and Arnold felt an affinity with Stoic thought.[161] But when we read the exact terms of the contrast which he drew between the 'ordinary' and 'best' self we can see that his fundamental debt was to an even more ancient line of thought. The ordinary self, he wrote, was 'manifold, and vulgar, and unstable, and contentious, and ever-varying'; the best self, on the other hand, was 'one, and noble, and secure, and peaceful, and the same for all mankind'.[162] These two lists replicate almost exactly the contrast made at the beginning of this book between two opposing views of the creative attribute (p.27).

III

When Owen wrote of 'this era of creation' (in 1817)[163] he was not referring only to the new possibilities for the 'creation of wealth' brought about by industrial developments.[164] They certainly occupied a central place in his thinking: 'mechanism', he observed, could 'be made the greatest of blessings to humanity', (and it was his own wealth obtained by these means which enabled him to promote his ideas).[165] But the 'era of creation' for him related above all to new social and human possibilities, which he described in terms of making a 'New Moral World'.[166]

As the application of new technologies and working methods had made the overcoming of scarcity an attainable goal, for the first time in human history, so the American and French Revolutions appeared to have made possible the realization of equality and justice. 'We have it in our power to begin the world over again', wrote Paine in 1776, shortly before the outbreak of the American Revolution; 'the birth day of a new world is at hand'.[167] In his *Rights of Man* (1791–92), defending the revolution in France, he hailed 'the present generation...[as] the Adam of a new world', able to bring into being 'a new era [for] the human race'.[168] In similar terms the young Wordsworth defended the execution of Louis XVI as part of a 'convulsion from which is to spring a fairer order of things', which will 'create a race of men who [will be] truly free'.[169]

Before the 18th century the main secular use of the word 'create' (derived from Roman practice) had been in politics. New legal entities were 'created', new titles likewise, (as occurs for example in Shakespeare's plays). When the American colonists broke away from British rule they 'created' new governments for themselves,[170] and Paine deliberately inverted this usage when he wrote of monarchs as 'beings of our own creating' who had 'become the gods of their creators'.[171] This was a typically republican attitude. A feature of republican politics had been the opportunities they gave for individual action, initiative and enterprise of a kind we would now call 'creative', as Paine indicated when he wrote of revolutions stimulating 'genius and talent', (the word 'genius' here implying creative ability).[172] We find this republican notion recurring in Britain in the first half of the 19th century — in J.S. Mill writing on Greece (under the influence of George Grote)[173] and on America (quoting Tocqueville).[174]

But Owen's 'era of creation' did not refer to either revolutionary or republican politics; rather, he envisaged an alteration of society and human behaviour so radical that those forms of politics would no longer be necessary. He adopted the same 'necessitarian' view of personality and character-formation as that set out by Godwin in his *Political Justice*: our individual qualities are the result of the circumstances of our upbringing, so better circumstances would produce better people. Owen recognized that the material conditions now existed 'to relieve the whole of the population from...misery, degradation and danger';[175] if, therefore, the social and educational environment was changed, if we set about 'creating entirely new surroundings',[176] then a new human nature could emerge. People would live in 'cordial unity and mutual co-operation', harmony would prevail within society and between nations, and 'real happiness will commence and perpetually go on increasing'.[177]

Towards the end of his life, Owen referred to his project as nothing less than 'the second creation of humanity'.[178] The similarity of this statement to those by Paine (quoted above) or Priestley (p.156) stems from their common background in Dissenting communities, where millenial ideas circulated. But comparable views on a new social order were formulated in France in this period on a wholly different basis. Saint-Simon had an equally clear perception of the new possibilities which economic and technological developments were introducing, and an equally robust wish to make political activity redundant. He was not concerned, as Owen was, with abolishing the division of labour, or with equality or common ownership. But he was convinced that those whom he saw as most important to the productive process, for him *les industriels* (entrepreneurial and scientific leaders), should replace politicians. Since 'an enlightened government only needs to be administered',[179] under their guidance the causes of social disorder would vanish, politics would become redundant, and co-operation and happiness would prevail.

Both Saint-Simon (born 1760) and Owen (born 1771) had lived through the years of revolutionary upheavals and Napoleonic excess, but their dislike of politics was not a reaction to these. The principal enemy for them was what was coming to be called 'individualism',[180] the view that human beings are motivated above all by self-interest and that that was desirable (and necessary) in conditions where economic prosperity depended on competition. For both men the democratic politics espoused in a limited way by liberals, like Constant or Macaulay, and in a more vigorous form by radicals, like French republicans or Chartists, were no more than a reflection of this prevailing individualism, and so could not be expected to reduce (let alone eradicate) it. Although Owen wrote that 'the creation of the circumstances to well educate man is a national work',[181] his approach to this task was essentially non-political, (hence the bitter quarrels between Owenites and Chartists). For him, politics were a symptom of the problem, not a means to its solution. Once the new moral world was in place co-operation would replace competition, politics would not be needed, and a flowering of human personality would occur.

In the mid-1840s, as Owen's final project was breaking up in acrimony, a similar vision of future happiness was being formulated in entirely new terms by Marx. Almost all the intellectual tools which Owen had had at his disposal had 'Made in Britain' stamped on them, (subsequently altered, in the eyes of Marx and Engels, to 'Failed in Britain'). Marx, on the other hand, combined an analysis of (mainly) British writings on political economy with a Hegelian philosophy of history which provided reasons for seeing future happiness and justice as not merely possible, but inevitable. Hegel's philosophy was an account of progressive development; political economy, in its founding text *The Wealth of Nations*, was implicitly the same. In his later political writings, however, Hegel's reservations about certain kinds of change led to his being regarded as a conservative; in similar fashion, Adam Smith's successors came to see political economy as a timeless set of rules. In both cases readers (of Hegel on politics and of Ricardo or James Mill on economics) came to see present conditions not as historical, but normative. The Prussian state, and the British economy, were taken to be not only how matters political or economic actually were, but also how they ought to be. The former was given a spiritual sanction, the latter the status of being natural, its economic prescriptions regarded as laws of nature.

Marx spent almost four years as a student in Berlin at a time when Hegel's influence was at its height. Soon after he left he read a book which fatally punctured Hegel's system — Feuerbach's *The Essence of Christianity* (1841). Building on Hegel's own perceptive remarks about psychological projection and compensation,[182] Feuerbach showed how religious beliefs could be understood as expressions of human unhappiness or wish-fulfillment; we project on to imaginary spiritual beings our own needs, in an idealized or inverted form.[183] His target (at this point) was Christianity, but since certain Christian doctrines had an important place in Hegel's thought, the implications of his analysis were plain. Two years later he made them explicit, in an attack on Hegel's idealism; what the latter had written about *Geist* should be understood as referring to humans. History was not the chronicle of *Geist* coming to know itself and be at home in the world; it was a record of human aspirations and achievements. Where theology had been, anthropology must be.[184]

Feuerbach's work had a decisive impact on young intellectuals living under the repressive Prussian monarchy; it helped them transform Hegel's thought from being a vindication of the status quo into a weapon against it. Hegel was wrong to suppose that freedom had been realized in history; in Germany, it had manifestly not yet arrived. He had, however, delineated correctly the dialectical manner in which progress did occur; their task, therefore, was to apply those insights to the present. For some of these young Hegelians, this meant accentuating 'the mighty power of the negative' (p.173). 'No one without the courage to be absolutely negative has the strength to create anything new' (Feuerbach), which is why 'the passion for destruction is a creative passion' (Bakunin).[185] For all of them the task was that of 'making human beings', 'creating the future', seeing history as a 'free, conscious creation'.[186] To Arnold Ruge, Hegel's crucial perception was that 'man's true being is that he is his own product'.[187] In the first place, 'the work of human beings...is the producing of human beings' by generating all the conditions necessary for social life; in the second place, the exercise of 'creative activity' is itself a formative process for individuals.[188]

For Ruge, with whom Marx for a short period was closely associated, the arena in which this activity should occur (to bring about true freedom) was democratic politics. Marx's own criticism of Hegel initially took the same form. But after he had moved to Paris (in 1843) he turned his attention to political economy, and a wholly new dimension of understanding came into view. Like Cortes 'when with eagle eyes / He stared at the Pacific...// Silent, upon a peak in Darien', facing a vast ocean never shown on any map,[189] Marx saw a new way of interpreting all human history. His writings of 1844 still convey the excitement of that discovery.

For Hegel, *Geist* was productive; for Feuerbach, human beings were productive.[190] For Marx, likewise, the distinctive feature of humans (that which set them apart from animals) was their productive capacity.[191] But while for Feuerbach, or Ruge, this attribute should be applied in new ways of thinking, or in making new social arrangements, for Marx the decisive field of action was material production. As we know, Marx came to hold the view that ways of thinking and social arrangements themselves actually depend on economic conditions. Not only that; he also made the character of economic life itself depend on the specific 'way of producing (*Produktionsweise*)' of any historical epoch.[192] The result was that the human productive capacity was seen as significant in three different ways. First, it was the distinctive feature of humans, anthropologically; second, the form it took was the decisive element in all economies; thirdly, this in turn determined (to a greater or lesser extent) the other forms of our lives — social, political, and intellectual.

There was no logical connection between the three (or more) levels of analysis; each could be independently true. The reason why Marx saw them as interdependent was that he was rereading the Hegelian *Geist* in terms of political economy's labour theory of value; the work (*Arbeit*) of the former was reinterpreted as the labour (*Arbeit*) of the latter. A new version of progress could then be formulated, in which material, social, individual and ethical advance could all be seen to move forward together. Since it was possible (in the 1840s) to envisage the future completion of human mastery over nature, Marx could write of world history as 'nothing other than the production of man through human labour, and the development of nature for man', of human history as a 'part of the history of nature and of nature's becoming man'.[193] It is difficult to imagine a more striking assertion of how the God-given had been supplanted by the humanly-made.

The ethical aspect of this progress was, as yet, far from being complete. But that an ethical component was integral to historical advance was implicit in Marx's initial definition of humanity. Since we can neither survive nor produce in isolation, human beings are naturally social, and out of our shared activity arises a common sense of humanity.[194] If we do not feel any community (*Gemeinwesen*) or commonality now, it is because with commercial and industrial developments self-interest and competition have come to prevail. However, while Political Economy put forward arguments why these aspects were necessary it also contained an element which would lead to its own destruction — the labour theory of value. If the value of something derived from the labour put into producing it, then those who did the labour should surely have a role in deciding about how it was made and distributed, and how much they should be paid. But the reality was the exact opposite. The workers had no say and low pay. Not only was this unjust, it was also inhumane, in the literal sense of violating our basic human nature.

At this point empirical evidence and Hegelian philosophy indicated the way ahead. Marx's contacts with French (and emigré German) workers in Paris, and Engels' account of the working-class in England,[195] showed that these men did share a sense of community as a living reality, and had the achievement of a just and equal society as their practical goal. Hegel's account of historical development provided the model for how this would occur: dissatisfaction leads to opposition and eventually to conflict, the outcome of which is a new and higher stage. Conflict in this case would take the form of revolution, and in 1848 — with revolutions breaking out all over mainland Europe — it seemed that this moment had arrived. The fact that it did not, suggested to Marx that the opposition and conflicts within existing economies had not yet reached the point of crisis, and it was to the task of identifying how present trends would lead to that inevitable moment that he devoted the rest of his working life.

The existing situation, of workers in capitalist societies, not only violated their social needs in terms of community, it also blocked their individual needs in terms of productive capacity. It was not only offensive ethically, it was also damaging psychologically. Productive activity is necessary for our emotional and mental well-being, as much as for our physical needs. Property is external to us, but our labour is what we immediately are, and, more importantly, the means by which we become what we can be; because it is in the act of producing something that we also realize our own personality. In this sense labour could be described as man's 'act of self-generation (*Selbsterzeugungsakt*)', the process by which we create our own selves.[196] Not to be able to do this was to be a stunted creature, more mechanical than human, living in a world where self-interest prevailed but which was so cruel that it effectively denied the majority even the chance to exist as a self. In other words, capitalism gave rise to a comprehensive 'alienation'.[197] The industrial worker was cut off from the sources of his own self, denied any meaningful productive activity, and isolated from his fellows: 'his activity is a misery to him, his own creation is like an alien power,...the essential bond connecting him to other men seems inessential...[and] he, the master of his creation, appears as the slave of his creation'.[198]

At the same time, however, the capitalist economy as a whole was eradicating all barriers between people. Every local, regional or national one-sidedness or self-sufficiency was being destroyed, all limitations and restrictions being broken down, by its 'cosmopolitan, universal energy', 'its colossal, productive forces'.[199] In so doing, it was preparing the way for a global economy in which particular interests would no longer stand as obstacles to general happiness. At the time of revolutionary transformation control of this universal economy would pass into the hands of the majority, who having experienced a real sense of community, and having known by their own suffering the evils of self-interest and private property, would institute that system of common ownership and free association which alone could do justice to human needs and potential.

Marx's accounts of this future state are notoriously vague, but about certain aspects he was consistent and clear. There would be no division of labour, and no exclusive or limited spheres of activity in either economic or social life. There would be equality and general participation. Above all, there would be 'conscious control' of the economy.[200] 'Communism creates a reality in which nothing is independent of individuals', for everything is subject to 'the power of united individuals'.[201] Isolation, separation, and division (both within us and between us) would disappear, and our sense of community and commonality would be fully realized. At the same time, with the material abundance which would then be available, we would move from the realm of necessity into that of freedom. We would at last be able to enjoy the free exercise of our productive abilities, the all-round development of our individual attributes and personality. 'The full development of human mastery over the forces of nature', in these future conditions, would make possible 'the development of all human powers as such [as] the end in itself'; in other words, we would see 'the absolute working out of man's creative potentialities'.[202] What form would this non-alienated labour take? Marx's answer was clear: it would possess 'the characteristics of art'.[203] Such work would be 'form-giving, purposive activity',[204] but with its purpose intrinsic to it, freely chosen and an end in itself.[205] It would be 'positive, creative activity (*positive, schaffende Tätigkeit*)'.[206]

At the heart of Marx's vision, therefore, was a view of creativity as the quintessential human value, and the model of creativity for him was artistic activity. His insistence on work having an intrinsic purpose or realizing form or expressing personality leave no doubt about this. On some aspects he is vague. At one point he envisages 'the utmost seriousness, the most intense exertion', like the activity of a composer;[207] on another occasion he writes of there being no individual artists but only individuals who paint, among their other activities,[208] for the barriers between free time and work would cease to exist and all-round development would replace specialisation.[209] Sometimes he insists on creative work as valuable for making personality evident: in a freely produced work you can see your own self as in a mirror, for 'as individuals express themselves, so they are'.[210] Elsewhere, he maintained that no such transparency exists, and that what distinguishes a notable work of literature is what goes beyond the personal.[211] But these different emphases or perspectives are details within what remained a permanent feature of Marx's thought, his conception of (in the words of Arnold which Marx himself might have written) 'free creative activity [as] the true function of man'.

It has been suggested that Engels' epitome of Marx's thought — as a synthesis of German idealist philosophy, French revolutionary politics, and British political economy — should be broadened to include a fourth component — German aesthetics (both Romantic and Weimar classical).[212] The suggestion is a good one, but it needs refining. It sometimes takes the form of a claim that Marx envisaged a future which would realize the ideas set out in Schiller's *On the Aesthetic Education of Man*.[213] But this is to misread both writers. Despite a common impression to the contrary, Schiller's text is not concerned with creativity. Its focus is on taste and beauty, the ways in which the development and exercise of our aesthetic capacities could overcome various kinds of dualism or alienation, and make possible true human freedom. For Schiller we come to freedom through beauty,[214] and this sense of beauty is cultivated not by being creative but by opportunities for play.[215] What Schiller wants is a 'complete revolution in [the] whole way of feeling', not in modes of action.[216] As far as Marx is concerned, he undoubtedly saw the good future as being aesthetically satisfying and the aesthetic capacity in general as important to human well-being. But that did not occupy the same pivotal role in his conception of human fulfillment as it did in Schiller's essay.

Marx did owe a debt to German aesthetics which was distinct from his debt to Hegel's philosophy of history or categories of thought, and that debt lay in his concept of creativity. As we have seen, Hegel's view of the creative process was that it tended to arise from a sense of lack or alienation, was often accompanied by selfishness and unhappiness, and inevitably led to opposition. Marx applied this view to the impersonal development of history but not to his model of truly free individual activity.

Here he adopted the ideas of Kant, Fichte or Schiller (in a work like *On Naive and Sentimental Poetry*), for all of whom there was an indissoluble bond between the creative and the moral. When Marx and his contemporaries began reworking Hegel's ideas in the 1840s they adopted Fichte's notion of creative action as a lucid, conscious and emphatically moral process.[217] In the writings of Cieszkowski, Hess and Edgar Bauer, there is a repeated attention to 'conscious' making,[218] (which has led to the comment that these writers should be called 'Young Fichteans' rather than 'Young Hegelians').[219] The same is true of Marx's account of the future realm of freedom. For him, as for Fichte, creativity and alienation are antithetical, freedom even being seen, on occasion, as a form of parthenogenesis ('my life is necessarily dependent on something external unless it is my own creation')[220] and true self-realization as intrinsically moral. From this perspective, if we are all creative we will all live in harmony. Although there are instances where he seems to admit that matters could be otherwise,[221] (and irrespective of the fact that some of his ideas about the future realm of freedom altered between the 1840s and 1860s), Marx does not appear to have changed his commitment to this idea. He did not question it, as Feuerbach did implicitly,[222] nor take account of the way Stirner attacked it explicitly (p.221).

At the centre of Marx's thought there are a number of puzzling features. Why should the *Produktionsweisen* exert so fundamental a role in explaining forms of society and historical change? Why had Marx so little appreciation of the importance of particular identity — individual, regional or national? How could the opportunity for us all to be creative remove social conflict to such an extent that individual rights will be superfluous and politics unnecessary? One answer to all these questions may be found in an awareness not just of the central place which the creative capacity occupied in Marx's thought, but (more especially) the form which his concept of creativity took. In fact, to understand this is to have a solution to the riddle of Marxism, in the sense that this can both unravel odd features of his thought and help to explain its grandeur and powerful appeal.

Marx was not alone is seeing the future as a time when general happiness would mean the flowering of all human capacities. The same was true of Fourier, Owen and the latter's associate William Thompson. Fourier envisaged a vast increase in the number of new Homers and Molières; in a world population of three billion he calculated that there would be 37 million of each.[223] Owen predicted a situation which would not only 'afford full scope for all the physical and intellectual powers of our nature', but one where 'new mental powers will be created'.[224] William Thompson saw a future in which (as co-operation replaced competition) each individual's faculties would become 'productive to the utmost' and lead to a dramatic rise in the amount of invention.[225] This was a new element in Utopian thought and it was a reflection of the central place which (during this period) creativity was coming to occupy as a human value. On this matter, as on so many others, Marx was both typical and extraordinary. His account of the natural and historical worlds as products of human making gave the most comprehensive explanation of why this value should now be central; and he put the exercise of this capacity at the heart of his image of the future.

As we know, Marx was a relentless opponent of all kinds of idealism and a merciless critic of that elite world which Coleridge or Arnold wanted to nurture and protect. Nothing could justify a situation where the majority had so little freedom, where injustice was so pervasive. When true freedom and justice came into being such distinctions would vanish, because the need for spiritual enclaves of that kind would no longer exist. But these hopes were not to be realized. Although the number of analyses and explanations for this outcome is such that by now the carcass of Marx's thought seems to have been picked bare, the aspect which is our concern here has been overlooked. Among the reasons why the future which Marx envisaged could not materialize was the fact that his notion of creativity was the same idealized view that we have seen in his German predecessors and in Coleridge or Arnold; it was of course broader, but it was no less flawed.

CHAPTER TEN

Radiant twilight

I

In the beginning European history had been good. For a short but magnificent moment — in fifth century B.C. Athens — humanity seemed to have realized its potential. As change in the 19th century became more disruptive, and the shape of the future more obscure, a counter-image of this kind had obvious appeal. Whether it was Arnold, concerned with culture, or Marx, looking for true democracy, classical Athens gave examples which showed that their ideals were not utopian. It is true that there were dark patches on the image — the existence of slavery, suggestions of pederasty, the distressingly amoral conduct of the Greek gods — but these were minor blemishes compared with the building of the Parthenon, the tragedies of Sophocles, or the career of Pericles. To know about these achievements, to see European civilization as built on these foundations, became a sign of true culture and the aim of good education. In a suitably Christianized form this image was transmitted to the young as the best possible hope for the future.

The central values of this classical ideal were harmony and balance. They were evident in the Delphic injunction 'Nothing in excess' or the Aristotelian concern for the (golden) mean, the 'calm greatness and noble simplicity' which Winckelmann had seen in Greek sculpture or the perfect proportions of Doric architecture which for Curtius reflected Greek character,[1] the joint attention to physical excellence and mental agility in Greek education or the integration of the individual into the community in Athenian society, with its combination of personal responsibility ('Know thyself') and public duty (described in Pericles' Funeral Oration). These values were seen as having been systematized and given their most exalted expression in that identity of the true, the beautiful and the good which formed the heart of Plato's philosophy. For Plato himself such an identity could exist fully only in the transcendent realm of the Forms; for 19th century scholars they had been realized once in history. But as metaphysics had (since Hegel) become historical this difference was hardly surprising.

Given the amount of attention paid to the classical world there was, of course, dissent from this view. Neither Grote writing about fifth century thought and politics, nor Preller discussing Greek mythology, agreed with the prevailing image.[2] But the works in which their arguments occurred were not animated by the desire to reject the classical ideal entirely. That only happened in 1872 when Nietzsche, then a twenty-eight year old Professor of Classical Philology at Basel, published *The Birth of Tragedy* and (for private circulation) his *Five Prefaces*. Nietzsche admired the Greeks as much as his predecessors and contemporaries, but for diametrically opposed reasons. Where they regarded Socrates as exemplary, the man who in his dedication to the truth had sacrificed his own life, Nietzsche saw him as a symptom of incipient decline. Where others were happy to belong to a philosophical tradition that went back to Plato, with his imposing metaphysics and his union of the aesthetic and the moral, Nietzsche was convinced that all transcendent belief was drastically mistaken and that the beautiful had nothing to do with the good. His two overriding convictions at this stage in his life were of the absolute value of art — 'the real metaphysical activity'[3] — and of the radical distinction between creative cause and aesthetic effect.

The Birth of Tragedy described tragic drama as the outcome of two forces, Dionysian and Apollonian, which were characterized by Nietzsche in ways which we do not need to examine here. What was most striking about the work (for our purposes) was its emphasis on the productive power of the dark, physical and painful. The Greeks created artistic masterpieces not out of serene insight and harmonious living, but, on the contrary, out of their perception of the 'horrors and terrors of existence', their acute need to overcome the 'eternal suffering', that 'eternal contradiction [which is] the father of things'.[4] The intensity of this pessimistic awareness might have overwhelmed them, but in fact they had been able to master it, first by creating their mythology, the Olympian deities (especially as portrayed in the Homeric poems), and secondly by their tragic drama. This combined music and poetry, impersonal chorus and isolated, mythical characters, to embody a vision of heroic endurance which both expressed the deep truth about reality and yet by its artistic form transcended that, and so provided redemption from it. The driving force, the impulse to create, was unaesthetic,[5] but the end-product was beautiful. In this way the Greeks had shown how art can provide a 'metaphysical supplement' to overcome nature.[6]

The tragedies of Aeschylus and Sophocles had achieved this kind of redemption. With the appearance of Socrates, however, and his insistence on everything being rationally analyzed and consciously understood, the ability to create such works had been lost. In the plays of Euripides, who had written under Socrates' influence, the loss was evident. 'Among all productive   people   the   instinct   [is]   the   affirmative,   creative power;...consciousness [is] critical and discouraging'.[7] For this reason the much-praised Greek 'serenity' had been unproductive,[8] and the continuation of philosophy along the lines set by Socrates had been a disaster. 'Art is more powerful than knowledge because it wants life.'[9] When the drive to know replaced the instinct for art the decline of European culture had begun.

In writing *The Birth of Tragedy* Nietzsche had made use of Schopenhauer's notion of life being propelled forward, like an ocean current, by an unconscious, impersonal will; on its surface floated conscious ideas, sharply delineated and clearly visible, but powerless to affect the speed or direction of the current. This view appealed to him because of its naturalism and pessimism, and also because of the special place which Schopenhauer gave to art, especially music. Nietzsche's application of these ideas to the Greek world was brilliantly illuminating, but it is doubtful whether this influence on its own would have given the work its coherence. That was due as much to his personal contact with the consummate man of the theatre, amateur classical scholar, musician and genius — Richard Wagner. From the time he read the piano scores and then heard performances of *Tristan und Isolde* and *Die Meistersinger*, Nietzsche had been a devotee of Wagner's music, and his move to Basel brought him close enough to the composer's home at that time (on Lake Lucerne) for frequent visits. The two men shared a hostility to the contemporary world and an admiration for Aeschylus' plays, Schopenhauer's philosophy, and Wagner's music; over the three years preceding the publication of *The Birth of Tragedy* they were in close contact.

While the impact of Wagner's works indicated to Nietzsche how life could be redeemed by art, the experience of Wagner as a person gave him ample evidence of how those works came into being, the different matter of creativity. The composer was utterly single-minded in the pursuit of his art, dedicated to a vision of a new kind of opera. He was also completely egotistical, unscrupulous and (if necessary) dishonest, in his ambition to achieve that; he once observed that he had only been able to fulfill his artistic calling by denying his moral self.[10] When Nietzsche made a distinction between a selfishly motivated artist and a true one, whose labours are impersonal — 'redeemed from individual will'[11] — and therefore immune to moral criteria, he was drawing on his knowledge of Wagner. This was also the case when he wrote about Aeschylus' Prometheus having 'the marvellous capacity of great genius...the harsh pride of the artist', accomplishing his aims with superb audacity, yet at the cost of immense suffering.[12] Unlike the Judaic Fall, in which humans went astray through weakness, the Promethean Fall had been an active sin, and was praised as such by Nietzsche. The Titan was not seduced, he chose to steal the fire. That he should suffer and be punished for this was inevitable; but that he performed his life-enhancing deed nevertheless, in the face of this penalty, made him exemplary. His 'glory of action' showed the irresistible power of the creative impulse.[13] In great tragedy we experience something of the same elemental 'fruitfulness' and 'productive joy',[14] an affirmation which is great because obtained at such cost.

The Birth of Tragedy dealt with this subject mainly in terms of metaphysics *à la* Schopenhauer and mythology *à la* Wagner. But Nietzsche also wrote two essays about ancient Greece, printed in his *Five Prefaces*, which dealt with the matter in a more directly historical manner. In 'The Greek State' he quoted Plutarch's distinction of the maker and the work (p.57) and then explained how this awareness of the gap between the beautiful and the conditions of its production stemmed not only from a (religious and metaphysical) sense of the horror of existence, but from a brutal social fact: there is no culture without slavery and cruelty.[15] 'This [truth] is the vulture gnawing at the liver of the Promethean promoter of culture.'[16] The Greeks were great because they did not just accept this fact, but welcomed it. In 'Homer's Contest' Nietzsche described their pleasure in conflict and destruction, their approval of rivalry and envy as stimulants to competition, their esteem for the ambition to be first and best[17] (like Achilles). There is 'a mysterious connection…between the battlefield and the work of art'; the aggressive and combative drives are in times of peace turned inwards and become the seeds of genius.[18] In subsequent notes he described the key to Greek achievement as residing in the qualities which Homer had portrayed — their pleasure in cunning, revenge, envy, invective and obscenity — and in their refusal to make a division between good and evil.[19] They were a people of genius who were both as naive as children and as cruel as adults.[20] By his own analysis they had genius because of these characteristics.

As well as being embodied in epic poetry and tragic drama these qualities had also occupied a place in pre-Socratic philosophy, above all in that of Heraclitus. Proud and isolated, gifted with extraordinary intuitive insight, Heraclitus had performed the true philosophical task: 'to allow the whole sound of the world resonate inside him, and then bring that forth as concepts'.[21] What he perceived was the impermanence of all reality and the productive power of conflict.[22] These insights had been possible because he had lived at a time when philosophy was still an integral part of a whole culture, when thought could express a philosopher's character as much as his ideas.[23] After Socrates, this had no longer been the case. Philosophers had become exiles, the spiritual had been separated from the physical, and ideas had been detached from the thinking person. In this field too genius had disappeared; instead, there was merely scholarship.[24]

This historical perspective placed Nietzsche himself in an awkward position. He was at this time, and throughout his life, convinced that any society had value insofar as it allowed for the appearance of genius. 'The goal of all culture', he wrote, is 'the production of genius'; 'my religion...lies in working for the production of genius'.[25] This belief caused him no difficulties as long as he was working for the recognition of Wagner's genius. But after the composer moved to Bayreuth to inaugurate his festival theatre he became increasingly involved in political issues. From being an opponent of contemporary reality he became a spokesman for German greatness; instead of living in proud isolation, he became part of a world which Nietzsche detested and in which there was no place for him. This precipitated a breach between the two men. Since the composer had (as a genius) become something more than a father-figure to Nietzsche, and his wife (as a young woman) something more than a mother-figure, the break-up was painful.

But the fault did not only lie with Wagner; the wound was also self-inflicted. As Wotan gave up an eye (and Alberich renounced love) to obtain power, so Nietzsche rejected Wagner in order to remake philosophy. He gave up the passive delight of being in the audience, sitting silently in the dark, spell-bound by the music, because he had begun to move away from the pessimism which made an experience of that kind satisfying. Just as Wagner himself had once abandoned his revolutionary hopes and turned to Schopenhauer, so now Nietzsche detached himself from Wagner to make his own revolution, in thought. Although his university post at Basel was in classical studies his own inclinations had drawn him towards philosophy. At the same time he had felt increasingly dissatisfied with philosophy in terms of knowledge, since that seemed inert and pallid. In pre-Socratic thought, as in Wagnerian music-drama, he felt in contact with something more comprehensive and profound. Before Socrates had turned philosophy into theory it had been alive: 'everything for the Greeks was living; with us it remains knowledge'.[26] There was an immense difference between these two, one which (Nietzsche was later to observe) had been recognized in the Book of Genesis by the fact that in the garden of Eden there had been a tree of knowledge distinct from the tree of life.[27]

The solution to this problem came with his perception that there is no true knowledge which is not itself created. There is no truth independent of what human beings construct. To know what things 'really' are is beyond our powers; language does not give us 'things themselves', only 'metaphors of things'.[28] There is an absolute gulf between the human and the non-human worlds; language does not bridge that gap, it merely provides us with a means of communication among ourselves. What we generally call truth is just the result of uniform agreement among 'the mass of metaphors, metonymies [and] anthropomorphisms'[29] which constitute language, and on which all our ideas depend. Developing this insight Nietzsche then asserted that our fundamental drive is that of forming metaphors, and instead of

lamenting the inadequacy (or aridity) of knowledge, we should recognize
that a human being has a unique capacity, 'a powerful genius to construct',
as an 'artistically creative subject'.[30] The philosopher, therefore, not only
has opportunity to be inventive; if he is to measure up to the implications of
this view he *must* be inventive. For Nietzsche, the realization of this fact
was a liberation: 'Not in *knowing,* [but] in *creating* lies our salvation!'[31]
The rest of his active mental life was devoted to elaborating this idea.

In itself the notion that only the maker knows was not new. It had
occurred in neo-Platonic thought and Christian theology and had (in
different ways) between central to the philosophies of Vico, Kant and
Hegel. With Nietzsche it took on new significance, for four reasons. Firstly,
his radical scepticism about the limits of language meant that all knowledge
was rootless and could have only a provisional character. Secondly, he
agreed with Heraclitus that everything is impermanent; there is no being,
only becoming, and as a result there is a constant need for the new. Thirdly,
the process of significant innovation was (as we have seen) perceived as
necessarily contestatory and amoral. But (fourthly) it was inherently
valuable in itself, precisely because it was creative.

We can see therefore that while Nietzsche shared the 19th century
belief in creativity as a value, he did so in a distinctly new way. While
Arnold and Marx saw the creative attribute as exemplary to a large extent
because they believed it also to be moral, Nietzsche regarded it as
supremely important despite (or because of) being amoral. While Hegel had
also viewed creativity in this light (as amoral), but maintained therefore that
the claims of creative as such must be moderated (seen only as a means
towards ethical existence), Nietzsche insisted, on the contrary, that it was
the claims of morality which must be denied. Just as 'being' is a fiction and
metaphysics an illusion, so the 'good' is harmful. In the name of creativity,
which for him meant an outstandingly creative individual, morality must be
replaced by a 'revaluation of all values'.[32]

Nietzsche's observations about language, and his recognition that 'in
creating lies our salvation', were written shortly after the publication of *The
Birth of Tragedy*; over the following years he developed and brought
together different strands of his thought to form the concept of a supremely
creative person (which he sometimes called the *Übermensch*), whose
existence could give meaning to life.[33] To do this he had to break free not
only of his early mentors, but of the German philosophical tradition in
which he had been educated. One way he did this was by exploring other
areas of thought (like French writers and moralists — Montaigne, La
Rochefoucauld, Stendhal) and by developing the implications of
Darwinism. The aspect of *The Origin of Species* which caused most alarm
to his contemporaries — the evolution of the human out of the animal —

was for Nietzsche a cause of delight; it destroyed the dualism of body and mind and showed the latter to be secondary and derivative. There could be no validity to any mental phenomenon that was not compatible with physical reality: thoughts are 'the shadows of our feelings', and 'soul is only a word for an aspect of the body'.[34] The sciences now, he wrote in 1878, have 'point by point taken up the threads of Epicurus' philosophy'; Epicurus 'still lives'.[35] As the latter had opposed Plato, so Darwin provided Nietzsche with arguments to attack two of his *bêtes noires* — Christianity and Kantianism.

In addition to its attention to physicality, Darwin's thought coincided with that of Epicurus in its emphasis on conflict in the development of new forms of life, in the role it attributed to chance, and in its overall perception of nature as indifferent. On none of these points did Nietzsche owe a special debt to Darwin, since the productive benefits of struggle was a commonplace of German thought and Schopenhauer had already persuaded him of the validity of the other ideas. But Darwin's account of the ever-changing character of nature, of the provisional status of all hierarchy and value, confirmed Nietzsche's insight into the makeshift and relative character of language; and it may also have sharpened his sense that life could have no meaning except that which humans beings themselves gave it.

The Darwinian perspective could induce a sense of helplessness and the futility of life, and there are passages in Nietzsche's writings which seem to convey this.[36] But he was saved from such a reaction by his feeling for nature's energy, abundance, prodigality.[37] On this subject he took issue with Epicurus. The latter had merely accepted the human condition; his philosophy was like a calming medicine, concerned with minimising pain.[38] It had not affirmed life in the way that Nietzsche insisted must be done. In place of his earlier pessimism he now believed in saying 'Yes' to life, in demonstrating human greatness in spite of, and in defiance at, nature's indifference. This occurred most evidently when nature's energy was harnessed and used by a gifted individual, as creativity.

Because of his belief in this kind of greatness Nietzsche also came to disagree with Darwin. The latter saw the struggle for existence as a matter of survival; in this process those with qualities most suitable to new conditions are those who come to be the strongest, and they enable the species to survive in an improved (i.e. better adapted) form. In Nietzsche's view the evidence of history showed the opposite to be the case: the strongest were generally defeated and as a result those who followed were inferior.[39] In his studies on ancient Greece he had given one example of such an evolution for the worse. In his subsequent writings he showed how this had been the case with European civilization in general. By using the

Darwinian method, delineating stages of development by which an original entity had been altered into something completely different, he demonstrated an anti-Darwinian outcome, not the development of civilisation out of barbarism, but the destruction of greatness by morality.

His most systematic account of this evolution, *On the Genealogy of Morals* (1887), describes how aristocratic values had come to be replaced by the rule of the 'herd instinct', in the form of what he called 'slave morality'.[40] Aristocratic values had been the expression of strong, healthy individuals who rejoiced in a 'triumphal affirmation of themselves', showing their superiority in 'war, adventure, hunting, dancing, [and] contests'.[41] They displayed the daring, restlessness and disregard for the fate of others which, according to Thucydides, the Athenians had possessed and which Nietzsche saw as having been reborn with Napoleon, 'this synthesis of the inhuman and superhuman (*Unmensch und Übermensch*)'.[42] In the completeness with which they had manifested 'the truly active emotions, like the drive to dominate [and] to possess', such individuals had realized to the full the 'actual will to life, which aims at power...at creating ever larger units of power'.[43] But they had also engendered a bitter sense of inferiority among the weak. Out of revenge and resentment the latter had therefore devised moral rules and common values which had thwarted the powerful and repressed all natural instincts. This 'sickly softening and moralizing' of humanity,[44] in which the life-affirming qualities had been turned inwards (against life), had begun with the Jews and been carried forward by the Christians; it had reached an extreme stage in German Protestantism and Kantian ethics. In erecting their ideal of the good the priests and philosophers had put a curse on mankind; what they called moral improvement was in fact degeneration.

'But he must come to us', exclaimed Nietzsche, 'the redeeming figure of great love and contempt, the creative spirit...This man of the future, who will redeem us from the ideal which has prevailed up to now,...will liberate the will once more [and] give back to the earth its purpose and to humans their hope'.[45] What he meant by this was described in *Thus spoke Zarathustra* (1883–85), where he writes about greatness in terms of the *Übermensch* — a strong, isolated individual whose 'creating, willing, valuing ego...is the measure and value of things'.[46] His three attributes (of willing, creating and valuing) were different aspects of a single energy, 'the will to power, the inexhaustible productive will of life'.[47] Someone who could 'remain true' to the earth and to the body[48] expressed and vindicated this life-force (which is what Nietzsche meant by giving back to the earth its purpose); if sufficiently gifted, such a person could also realize the specifically human form of willing, in being creative.[49] Since there is no God or anything else beyond this life, since everything is in flux, and since each body is unique, the most complete employment of such ability must be entirely self-generated, not only in terms of energy but also as value. So willing becomes creating which is also valuing. The 'higher men' whom Zarathustra addressed were 'creators' and he himself was 'a visionary, a willer, a creator, a future himself and a bridge to the future'.[50] He was exemplary in showing how life should be lived; by so doing, he pointed the way ahead.

However, he did not do more than point; he was only a bridge. If he had shown not just how to proceed but also where to arrive he would have set up a new goal or ideal,[51] and so limited his own future activity. While in his first writings Nietzsche had seen redemption in the aesthetic work of art, he how saw it achieved purely by being creative. 'To create — that is the great redemption from suffering'.[52] This activity alone can fulfill a life and justify life. In one of his notebooks he asked, 'How have I endured [life]?', and replied 'By creating'.[53]

It will by now be clear that Nietzsche's account of creativity was in effect a recovery of what I have called the lost tradition. Coming to his writings after the enquiry recorded in this book is like hearing a recapitulation of its opening theme. In his work all the elements of the lost tradition were recognized: multiplicity, physicality, restlessness, disorder and conflict. He celebrated the defiant ambition of Prometheus, the lion-hearted daring of Achilles, and chameleon versatility like that of Odysseus.[54] He admired the polytheistic and the Protean.[55] His statement that 'the terms "autonomous" and "moral (*sittlich*)" are mutually exclusive'[56] could have been an echo of the chorus in Sophocles' *Antigone* (p.18); he cited Thucydides on the causes of Athenian greatness (p.33), and he had words of praise for Alcibiades and Caesar.[57] He emphasized the roots which make flowers possible (p.34), or the dung that enriches the soil for future harvests (p.111);[58] he associated the creative with storms or sexuality (p.117),[59] with the childlike (pp.113 and 144),[60] the mad (pp.51, 118 and 194) and the criminal (pp.219 and 222).[61] He recognized in Machiavelli a kindred spirit who had delineated the true features of (creative) *virtù* — its boldness, its use of cunning and dissimulation, its mixture of animal instinct and human insight.[62] Although he seems to have read little Diderot, he delighted in the works of the latter's friend Galiani (who had been one of the inspirations for *Le Neveu de Rameau*).[63] Above all, he looked to Goethe as the richest embodiment of human creativity.[64]

The most important step to seeing this attribute in its true light was to recognize its utter incompatibility with the morally good. Again and again Nietzsche insisted on this point: 'look at the good and the just. Whom do they hate the most?...The creative';[65] 'the good...are *incapable* of creating'.[66] The relationship between the true, the good and the beautiful is one of antagonism.[67] He ridiculed Kant for falling into the ergonic fallacy,[68] and echoed him (sarcastically) when he pointed out that there were no people of any interest in heaven.[69] An example of such idealistic nonsense was the notion of the higher man being half saint and half genius.[70] For him, the higher man must be the exact opposite of a saint — hard, powerful, contemptuous of others, attentive to his own energies and insights, and able to draw on the immense bounty of '*chaos sive Natura*',[71] that primordial turmoil from which all life stems.

II

In his essay *On Naïve and Sentimental Poetry* (1795/6) Schiller stated that 'we know little of the private life of great geniuses', but what we do know confirms our intimations that they were moral, chaste, modest and altogether exemplary in their conduct.[72] When he wrote this the first part of his statement was true; only with the publication of Rousseau's *Confessions* (1782–89) and Boswell's *Life of Johnson* (1791) did the private, as distinct from professional, life of writers start to become matters of general interest.[73] But even allowing for scarcity of information the second part of Schiller's statement is surprising, given the amount of evidence which appeared to suggest otherwise. It is true that where details of a life are not available we must be cautious about making inferences based on the works. It is also true that when details of a life are available they may conform to certain stereotypes,[74] and, to the extent that they are autobiographical, they may not be any more reliable than the works; which likeness is true in a hall of mirrors? But even making allowance for these limiting factors Schiller's remark was ill-informed.

Within a generation it had also become anachronistic, because by then a writer of undoubted genius had become famous as much for his scandalous conduct as for the brilliance of his poetry. Byron established his reputation with the publication of the first part of *Childe Harold's Pilgrimage* (1812); four years later the break-up of his marriage, and the circumstances leading to his departure from Britain, made him notorious. His subsequent publications confirmed his eminence as a writer, while his death in Greece gave him iconic status. 'Since the Thunderer sank to night in Missolonghi's fatal marsh, the intellectual throne has remained vacant', wrote the young Disraeli;[75] and Macaulay observed (in 1831) that Byron was the most celebrated Englishman of the 19th century.[76] For the latter, however, this reputation was not deserved; his brilliance as a poet could not outweigh the bad influence he had had, encouraging a belief that 'the two great commandments were, to hate your neighbour and to love your neighbour's wife'.[77] This judgement, recognising the ability but deploring the immorality, was a common reaction to Byron's work and it was the result either of conflating the life and the work or of hostility to distinct features of the poetry. For Hazlitt, for example, the poetry suffered from a morbid elegance which arose from 'a mind preying upon itself', the way in which Byron was 'self-dependent',[78] as if (citing Shakespeare) 'a man were author of himself / And knew no other kin'.[79] For others the antagonism was to the way his verse portrayed the universe as indifferent to human striving, or how it celebrated those who defied convention — Cain, Don Juan and (of course) Prometheus. In his writings the powers representing the good are never endorsed and the outsider alone can see truth.

Byron's outlaws, wanderers and other free (and lonely) spirits were in good literary company, because the sense of not belonging — in the world or in a given society — was a common theme in Romantic literature. In France, in the middle years of the century, this association of artistic endeavour with being an outsider came to be formulated in the phrase *la vie de Bohème*, the life of a gypsy. (Mérimée's *Carmen* (on gypsy life) was published in 1845, Murger's *Scènes de la vie de Bohème* (on artistic life in Paris) appeared between 1845 and 1849.)[80] In the eyes of the artistic *bohèmiens* the values of the Parisian bourgeoisie — their obsession with money, their belief in progress, their sanctimonious and censorious attitude to anything beyond their own limited experience — meant that that society could only be rejected entirely.

Action against such a society could take a number of forms. The most thorough-going was revolution, which occurred in 1848 but the achievements of which were soon overturned. The most immediate was crime, and in his *Père Goriot* (1835) Balzac portrayed a master-criminal, Vautrin, as an embodiment of the spirit of revolt. A man of genius, of profound insight and ferocious energy, of cold calculation and multiple disguise, Vautrin exerts a magnetic spell over the young Rastignac. While his amoral advice — 'there are no principles, there are only events; there are no laws, there are only circumstances'[81] — is chilling, and in his moment of unmasking he seems to be Lucifer reborn,[82] he nevertheless compels our admiration. His energy, daring and resourcefulness, set in relief to (and in opposition against) the mean-spirited world of Goriot's daughters, attains a kind of nobility which justifies his own claim to be 'a great poet', not in verse but 'in actions and feelings'.[83]

This was certainly the verdict of a young writer in 1846. In his review of that year's Salon, Baudelaire discussed heroism in contemporary life. He could see it only in such social misfits as an aristocratic dandy and an underworld criminal like Vautrin.[84] In subsequent writings he explored the interdependence which existed between the diabolical and the angelic,[85] and the duality of artistic temperament, 'the power to be at one and the same time oneself and another'.[86] These perceptions were confirmed by his reading the stories and essays of Edgar Allen Poe — 'this Byron adrift in an evil world'[87] — and he adopted Poe's threefold division of human attributes in which taste, the faculty by which we create and judge beauty, is wholly distinct from those of intellect (for science) and duty (in morality). The terms of the latter are inappropriate and irrelevant to art; poetry aims to be nothing but itself.[88] A poem's validity lay entirely in its own beauty and originality: 'Take us to heaven or hell. Who cares which? / As long as at the heart of the unknown we find the *new*'.[89] The aesthetic equivalent of the criminal, for Baudelaire, was the dandy, 'that supreme incarnation of the idea of beauty, transported into ordinary life'; he was the product of 'a character of opposition and revolt', 'in love above all with distinction'. He was outside the laws because he was above them, not only in his aristocratic disdain for what others might admire, but in his 'burning need' to make himself original. His life was devoted to 'a cult of himself', and for the opinions of others he had nothing but impassive disdain.[90]

The writings of Byron, Balzac's character of Vautrin, and the essays of Baudelaire all located value outside moral norms and social conventions. The status of the outsider was one which they admired, at times even relished, because alienation for them was a precondition for seeing and expressing their individual truth. Instead of being an obstacle to creative fulfilment (as it was for Marx) alienation for them was its necessary precondition. This view was a consequence of two of their basic assumptions: first, that humans are essentially isolated and fulfilment can only be achieved and measured in individual terms; second, that there is no progress, in terms either of some gradual improvement or of any sudden transformation.

Accounts of the *vie de Bohème* have sometimes related its appearance in the mid-19th century to economic developments in France and the actual conditions facing writers and artists at that time in Paris.[91] With the introduction of copyright certain kinds of writing — prose fiction, journalism, plays — could provide a good income, but other kinds (notably poetry) did not. As a result, those engaged in what had previously been regarded as the most exalted form of writing were now, in market conditions, those who were most neglected. On the other hand, the existence of a dynamic market generated a sense of continual possibility, there was extensive freedom of expression, and one legacy of the Revolution was an immense confidence in the power of ideas. In this respect, writers were beneficiaries as well as victims of these new circumstances, a part of this world as well as apart from it. The failure of the 1848 revolution may have contributed to, or reinforced, the sense of art as existing in a realm of its own[92] — in an 'ivory tower', as 'art for art's sake'[93] — but that did not destroy the sense of utter conviction and dedication with which those beliefs were held. On the contrary, to be on the margins of such a society could be seen as a sign of integrity.

To occupy such a position, however, was not perceived as being in any state of grace; it was rather to be a *poète maudit*, under a curse. This was because exclusion and rejection meant that there was nowhere such writers could feel they belonged. Their situation was that depicted in Baudelaire's prose poem *L'Étranger*, which describes an encounter with an 'enigmatic man' who has no family, friends or home and whose only love is the clouds, 'the clouds which drift over...far away...far away...the wonderful clouds'.[94] The word *étranger* can be translated as 'stranger' or 'foreigner' (or 'outsider'), and each of these words conveys the idea of someone who not only does not belong here, but who experiences that condition as one of absence or loss. The poet's power of insight or vision was inextricably bound up with a feeling of something missing; and the more captivating and beautiful the alternative worlds embodied in the poetry (nowhere more strikingly than in *Les Fleurs du mal*) the greater the sense of alienation.

An attempt to overcome this problem was made in a remarkable book published in Berlin in 1844, Max Stirner's *Der Einzige und sein Eigentum*. Literally translated the title means *The Unique One and his Ownership* (or, *his Own*) and the work is a defiant assertion of uniqueness as a self-sufficient value. Applying the criticism Feuerbach had used to undermine Christianity and Hegelianism, Stirner insisted that not only are such abstract concepts as 'goodness' or 'equality' mere projections of individual wishes, but so too are such ideals as Feuerbach's 'humanity' or the 'rational order' of the liberals or the 'social duty' of the socialists.[95] Moreover, these political goals are as unrealisable and as potentially oppressive as the religious beliefs which Feuerbach had attacked. For Stirner, whatever is external or foreign to the individual is an enemy to true life. Value and truth can only lie in what each person creates. Each of us should be 'the creator [and] the judge, who continually creates anew'.[96] Our motto should be not 'Know thyself' but 'Realize yourself (*Verwerte dich!*)'.[97]

This extreme position stemmed from Stirner's view of uniqueness as something which is not given, but made. My basic sense of a self derives from my awareness that I am the 'creator and owner' of what I think;[98] 'I only am myself insofar as I make myself, i.e. no other person makes me but I must be my own work'.[99] We can do this because humans have creative powers; and like all living creatures they need to exercise their powers. To be human means to be active, expressing these capacities in individual ways.[100] Inevitably, this will mean coming into conflict with others and with the laws: 'the unrestrained I...is the perpetual criminal in the state'.[101] But no state, in Stirner's view, can be legitimate. Even words, being secondhand, have something alien about them; and (he continued) 'my own creatures are already foreign to me after the act of creation'.[102] Only works of art may be immune to this problem, inasmuch as they may retain the individuality which generated them.[103]

By making creativity the source of all value[104] (as well as of the individual self) Stirner abolished the problem of alienation. Obviously, the unique person did not belong in society, but by Stirner's definition the very idea of belonging was (like that of 'society') a delusion. I can only be at home with what is entirely mine. In effect, he rewrote the Stoic injunction 'To thine own self be true' by transforming what for the Stoics was given (the evidence and presence of a higher order) into something wholly made. I can only be true to my self by exercising my creative powers to the utmost, making a wholly new and original self. 'I am...the creative nothing,...out of which I myself as creator create everything'.[105] The activity is simultaneously self-constituting and self-justifying.

In Stirner's book these ideas rarely went beyond forceful assertion; in Nietzsche's hands they were developed and deepened with extraordinary flair. The former refused to accept that abstract nouns or words for collective entities were anything more than the fantasies or projections of inadequate individuals, but he provided no arguments to support this view. Nietzsche, by contrast, conducted a relentless attack on metaphysics since Plato, on Christian theology and morality, on Cartesian and Kantian dualism, on teleologies of history and existing political ideologies. The results of this were, initially, drastic; if you conduct a scorched earth policy you end up with nothing to live on. It seemed that we can have no 'truth' to guide us, nor even any 'self' to pursue it. But what this then meant was that there was an overwhelming need to make new truths and to construct our selves. The genealogies of destruction opened the way for the rhapsodies of creation.

The ancient injunction 'Know thyself' had to be replaced, since there was no given self to be known. For Nietzsche the alternative formulation was 'Will a self, in order to become a self',[106] or, more succinctly, 'Become who you are'.[107] Each person, in his account, is a collection of forces; in some people these forces are stronger than in others. The especially gifted person who can harness and direct powerful forces in a distinct fashion can acquire in that process an individual identity, a 'self'. The kind of impersonality Nietzsche had observed in Wagner, or the way in which a work may develop involuntarily,[108] could mean that only through the work did the artist actually achieve a self; in other words, it could be that 'the work invents its creator'.[109] His most evocative statement of this insight occurred in *Beyond Good and Evil*: 'in man, *creature* and *creator* are united; in man there is matter, fragment, excess, clay, mud, madness, chaos; but in man there is also creator, sculptor, the hardness of the hammer, the divine spectator and the seventh day'.[110] The chaos is not a self, but in the exercise of its innate creative power it can become a self; this is the way in which a person could be described as 'self-creating'.[111]

In his inaugural lecture at Basel Nietzsche had attacked the view that genius owes anything to external conditions, and soon after he wrote that a 'productive uniqueness' forms the core of each person.[112] These views informed his later writings. A chaos may not be a self, but its creative powers are quite distinct, unique to this configuration of forces in this individual body. The exercise of these powers, in 'overcoming' the chaos, is the manifestation of the will to power. Zarathustra describes this as follows:

> To redeem the past and to transform every 'It was' into an 'I wanted it thus!' — that alone do I call redemption!
> Will — that is what the liberator and bringer of joy is called...
> Willing liberates...
> I taught you: 'The will is a creator'.
> All 'It was' is a fragment, a riddle, a dreadful chance — until the creative will says to it: 'But I willed it thus!'
> Until the creative will says to it: 'But I will it thus! Thus shall I will it!'[113]

The repetition in these sentences is not only for the variations in tense (past, present, future) but to stress the three different components — the 'I', the 'willing', and the result ('thus') — which could be termed the uniqueness, the action, and the quality. These also provide three separate vindications, in terms of self-reliance (or self-generation), the exercise of the most affirmative element of life (creating), and the achievement of something which commands respect and admiration. Together they produce an instance of greatness.

This greatness could be manifest in works of art (as with Goethe) or in actions (as with Napoleon) or in character (as in both of them). Whatever the form in which distinction was achieved, the creative person was above others, and sole arbiter of what was 'good' or 'right'. For Nietzsche, therefore, there was never a problem about alienation, in part because (like Stirner) he recognized no possible 'home' or place to belong, but more importantly because he did not accept that the creative and non-creative spoke the same language. His own terminology was one of separation, measured by height, with a radical break between the eminent few and the worthless many. The mountain imagery he was fond of using conveyed this attitude perfectly. Not only were very few able to scale the peaks, and then able to see farther than anyone else, but there was also only room for very few at the top.

In the contests at the ancient Olympic games there was only one prize, for the person who came first. The Nietzschean *Übermensch* would be the winner in a similar kind of contest. On this point Nietzsche was absolutely uncompromising; and the determined way in which he worked out the implications of this continues to make his thought shocking. One example of this is the way in which he used the idea of 'economy (*Ökonomie*)' to describe the internal arrangement or organization of an entity and the interdependence of all the elements within it. He applied the concept to both an individual person and to society as a whole. In the individual case he saw that 'in the great economy of the whole' the most terrible impulses or desires, (as also illness or dreams), could be productive and beneficial.[114] With respect to society he put forward (first in 'The Greek State' and then at intervals through his work) the radical notion that there is no culture without slavery and cruelty.[115] High achievement depends on 'darkness,…depth,…evil',[116] in the social as well as the individual dimension. 'The basic phenomenon: countless individuals [are] *sacrificed* for the sake of the few, to make them possible'; the higher man 'needs the opposition of the masses…He stands on them, he lives off them'.[117]

In earlier versions of 'economy' (such as providential ideas of the 'divine economy') the emphasis was usually on balance (or compensation) within an overall harmony.[118] For Nietzsche there should never be an end to struggle and suffering, because that was what produced greatness. Conflict could not end because life itself was an instinct for growth and power, and the overpowering of what was foreign or weak.[119] Given these dynamic and expansive tendencies, the realisation of the will to power by one person inevitably entailed the defeat and subjection of others. Power of this kind cannot exist in isolation; in Nietzsche's view mastery entailed slavery, which is why he called for a renewal of the latter as well as the former, a new slavery as well as a new 'dominating caste'.[120]

Although Nietzsche came to express certain reservations about 'artists',[121] most of the examples of greatness that he gave were of writers, artists, composers. The aristocracy he wanted was a spiritual elite. Individuals of this kind tend to be isolated, enjoying the solitude which Zarathustra welcomes as his home,[122] and this raises the possibility that their power need not depend on the slavery of others. Nietzsche insisted that it does. Every kind of social levelling undermined cultural vitality. Greatness is exceptional, and exceptions need a contrasting rule: 'a high culture is a pyramid; it can only stand on a broad base'.[123] A mass of mediocrity alone enables the great and exceptional to exist. Nietzsche's point here was not merely one of quality being in inverse proportion to quantity; other factors were involved. First, there was what he called the 'pathos of distance':[124] aristocracy demands a gulf between the noble and the rest in order to generate a feeling of distinction, superiority, high calling, great gifts. Secondly, evil and cruelty are beneficial because they are productive: 'almost all that we call culture depends on the spiritualizing and intensification of cruelty'.[125] What he had perceived in the Greeks he here made into a general rule, sometimes referring to it as 'sublimation'.[126] But this was not a process which acted like *katharsis*, obviating the need for actual cruelty. On the contrary, it arose out of the real experience of cruelty, which it intensified (as well as 'deified').[127] This was why he could write of 'a noble mode of thought' as one which 'believes in slavery',[128] and why he called not only for a new 'mighty aristocracy,...philosophical men of power, artist-tyrants',[129] but also for 'collective enterprises in discipline and breeding' and 'the merciless annihilation of all parasites and degenerates'.[130] Underpinning all these views was his notion of economy: 'in the great economy of the whole, the most appalling aspects of reality...are more necessary...than the so-called "good"'.[131]

In addition, in his focus on excellence being *primus super omnes* (or, in the words of a contemporary writer, 'it is not enough to succeed, others must fail').[132] Nietzsche was articulating in an extreme form the problem of significance, that aspect of creativity which distinguishes it from novelty (p.8). Although the heroic individual whom Nietzsche envisaged would be wholly self-sufficient and act according to his own value, the greatness of his achievement depends on how that compares with what others have done. The power Nietzsche was concerned with was that of ideas and beliefs, which do not hold sway because of force but because they articulate certain needs, intimations, aspirations or feelings, within a common network of assumptions and meanings. It is this which produces significance. New ideas can only become significant by engaging with that network, in order to change it. While it may be true that there can be an unlimited number of interpretations,[133] it is not true that there can be an unlimited quantity of significant meanings. We can each have our own perspective, but if that does not go beyond the personal (i.e. if it does not win recognition from others) then it is merely trivial. At any one time only a certain number of perspectives are likely to have some degree of general validity. The quantity of meanings is therefore finite and significance may always have to be contested. It is because a creative work or action (in whatever form) engages with or denies some existing significance, in order to introduce its own, that it is usually disruptive.[134]

In his excited, and only intermittently coherent, conception of the heroic figure who would show mankind 'a new untrodden way to becoming greater',[135] Nietzsche was not confined to an aesthetic model. The will to power, which this figure embodies and harnesses, is not intrinsically aesthetic, any more than the genius of Napoleon was aesthetic. What most characterizes the will to power in human beings is the ability to be creative, and it often seems that what Nietzsche wanted to describe was greatness as sheer creativity. This is what he meant by describing 'the supreme will to power' as 'imposing on *becoming* the character of *being*', something which art — as 'the will to overcome becoming', with its concern for lasting form — could impede.[136] Sheer creativity was 'becoming as invention, [a] willing,...an action, a positing',[137] an innovative force so comprehensive and profound that the present moment becomes everything. The mature Nietzsche is in thrall to this idea, but it is one which is always eluding him. He wants to describe the features, and convey the intoxicating energy, of the creative moment — the vision and the charge, the conviction and the need — building a bridge to who knows where? But it is only a moment, poised between unconscious origin and all-too-specific result, the former being beyond language and the latter needing definite terms (if it is to attain significance) and so threatening to become permanent (and therefore a possible obstacle to further creativity).

Nietzsche lived in a time of heroic enterprises and he sometimes displayed a similar confidence in the future. The twilight, in which the obsequies of the gods and idols were being performed, was for him radiant with the promise of a new dawn. He sang the praises of a new kind of hero who would throw off the past and, like Prometheus, fashion humanity anew.[138] Given the variety of arguments he put forward and positions he supported, (as well as the problems about the status of his unpublished texts),[139] there are many difficulties in assessing exactly what he meant by that. At its outer reaches his thought frays into a number of loose ends. But there is no doubt that in his writings we find the most complete expression and exploration of what I have called the lost tradition about the character of creativity.

Nietzsche did not only recover that; he also took it to the limit. He accentuated to a harsh and unpalatable degree those aspects which had led Goethe to observe that when writing he did not care about the consequences.[140] But while in this way he destroyed every possible link between the creative and the moral, and could be said therefore to have de-moralized the concept, he did not de-aestheticize it. Despite his reservations about the 'artist-type' his thought-world was almost entirely confined within the limits of 19th century *Kultur*. Whereas Marx had wanted to break down the barriers between *Kultur* and *Zivilisation*, mutually transforming both, Nietzsche wanted to intensify and increase to the utmost the distance between them. Each of these men could be seen as the culmination of the two traditions which this study has described. For Marx the future would bring creative fulfilment which will be central to, and synonymous with, social harmony and unity; for Nietzsche creative achievement worthy of the name would entail conflict, domination and subjection. In their writings each conveys a tremendous sense of energy and possibility, like the voice of a *Heldentenor* soaring out above an orchestra of a hundred musicians. But the confidence which inspired them is no longer one which we can share.

CHAPTER ELEVEN

Epilogue: the fire and the fennel-stalk

I

Over the course of the last century, in the Western world, an ever greater number of human attributes came to be crowned with the laurel wreath of 'creativity'. In 1907 Bergson placed humanity in an evolution which was 'creative';[1] in 1911 Schumpeter gave prominence to the entrepreneur and made his role in 'creating' central to economic life;[2] in 1916 Russell redefined the ancient opposition between 'doing' and 'having' as one between being 'creative' and being 'possessive'.[3] In the 1930s books were published on 'creative' mind and intelligence,[4] and Valéry wrote that 'every person creates without knowing it'.[5] Since the 1950s this idea has featured in studies of the brain and language ability,[6] and writers and public figures of an ever wider variety — politicians of right and left,[7] hard-nosed strategists and articulate feminists,[8] people who on almost every other issue have been diametrically opposed — have been at one in wishing to increase opportunities for 'creative' lives.

A number of these uses of the word are (in terms of the definition used in this book) inappropriate. To describe the quasi-automatic functioning of the human brain, or the preconscious acquisition (or generation) of language, as 'creative', is to ignore the role of agency which has always been central to the meaning of the word. But that the use of the word should have become so widespread is itself indicative of important developments, and it seems reasonable to see these in terms of the same factors which (if the account given here is correct) initially gave rise to creativity as a value in the 19th century: scientific and technological advances which gave promise, and were evidence, that new forms of human making were possible, economic conditions which made continual innovation necessary, and a view of the future which made the new itself desirable. With regard to the first, the last century brought achievements which (in 1900) were scarcely imaginable, let alone thought practicable — splitting the atom and releasing immense power, travelling out of the earth's biosphere, decoding the genetic structure of living creatures, developing satellite communications and information technologies. With regard to economics, the benefits of free-market economics came to be widely accepted as it became evident that in conditions of increasing complexity only an open market was efficient enough (in transmitting information), and flexible enough (in fostering innovation), to ensure continuing growth. In addition, there was an expansion of service industries and greater interaction between national economies; together, these accelerated the pace of change and increased the vulnerability of any particular economy, leading to the view that only 'the quick and the creative will survive'.[9]

In this way scientific, technological and economic developments over the last hundred years have intensified and accelerated previous trends. With regard to ideas about the future, on the other hand, the reverse has been the case. The belief in progress (which made the new seem desirable) has come to be undermined in increasingly sombre ways, the horrors of the First World War being succeeded by the enormities of the Second, and ecological constraints now throwing an ever darker shadow over what lies ahead. Yet a limited belief in progress remains, if not historically then personally, for the individual. This is in large part due to that new understanding of human psychology initiated by Freud, in which certain central features of personality came to be seen as amenable to change: 'where id was, there ego shall be'.[10] To some extent this was seen as possible because of the notion that everyone has a 'creative' unconscious,[11] and it has given rise to a new kind of self-improvement, one which is not moral but a matter of psychic health.

Confidence in such a process is due not only to the plausibility of the theories on offer, but also to the contraction of value into the self which has gradually been taking place. Among the reasons for this has been one feature common to many of the technological innovations in this period: from the radio, telephone and motor-car to television, compact discs, computers and their many accessories, a large number of modern inventions has made available in private what previously had to be shared in the company of others. It is no longer necessary to travel together with other people and sit among them in order to see a politician or a football match or a concert. Politics, sport, cultural activities (and much else) are accessible to each of us in isolation. The continual increase in the number of experiences available in the private space has enlarged the sense of individual possibility and, at the same time, undermined the status of much that formerly was shared.

In these circumstances it is no surprise that discussions of Nietzsche's thought now have an entirely different focus and emphasis from those in the years after his death. His first readers lived in a time conscious of its power, which in certain of its forms (capitalist industry, authoritarian and imperialist policies) was inseparable from mastery and domination, and with which some of his own preoccupations seemed fully compatible. In our time the situation has changed comprehensively; we are more concerned now with the way in which almost all certainties have collapsed (epitomized in Nietzsche's statement that 'God is dead'),[12] and with the problematic character both of language and of establishing any objective view (i.e. of going beyond the perspectivism which he described).[13] It seems that the bankruptcy of the rich intellectual capital of Europe, which he announced, has become our inheritance.

However, while these aspects of his analysis may be seen as compelling, Nietzsche's prescription for the future, a new 'mighty aristocracy' (p.223), is entirely out of favour. In place of a realisation of the will to power which is great and heroic, contemporary Nietzscheans envisage solutions which are tame and domestic. For them, the way ahead lies in his statements about life being 'an experiment for the person who seeks to know',[14] or of knowledge itself being 'a world of dangers and victories,…dance and play'.[15] In other words, each of us can and should search out and embody a distinct way of living which is justified in individual terms. To achieve a distinctly personal value in this manner is to exercise and fulfill the capacity 'to be the poets of our life'.[16]

The drastically reduced ambition of such a project (in comparison with that announced in *Thus spoke Zarathustra*) is in part due to, and is itself a manifestation of, that contraction of value into the self mentioned above. As such (and also) it is related to a new kind of emphasis on each self being inescapably and substantially unique. The discovery of the unconscious — as a repository of individual drives and experiences, source of fierce energies and unwelcome fears — has made redundant previous ideas of achieving self-knowledge, since now there is no given self to be known. Instead, there is a new need or aspiration to *make* our own self. Only the individual can perform this activity because only she or he has access to the relevant material. Even shared language may be inadequate to do justice to each person's uniqueness, in which case we must speak in metaphors. But far from being a drawback, this may be an advantage; because uniqueness plus metaphor can equal poetry.

A uniqueness which has aesthetic distinction (which has, in Nietzsche's word, 'style'),[17] is the mark of someone who has become the poet of her or his own life. Since the aesthetic realm both provides the greatest scope for individual freedom and enables individuality to become visible, an ideal of this kind has obvious appeal. But as the number of such 'poets' increases their lives seem ever less interesting. There are many reasons for this. One is the discrepancy between our attitude to art (based on past achievements and the promise which the aesthetic can always offer) and what contemporary art (visual, musical and literary) actually delivers. On one hand, the fact that we have available, at the touch of a button, a vast number of the visual objects, musical works and literary texts which have been produced in earlier centuries, has undermined our *need* for new art. On the other hand, in certain areas (e.g. music and the visual arts) the shared symbolic languages and conventions of the previous five centuries have broken down. As a result there seems to be an abundance of talent — invention, wit and brilliance — but a scarcity of significance.

This situation has important implications for the subject of this study. To define creativity in the way it was understood when it became a value, that is, as innovation which is significant, means that an action or an artefact is not 'creative' if it is of little or no consequence to people other than the agent. It may be imaginative, playful, or dazzling, and valid in those terms; but that value is of a different order from something which, attaining significance, justifies the use of the word creative. A familiar example of this distinction can be seen in the paintings done by children. Since it is rare for such art to hold any interest for anyone beyond the immediate family it is wrong to call it 'creative'. As one expert on childhood, Iona Opie, has observed, 'children aren't really creative...[They] invent nothing. They adapt things...They are Tories of the whole and anarchists of the particular'.[18] Because the children are engaged in art and doing something new (not an exercise in copying), the result of their efforts is called 'creative'. It should rather be called 'individual'.

A similar criticism applies to the ambition of the domestic Nietzscheans to be the poets of their own lives. To realize uniqueness in terms of personal authenticity is not hard to imagine, and may not be difficult to achieve. But doing that need not amount to any more than being the journalist of your own life. To be a poet of this kind, however, and achieve an authenticity which has aesthetic status, is a task of a different order, to which many may feel called but few seem to be chosen. It is not a matter of embodying a personal aesthetic. That may bring satisfaction to the person concerned, but does it win recognition from others? Would it command interest if the agent was unknown (like a poem which is anonymous)? In other words, does it have independent aesthetic status? If not, it is without general significance and therefore not 'creative', only 'individual' or 'novel'.[19]

Nietzsche's conception of a life which was self-created was a new version of that Stoic ideal which (in the modern period) took shape in the writings of Shaftesbury and the German notion of *Bildung*. His links with this tradition are clear from his admiration for the writer he called his 'brother-soul', Emerson;[20] but whereas the latter aspired to a self-realisation which was in harmony with a transcendent and immanent moral order, Nietzsche depicted an integration of discordant elements of the self into a form which was aesthetically compelling. In both cases the activity was akin to parthenogenesis (and at times Nietzsche himself used a neo-Platonic vocabulary of 'overflowing' or 'streaming out of a single fountain').[21] This was because he believed that the activity of shaping the self — whether to an ethical or an aesthetic end — had to be wholly autonomous. However, the move from a moral to an aesthetic framework of value made self-creation an infinitely harder task, since it transformed that from being a realisation of a universal in the particular to the creation of a particularity which aspired to as great a degree of universality as might be attainable.

Nietzsche was fully aware of this problem. It lies at the heart of what is nowadays referred to as his 'elitism'[22] and was a key factor in giving rise to those aspects of his thought which are (to say the least) objectionable. There are excellent reasons for wishing to evade this problem, but the alternative is a notion of self-creation or creative activity which tends to be merely personal and so of little interest to anyone beyond the agent (plus close friends and family), in other words a result which is trivial, (meaning not that it is worthless but of very limited interest). If terms like 'self-realisation' or 'individuation' are used, or the goal is merely one of 'play', no difficulties arise. But to applaud the pursuit of individuality on the supposition that that automatically makes one 'creative' is misleading; it is to stretch the meaning of the word beyond the limits which give it its distinctness.

In addition, the desire to be 'creative' in these contemporary terms is in many respects perpetuating the false expectations of Arnold or Marx. Twenty years ago what was described as 'the grand illusion of American culture' was the belief 'that creativity is necessarily good for you and that contact with works of art is morally improving'.[23] Today this observation could probably be applied to most of the Western world. (For domestic Nietzscheans, of course, the word 'morally' would need to be altered to 'personally' or 'individually', but they would otherwise be riding the crest of the same wave.) This attitude is based on two beliefs: first, that the creative and aesthetic are interlinked, and, second, that each is necessarily beneficial. We have plentiful evidence to be doubtful about both.

The fact that we could put Arnold and Nietzsche in the same lineage derives from their common assumption that cultural and intellectual matters (*Kultur*) are radically different from, and superior to, political and economic concerns (*Zivilisation*). Even more than Arnold Nietzsche despised the political movements of his time and had contempt for financial, commercial or industrial activities. In his ignorance of these fields he fell into the same trap which he had accused Kant of falling into, with regard to art, making no distinction between the origin and the end-result; in other words, he succumbed to the ergonic fallacy himself.[24] (As Kant assumed that the aesthetic harmony of a successfully completed artwork must also have been present in the genius, so Nietzsche supposed that an industrialist was as crass or unattractive as his products.)[25] While he attacked 'cultural philistines' for their superficial attitude to art,[26] most of his own judgements outside the intellectual and cultural sphere were equally superficial. As a result, while he reversed the evaluation of the two traditions — attacking the tradition of the Creator with remorseless brilliance and giving the tradition of creativity more complete expression than had ever occurred before — the effect of his writings was to reinforce the separation between the cultural sphere and that of politics and economics.

The tradition of creativity depicted the creative impulse as amoral, as being (in the words of Blake or Goethe) indifferent to the consequences.[27] At the heart of that impulse is an animating force, which may stem from deep conviction, tenacious need, strong ambition, or something else. Without that force the creative insight would be stillborn, no more than a bright idea. This is not simply because the insight has to be given 'a local habitation and a name',[28] but because it usually has to push aside the known or the conventional to make space for itself and so may be perceived as a threat or danger. Here we come to the heart of what is at issue over whether an action or innovation is significant. The decisive question is not 'Is it new?' but rather 'Does it matter?'. When Nietzsche wrote 'Live dangerously!'[29] he was advocating a life of creative action; he knew that that could only be one of taking risks and violating norms, because there is no other way of putting a shape on the future that will make a difference. For him, the shape was intellectual or aesthetic; for others it can equally well be political or economic. While this latter (economic) dimension has come to be given recognition in recent years the full implications of what that involves seems to pass people by. That is to say, when the adjective 'creative' is applied to economic action there is little scent of danger. But there should be.[30]

This study has argued that creativity became a value as a result of the fundamental changes which occurred in the relationship between human beings and the natural world. Where once people had been dependent on, and derived meaning from, non-human forces, they slowly came to see themselves as makers of their own lives, both materially and (in the broadest sense) morally. In this perspective material independence (the outcome of scientific and technological advances in combination with free market economics) was the precondition for this new kind of human autonomy; that is to say, these new developments came to erode the need for (and efficacy of) non-human sanctions to morality and politics. So the belief arose that 'the exercise of a creative power...is the true function of man' (p.196). Over the second half of the last century, in the Western world, there was an expansion and acceleration of the processes which led to this self-image. The increase in knowledge and power enhanced the sense of human achievement, the result of our own creative ability. Both in the collective and in the singular people became more aware of this capacity.

And because the word 'creative' has had such overwhelmingly positive associations, in European thought, we regard this situation as satisfactory. With those matters which we are not happy about, we do not see the problem arising from an excess of creativity; on the contrary, the general attitude seems to be that the more that people are creative the better it will be for them individually, and the better it will be for us all.

This view rests on three false assumptions. The first is that which the evidence set out in this book puts in doubt, namely, the belief that the human creative attribute is unproblematically benign. The second and third assumptions relate to different types of 'independence', one individual, the other general. With respect to the former, contemporary society offers individuals a high degree of personal freedom; and (as we have seen) the need to *be* individual, to realize a unique self, has become a new kind of imperative. But the very conditions which have made this possible also deny its fulfilment. The social fragmentation which has accompanied this change (the ever more attenuated sense of belonging in a wider society) has undermined the degree of recognition that can validate such uniqueness. At the beginning of the last century the undiscovered country was that which lay within; at the start of this century the vanishing continent is that of collective experience, or common identity, or shared ideals. What we are left with is an increasingly pronounced individualism delivering ever more diminishing returns.

The third false assumption is that human beings as a whole are independent, dwelling in a world entirely of their own making. We have learnt that that is not the case. Just as we rely on our social world for essential aspects of meaning, so we rely on the natural world for our physical survival. We have become conscious of our dependence on natural resources and the limits which these impose on all human enterprises. The view of earth from the Apollo spacecraft was the Archimedean point which made us see everything anew. The longing for infinity, to explore every unknown, to cross the last frontier, not accepting even the sky as the limit, was fulfilled; and the infinite was revealed as dark, cold, and unwelcoming, an immense emptiness in which a few barren rocks seemed to have been thrown at random. We have seen that we belong on earth, and that our survival depends on accepting its finitude.

The modern world distinguished itself from the ancient world by rejecting the authority of the past and installing in its place a belief in the future. As Newton, in framing a theory which would apply to a universe which was infinite, replaced the circle (as the basic geometrical form) with the straight line, so in the late 18th century the conception of history changed from a cyclical model to become one of linear progress. The confidence in human powers which this change demonstrated was also evident in poetry, where the previous aim of imitating nature (or earlier poets) gave way to one of expressing individual perception and ability. This shift has been characterized as a move from an image of the poet as a mirror, reflecting an external reality, to that of the poet as a lamp, shining out with its own power.[31] But what this image overlooked, and what is now our concern, is that the independence of the lamp is an illusion; because its flame depends on the invisible oxygen in the air.

The awareness that our survival in physical terms is fragile and uncertain is matched by our intellectual insecurity. Heirs to Nietzsche's nihilism we have been cut loose from the *terra firma* of continuity with the past and have little idea of where we can find a secure mooring. More than in any previous era our time has (in Habermas's words) 'to create its normativity out of itself'.[32] We have no alternative to making our thought-world and our material and social worlds ourselves. But we have become more aware than ever before of the ambivalent character of much that that involves. There is nothing new in the perception that scientific and technological advances may be dangerous, as the regular retelling of the Frankenstein story shows. Likewise, the knowledge that free market economics can be alarmingly volatile and wasteful (in both human and material terms) is a commonplace. In recent years, however, the phrase which Schumpeter coined to describe this problem — 'creative destruction'[33] — has acquired wider resonance, as we have seen the destructive aspects of our economies affect so much more of our lives, tending to exacerbate inequalities, undermine social cohesion, and threaten ecological survival.

Just as the belief in progress arose when awareness of actual (or possible) material improvement reached a critical mass, so our sense of the dangers which are inherent in the continuation of that improvement may now also be reaching a critical mass. To envisage a future which is no more than an extrapolation of the currently dominant trends is to see a prospect of gradual collective suicide. And it may be that that will be our fate. We will only avoid it by either some wholesale reversion to pre-modern attitudes (which is hard to imagine taking place) or by making the notions of limits and interdependence central to our perceptions and decisions. The first (pre-modern) solution would mean rejecting creativity as a value; the second change would mean that creativity would cease to have the exemplary status which it has come to possess over the last hundred and fifty years. If that were to be the case this book would merely be the first of many obituaries.

It is possible that, since human beings are so clever, solutions to these difficulties will be found and (although this seems less likely) those solutions will then be applied. But for that to happen our values would have to change. In a world in which many forms of life (including our own) could only survive in controlled environments we would esteem resourceful skills of reproduction as highly as (or more highly than) energetic and significant production. We would value the curator as much as (perhaps more than) the creator. And our highest aesthetic admiration would not be for heroic individual achievement — a landscape painted by Van Gogh — but rather for a subtle dialogue with nature — a Japanese garden.

II

Throughout European history one figure above all has been seen as embodying the creative attribute — Prometheus. The way in which people have regarded him has been synonymous with their attitude to, and belief about, creativity. We need, now, to see Prometheus in a new way, that is to say, to see him whole.

He was not only a creature of astonishing courage and daring, of defiance and independence. He also possessed expert knowledge and skill. What we have consistently overlooked is that this knowledge was not simply one about what fire could do. It was also, and equally importantly, about how it could be contained.

Prometheus stole the fire from the gods. How did he do that? By hiding it in a giant fennel-stalk. By that means he was able to carry the fire away from Olympus, down to human beings. It was the fennel-stalk, *ferula communis*, with its soft pith and hard rind, which made his gift possible.[34] The knowledge Prometheus brought us was not only about creative capacity and power; it was also about how to contain it.

Notes

Where no translator is given the translation is my own.

Chapter One

1. M. Shelley, *Frankenstein*, ed. M. Hindle (Harmondsworth, 1992), pp.203 and 28.
2. Ibid., p.46.
3. Ibid., p.47.
4. Ibid., p.54.
5. Ibid., p.97.
6. Ibid., pp.142 and 97.
7. Ibid., p.54.
8. Ibid., p.142.
9. Ibid., p.159.
10. Ibid., p.13.
11. Ibid., p.20.
12. Ibid., p.27.
13. Ibid., p.29.
14. Ibid., p.207.
15. Ibid., p.210.
16. Ibid., p.54
17. It was reinforced by revisions made by Mary Shelley to the third edition (1831) of the novel. See Maurice Hindle's Introduction to his 1992 edition, p.xlvii.
18. *Frankenstein*, p.210.
19. Ibid., p.50.
20. For other discussions of the novel which emphasise this theme see, in addition to the Introduction cited in Note 17, C. Small, *Ariel like a Harpy* (London, 1972) and P. Cantor, *Creature and Creator* (Cambridge, 1984), pp.109ff.
21. B. Disraeli, *Contarini Fleming* (London, 1832), IV, 222.
22. K. Marx, *Grundrisse* (Berlin, 1953), p.507.
23. M. Arnold, 'The Function of Criticism at the Present Time', *Prose Works*, ed. R.H. Super (Ann Arbor, 1960-77), III, 260.The text quoted here is that given when the essay first appeared, initially in the *National Review* (November, 1864) and then in the first two editions (1865 and 1869) of *Essays in Criticism*. In the third edition (1875) of that collection Arnold altered the phrase 'true function' to 'highest function' (see *Prose Works*, III, 530), and that is the version given in Super's edition.
24. Psalms, 24, 1; 100, 3.
25. *Second Treatise of Government*, V, §40; ed. P. Laslett (Cambridge, 1988), p.296.
26. For examples, see entries under 'Creatio', 'Creator' and 'Creatrix' in the *Thesaurus Linguae Latinae*, ed. A. Leski et al. (Leipzig, 1906-9). Lucretius' phrase occurs in *De rerum natura* I, 629 and V, 1362.

27. In the Septuagint (the earlier Greek translation of the Torah and the Prophets) the first sentence of Genesis used the verb *poein*, but that did not allow for a distinction between 'making' and 'creating'.

28. See S.S. Friedman, 'Creativity and the childbirth metaphor', *Feminist Studies* 13 (1987), 49-82, S.M. Gilbert and S. Gubar, *The Madwoman in the Attic* (New Haven, 1979), pp.3ff., and C. Battersby, *Gender and Genius* (London, 1989); on *Frankenstein* see also A.K. Mellor, *Mary Shelley: her life, her fiction, her monsters* (London, 1989), pp.40ff. On this subject see also below Ch.2, note 95.

29. In 18th century discussions of genius this aspect was one feature that was seen to distinguish genius from mere originality; see for example C.A. Helvétius, *De l'Esprit* (1758), Discours IV, Ch.1, note *a*, and I. Kant, *Kritik der Urteilskraft* (1790), § 46; where I use the word 'significant' Kant used the word 'exemplary'. For a modern equivalent of this distinction see A. Rottenberg and C.R Haussman (eds), *The Creativity Question* (Durham, N.C., 1976), p.6, where the distinct features of 'creative' activities are seen as 'newness' and 'value'.

30. See W.K. Wimsatt and M.C. Beardsley, 'The Intentional Fallacy', in W.K. Wimsatt, *The Verbal Icon* (Lexington, 1954), pp.3-18, and W.K. Wimsatt, 'Genesis: a fallacy revisited', in P. Demetz (ed.), *The Discipline of Criticism* (New Haven, 1968), pp.193-225.

31. Psalms, 19, 1; Epistle to the Romans, 1, 20.

32. *Laws*, 889ff; *Timaeus*, 47b-c; Cicero, *De natura deorum*, II, 4, 15-18, 29, 42 and 54; Plotinus, *Enneads*, I, 6, 2-7.

33. Cicero, *De natura deorum*, II, 35 and 37; Seneca, *Epistulae morales*, LXV, 3; Plotinus, V, 8, 1.

34. Euripides, *Suppliants*, 180-83; Aristotle, *Poetics*, 1455a 32; Horace, *Ars poetica*, 102-3, in which formulation – '*Si vis me flere...*(If you want to move me, you must first feel grief yourself)' – it became proverbial.

35. Isocrates, *Nicocles*, 7; Cicero, *Orator*, 132; Quintilian, *Institutio oratoria*, XI, I, 1.

36. T.S. Eliot's essay 'Tradition and the Individual Talent', first published in *The Sacred Wood* (1920) has become the classic statement of this position.

37. The Oxford English Dictionary (2nd. edn., 1989) gives the same definition for both 'creativeness' and 'creativity', namely, 'creative power or faculty; ability to create'.It gives 1820 as the first recorded instance of the former (although it was used by Coleridge in 1796, see Chapter Eight, note 83) and 1875 for the latter.

38. See P. Imbs et al., *Trésor de la langue francaise* (Paris, 1971-94), VI, 444; J. Ritter et al., *Historisches Wörterbuch der Philosophie* (Darmstadt, 1971-), IV, 1195.

Chapter Two

1. The interpretation of myth is, of course, a perenially vexed question. My remarks about creation myths are not intended to be either comprehensive or exclusive, with respect to their meaning. Nor am I suggesting that there is a direct correlation between the myths and subsequent attitudes to creativity in a specific society. I do suggest, however, that there is a continuity of belief about the character of creativity, that the myths reveal certain beliefs which are also evident later, and that the similarities of these beliefs are significant. For a comparable attitude to myth to that used here see W. Burkert, *Structure and History in Greek Mythology and History* (Berkeley, 1979), especially pp.17-23.

2. M. Eliade, *The Quest* (Chicago, 1969), p.163.

3. Ibid., p.159.
4. M. Eliade, *A History of Religious Ideas* vol.1 (Chicago, 1978), p.139 and n.9.
5. Ibid., p.200.
6. M. Eliade, *Patterns in Comparative Religion* (London, 1962), p.75.
7. E.O. Turville-Peter, *Myth and Religion of the North* (London, 1964) pp.35-65.
8. M.L. Ricketts, 'The North American Indian Trickster', *History of Religions* 5 (1966), pp.327 and 340. See more generally, W.J. Hynes et al. (eds), *Mythical Trickster Figures* (Tuscaloosa, 1993).
9. T. Jacobsen, in H. Frankfurt et al., *Before Philosophy* (Harmondsworth, 1961), p.160.
10. M. Eliade, *The Forge and the Crucible* (London, 1962), pp.25, 89-90.
11. See M.L. Ricketts, article cited in n.8, pp..335-41, on the trickster as opponent of the 'high god' or of priestly cults.
12. *Theogony*, 70ff. The manner of their own births was also seen by Hesiod as complementary; see *Theogony*, ed. M.L. West (Oxford, 1966), p.402.
13. Lucian, *Hermotimus*, 20.
14. W. Burkert, *Greek Religion: Archaic and Classical*, tr. J. Raffan (Oxford, 1985), p.141. See also Burkert's comments on Hephaestus as a 'model of all-fashioning creator', p.168.
15. Aristotle, Politics 1341b, tr. E. Barker (Oxford, 1946).
16. Burkert, Greek Religion: Archaic and Classical, p.158.
17. *Iliad*, XXIV, 334; tr. R. Lattimore (Chicago, 1961).
18. *Iliad*, XVIII, 590-93.
19. For Athene, see *Theogony*, 896-97; for Hephaestus, see *Iliad*, XXI, 355; for Hermes, see *Homeric Hymn*, 155. Athene was the daughter of Metis, the goddess who embodied this attribute and whose children could present the severest threat to the stability of Zeus' rule. The hero who epitomised this cunning was Odysseus, one of whose epithets was 'inventive' (*polymechanos*), *Odyssey* I, 205, etc. On this subject generally see M. Detienne and J.-P. Vernant, *Cunning Intelligence in Greek Culture and Society*, tr. J. Lloyd (Hassocks, 1978).
20. Burkert, *Greek Religion: Archaic and Classical*, p.156.
21. Hesiod, *Works and Days*, 77; tr. R. Lattimore (Ann Arbor, 1959).
22. *Theogony*, 925-26; tr. N.O. Brown (New York, 1953).
23. *Iliad*, VIII, 421-22; tr. R. Lattimore.
24. Detienne and Vernant, *Cunning Intelligence in Greek Culture and Society*, p.33.
25. A. Brelich, *Gli eroi greci* (Rome, 1958), pp.166-74.
26. Ibid., pp.99, 299, 305-6.
27. Ibid., pp.282, 298, 300.
28. Ibid., pp.244ff.
29. Ibid., pp.264 and 237.
30. Ibid., pp.255.
31. Ibid., pp.240-44.
32. Ibid., pp.255-59.
33. *Odyssey*, XIX, 395-97.
34. Apollodorus, *Epitome to the Library*, III, 8.
35. Apollodorus, *The Library*, III, 15, 8; Ovid, *Metamorphoses*, VIII, 237ff. The mythical creatures the Telchines and Dactyles provide another example of this combination of inventive abilities as both 'admirable and dangerous', and this has been seen as 'pervad[ing] the Greeks' image of the artist', E. Kris and O. Kurz, *Legend, Myth and Magic in the Image of the Artist* (London, 1979), pp.89-90.

36. Deceitfulness — *Theogony,* 537, 540, 565, etc.; daring — *Prometheus Bound,* 180, 237; for his close links with Hephaestus, see J. Duchemin, *Promethée* (Paris, 1974), pp.42, 55.

37. *Theogony,* 507-616; *Works and Days,* 47-104. See the editions of these works by M.L. West (Oxford, 1966 and 1978 respectively).

38. For a succint discussion of the authorship see D.J. Conacher, *Aeschylus' Prometheus Bound* (Toronto, 1980), pp.141-74.

39. *Protagoras,* 320d.

40. *Theogony,* 563.

41. *Prometheus Bound,* 109-11; 254.

42. See D. Conacher, *Aeschylus' Prometheus Bound,* pp. 84 and 92, and M. Griffith, *Prometheus Bound* (Cambridge, 1983), pp.167 and 178.

43. *Protagoras,* 322c; tr. W.K. Guthrie, *Collected Dialogues* ed. E. Hamilton and H. Cairns (Princeton, 1961).

44. Ibid., 322d. The resolution of the trilogy, of which *Prometheus Bound* is presumed to be the first part, has plausibly been conjectured as depicting Zeus giving justice to humanity: see H. Lloyd-Jones, *The Justice of Zeus* (Berkeley, 1971), pp.99-102.

45. *Birds,* 1545 and 1547.

46. The extent to which Hesiod does in fact do this (as suggested, for example, by B.C. Dietrich, *The Origins of Greek Religion* (Berlin, 1974), p.58) is a matter of dispute; both as to whether the Hesiodic Zeus can be taken to represent justice (see A.W. Adkins, 'Cosmology and Order in Ancient Greece' in *Cosmogony and Ethical Order,* ed. R.W. Lowin and F.E. Reynolds, (Chicago, 1985), pp.55-61), and as to whether Hesiod himself endorsed the view of Zeus he portrayed (see J. Shklar, 'Subversive Genealogies', *Daedalus* 101 (1972), pp.130-36).

47. *Theogony,* 219; also 514, 516.

48. Apollodorus, *The Library,* I, 6, 1. For a philosophical interpreatation of this war see Plato, *Sophist,* 246aff. On the subsequent use and different versions of the Prometheus myth see L. Awad, *The Theme of Prometheus* (Cairo, 1963) and R. Trousson, *Le Thème de Promethée dans la littérature européenne* (Geneva, 1964).

49. *Prometheus Bound,* 936, 963, 1010.

50. B. Knox, *The Heroic Temper* (Berkeley, 1964), pp.22ff.

51. B. Knox, *Oedipus at Thebes* (New Haven, 1957), pp.50, 66, 99, 104.

52. *Antigone,* 332ff.; tr. E.F. Watling (Harmondsworth, 1947).

53. *Mechanoen technas,* glossed by Jebb as 'the inventive quality in his skill'; *Antigone,* ed. R.C. Jebb, (Oxford, 1888), p.76.

54. For a similar reading of this passage see V. Ehrenberg, *Sophocles and Pericles* (Oxford, 1954), pp.60-65. For a refusal to see it in this light see E.A. Havelock, *The Liberal Temper in Greek Politics* (New Haven, 1957), p.407.

55. *Hippolytus,* 916ff.; see *Hippolytus,* ed. W.S. Barrett (Oxford, 1964), p.339; also, on lines 377-378, p.227.

56. *Politics,* 1253a 21.

57. Knox has pointed out how closely the character of Prometheus resembles the Sophoclean hero: *The Heroic Temper,* p.50.

58. *Phaedrus,* 274cff.; tr. R. Hackforth, *Collected Dialogues.*

59. *Politics,* 1277b, 1282a.

60. *Republic,* 601c-e; *Cratylus,* 389a-390b.

61. J.-P. Vernant, *Myth and Thought among the Ancient Greeks* (London, 1983), pp.261ff.

62. *Republic,* 330c. Cicero made a similar observation about poets: in poetry, 'more than in other arts, it somehow happens that everyone finds his own work excellent; so far I

have never known the poet...who did not think himself the best', *Disputationes Tusculanae*, V, 22, 63; tr. J.E. King (London, 1945).

63. *Statesman*, 271d.
64. Ibid., 272a; 273b-c, tr. J.B. Skemp, *Collected Dialogues*.
65. Ibid., 274a.
66. Ibid., 274c-d.
67. P. Vidal-Naquet, 'Plato's Myth of the Statesman', *Journal of Hellenic Studies* 98 (1978), p.139.
68. *Republic*, 363eff., 377d, 379d, 386aff., 392b, 568aff., 598d.
69. Ibid., 424c.
70. *Phaedrus*, 265b. For the novelty of Plato's theory of inspiration see R. Harriot, *Poetry and Criticism before Plato* (London, 1969), pp.50, 78 and 83.
71. *Phaedrus*, 248d-e.
72. *Laws*, 892d, tr. A.E. Taylor, *Collected Dialogues*.
73. See, for example, the *Kulturgeschichte* of Dicaearchus, in A. Lovejoy and G. Boas, *Primitivism and related ideas in Antiquity* (New York, 1935), pp.93-96, and that of Diodorus Siculus, *History*, I, 15; see also T. Cole *Democritus and the Sources of Greek Anthropology* (Ann Arbor, 1967), pp.26 and 33.
74. *Epistulae morales*, XC, 38 and 40.
75. Ibid., XC, 3, 36 and 38.
76. Ibid., XC, 11.
77. Ibid., XC, 24.
78. Ibid., XC, 14, tr. R.M. Gummere (London, 1920).
79. Diogenes Laertius, *Lives of Eminent Philosophers*, X, 32, tr. R.D. Hicks (London, 1925).
80. Ibid.,X, 78.
81. *De rerum natura*, II, 573 and V, 392.
82. Ibid., I, 56, 629 and 632-33; II, 62; V, 186 and 1362.
83. *Sophist*, 246a-c.
84. *De rerum* natura, V, 1091 ff. and 1241 ff.
85. Ibid.,V, 1361 and 1379.
86. Ibid.,V, 1028ff.
87. Ibid.,V, 1031 and 1059-90.
88. Ibid.,V, 1452. C. Bailey translates '*impigrae ... experientia mentis*' as 'inventiveness' in his edition (Oxford, 1947), p.1549.
89. *De rerum natura*, V, 1107, tr. W.H.D. Rouse (London, 1937).
90. Ibid., V, 1105ff. See the comments by C. Bailey ad loc, disputing the reading of the text which would make these men philanthropic (*benigni*).
91. Diogenes Laertius, *Lives*, X, 118-20.
92. Ibid., X, 117.
93. Heraclitus, Fragment 53 (Diels-Kranz); Empedocles, Fragment 17 (Diels-Kranz). Both men also emphasised the importance of the senses, as a means to knowledge, and both wrote in an allusive or poetic way. These are significant facts. It was only by refusing to subordinate the evidence of the senses and the possibilities of language to the demands of rational consistency and clarity that these two men could formulate and express their ideas. Heraclitus, in particular, should perhaps occupy a more prominent place in this history than that suggested here. The reasons for not giving him that are twofold: firstly, the obscurity of his thought, and, secondly, the fact that in the Hellenistic period his ideas were incorporated within a Stoic framework. As a result

the philosophy of Epicurus was of greater importance as the bearer of the belief that disorder and conflict are necessary to production.

94. It surely must be more than a coincidence that it was the Epicurean poet and philosopher Philodemus of Gadara who opposed that aesthetic (most fully evident in Horace's *Ars poetica*) which emphasized the unity of writer and work and the moral function of poetry. While other poets (e.g. Catullus, Ovid, Callimachus) implicitly or explicitly opposed this ideal, only the fragments we have of Philodemus' *On Poems* provides an extended attack on it. For a new version of this text (first published in 1923) see C. Magnoni, *Filodemo: La Poesia V* (Naples, 1993); this has been translated by D. Armstrong in D. Obbink (ed.), *Philodemus and Poetry* (Oxford, 1995), pp.256-69. See also the essays in the same volume by Obbink (pp.189-209) and E. Asmis (pp.15-34 and 148-77).

95. These comments apply to the first version of the Creation Story, Genesis 1, 1-2, 4a. The priority of the male (and subordination or exclusion of the female) was of course a widespread feature of ancient, medieval and early modern European thought. In terms of creativity this was manifest as much in biology or physiology as in theology, as for example in Aristotle's assertion that the decisive form-giving agent in conception was the male semen; see his *Generation of Animals*, 727b 30ff, 729a 11ff, 731b 18ff and 766a 30ff.

96. Psalms, 33, 9. All Biblical quotations are from the Jerusalem Bible.

97. Genesis, 1, 26.

98. Exodus, 3, 14.

99. Psalms, 90, 4.

100. Genesis, 2, 4bff.

101. For a brief account of this material, see the Introduction to *Creation in the Old Testament*, ed. B. Anderson, (London, 1984).

102. Job, 38, 4-33. The interpretation of the final chapters of Job is disputed. For some, Yahweh's replies are not justifications but indications of a supra-human mystery. For a similar reading to that given here, see J.L. Crenshaw, *Studies in Ancient Israelite Wisdom* (New York, 1976), p.31.

103. Isaiah, 29, 16.

104. There are instances of Zeus exercising creative power — in the Orphic cosmology preserved in the Derveni papyrus (possibly sixth century) and the fragmentary speculations of Pherecydes of Syros (sixth century), see G.S. Kirk et al., *The Presocratic Philosophers* (Sec.edn., Cambridge, 1983), pp.31-33, 60ff. But these do not represent the general Greek belief; see W.K. Guthrie, *In the Beginning* (London, 1957). The fact that Zeus' powers were limited also meant that there were doubts as to whether his order would always prevail; see Hesiod, *Theogony,* 886-900; Pindar, *Isthmian Ode,* VIII, 27ff.

105. Diogenes Laertius, *Lives*, VII, 134-136 and 156.

106. Epictetus, *Discourses*, II, 8, 2, tr. P.E. Matheson (Oxford, 1916).

107. Seneca, *Epistulae morales*, XXXI, 6; *De vita beata*, XXIV, 4.

108. Epictetus, *Discourses*, II, 8, 3, and Seneca, *Epistulae*, LXV, 2-3.

109. Epictetus, *Discourses*, III, 22, 20.

110. This idea, derived from *Republic*, 597b-c, was developed by the Middle Platonists and first evident in Cicero, *Orator*, 7ff.; his source was probably Antiochus of Ascalon. See J. Dillon, *The Middle Platonists* (London, 1977), pp.95 and 138, and A.A. Long, *Hellenistic Philosophy* (London, 1974), pp.222-29.

111. *Enneads*, V, 2, 1, 7-9; tr. A.H. Armstrong (London, 1984).

112. See, for example, the comparison of a sculptor acting in the same way as Soul, *Enneads*, V, 8, 1, 34-40. But the emphasis here (and elsewhere) is on the realization of a pre-existing form, not the generation of something new.

113. *Enneads*, V, I, 6, 38.

114. Colossians, 1, 16-17.

115. See T. Bosloper, *The Virgin Birth* (London, 1962), pp.29ff., and 'Virgin Birth' in *The Encyclopedia of Religion*, ed. M. Eliade et al. (New York, 1987), XV, 272-76.

116. Cicero, *De natura deorum*, III, 69 and 75. The problem was much more acute for the Stoics since they had to explain why reason, the presence of *logos* in man, was put to bad use as much as to good. In addition, neither to them nor to neo-Platonists was available the most plausible answer given to Job, namely, that human understanding is inadequate to comprehend the ultimate realities, Job, 33, 12.

117. Lactantius, *De ira* Dei, as quoted in Voltaire, *Dictionnaire philosophique*, ed. C. Mervaud et al., (Oxford, 1994), I, 421, article 'Bien (tout est)'.

118. *Epic of Gilgamesh*, tr. N.K. Sandars (Harmondsworth, 1960), p.63.

119. See, for example, E.A. Speiser, *Genesis* (New York, 1964), p.26.

120. Genesis, 3,1 and 22.

121. J. Bowker, *The Targums and the Rabbinic Literature*, (Cambridge, 1969), p.125.

122. C. Westermann, *Genesis, 1-11: a Commentary,* tr. J.J. Scullion (London, 1984), p.289. 'Cain' can be translated as 'create; see ibid., p.290, and D. McCarthy, *Creation in the Old Testament,* ed. B. Anderson, (London, 1984), p.78. Cain has also been seen as a Prometheus figure; see H. Blumenberg, *Work on Myth*, tr. R.M. Wallace (Cambridge, Mass., 1985), pp.368-71.

123. Genesis, 4, 21-22.

124. Ibid., 4, 12.

125. Ibid., 5, 3.

126. Ibid., 4, 26.

127. See, for example, *A Catholic Commentary on Holy Scripture,* ed. B. Orchard et al., (London, 1953), p.189.

128. Genesis, 6, 2-4.

129. Enoch, 7, 1, as translated in *The Apochryphal Old Testament,* ed. H.F.D. Sparks (Oxford, 1984).

130. Ibid., 8, 1-2.

131. Ibid., 65, 6; 69, 9.

132. Ibid., 9, 6.

133. Ibid., 65, 10.

134. Genesis, 11, 4.

135. R. Davidson, *Genesis1-11* (Cambridge, 1973), pp.35 and 107.

136. In his monumental commentary (see note 122) Claus Westermann opposes the point of view suggested here. He takes issue with those who have seen the tree of knowledge as initiation into magic and the serpent as a trickster figure (pp.237-38). He sees no Promethean theft in the Old Testament, 'no culture hero to rise in revolt against the gods... Civilisation and its effects have a positive emphasis in Israel from the very beginning' (p.343). Yet in detail his commentary supports the position adopted here. The promise 'to be like God' is 'concerned with a divine and unbridled ability to master one's existence', (p.251). What occurs to Eve after she has eaten the apple 'is a sort of magic' (p.240), which involves not only a loss of innocence but also something positive: Adam and Eve now have the knowledge of ability to cover themselves and 'the narrator intends this to indicate progress: they have become clever' (p.251). More precisely, 'what the man and woman do here corresponds

externally to what God does in 2, 8...both "create" something to help the situation' (p.252). These comments undermine Westermann's general position, which is based largely on his reading of 1, 26b and 28b and 12, 1-3. That he sees no discrepancy is due to the fact that he is unaware of the general problem which was so apparent to the Greeks. He writes that in most mythologies the civilising hero 'either takes his stand with the creator or is identified with him' (p.59), which is not merely incorrect but an inversion of much of the evidence.

137. Knight, 'Cosmogony and Order in the Hebrew Tradition', in *Cosmogony and Ethical Order*, ed. R.W. Lowin et al., (Chicago, 1985), p.148.
138. *Enneads*, V, 1, 1, 1-6, tr. A.H. Armstrong (amended).
139. *De civitate Dei*, XXII, 24. See E.R. Dodds, *Pagan and Christian in an Age of Anxiety* (Cambridge, 1965), p.24.
140. *Enneads*, III, 2, 2, 10ff.; *De civitate Dei*, XII, 24.
141. *Enneads*, III, 5, 1.
142. *De civitate Dei*, XII, 26 and XXII, 24.

Chapter Three

1. *Iliad*, XI, 784, tr. R. Lattimore (Chicago, 1951); see also VI, 208.
2. Ibid., IX, 443.
3. Ibid., XI, 653.
4. Ibid., XX, 490; XXI, 214, 314, and 542; XXII, 345 and 418.
5. *Odyssey*, I, 205; V, 203; XI, 60; XI, 405 and 473; tr. R. Lattimore (New York, 1975).
6. Ibid., III, 120-22; IX, 19 and 422; XIX, 203.
7. Ibid., XIII, 291.
8. *Iliad*, XXIV, 41-43.
9. M. Detienne and J.-P. Vernant, *Cunning Intelligence in Greek Culture and Society*, tr. J. Lloyd (Hassocks, 1978), pp.33-37.
10. *Isthmian Ode*, IV, 49-50, tr. L.R.Farrell, *The Works of Pindar* (London, 1930-32).
11. Solon, Fragments 1 and 2, in *Early Greek Political Thought from Homer to the Sophists*, tr. and ed. M. Gagarin and P. Woodruff (Cambridge, 1995), pp.25-26.
12. A.W. Adkins, *Moral Values and Political Behaviour in Ancient Greece* (London, 1972), pp.67ff.
13. Thucydides, *History of the Peloponnesian War*, I, 138, 3, tr. R. Warner (Harmondsworth, 1972), p.117. The literal meaning of the words translated here as 'genius' was 'strength *(hischun)*' and 'power *(dunamei)*', mental qualities which, in conjunction with the innate insight and wisdom also attributed to him in this passage by Thucydides, were synonymous with genius in the modern sense of the word.
14. Plutarch, *De malignitate Herodoti* 869ff, tr. L. Pearson and F.H. Sandbach, *Moralia* (London, 1965).
15. Plutarch, *Themistocles*, 5, 2 and 22, tr. B. Perrin, *Lives* (London, 1915).
16. Thucydides, *History*, 6, 15; Plutarch, *Alcibiades*, 10, 2ff, and see also his *Comparison of Alcibiades and Coriolanus*, 1ff.
17. Thucydides, *History*, 6, 15, 4, tr. Warner, p.418.
18. Aristophanes, *Frogs*, 1431-32.
19. Plutarch, *Alcibiades*, 23, 4, tr. I. Scott-Kilvert, *The Rise and Fall of Athens* (Harmondsworth, 1962), p.267.
20. Thucydides, *History*: on restlessness — 1, 70, 2; 2, 64, 4; 6, 87, 3; on ambition — 3, 87, 8; on novelty — 1, 70, 1; 1, 102, 3.

21. Ibid., 1, 144, 3; 2, 64ff.
22. Ibid., 1, 144,4; 2, 43, 3; 2, 89, 7.
23. Ibid., 1, 70, 1; 1, 74, 2; 1, 90, 1; 1, 91, 5; 1, 102, 3.
24. Ibid., 6, 18, 3ff. V. Ehrenburg, '*Polypragmosyne*: a study in Greek politics', *Journal of Hellenic Studies* 67 (1947), pp.46-67, described this need for action as a 'restless audacity' (p.51), which has a 'Janus-face' (p.53), and of which Odysseus was the archetypical example (p.60).
25. Sophocles, *Oedipus Tyrannos*, 880, tr. R. Fagles.
26. Plato, *Statesman*, 291b-c, tr. J.B. Skemp, *Collected Dialogues* (Princeton, 1963).
27. Aristotle, *Nicomachean Ethics*, 1144a 25 and 1141a 25, tr. W.D. Ross.
28. Ibid., 1181a 1.
29. Aristotle, *Poetics*, 1451b.
30. Isocrates, *Antidosis*, 253ff. (= *Nicocles*, 5ff.). The poets' claim was embodied in myths about Orpheus and Amphion; see Horace, *Ars poetica*, 391ff.
31. Isocrates, *Antidosis*, 255 (= *Nicocles*, 7); Quintilian, *Institutio Oratoria*, XII, 1,1-9. On Isocrates see B. Vickers, *In Defence of Rhetoric* (Oxford, 1988), pp.149ff.
32. H.I. Marrou, *A History of Education in Antiquity*, tr. G. Lamb (London, 1956), p.282. In Rome this statement was attributed to the elder Cato, (*Grammatici Latini*, ed. H. Keil (Leipzig, 1857), I, 310: '*Marcus Porcius Cato dixit litterarum radices amaras esse, fructus iocundiores*'), and was later adapted by Cicero in his *Orator*, 147, tr. H.M. Hubbell (London, 1952), p.421: 'it is with all major arts as it is with trees; their height delights us, but their roots and stems do not (*altitudo nos delectat, radices stirpesque non item*); but the former are not possible without the latter' (translation amended).
33. *De Oratore*, III, lvi, 214-lvii, 217; tr. H. Rackham (London, 1952), pp.171-73.
34. Vickers, *In Defence of Rhetoric*, pp.26-27, 34 and 45-46.
35. See Aristotle, *Rhetoric*, 1388a 10ff. The problem had been foreshadowed in Hesiod's distinction between good and bad *Eris, Works and Days*, 11-29.
36. Tacitus, *Dialogus de oratoribus*, 40; tr. W. Petersen (London, 1946), p.123.
37. Sallust, *Historia*, I, 7, cited in R. Syme, *Sallust* (Berkeley, 1964), p.249 and n. 52.
38. Cicero, *De Officiis*, I, xviii, 26 and I, xix, 64; tr. W. Miller (London, 1913), pp.27 and 67.
39. B. Latini, *La Rettorica*, ed. F. Maggini (Florence, 1915), pp.14-17, translating Cicero's *De Inventione*.
40. Latini, *Li Livres dou Tresor*, ed. F. Carmody (Berkeley, 1948), p.318.
41. Marsilio, *Defensor Pacis*, tr. A. Gewirth (New York, 1956), I, xii, 6.
42. Ibid, I, xii, 2: the command which makes law is given by the '*legis latorem sive factorem*'. The revival of Roman law brought a similar emphasis on human making, e.g. Baldus: '*civitas est quid factibile, et non solum nascitur sed creatur*', P. Riesenburg, 'Civism and Roman Law in 14th century Italian society', *Explorations in Economic History* 7 (1969), p.244; see also, J. Kirschner, '*Civitas sibi faciat civem*: Bartolus' doctrine on the making of a citizen', *Speculum* 47 (1973), pp.694-713, especially 698-99.
43. Quoted in H. Baron, *The Crisis of the Early Italian Renaissance* (Second edn., Princeton, 1966), p.419. Bruni's source was Sallust, *De conjuratione Catilinae*, 7.
44. L.B. Alberti, *Opere volgari*, ed. C. Grayson (Bari, 1960), I, 201 and 132; Cicero's quotation occurs in *De Finibus*, II, xiii, 40.
45. *Defensor Pacis*, I, xvi, 7.
46. Ibid., I, xiii, 3. It is a measure of Marsilio's insight and originality that although he derived this make/value distinction from Aristotle (*Politics* 1277b and 1282a), he re-

interpreted it in the sense in which it had been used by Plato (see p.21), stressing the need to guard against the unreliability of the maker.

47. N. Rubinstein, 'Machiavelli and Florentine republican experience', *Machiavelli and Republicanism*, ed. G. Bock et al. (Cambridge, 1990), p.8.

48. Quoted in D.J. Wilcox, *The Development of Florentine Humanist Historiography* (Cambridge, Mass., 1969), p.76.

49. Alberti, *Opere volgari*, I, 180 and 183. For a similar view of the Romans, see N.J. Gilbert, 'A Letter of Giovanni Dondi dall'Orologio...', *Viator* 8 (1977), pp.334 and 343.

50. Petrarch, *De remediis utriusque fortunae*, quoted in C. Trinkaus, *In our Image and Likeness* (London, 1970), pp.193 and 399. Petrarch's specific subject in this passage was the origin of physical life, i.e. sexuality; but that he had a wider reference in mind can be inferred from his use of the Ciceronian topos (n.32) and from the experience described in his *Secretum*, his difficulty reconciling his desire for fame as a poet with Christian moral requirements.

51. L. Valla, *Oratio...*(1455), quoted in M. Baxandall, *Giotto and the Orators* (Oxford, 1971), pp.118-19 and 176-77.

52. Valla, *On Pleasure: De voluptate*, tr. A.K. Hieatt and M. Lorch (New York, 977), III, vi, 1 (p.258) and III, xxii, 1 (p.290). In similar fashion we can see moves to vindicate anger in the writings of Ficino (*Commentarium in Phedrum*, Summa 31), Pico (*Heptaplus*, IV, 5) and Poliziano (see D. Summers, *Michelangelo and the Language of Art* (Princeton, 1981), p.247).

53. Manetti's biography was included by Vespasiano di Bisticci in his *Vite di Uomini Illustri*, ed. P. d'Ancona et al. (Milan, 1951), pp.259-89; for modern accounts see L. Martines, *The Social World of the Florentine Humanists* (Princeton, 1963), pp.133-38 and 176-90, and H.W. Wittschier, *Giannozzo Manetti: Das Corpus der Orationes* (Cologne, 1968), pp.19ff.

54. G. Manetti, *De dignitate et excellentia hominis*, ed. E.R. Leonard (Padua, 1975), pp.57-58.

55. Ibid., pp.77-78.

56. Ibid., p.91 and pp.92-93.

57. Ibid., pp.59 and 60.

58. G. Gentile, in an article of 1916 reprinted in *Giordano Bruno e il pensiero del rinascimento* (Florence, 1920), pp.153-78, first described this work in these terms, which were adopted by E. Cassirer in his *Individuum und Kosmos in der Philosophie der Renaissance* (Leipzig, 1927), p.88, and expanded by W. Zorn in the first full modern account, *Giannozzo Manetti: seine Stellung in der Renaissance* (Freiburg, 1939). E. Garin drew attention to the patristic antecedents of the work, 'La "Dignitatis Hominis" et la letteratura patristica', *Rinascita* I (1938), pp.102-46 (see especially pp.108-10 and 145-46), while at the same time recognising the importance which Manetti gave to the active life, see *Medievo e rinascimento* (Bari, 1961), p.298. This latter aspect has been stressed by H. Wittschier (n.53) and contested by N. Badaloni, 'Filosofia della mente e filosofia delle arti in G. Manetti', *Critica storica* II (1963), pp.395-450. For recent accounts see Trinkaus, *In our Image and Likeness*, pp.230-58, and *The Scope of Renaissance Humanism* (Ann Arbor, 1983), pp.364-403.

59. *De dignitate*, p.97. All the passages quoted here are from Book III. In his *Vite...*(n.53), pp.260 and 284, Vespasiano described how Manetti's own success, both as a scholar and a politician, aroused extreme envy among his contemporaries.

60. N. Machiavelli, *Il Principe e Discorsi*, ed. S. Bertelli (Milan, 1960), p.98 [Ch.25].

61. Machiavelli, *Arte della guerra*, ed. S. Bertelli (Milan, 1961), p.514.

62. See J.G.A. Pocock, *The Machiavellian Moment* (Princeton, 1975), pp.154 and 166ff.
63. *Il Principe*, p.65 [Ch.15].
64. Ibid., p.92 [Ch.21].
65. Ibid., pp.73-74 [Ch.18].
66. Ibid., p.74 [Ch.18].
67. Ibid., p.73 [Ch.18].
68. Ibid., p.47 [Ch.9].
69. Ibid., p.50 [Ch.10] and p.101 [Ch.25].
70. Ibid., p.72 [Ch.18].
71. Ibid., p.72 [Ch.18].
72. *Discorsi*, p.144 [Bk.I, Ch.6].
73. Ibid., p.384 [III, 1].
74. Ibid., p.458 [III, 25].
75. Ibid., p.463 [III, 28].
76. Ibid., pp.436-37 [III, 16].
77. Ibid., p.123 [I, Proemio].
78. Ibid., p.486 [III, 37].
79. *Il Principe*, p.32 [Ch.6], and see p.97 [Ch.24]; on physical activity pp.63-64 [Ch.14].
80. Ibid., p.53 [Ch.12].
81. Ibid., p.50 [Ch.10].
82. *De officiis*, I, iv, 11-12 and I, xvi, 49-50.
83. Ibid., I, xxv, 85 and *De republica*, II, 42; see Q. Skinner, 'Machiavelli and the pre-humanist origins of republican thought', *Machiavelli and Republicanism*, pp.129ff.
84. *De officiis*, I, xxii, 75-76.
85. Ibid., I, xix, 63. (See Plato, *Menexenus*, 246eff. and *Laches*, 197bff.)
86. *De officiis*, I, xxviii, 101; II, xii, 43 and III, xvii, 68.
87. *De republica*, VI, xiii,13 and VI, xvi, 16.
88. See F. Gilbert, *Machiavelli and Guicciardini* (Princeton, 1965), pp.192ff. Machiavelli's knowledge of Epicurean ideas is evident from the fact that he copied a manuscript of Lucretius' *De rerum natura* (see S.Bertelli, 'Noterelle Machiavelliane', *Rivista Storica Italiana* 73 (1961), pp.544-53 and 76 (1964), pp.544-53). It is worth pointing out that there are some notable resemblances between aspects of the *Discorsi* and Epicurean thought: the role of chance in the development of societies and institutions (e.g. p.131 [I, 2]) which is distinctly different from Polybius on this matter), the productive power of conflict (p.309 [II, 12] and passim) and of necessity (p.136 [I, 3]), the emphasis on continual flux and *diversità* (e.g. p.417 [III, 9]), the stress on physicality in general, and the perception of nature as 'harsh...[and] unreasonable' (H. Mansfield, *Machiavelli's New Modes and Orders* (Ithaca, 1979), pp.50-51) or, in other words, her indifference to human well-being. Almost all these elements could be seen to derive from other sources, but their combination in this work may be significant.
89. *Il Principe*, p.87 [Ch.20].
90. *Discorsi*, p.136 [I, 4].
91. Ibid., p.195 [I, 27].
92. *Arte della guerra*, p.519.
93. *Discorsi*, p.124 [I, Proemio].
94. *Arte della guerra*, p.518; *Il Principe*, p.31 [Ch.6] and pp.101-2 [Ch.26].
95. *Istorie fiorentine*, ed. F. Gaeta (Milan, 1962), pp.70-71.
96. E. Panofsky, *Renaissance and Renascences in Western Art* (London, 1970), pp.10ff.
97. Genesis, I, 26. See Trinkaus, *In our Image and Likeness*.

98. Plotinus, *Enneads*, I, 6, 8 and V, 9, 1.

99. M. Ficino, *Commentarium in convivium Platonis sive de amore*, ed. R. Marcel (Paris, 1956), p.142 [I,4], p.145 [II,1], p.146 [II,2]. Subsequent references to this work will be to its short title (*De amore*).

100. M.J.B. Allen, 'Ficino and the *Timaeus*', *Supplementum Festivum: studies for Paul Kristeller*, ed. J. Hankins et al. (Binghampton, 1987), pp.399-439. On Ficino's debt to the writings of Hermes Trismegistus, see F.A. Yates, *Giordano Bruno and the Hermetic Tradition* (London, 1964), pp.12ff. and 20ff.

101. M. Ficino, *Theologia platonica de immortalitate animorum*, ed. R. Marcel (Paris, 1964), Vol. I, p.141-42 [III, 2].

102. Ibid., II, 228 [XIII, 3].

103. Ibid., II, 223 [XIII, 3].

104. Ibid., II, 224.

105. Ibid., II, 224.

106. Ibid., II, 224.

107. Ibid., II, 225.This did not mean for Ficino that humans were literally 'creative' in the same way as God. Only the latter could 'create'; humans could 'generate'. See M.J.B. Allen, *The Platonism of Marsilio Ficino* (Berkeley, 1984), p.80.

108. *Theologia platonica*, II, 226.

109. Ibid., II, 260-62 [XIV, 4].

110. Ibid., II, 229 [XIII, 4].

111. Plotinus, *Enneads*, V, 1, 1; tr. A.H. Armstrong (London, 1984).

112. *De amore*, p.145 [II, 1].

113. *Commentarium in Phedrum* (Ch.9) in M.J.B. Allen, *Marsilio Ficino and the Phaedran Charioteer* (Berkeley, 1981), pp.108-9.

114. *De amore*, p.207 [VII, 6]. On this subject see E. Panofsky, *Idea; a concept in art theory*, tr. J.J. Peake (New York, 1968).

115. Michelangelo, *Rime*, ed. E. Barelli (Milan, 1975), nos. 44 and 83; Castiglione, *Il Cortegiano*, Bk. IV, tr. C. Singleton (New York, 1959), pp.342ff. and 352ff.

116. *Theologia platonica*, I, 230 [VI, 2].

117. *De amore*, p.142 [I, 4].

118. Ibid., p.199 [VI, 1]; *Theologia platonica*, I, 321 [VIII, 12].

119. *De amore*, p.182 [V, 3].

120. *De divino furore* in *The Letters of Marsilio Ficino* (London, 1975) tr. Members of...the School of Economic Science, Vol. I, p.45. On the music of the spheres (the classic account of which was Macrobius' version of Cicero's *Somnium Scipionis*) see J. James, *The Music of the Spheres* (New York, 1993).

121. *De divino furore*, p.44.

122. *Commentarium in Phedrum*, pp.85 and 143.

123. *De amore*, (VII, 13 and 14) pp.257-58.

124. *Commentarium in Phedrum*, pp.156-57.

125. *De amore*, p.155 [II, 7].

126. Ibid., p.160 [III, 1] and p.165 [III, 3].

127. Ibid., p.158 [II, 8].

128. Ibid., p.165 [III, 3].

129. *De divino furore*, pp.45-46.

130. Ibid., p.46.

131. Ibid., p.46.

132. *Sylvae*, IV, 70ff. in *Poeti latini del quattrocento*, ed. F. Arnaldi et al. (Milan, n.d.), pp.1094-96. This idea also occcurred in Bartolomeo della Fonte's poetics (written

around 1490), which drew heavily on Horace's *Ars poetica*; see C. Trinkaus, 'The Unknown Quattrocento Poetics of Bartolomeo della Fonte', *Studies in the Renaissance* XIII (1966), pp.103 and 106.

133. C. Landino, *Scritti critici e teorici*, ed R. Cardini (Rome, 1974), p.141.

134. Ibid., p.142. The Aristotle reference is given below (note 189).

135. *Iliad*, II, 484-86. The epithet 'divine' was applied by Aristotle to Homer (*Poetics* 1459a30) and by Horace to the first poets (*Ars poetica*, 400). Petrarch and Boccaccio had both made use of this notion, drawing on Aristotle or on Cicero's *Pro Archia*, in their attempts to rehabilitate poetry: see Petrarch's Coronation Oath (in E.H. Wilkins, *Studies in the Life and Work of Petrarch* (Cambridge, Mass., 1955), p.301) and his *Rerum familiarum libri*, X, 4; likewise, Boccaccio, *Genealogia deorum gentilium*, XIV, 6-8, and see his *Trattatello in laude di Dante*, in *Opere in Versi,[&]..Prose*, ed. P.G. Ricci (Milan, 1965), pp.621 and 637. It was in this *Trattatello* that Boccaccio was the first person to describe Dante's *Commedia* as 'divine', ibid. p.634.

136. *Scritti critici*, p.142. See on this subject E.N. Tigerstedt, 'The Poet as Creator: origins of a metaphor', *Comparative Literature Studies* 5 (1968), pp.455-88.

137. C. Salutati, *Epistolario*, ed. F. Novati (Rome, 1891-1905), I, 176 and 183 (letter to R. Guidi, 16 August 1374), tr. D.T hompson et al., *Three Crowns of Florence* (New York, 1972), pp.3 and 9.

138. G.B. Fuscano, *Della oratoria e poetica facultà* (1531) in *Trattati di poetica e retorica del cinquecento*, ed. B. Weinberg (Bari, 1970), I, 192. Fuscano's debt to Landino is clear from the text.

139. J.C. Scaliger, *Poetices libri septem* (1561), tr. F.M. Padelford (New York, 1905), p.8; T. Tasso, *Discorsi dell'arte poetica* (1570) and *Discorsi del poema eroico* (1594) in *Prose*, ed. E. Mazzali (Milan, 1959), pp.387 and 589.

140. G. Vasari, *Le Vite de' più eccellenti pittori...*, ed. G. Milanesi (Florence, 1908), I, 215-16. According to Panofsky the words 'creator' and 'creating' began to be used in Italy in connection with painters around 1540/1550, *Renaissance and Renascences*, p.188, note 3.

141. See on this subject M.J.B. Allen, *The Platonism of Marsilio Ficino* (Berkeley, 1984), pp.43ff.

142. *De amore*, p.160 [III, 1].

143. *Theologia platonica*, II, 229ff [XIII, 4].

144. Ibid., II, 247 [XIV,1].

145. *De amore*, p.160 [III, 1].

146. P. Kristeller, *Eight Philosophers of the Italian Renaissance* (London, 1965), p.45.

147. E. Cassirer, 'Giovanni Pico della Mirandola', *Journal of the History of Ideas* 3 (1942), pp.330 and 333. For a critique of this view see W.G. Craven, *Giovanni Pico della Mirandola* (Geneva, 1981), pp.32ff. and 84ff. In the case of Pico there is perhaps as unavoidable ambivalence, as suggested in E. Garin, *La cultura filosofica del rinascimento* (Florence, 1961), p.337.

148. *De vita triplice*, ed. and tr. C.V. Kaske and J.R. Clark (Binghampton, 1989), pp.116-17.

149. *Problemata*, XXX, 1, translated in R. Klibansky, E. Panofsky and F. Saxl, *Saturn and Melancholy* (London, 1964), p.18.

150. Ibid., p.25.

151. Ibid., p.26.

152. *De vita*, pp.116-17.

153. Ibid., pp.120-21.

154. *Iliad*, II, 484-85 and 594-600; Pindar, *Isthmian*, VI, 10ff. On this subject see R. Harriott, *Poetry and Criticism before Plato* (London, 1969), pp.61 and 94-5, and,

more generally, P. Murray, 'Poetic genius and its classical origins', *Genius: the history of an idea*, ed. P. Murray (Oxford, 1989), pp.9-31.

155. *Ars poetica*, lines 295, 408-15, 453ff. He also ridiculed the idea of needing to be melancholic (line 302).

156. *Poetics*, 1455a; tr. I. Bywater.

157. *De tranquillitate animi*, XVII, 10-11, tr. J. Basore, *Moral Essays* (London, 1935), II, pp.284-85 (translation amended).

158. Pindar, *Olympian*, IX, 82 and XIII, 11; Horace, *Ars poetica*, 10.

159. Virgil, *Aeneid*, VI, 823.

160. 'Longinus', *On the Sublime*, I, 4 and passim. See also Dio Chrysostom's *Olympic Discourse*, XII, 65.

161. Plato, *Symposium* 196e.

162. Juvenal, *Satires*, I, 79.

163. Horaces, *Epistles*, I, 2, 62. See also *Odes*, I, 16.

164. Ovid, *Amores*, III, 12, 41; Horace, *Satires*, I, 10, 37 and *Epistles*, I, I, 10-11. The first self-conscious advocates of this attitude had been Callimachus (see B. Snell, *Poetry and Society* (Bloomington, 1961), pp.103ff) and his pupil Eratosthenes (see R. Pfeiffer, *A History of Classical Scholarship* (Oxford, 1968), p.167).

165. Hesiod, *Theogony*, 22-26.

166. Gellius, *Noctes Atticae*, XI, 2, 5, tr. J.C. Rolfe (London, 1927), II, 304-5, reading *grassator* rather than *crassator*, as suggested in the *Oxford Latin Dictionary* (Oxford, 1968), p.772.

167. *Odyssey*, VIII, 62-64 (on Demodocus), and Homer himself was believed to have been blind.

168. *Theogony*, 27.

169. *Olympian*, I, 28-34, and *Nemean*, VII, 20-24, tr. M. Bowra (Harmondsworth, 1969), pp.65 and 159. Aristotle quoted a proverb 'Poets tell many a lie' (which was attributed to Solon), *Metaphysics*, I, ii, 983al.

170. Gorgias, *Encomium on Helen*, tr. R. Harriott, *Poetry and Criticism before Plato*, pp.119ff; see also on this subject G.B. Walsh, *The Varieties of Enchantment* (Chapel Hill, 1984), pp.81ff.

171. Horace, *Epistles*, II, 2, 102. The archetypical example of such rivalry was the savage revenge Apollo took on Marsyas after their poetic contest, Ovid, *Metamorphoses*, VI, 382ff.

172. *Genealogia deorum gentilium*, XIV, 5, tr. C.G. Osgood, *Boccaccio on Poetry* (Princeton, 1930), pp.32ff.

173. I. Maier, *Ange Politien* (Geneva, 1966), p.184.

174. F. Berni, *Poesie e Prose*, ed. E. Chiòrboli (Florence, 1934), p.269.

175. Ibid., pp.273, 274, 275, 289 and 290.

176. *Lettere*, ed F. Flora (Rome, 1960), p.45. (The Biblical source was Jeremiah, IX, 5.)

177. Ibid., p.131.

178. *Orlando furioso*, IV, 18, 1.

179. Ibid., XI, 2, 7-8.

180. Ibid., IV,1, 1-4; tr. B. Reynolds (Harmondsworth, 1975-77).

181. Ibid., X, 15, 1-4.

182. Ibid., XXXV, 23-27.

183. *Prosatori latini del quattrocento*, ed. E. Garin (Milan, 1952), p.904.

184. The remark occurs in the margin of a letter, see *Lettere*, ed. F. Gaeta (Milan, 1961), which is now thought to have been written in 1506; see the notes to the translation by

R. Price in *The Prince* (Cambridge, 1988), pp.95-99. The phrase might be an echo of Sallust, *Bellum Jugurthinum*, VII, 1.

185. *Prosatori latini*, p.902.

186. W.H. Woodward, *Vittorino da Feltre and other humanist educators* (Cambridge, 1897), p.141, citing A.S. Piccolimini.

187. M.T. Herrick, *The Fusion of Horatian and Aristotelian Literary Criticism* (Urbana, 1946); B. Weinberg, *A History of Literary Criticism in the Italian Renaissance* (Chicago, 1961), pp.107 and 810.

188. *Poetics*, 1451b, tr. I. Bywater.

189. *Metaphysics*, I, iii, 983b27 (referring to Plato, *Cratylus*, 402b, on Homer and Hesiod).

190. *Poetics*, 1449b. On the variety of ways in which this was thought to happen, see B. Hathaway, *The Age of Criticism* (Ithaca, 1962), pp.205ff.

191. *Poetics*, 1448a, 1454a, 1453a.

192. *Ars poetica*, 343. This notion of the moral benefit of poetry had subsequently been attacked by Seneca in his *Epistula* 88, §§ 2, 5 and 32.

193. *Poetics*, 1449b and 1451a.

194. *Ars poetica*, 23.

195. See D. Javitch, *Proclaiming a Classic: the canonisation of* Orlando furioso (Princeton, 1991).

196. *Poetics*, 1447a, 1448b and 1450a (on tragedy); also *Rhetoric*, 1371b, and *Politics*, 1340a.

197. B. Hathaway, *Age of Criticism*, p.333, citing D. Barbaro (1557). With reference to art see M. Kemp. 'From *Mimesis* to *Fantasia*', *Viator* 8 (1977), pp.347-98, and D. Summers, *Michelangelo and the language of art* (Princeton, 1981), pp.103ff. On Dante see M.W. Bundy, *The Theory of Imagination in Classical and Medieval Thought* (Illinois, 1927), pp.226ff.

198. B. Weinberg, 'The Poetic Theories of Minturno', *Studies for F.W. Shipley* (St. Louis, 1942), p.108.

199. L. Castelvetro, *Poetica d'Aristotele...*(1576), tr. A.H. Gilbert, *Literary Criticism: Plato to Dryden* (New York, 1940), p.307.

200. Ibid., p.353.

201. Ibid., p.317.

202. Ibid., pp.331 and 351.

203. Ibid., p.305.

204. Ibid., pp.320ff. For this reason Castelvetro is severely critical of literary theft, see pp.323ff.

205. C. Curcio, *Dal Rinascimento alla Contrariforma* (Rome, 1934), p.51.

206. J. Mazzoni, *Della difesa della Commedia di Dante* (1587), in Gilbert, *Literary Criticism*, p.374.

207. Plutarch, *Life of Pericles*, I, 1, 4, tr. B. Perrin (London, 1906), p.5.

208. Lucian, *The Dream*, 9.

209. Catullus, XVI, 5-6; Martial, I, 4, 8 and XI, 15, 13; Ovid, *Tristia*, II, 353ff. Since in these instances the poets may have had reason to disassociate themselves from their writings (because of their obscene or provocative character) we cannot necessarily take these statements to be true (any more than with those instances of poets making the opposite claim, i.e. about their poems displaying their own moral rectitude). If we have no other evidence apart from the poems themselves then the matter remains inconclusive. However, such evidence as we do have up to this time appears to give more weight to the idea of the disunity (rather than of the unity) of the maker and the work.

Chapter Four

1. Montaigne, *Essays*, III, 6: all previous and existing knowledge is now 'less than nothing compared with what is unknown', tr. D. Frame, *The Complete Essays* (Stanford, 1965), p.692.
2. *Francis Bacon*, ed. B. Vickers (Oxford, 1996), p.169.
3. *Novum Organum*, [1620] I, xciii. On the confidence which inspired the voyages of discovery see J.H. Parry, *The Age of Reconnaissance* (London, 1973), pp.257ff.
4. *Francis Bacon*, p.196.
5. Ibid., p.184.
6. *Préface sur le traité sur le vide, Oeuvres complètes*, ed. J. Chevalier (Paris, 1957), pp.533-34. Written around 1647, this fragment was first published in 1779. Bacon made a similar point in his *Novum Organum*, I, lxxxiv, and Fontenelle was to do the same in his *Digression sur les anciens et les modernes* [1688], *Textes choisis*, ed. M. Roelens (Paris, 1986), p.256.
7. *De sapientia veterum*, XXVI, *Works*, ed. J. Spedding et al. (London, 1857-59), VI, 748-49.
8. *Novum Organum*, I, xcii, xcvii and cviii.
9. Ibid., Preface and I, lxxi.
10. *Francis Bacon*, p.480 [*New Atlantis*].
11. *Novum Organum*, I, cxxix, tr. M. Silverthorne (Cambridge, 2000), p.99.
12. See on the conceptual aspects of this A. Pérez-Ramos, *Francis Bacon's Idea of Science and the Maker's Knowledge Tradition* (Oxford, 1988); for an account of the practical aspects see P. Rossi, *Philosophy, Technology and the Arts in the Early Modern Era*, tr. S. Attanasio (New York, 1970). On the subsequent development of these ideas in the 17th century see R.F. Jones, *Ancients and Moderns* (Second edn., St. Louis, 1961), C. Webster (ed.), *The Intellectual Revolution of the 17th century* (London, 1974) and C. Webster, *The Great Instauration* (London, 1975).
13. *England's Treasure*, Ch.3, §12, in *Early Economic Thought*, ed. A.E. Monroe (Cambridge, Mass., 1924), p.178. This text was published in 1664 but had been written in 1623; see J. Appleby, *Economic Thought in 17th century England* (Princeton, 1978), p.37.
14. *Francis Bacon*, p.193 [*Advancement*].
15. Webster, *The Great Instauration*, p.357.
16. J. Donne, 'An Anatomie of the World: the first anniversary' [1611], line 213, *Poems*, ed. H. Grierson, (Oxford, 1933), p.214.
17. *Leviathan*, ed. C.B. Macpherson (Harmondsworth, 1968), p.295 [Ch.24].
18. *On the Citizen*, ed. and tr. R. Tuck and M. Silverthorne (Cambridge, 1998), p.24.
19. *De homine*, ii, 10, cited in A. Pérez-Ramos, *Francis Bacon's Idea of Science*, p.187.
20. *De homine*, ii, 10, as note 19.
21. *Leviathan*, p.407 [Ch.31].
22. Ibid., pp.106, 165, 328.
23. Ibid., p.233 [Ch.18].
24. Ibid., p.81 [Introduction].
25. *The Elements of Law*, ed. F. Tönnies [1889] (London, 1969), p.108, [II, I, 1].
26. *Leviathan*, pp.81-82 [Introduction].
27. Ibid., pp.220-21 [Ch.16]) and pp.227ff. [Ch.17 and 18]. See I. Hampsher-Monk, *A History of Modern Political Thought* (Oxford, 1992), pp.40-42.
28. *Leviathan*, p.227 [Ch.17], and *On the Citizen*, p.9.
29. *Leviathan*, p.397 [Ch.31], and see p.260 [Ch.20].

30. Ibid., p.398 ([Ch.31].
31. See W.B.Glover, 'God and Thomas Hobbes', *Hobbes Studies*, ed. K.C.Brown (Oxford, 1965), pp.141-68, especially pp.163ff. See also R.J. Halliday et al., 'Hobbes's Belief in God', *Political Studies* 31 (1983), pp.418-33.
32. M. Oakeshott, 'Introduction', *Leviathan*, (Oxford, 1947), p.lii.
33. *Pensées*, ed. L. Lafuma (Paris, 1962), no.421.
34. Ibid., no.913.
35. Algernon Sidney, *Discourses concerning government*, I, vi, (Indianapolis, 1990), p.20; see also pp.357, 373, 464. This work was first published in 1698, fifteen years after Sidney's death.
36. *Complete Prose Writings* (Yale, 1953-82), IV, 390-91.
37. Ibid., VII, 432ff.
38. *Paradise Lost*, XI, 606.
39. Ibid., V, 609-10.
40. Ibid., V, 860 and 864.
41. Ibid., I, 603.
42. Ibid., VI, 290.
43. Ibid., IX, 129-30.
44. Ibid., II, 386.
45. Ibid., X, 440-41.
46. Ibid., III, 681; IV,121; V,243 (and see III, 392).
47. Ibid., IX, 665ff.
48. Ibid., IX, 1135ff.
49. Ibid, IV, 774-75.
50. Ibid.,VII, 120ff; VIII, 66ff; VIII, 167; XII, 575ff. There is a parallel emphasis on the importance of limits: IV, 774-75; VIII, 188ff.
51. Ibid., VII, 121.
52. Ibid., VIII, 188-89.
53. Ibid., VIII, 173-75.
54. Ibid., X, 1078-81.
55. Ibid., XI, 610-12.
56. For an example of this see the preface of Theophilus Presbyter's *De diversis artibus* (c.1120) / *On Divers Arts*, tr. J.G. Hawthorne et al., (Chicago, 1963), p.11; and, on this topic generally, see G. Post et al., 'The Medieval Heritage of a Humanist Ideal: *Scientia donum Dei est*', *Traditio* 11 (1955), pp.195-234.
57. *Paradise Lost*, XI, 607-8.
58. Ibid., XII, 470. On this subject see A. Lovejoy, 'Milton and the paradox of the Fortunate Fall', *Essays in the History of Ideas* (New York, 1955), pp.277ff.
59. *Complete Prose Writings* II, 514ff.
60. *Complete Writings*, ed. G. Keynes (Oxford, 1976), p.150.
61. 'A Defence of Poetry', *Selected Poetry, Prose and Letters*, ed. A.S.B. Glover (London, 1951), p.1044.
62. D. Norbrook, *Writing the English Republic* (Cambridge, 1999), pp.433ff.
63. B. Worden, 'Milton's republicanism and the tyranny of heaven', G. Bock et al. (eds), *Machiavelli and republicanism* (Cambridge, 1990), pp.225ff.
64. M.A. Radinowicz, 'The Politics of Milton', A. Patterson (ed.), *John Milton* (London, 1992), pp.120ff.
65. See R.J.Z. Werblowsky, *Lucifer and Prometheus* (London, 1952), *passim*; P. Conrad, *To be continued* (Oxford, 1995), pp.164ff. On Milton's own account of divine creation see C.A. Patrides, *Milton and the Christian tradition* (Oxford, 1960), p.93ff. On Satan

and that later Promethean figure, Frankenstein, see P. Cantor, *Creature and Creator* (Cambridge, 1984), pp.103ff.

66. *History of the Royal Society* (London, 1667), p.321.
67. Ibid, pp.83 and 392.
68. Ibid., p.124.
69. Ibid., p.89.
70. Ibid., p.85.
71. Ibid., p.392.
72. Ibid., pp.42 and 152.
73. J.R. Hale, 'Gunpowder and the Renaissance', C.C. Caster (ed.), *From Renaissance to Counter-Reformation* (London, 1966), p.115.
74. *Paradise Lost*, VI, 470ff.
75. Ibid., I, 740ff.
76. Ibid., II, 260.
77. H. Power, *Experimental Philosophy* (London, 1664), p.192.
78. Ibid., p.191.
79. Ibid., Preface.
80. P. Hazard, *La Crise de la conscience européene* (Paris, 1935), II, 117, quoting Fontenelle's preface to the *Histoire du renouvellement de l'Académie royale des sciences* (1702). For the latter's arguments about the benefits of mathematics and physics see *Textes choisis*, ed. M. Roelens (Paris, 1966), pp.267ff.
81. For a short account of the quarrel see G. Highet, *The Classical Tradition* (New York, 1949), pp.262ff. For a selection of relevant French texts, see *Antike und Moderne in der Literaturdiskussion des 18 Jahrhunderts*, ed. W. Krauss et al. (Berlin, 1966); for English texts see *Critical Essays of the 17th century*, ed. J.E. Spingarn (Oxford, 1908).
82. On this topos see R. Merton, *On the Shoulders of Giants* (New York, 1965).
83. Fontenelle, *Digression sur les anciens et les modernes* (1688), *Textes choisis*, p.256.
84. Psalms, 24, 1;100, 3.
85. See D.P. Walker, *The Decline of Hell* (London, 1964).
86. G. Bollenbeck, *Bildung und Kultur: Glanz und Elend eines deutschen Deutungsmusters* (Frankfurt, 1994), pp.55ff.
87. *Two Treatises on Government*, ed. P. Laslett (Cambridge, 1988), p.296 [II, § 40].
88. *An Essay concerning Human Understanding*, ed. P. Nidditch (Oxford, 1979), p.100 [I, iv, 23].
89. *Essay*, pp.119-120 [II, ii, 2] and p.164 [II, xii, 2]; *Two Treatises*, p.332 [II, § 97].
90. *Essay*, p.163 [II, xii, 1]. On the theme of making in the *Essay* see R.S. Crane, 'Notes on the Organisation of Locke's *Essay*', *The Idea of the Humanities and other essays* (Chicago, 1967), I, 288ff.
91. *Essay*, p.292 [II, xxii, 9].
92. *Some Thoughts concerning Education*, ed. J.W. and J.S. Yolton (Oxford, 1989), p.83.
93. *Essay*, p.549 [IV, iii, 18].
94. *Two Treatises*, p.271 [II, §6].
95. *Essay*, p.541 [IV, iii, 6].
96. Cited in J. Yolton, *John Locke and the way of ideas* (Oxford, 1956), p.61.
97. *Two Treatises*, pp.161-62 [I, §30].
98. *Essay*, p.325 [II, xxvi, 2]. See, on this subject, A. Ryan, *Property and Political Theory* (Oxford, 1984), pp.28-29.
99. *Two Treatises*, p.292 [II, § 35].
100. Manuscript note (1693) cited in J. Dunn, *The Political Thought of John Locke* (Cambridge, 1969), p.245 n.2.

101. *Two Treatises*, p.291 [II, § 34].
102. Ibid., p.182[I, § 58].
103. *Essay*, pp.262 and 261 [II, xxi, 45].
104. Ibid., p.293 [II, xxii, 10].
105. Ibid., p.252 [II, xxi, 34].
106. Manuscript early draft of the *Essay*, in J. Dunn, *Political Thought*, p.230; and see *Two Treatises*, pp.298-99 [II, §41].
107. *Observations upon the United Provinces of the Netherlands* [1673] (Cambridge, 1932), p.128.
108. Ibid., p.100.
109. Ibid., pp.98-99, 105-6, 141-42.
110. Ibid., p.150.
111. *A Discourse of Trade* (London, 1690), p.1.
112. *A Plan of the English Commerce* (Fifth edn., London, 1749), pp.1-2.
113. Ibid., p.75.
114. Ibid., pp.vii, xiii and xiv.
115. Ibid., p.17.
116. Ibid., p.32.
117. J. Addison and R. Steele, *The Spectator*, no.2 (2 March, 1711) and subsequently.
118. *The Complete English Tradesman* [Second edn, 1727] (New York, 1969), I, 310.
119. C. Davenant, *Essay upon...the balance of trade* (1699), quoted in J. Sekora, *Luxury: the concept in Western thought* (Baltimore, 1977), p.79.
120. Augustine, *De civitate Dei*, XVII, 13; Boethius, *De consolatione philosophiae*, II, 30; E. Spenser, *The Faerie Queene*, Bk.VII, Cantos 6 and 7.
121. N. Barbon, *A Discourse of Trade*, p.65; the text continues, 'it is an invention to dress a man as if he lived in a perpetual spring; he never sees the autumn of his clothes'.
122. B. Mandeville, *The Fable of the Bees*, ed. F.B. Kaye (Oxford, 1924), I, 325 and 330.
123. James Steuart, *An Inquiry into the Principles of Political Economy* [1767], ed. A. Skinner (Edinburgh, 1966), I, 184. This passage was reproduced (unacknowledged) in the article on 'Commerce' in the *Encyclopaedia Britannica* (Edinburgh, 1771), II, 238.
124. *Considerations upon the East-India Trade* (London, 1701), p.66.
125. Ibid., p.67. On Martyn, and the economic debate in which he was engaged, see I. Hont, 'Free trade and the economic limits to national politics', *The Economic Limits to Modern Politics*, ed. J. Dunn (Cambridge, 1990), pp.41-120, especially pp.101ff.

Chapter Five

1. *The Fable of the Bees*, ed. F.B. Kaye (Oxford, 1924), Vol. I, pp.6 and 13.
2. Ibid., I, 34-35 ('acorns'), 37 and 242.
3. Ibid., I, 104.
4. Ibid., I, 183; II, 285 and 305.
5. Ibid., I, 231-32.
6. Ibid., I, 269 and 308; II, 259-60.
7. Ibid., I, 231-32.
8. Ibid., I, 6.
9. Ibid., I, 25, 250, 327ff.
10. Ibid., I, 135 and 232; II, 260.
11. Ibid., I, 244.
12. Ibid., I, 61 and 134ff.

13. Ibid., I, 6, 183 and 197.
14. Ibid., I, 6; II, 59.
15. Ibid., I, 343; II, 269.
16. Ibid., II, 178 and 271.
17. Ibid., I, 42.
18. Ibid., II, 187.
19. Ibid., II, 279.
20. Ibid., II, 353.
21. Ibid., I, 168; II, 136.
22. Ibid., I, 3.
23. Ibid., II, 64.
24. Ibid., II, 74.
25. Ibid., II, 81.
26. Ibid., II, 130; I, 124.
27. Ibid., II, 92.
28. Ibid., I, 68, 135; II, 89, 138.
29. Ibid., I, 130.
30. Ibid., I, 127.
31. Ibid., I, 128.
32. Ibid., I, 130.
33. Ibid., I, 26 and 366.
34. Ibid., II, 142.
35. Ibid., II, 144-45.
36. Ibid., II, 21. On this (and other) aspects of Mandeville's thought see E.J. Hundert, *The Enlightenment's* Fable: *Bernard Mandeville and the Discovery of Society* (Cambridge, 1994), pp.45ff. and 95-96.
37. *Free Thoughts on Religion* (London, 1720), pp.99-103.
38. *Fable*, II, 243-52.
39. *Typhon: or the wars between the Gods and the Giants* (London, 1704). The work is based on Scarron's burlesque of the same name (1694) but unlike that text Mandeville's poem is devoid of any literary merit.
40. Hundert, *The Enlightenment's Fable*, p.248.
41. The accuracy of this analogy depends on the extent to which Mandeville's 'skilful politicians' (*Fable*, I, 47) were doing more than pursuing their private ambitions or gratifying their own vanity, i.e. the extent to which they consciously envisaged a generally beneficial result. In *An Enquiry into the Origin of Honour* (London, 1732), p.41, the process is not seen as an individual invention but rather as 'the joint labour of many', which took time, like other great achievements, described in the *Fable* as the result of the 'experience of many generations' (note 34, above). Elsewhere, however he wrote of the deliberate 'dexterous management of a skilful politician' turning 'private vices…into public benefits', *Letter to Dion* [1732] (Los Angeles, 1953), p.36.
42. The subtitle of the work, and see *Fable*, II, 120-21.
43. Ibid., I, 343; see also 325 and 331.
44. Ibid., I, 344 and 44.
45. Ibid., I, 373ff. On sexuality, see I, 65-66, 73-74 and 142ff.
46. Ibid., I, 41ff.
47. Ibid., II, 144-45.
48. Ibid., I, 91.
49. Ibid., I, 369.

50. Pope obesrved, in his *Essay on Man* (II, 191-92), that 'Envy, to which the ignoble mind's a slave, / Is emulation in the learn'd or brave'.

51. *The Complete English Tradesman* [Second edn., 1727] (New York, 1969), I, 234-35; 'Religion is one thing, trade is another', wrote Mandeville, *Fable,* I, 356.

52. *Review* (21 June, 1709), see B. Dijkstra, *Defoe and Economics* (London, 1987), p.7.

53. *A Treatise of Human Nature,* ed. P. Nidditch (Oxford,1978), p.469 [Bk.III, Part I, Sect.1].

54. Ibid., pp.xv and xix [Introduction].

55. *Essays Moral, Political and Literary,* ed. T.H. Green et al. (London, 1875), 'Of Eloquence', I, 171 n.2. This statement occurs in a footnote which Hume omitted in his last edition, the text of which is used in all subsequent references (see note 59).

56. *Treatise,* p.466 [III, I, 1].

57. Ibid., p.265 [I, iv, 7].

58. Ibid., p.250 [IV, iv, 5]; *Enquiries concerning the Human Understanding and... Principles of Morals,* ed. L.A. Selby-Bigge (Oxford, 1902), p.164 [XII, iii, § 132].

59. *Essays Moral, Political and Literary,* ed. E.F. Miller (Indianapolis, 1985), 'Of Commerce', p.254.

60. Ibid., 'Of the Standard of Taste', p.246; *The Natural History of Religion,* ed. A.W. Colver (Oxford, 1976), II, pp.26-27.

61. *Treatise,* p.225 [I, iv, 4].

62. *Essays,* 'Of Interest', p.300.

63. Ibid., 'Of Refinement in the Arts', p.270.

64. *Treatise,* p.353 [II, ii, 4].

65. Ibid., p.451 [II, iii, 10]; see also *Essays,* 'The Stoic', p.149.

66. The theme was, as it were, announced by Locke, *Essay,* II, xxii, 50.

67. *Treatise,* p.484 [II, ii, 1].

68. *Essays,* 'Of Refinement in the Arts', p.270.

69. *An Essay on the history of civil society,* ed. F. Oz-Salzberger (Cambridge, 1995), pp.46 and 51.

70. Ibid., p.52.

71. Hume, *Treatise,* pp.433-34 [II, iii, 8].

72. *Essays,* 'Of Commerce', p.264.

73. *Treatise,* p.311 [II, i, 10].

74. *Enquiry...Understanding...,* p.83 [VIII, i, § 65].

75. *Essays,* 'Of Refinement in the Arts', pp.269ff.

76. Ibid., p.277.

77. Ibid., p.276ff.

78. Ibid., p.271; also pp.273-74.

79. Ibid., p.271.

80. *Treatise,* p.434 [II, iii, 18].

81. D. Mallet, *The Excursion,* I, 95; E. Young, *Night Thoughts,* IX, 1061ff; J. Thomson, *Liberty,* III, 107ff (blending neo-Platonic emanation with Newtonian cosmology and republican fraternity). See also Hume, *Essays,* 'The Stoic', p.152.

82. *Essays,* 'Of the Rise and Progress of the Arts and Science', p.114.

83. Ibid., 'Of Interest', p.299.

84. Ibid., 'Of Commerce', p.267.

85. *Treatise,* pp.477ff. [III, ii, 1ff].

86. *Letters,* ed. J.Y.T. Greig (Oxford, 1932), p.32 (17 September 1739).

87. *Treatise,* pp.86ff [I, iii, 6].

88. Cited in *The Leibniz-Clarke Correspondence*, ed. H.G. Alexander (Manchester, 1956), p.166; and see pp.182-83.
89. *Enquiry...Understanding*, p.135 [XI, § 105].
90. Ibid., p.136.
91. *Dialogues concerning natural religion*, ed. R.H. Popkin (Indianapolis, 1980), p.36 [V].
92. Ibid., p.52 [VIII];and see pp.46-47 [VII].
93. Ibid., p.63 [X].
94. Ibid., p.74 [XI].
95. N. Kemp Smith, Introduction to his edition of the *Dialogues* (Indianapolis, 1947), pp.57ff; E.C. Mossner, 'Hume and the legacy of the *Dialogues*', *Bicentenary Papers* (Edinburgh, 1976), pp.2ff.
96. F.-M. Arouet de Voltaire, *Lettres philosophiques*, XXV, 3 and 4.
97. C. de Secondat, Baron de Montesquieu, *De l'Esprit des lois, Oeuvres complètes*, ed. R. Caillois (Paris, 1958), ii, 586 [Bk.XX, Ch.2].
98. Ibid., ii, 578 and 581 [XIX, 27].
99. Ibid., ii, 486-87 [XIV, 13] and ii, 582 [XIX, 27].
100. Ibid., ii, 333-34 [VII, 1].
101. Ibid., ii, 583 [XIX, 27].
102. *Lettres philosophiques*, XVIII, first paragraph.
103. J.-F. Melon, *Essai politique sur le commerce*, in *Economistes-financiers du XVIIIème siècle*, ed. E. Daire (Paris, 1843), p.720.
104. D. Diderot et al., *Encyclopédie, ou Dictionnaire raisonnée sur les sciences, les arts et les métiers* (Paris, 1751-65), III, 832b ('Commerce'), 697a and 699a ('Concurrence'), both written by Véron de Forbonnais.
105. Ibid., V, 601b-602a ('Emulation') and 734b-735a ('Envie').
106. Ibid., XIII, 391b ('Privilège'). Likewise, Voltaire wrote that envy 'sharpens genius', *Traité de métaphysique*, ed. H.T. Patterson (Manchester, 1967), p.54.
107. *Encyclopédie*, IX, 765a-766a and 769b ('Luxe'); and see his article 'Législateur', IX, 362b-363a.
108. Ibid., III, 695a ('Commerce').
109. Ibid., VII, 74a ('Fondation'), written by Turgot.
110. Ibid., VII, 74b.
111. V. de Riqueti, Marquis de Mirabeau, *Philosophie rurale...*(Amsterdam, 1766), I, vii and xxxv-vi; see also, xxxix.
112. Ibid., II, 22-25.
113. Ibid., II, 13.
114. Ibid., I, xxxix and III, 9 — on theocracy; Le Mercier de la Rivière, *L'Ordre naturel et essentiel des sociétés politiques* (Paris, 1767), pp.166ff and 185 — on legal despotism.
115. References to Smith's works are given in the standard format of the Glasgow edition (Oxford, 1976-80): titles abbreviated — WN for *The Wealth of Nations*, ed. R.H. Campbell and A.S. Skinner, TMS for *The Theory of Moral Sentiments*, ed. A.L. Macfie and D.D. Raphael — followed by (for WN) Book, Chapter, Division, Paragraph, and (for TMS) Part, Section, Chapter, Paragraph. This phrase occurs in WN, IV.ix.51. On Smith's thought see *Essays on Adam Smith*, ed. A.S. Skinner and T. Wilson (Oxford, 1976), *Wealth and Virtue*, ed. I. Hont and M. Ignatieff (Cambridge, 1983), and *Adam Smith's* Wealth of Nations: *new interdisciplinary essays*, ed. S. Copley and K. Sutherland (Manchester, 1995).
116. WN, IV, ii, 43.
117. TMS, I, i, 5, 5.
118. TMS, IV, 1, 11.

119. TMS, III, 1, 5.
120. TMS, III, 1, 2.
121. TMS, III, 2, 32.
122. TMS, III, 3, 37.
123. TMS, IV, 2, 8 and VI, 1, 6.
124. WN, II, iii, 25.
125. WN, II, iii, 36, and see I, x, b, 38.
126. WN, V, i, f, 4.
127. WN, I, xi, p, 8.
128. WN, V, i, f, 50.
129. WN, V, i, f, 50.
130. WN, I, x, b, 42-43.
131. WN, III, iv, 3.
132. WN, II, iv, 15.
133. WN, IV, iii, c, 9.
134. WN, I, xi, p, 10.
135. WN, IV, ii, 21 and IV, ii, 43.
136. WN, II, v, 14.
137. WN, V, iv, 1.
138. WN, I, iv, 1, 139.
139. WN, IV, iii, c, 9, and see I, xi, p, 10.
140. WN, V, i, f, 4.
141. TMS, I, iii, 3, 2, and I, iii, 2, 1.
142. TMS, I, iii, 2, 5.
143. TMS, I, iii, 3, 8.
144. TMS, III, 3, 37.
145. TMS, VI, 3, 30.
146. TMS, III, 2, 35.
147. TMS, VI, 1, 12; and see VI, I, 6 and 9.
148. TMS, I, iii, 3, 2.
149. *Essays on Philosophical Subjects*, ed. W.P. Wightman et al. (Oxford, 1980), pp.45-46.
150. Ibid., p.66.
151. Ibid., p.105.
152. Ibid., pp.46 and 61-62.
153. TMS, VI, ii, 3, 2.
154. TMS, IV, 1,10.
155. See my article 'Materialism and history: Diderot and the *Histoire des Deux Indes*', *European Review of History* 3 (1996), pp.151-60.
156. WN, IV, ii, 39.
157. WN, IV, vii, c, 74-75, and IV, ii, 39.
158. *Lectures on Jurisprudence*, ed. R.L. Meek et al. (Oxford, 1978), pp.350-52; WN, I, I, 8-9, and see the editors' notes to these paragraphs. In WN, II, Introduction, 4, the owner/investor is also seen as inventive. On Smith's limitations in this respect see the editors' General Introduction, WN, p.49; R. Koebner, 'A. Smith and the Industrial Revolution', *Economic History Review*, 2nd. series, 9 (1959), pp.381-91; and D.C. Coleman, 'A. Smith, Businessmen, and the Mercantile System...', *History of European Ideas* 9 (1988), pp.161-70.
159. H. Martyn, *Considerations upon the East-India Trade* (London, 1701), p.74.
160. J. Cary, *An Essay towards regulating the trade...*(Second edn. London, 1719), p.99.
161. D. Defoe, *A Plan of English Commerce* [1729] (Fifth edn, London, 1749), p.ix.

162. E. Young, *Love of Fame, the Universal Passion* [1728], Satire V, line 170; G. Berkeley, *The Querist* [1735-37], *Works*, ed. T.E. Jessop (London, 1953), VI, 105; S. Johnson, *The Adventurer* no. 67 (26 June, 1753), *Works* (Yale, 1958-), II, 387.

163. Quoted in N. McKendrik et al, *The Birth of Consumer Society* (London, 1982), p.50.

164. J. Dalton, 'A Descriptive Poem…[about] the mines, near Whitehaven' [1755], *The New Oxford Book of 18th century Verse*, ed. R. Lonsdale (Oxford, 1987), p.469. This text has been seen as 'perhaps the first poem to describe a steam-engine', A. Briggs, *Iron Bridge to Crystal Palace* (London, 1979), p. 34.

165. WN, I, x, c, 26; II, ii, 32; IV, i, 10; IV, vii, c, 7 and 48 and 50; IV, ix, 22 and 23. Similarly, Saint-Lambert stated that industry and commerce 'create' new wealth, *Encyclopédie*, IX, 767a; Morellet wrote that new types of demand 'create' new production, cited by Diderot in his *Apologie de l'abbé Galiani* [1770], *Oeuvres Politiques*, ed. P. Vernière (Paris, 1963), p.115; and in Raynal's *Histoire des Deux Indes* [1770-80], (Geneva, 1783), IX, 172 [Bk.XIX, Ch.6], we read that 'war destroys, while commerce creates'.

166. The word *entrepreneur* was used in a form approximating to its modern meaning in Cantillon's *Essai sur la nature du commerce en général* [written c.1730, published 1755], ed. H. Higgs (London, 1931), pp.46ff (on which see A.E. Murphy, *Richard Cantillon* (Oxford, 1986), pp.255ff). However, neither the terminology nor the precise role of such a figure was clearly delineated in the 18th century.

167. J. Steuart, *An Inquiry into the Principles of Political Economy*, ed. A.S. Skinner (Edinburgh, 1966), I, 46, 123, 156-67, 166 and 184 (on manufacturers), I, 74 (on Colbert, Law and Walpole).

168. D. Stewart, *Collected Works*, ed. W. Hamilton (Edinburgh, 1845-60), VIII, 192 and 196, 'Lectures on Political Economy' (written c.1800, with additions 1809-10).

169. Ibid., pp.318-19 and 321. The article 'Commerce' in the *Encyclopedia Britannica* (Edinburgh, 1771), II, 230 (which drew unacknowledged on J. Steuart's *Inquiry* (ed. cit.) I, 106) also credited manufacturers as much as workmen with 'ingenuity'; see also Thomas Hearn (1793) on 'the ingenuity of the artist…and the enterprise of the merchant', cited in *Republicanism, Liberty, and Commercial Society, 1649-1776*, ed. D. Wootton (Stanford, 1994), p.40. Traces of this view (of the central role of invention in commerce) also appeared in the writings of Malthus (in 1814), cited by D. Winch in J. Burrow et al., *That Noble Science of Politics* (Cambridge, 1983), p.74, and in A. Ure, *The Philosophy of Manufactures* (London, 1835), p.446.

170. D. Stewart, *Collected Works*, VIII, 194.

171. WN, I, xi, n, 9.

172. WN, II, v, 12.

173. G.-L. Leclerc, Comte de Buffon, *Epoques de la nature* [1779], ed. G. Gohau (Paris, 1998), p.220.

174. WN, II, v, 12.

175. D. Stewart, *Collected Works*, X, 68.

176. TMS, II, iii, 3, 3.

177. J. Bentham, *Economic Writings*, ed. W. Stark (London, 1952), I, 171.

178. Ibid., I, 168.

179. Ibid., I, 177.

180. Ibid., I, 180.

181. *Journal de Commerce* (Paris, 1759), pp.56-57. (Some of this article also appeared in Bk.XIX, Ch.6 of Raynal's *Histoire des Deux Indes* (Geneva, 1783), IX, 173.)

182. Ibid., pp.57 and 61.

183. Ibid., p.56.

184. J.G.A. Pocock, *The Machiavellian Moment* (Princeton, 1975), pp.452ff., citing Defoe and others; see also Montesquieu, *Lettres persanes*, CXLII, on John Law's 'empire de l'imagination', *Oeuvres complètes*, i.,351.

185. For an early example see N. Barbon's *Discourse on Trade* [1690] in W. Letwin, *The Origins of Scientific Economics* (London, 1963), p.72. The theme became common, often as an element in the attack on luxury. For a recognition of the historical significance of this development see Hume, *A History of England*, 'Appendix to the Reign of James I', [1754-62] (Indianapolis, 1983), V, 140.

186. R. Cantillon, *Essai sur la nature du commerce*, pp.28, 46, 58; also, Montesquieu, *De l'Esprit des lois*, VII, 1 (ii, 334), and XIX, 27 (ii, 580).

187. W. Duff, *Essay on Original Genius* (London, 1767), p.19.

188. *Discorsi*, I, 5; II, 2; III, 1 and 9 and 21 and 49.

189. A. Sidney, *Discourses concerning government* [1698] (Indianapolis, 1990), p.273.

190. *Fable of the Bees*, I, 17.

191. F. Quesnay, *Dialogues sur le commerce* [1768], cited in F. Acomb, *Anglophobia in France 1763-1789* (Durham, N.C., 1950) p.63. See also Mirabeau, *Philosophie rurale*, II, 24.

192. J.G.A. Pocock, 'Machiavelli, Harrington and English political ideologies in the 18th century', *Politics, Language and Time* (Sec.edn. Chicago, 1989), pp.104-47. This Venetian-Roman contrast was not entirely clear-cut insofar as the former was strongly influenced by Polybius' analysis of the success of the Roman republic (which itself became well-known through Machiavelli's *Discourses*). For a succint account of the contrast see I.Hampsher-Monk, *A History of Modern of Political Thought* (Oxford, 1992), pp.206ff.

193. In his poem *Liberty* (1734-36), V, 94, James Thomson called such virtue 'the social cement of mankind'.

194. G. Berkeley, *An Essay towards preventing the ruin of Great Britain* [1721], *Works* (see note 162), VI, 79. Later in the century there was support among republicans for commerce, on the grounds of its increasing wealth in general and its fostering peaceful relations between states (by trading rather than fighting). See, for example, with reference to Paine, D. Wootton, 'Introduction', *Republicanism, Liberty, and Commercial Society, 1649-1776*, pp.33ff. But to the best of my knowledge this did not lead Paine to praise commercial activity *qua* action.

195. A. Ferguson, *An Essay on the history of civil society*, p.12. See also his *Institutes of Moral Philosophy* [1769] (Edinburgh, 1773), p.17, and his *Principles of Moral and Political Science* (Edinburgh, 1792), p.122.

196. *Principles*, p.267.

197. *Essay*, p.205.

198. Ibid., p.25.

199. Ibid., p.47.

200. Ibid., p.47.

201. Ibid., p.47.

202. *Principles*, p.254.

203. *Essay*, pp.24, 140-41, 206-7, 226.

204. *Principles*, p.227.

205. Ibid., p.254.

206. *Enquiry* (see note 41), pp.179-81 and 230-31.

207. *Fable*, II, 111.

208. Ibid., II, 117.

209. Francois, Duc de la Rochefoucauld, *Maximes* no.468, ed. J. Truchet (Paris, 1967), p.106.

210. *Essay on Man*, IV, 287ff, *The Poems of A. Pope*, ed. J. Butt (London, 1963), p.544. For a similar view see Addison's discussion of ambition in *The Spectator* nos. 255-57 (22-25 December 1711).

211. H. Fielding, *Jonathan Wild* (Harmondsworth, 1982), pp.31-32, 39-40, 168 and 219.

212. Ibid., pp.53, 77, 89, 90, and 215.

213. Ibid., pp.153 and 215.

214. Ibid., p.102. Another striking portrayal of an unscrupulous and inventive man of action occurs in the character of Begéarss in Beaumarchais' *La Mère coupable* (1792); see his *profession du foi* in Act IV, Scene 4.

215. *Cambridge Economic History of Europe*, ed. P. Mathias and M.M. Postan (Cambridge, 1978), VII, 184.

216. J. Boswell, *Journal of a Tour of the Hebrides* [1785], (Oxford, 1970), p.381 (18 October, 1773), italics added. Fielding made a similar point with regard to politics, *Jonathan Wild*, p.154. Johnson's comment was not only about visibility since he went on to concede that 'a merchant may, perhaps, be a man of an enlarged mind; but there is nothing in trade connected with an enlarged mind'.

217. D. Defoe, *The Life and Adventures of Robinson Crusoe* (Harmondsworth, 1965), pp.31, 103, 198 and 269.

218. Ibid., pp.27-28.

219. Ibid., p.58.

220. Ibid., p.60.

221. Ibid., p.297.

222. *Plan of English Commerce*, pp.xiii and xv.

223. *Weekly Review*, Vol. I, no.42 (6 January, 1712), paginated as p.82 (although actually p.84).

224. *The History of the Adventures of Joseph Andrews* (Everyman edn., London, 1993), p.217 [Bk.III, Ch.1].

225. Ibid., Preface, pp.48 and 52.

226. Ibid., p.217 [Bk.III, Ch.1]; *The History of Tom Jones* (Everyman edn., London, 1957), Vol. I, p.393 [Bk.IX, Ch.1].

227. *Macbeth*, Act II, Scene 1, line 38; *Hamlet*, II, iv, 139. In *Jonathan Wild* Fielding observed that 'readers of romances...agree to be deceived' (pp.154-55). The verb 'create' was also used in a neutral sense for engendering or stimulating an emotion, as in 'create a liking' (Locke, *Some Thoughts concerning Education*, § 49) or 'create' fear or courage (Mandeville, *An Enquiry into the origin of honour* (London, 1732), pp.42 and 60).

228. *Tom Jones*, I, 391 [Bk.IX, Ch.1].

229. Ibid., I, 393.

230. Ibid., I, 315ff [Bk.VIII, Ch.1].

231. Ibid., I, 39 [Bk.II,Ch.1].

232. Ibid., I, 153 [Bk.V, Ch.1].

233. Ibid., II, 15 [Bk.X, Ch.1].

234. Ibid., II, 101-2 [Bk.XII, Ch.1].

235. *The Tatler*, no. 101 (1 December, 1709).

236. W. Enfield, *Observations on Literary Property* [1774], cited in M. Rose, 'The Author as Proprietor: Donaldson v. Becket and the Genealogy of Modern Authorship', *Representations* 23 (1988), p.59. See ibid., p.80 for a similar statement by Lord Mansfield.

237. W. Blackstone, *Commentaries on the Laws of England* (Oxford, 1765-69), II, 407.

238. M. Rose, *Authors and Owners: the Invention of Copyright* (Cambridge, Mass., 1993), pp.72-73; and see ibid., p.12, citing F. Hargreave, *An argument in defence of literary property* [1774]. See also on this point Blackstone, *Commentaries*, II, 406. On the background to the distinction between the liberal and mechanical arts, a development of the ancient hierarchy of mental and manual work, see D. Summers, *The Judgement of Sense* (Cambridge, 1987), pp.244 and 251ff.

239. Anon. [1735], cited in M. Rose, *Representations* 23 (1988), pp.56-57.

240. J. Boswell, *The Life of Samuel Johnson* [1791] (Oxford, 1953), p.546.

241. Anon. [1770], cited in T. Ross, 'Copyright and the invention of tradition', *Eighteenth-Century Studies* 26 (1992), p.24.

242. Ibid., p.9, citing Sir Ilay Campbell [1773]. On this debate in general see J. Feather, *A History of British Publishing* (London, 1983), pp.74ff.

243. *An Epistle to Dr. Arbuthnot*, line 265, *Poems*, p.606.

244. J.W. Saunders, *The Profession of English Letters* (London, 1964), p.137.

245. See also Johnson's famous letter (February, 1755) to Lord Chesterfield, included in Boswell's *Life* (Oxford, 1953), pp.184-86. On the attack on patronage see A.S. Collins, *Authorship in the Days of Johnson* (London, 1927), pp.189ff.

246. Horace, *Epistles*, II, 2, 102.

247. *Fable of the Bees*, I, 136-37 and II, 343; A. Smith, TMS, III, 2, 23; E. Young, 'On Lyric Poetry', *Ocean, an Ode* (London, 1728), pp.15-16; T. Smollett, *Peregrine Pickle*, Ch.101 on the 'College of Authors'.

248. O. Goldsmith, *Collected Works*, ed. A. Friedman (Oxford, 1966), II, 85, *The Citizen of the World* [1762], Letter 20.

249. Ibid., II, 344, Letter 84.

250. J. Ralph, *The Case of Authors by Profession or Trade* (London, 1762), p.1.

251. Ibid., pp.8 and 58. Ralph (who was among the Grub Street hacks vilified by Pope in *The Dunciad* (III, 165)) ended his pamphlet with a call for writers 'to find out the force and benefit of combinations. Combine!...and you might out-combine the ugly booksellers themselves', p.75. On Grub Street see P. Rogers, *Hacks and Dunces: Pope, Swift and Grub Street* (London, 1980).

252. All references are to *The Dunciad in Four Books* (1743), in *The Dunciad*, ed. J. Sutherland (London, 1943); this reference is to I, 11-12 and 16, pp.269-70.

253. Ibid., IV, 654, p.409.

254. Ibid., IV, 478-80, p.388.

255. Ibid., IV, 484, p.389, and II, 414, p.317. See also I, 275, where Dulness instructs (in quasi-Epicurean fashion) 'How random thoughts now meaning chance to find', p.290.

256. *The Lives of the English Poets* [1779-81] (Everyman edn., London 1953), II, 205.

257. See E. Jones, 'Pope and Dulness', *Proceedings of the British Academy* LIV (1968), pp.231-63. For a somewhat similar debate in Germany at the end of the century see M. Woodmansee, 'Aesthetic autonomy as a weapon in cultural politics', *The Author, the Art and the Market* (Columbia, 1994), pp.57-86.

258. Virgil, *Aeneid*, VI, 823.

259. The flaying of Marsyas is described in Ovid, *Metamorphoses*, VI, 384ff; the blinding of Thamyris and killing of Linus are recorded in Pausanias, *Description of Greece*, Bk.IX, Ch.29, §§ 6 to 9, and Ch.30, §2. On this aspect of Apollo's character see M. Detienne, *Apollon le couteau à la main* (Paris, 1998), p.11 and passim.

260. *The Rambler*, 145 (6 August, 1751).

261. Boswell, *Life of Johnson*, p.225. Italics added.

262. E. Young, *Conjectures on Original Composition* (London, 1759), pp.55 and 54.

263. Ibid., p.12.
264. See note 260.
265. Young, *Conjectures*, pp.54 and 68.
266. *The Spectator* no.283 (24 January, 1712), ed. D.F. Bond (Oxford, 1965) III, 3-4.
267. Ibid., III, 5.
268. *Complete English Tradesman*, I, 226.
269. *Conjectures*, p.22.
270. *Economic Writings*, I, 177.
271. M. Weber, *The Protestant Ethic and the Spirit of Capitalism* [1904-20], tr. T. Parsons (New York, 1958), pp.39 and 43; H. Trevor-Roper, in M.J. Kitch (ed.), *Capitalism and the Reformation* (London, 1967), pp.31ff; P. Payne, in *Cambridge Economic History of Europe*, VII, 180ff; likewise, J. Kocka, in ibid., p.513.
272. Horace, *Ars poetica*, 322ff.
273. P. Mathias, *The First Industrial Nation* (Sec.edn, London, 1983), pp.3, 13, 56; H. Jennings, *Pandaemonium* (London, 1987), pp.65-66 and 110-11.
274. Smith, WN, V, i, f, 50, 60 and 61.
275. J. McVeagh, *Tradeful Merchants* (London, 1981), pp.86 and 97; J. Raven, *Judging New Wealth* (Oxford, 1992), pp.197, 224 and 234.
276. *Inquiry*, II, 6. This also appeared in the article on 'Commerce' in *Encyclopedia Britannica* (1771), II, 231.
277. G. Raynal, *Histoire des Deux Indes* (Geneva, 1783), IX, 309ff [Bk.XIX, Ch.15].

Chapter Six

1.   *On the Sublime*, I, 4.
2.   Ibid., II, 2, *Ancient Literary Criticism*, ed. and tr. D.A. Russell (Oxford, 1972), p.463.
3.   J. Addison, *The Spectator* nos. 333, 339, 412-14, 417-18 (1712); D. Hume, *Treatise*, II.iii.8 (1739-40); W. Smith, *Dionysius Longinus: On the Sublime,...with notes and observations* (Dublin, 1740), pp.63-64 and 93; J. Baillie, *An Essay on the Sublime* (London, 1747), pp.4, 9, 14, 20-21.
4.   Baillie, *Essay on the Sublime*, p.25.
5.   Ibid., pp.26-27
6.   *A Philosophical Enquiry into the Origins of our Ideas of the Sublime and Beautiful*, ed. J. Boulton (London, 1958), pp.124-25 [III, 27].
7.   Ibid., pp.42-43 [I,10].
8.   Ibid., p.124 [III,27].
9.   Ibid., pp.40, 57 and 59 [I,7; II, 2 and 3].
10. Ibid., pp.61 and 83 [II, 4, 18 and 19].
11. Ibid., pp.64ff [II, 5].
12. Ibid., p.82 [II, 17].
13. Ibid., p.86 [II, 22].
14. Ibid., pp.51 and 86 [I, 18 and II, 22].
15. Ibid., pp.40 and 135-36 [I, 7 and IV, 6].
16. Ibid., pp.51 and 158 [I, 17 and V, 24].
17. Ibid., p.50 [I, 17].
18. *Conjectures on Original Composition* (London, 1759), pp.13-14.
19. Ibid., p.39.
20. Ibid., p.10.
21. Ibid., p.45.

22. Ibid., p.66.
23. Ibid., pp.55 and 12.
24. Ibid., p.42.
25. Ibid., p.53.
26. J. Boswell, *Journal of a Tour of the Hebrides* (Thursday, 30 September), ed. R.W. Chapman (Oxford, 1930), p.341.
27. A. Pope, Preface to *The Works of Shakespeare* (London, 1725), p.ii; Addison, *Spectator* no.160 (3 September, 1711), criticising Milton for being too imitative and restricted by rules (unlike Homer, Pindar, or Shakespeare).
28. *Ocean, an Ode* (London, 1728), p.27.
29. *Conjectures*, p.41.
30. Ibid., p.41.
31. Ibid., p.49.
32. Ibid., p.71.
33. *Commentaries on the Laws of England* (Oxford,1765-69), II, 406.
34. F. Hargreave, *An Argument in defence of literary property* (1774), cited in M. Rose, *Authors and Owners* (Cambridge, Mass., 1993), p.125.
35. *Conjectures*, p.54.
36. For different views of these issues see M. Woodmansee, 'The Genius and the Copyright', *The Author, Art and the Market* (Columbia, 1994), pp.35-55; D. Saunders, *Authorship and Copyright* (London,1992), pp.222ff. and 236ff.
37. E. Zilsel, *Die Entstehung des Geniebegriffes* (Tübingen, 1926); C.S. Lewis, *Studies in Medieval and Renaissance Literature* (Cambridge, 1966), pp.169ff. and *Studies in Words* (Cambridge, 1967), pp.89ff; J.C. Nitzsche, *The Genius Figure in Antiquity and the Middle Ages* (New York, 1975). Johnson's definitions of 'Genius' in his *Dictionary of the English Language* (1755) covered most of these senses, but not invention or fertility.
38. R. Wolseley, Preface to Rochester's *Valentinian*, in *Critical Essays of the 17th century*, ed. J.E. Spingarn (Oxford, 1908), III, 16.
39. W. Temple, 'Of Poetry', *Critical Essays*, ed. Spingarn, III, 74-75.
40. On the background and development of this usage see L. Pearsall Smith, *Four Words* ['Romantic', 'Originality', 'Creative', 'Genius'] (London, 1924), pp.19 ff; with reference to the gendered assumption and characterisation see Ch.1, note 28 and Ch.2, note 95.
41. Quoted by J. Bunyan, *The Pilgrim's Progress*, Everyman edn (London, 1955), p.145, where the similar statement in Genesis 6, 5 is also quoted. In both cases the Vulgate text has *cogitatio*.
42. S. Parker, *A Free...Censure of the Platonic Philosophy* [1666], cited in B. Vickers and N. Struever, *Rhetoric and the Pursuit of Truth* (Los Angeles, 1985), p.43.
43. Satan seduced Eve by 'the organs of her fancy' (*Paradise Lost*, IV, 800), and see Montaigne's essay 'On the Power of the Imagination', *Complete Essays*, tr. D. Frame (Stanford, 1965), pp.68-76. On this subject generally see M.-H. Huet, *Monstrous Imagination* (Cambridge, Mass., 1993).
44. W. Davenant, Preface to *Gondibert* (1650), in *Critical Essays*, ed. Spingarn, II, 20-21; and Z. Mayne, *Two Dissertations concerning sense and the imagination* (London, 1728), p.74.
45. Davenant, *Critical Essays*, ed. Spingarn, II, 27-28.
46. Horace, *Ars poetica*, 295 and 408-18; 'Longinus', *On the Sublime*, XXXVI, 4 and II, 2.
47. J. Dryden, Preface to *The Rival Ladies* (1664), *Of Dramatic Poesy and other critical essays*, ed. G. Watson, Everyman edn (London, 1962), I, 8.

48. R. Blackmore, Preface to *King Arthur* (1697), cited in K. Simonsurri, *Homer's Original Genius* (Cambridge, 1979), p.83. Likewise, W. Temple, 'Of Poetry', *Critical Essays*, ed. Spingarn, III, 81; Addison, *Spectator* no.160 (1711); and A. Pope, Preface to *The Iliad* [1715], *The Poems of Alexander Pope*, ed. M. Mack (London, 1967), VII, 5, 8-9 and 12.

49. On this development for the previous period see W. Rossky, 'Imagination in the English Renaissance', *Studies in the Renaissance* 5 (1958), pp.49-73; and B. Southgate, 'The "Power of Imagination"...in 17th century England', *History of Science* 30 (1992), pp.281-94; for the 18th century see R.S. Crane, 'Suggestions towards a genealogy of the "Man of Feeling"', *The Idea of the Humanities* (Chicago, 1967), pp.188-213, E. Tuveson, *The Imagination as a means of grace* (Berkeley, 1960); and J. Engell, *The Creative Imagination* (Harvard, 1981) (on some of the limits of which see C. Siskin, *The Historicity of Romantic Discourse* (Oxford, 1988), pp.16ff and 37ff).

50. A. Pope, Preface to *The Iliad*, VII, 22 and 4.

51. Ibid., VII, 12 and 3.

52. See C. Thacker, *The Wildness Pleases* (London, 1983); the phrase (of this title) is taken from Shaftesbury, 'The Moralists', *Characteristics of Men, Manners, Opinions, Times* (London, 1711), II, 388. For a mid-century example of this shift see R. Desmond, *Kew: the history of the Royal Botanic Gardens* (London, 1995), p.361: '1757– Robert Greening submits plans for converting the nursery into a wilderness'.

53. T. Blackwell, *An Enquiry into the Life and Writings of Homer* (London, 1735), p.148.

54. Ibid., p.104.

55. Ibid., pp.71 and 121.

56. Ibid., p.125.

57. Ibid., p.65.

58. Ibid., pp.40-41.

59. J. Locke, *Some Thoughts concerning Education,* ed. J.W. and J.S. Yolton (Oxford, 1989), p.221: 'the natural temper of children disposes their minds to wander. Novelty alone takes them'; and Diderot, *Eléments de physiologie*, ed. J. Mayer (Paris, 1964), p.250: 'the imaginative man walks about in his head like a busybody in a palace, every moment going off in a different direction at the sight of something of interest...The imagination is the image of childhood, which is attracted by everything without distinction'. For later examples, see Coleridge, *Biographia Literaria*, Ch.4, ed. J. Engell and W.J. Bate (Princeton, 1983), I, 81, and Baudelaire, *Oeuvres complètes*, ed. C. Pichois (Paris, 1976), p.690 [*Le Peintre de la vie moderne*, III].

60. G. Vico, *The New Science*, §§375 and 376, tr. T.G. Bergin and M.H. Fisch (Cornell, 1968), pp.116-17. This kind of creation was, as Vico indicated, 'infinitely different from that of God'; it was the product not of knowledge but of a 'wholly corporeal imagination (*una corpolentissima fantasia)*'.

61. Vico, *New Science*, § 916, p.336.

62. J. Warton, *Odes on various subjects* (London, 1746), p.6.

63. 'Ode to Fancy', ibid., pp.7-9.

64. J. Warton, *An Essay on the Writings and Genius of Pope* (London, 1756), pp.iv-v.

65. Ibid., p.105.

66. Ibid., p.204.

67. S. Johnson, *The History of Rasselas* [1759] (Harmondsworth, 1976), p.60 [Ch.10].

68. Warton, *Essay on...Pope*, p.x.

69. T. Gray, Note (added in 1768) to 'The Progress of Poesy', II, 2; *The Poems of Thomas Gray, William Collins, Oliver Goldsmith*, ed. R. Lonsdale (London, 1969), p.168.

70. H. Blair, *A Critical Dissertation on...Ossian* (London, 1763), p.2.

71. Ibid., p.209.
72. W. Duff, *An Essay on Original Genius* (London, 1767), pp.97 and 162ff.
73. Ibid., pp.260 and 264ff.
74. Ibid., p.181.
75. Montesquieu, *De l'Esprit des lois*, XIX, 5, *Oeuvres*, ii, 559; J.-J. Rousseau, *Oeuvres complètes*, ed. B.Gagnebin et al. (Paris,1959-96), III, 8, and IV, 324. This edition of Rousseau's works will be referred to hereafter by the initials OC.
76. J.le Rond d'Alembert, 'Discours préliminaire', *Encyclopédie*, (Paris, 1751-65), I, xiv and xvi; Buffon, *Histoire naturelle* (Paris, 1749-1804), IV, 68; J.-F. Marmontel, 'Génie', *Encyclopédie: Supplément* (Paris, 1776-80), III, 203a.
77. J.-B. Dubos. *Réflexions critiques sur la poésie et sur la peinture* (Paris, 1719), II, 5, 12-15 and 41-42; Voltaire, 'Imagination', *Encyclopédie*, VIII, 561bff; and 'Génie', *Questions sur l'Encyclopédie* [1771], *Oeuvres complètes* (Paris, 1877-85), XIX, 246.
78. J.O. de la Mettrie, *Histoire naturelle de l'âme* (La Haye, 1745), pp.119-20 and 185ff; A.-R.-J. Turgot, *Tableau philosophique*...[1750], *Oeuvres*, ed. G. Schelle (Paris, 1913-23), I, 223-24; Turgot distinguishes between minds like diamonds, which reflect light, to those of geniuses, which are like torches shining by themselves; F.-V. Toussaint, *Observations périodiques* [1757], cited by A. Becq, *Genèse de l'esthétique française moderne* (Pisa, 1984), p.695.
79. *Encyclopédie*, VII, 582a-584a.
80. On this subject see H. Dieckmann, 'Diderot's conception of genius', *Journal of the History of Ideas* 2 (1940), pp.151-82; the comments of P. Vernière in his edition of Diderot, *Oeuvres esthétiques* (Paris, 1968), pp.5-8; and J. Chouillet, *L'Esthétique des lumières* (Paris, 1974), pp.128ff.
81. *Oeuvres esthétiques*, p.261. Voltaire had given an example of this in his account of Renaissance Italy, *Essai sur les moeurs*, ed. R. Pomeau (Paris, 1963), I, 766.
82. *Encyclopédie*, V, 636a ['Encyclopédie'].
83. *Oeuvres philosophiques*, ed. P. Vernière (Paris, 1956), p.123.
84. Ibid., pp.229 and 182 [*Pensées sur...la nature* (1754), §§L and VI].
85. *Encyclopédie*, IX, 625b ['Locke'].
86. *Oeuvres philosophiques*, p.300; this work was written in 1769, and published in 1830.
87. Ibid., pp.182 and 189 [*Pensées sur...la nature*, §§ VI and XV]; *Encyclopédie*, V, 296b ['Eclairé']; and VII, 582b and 583b ['Génie'].
88. *Oeuvres complètes*, ed. J. Assézat & M. Tourneux (Paris, 1875-77), II, 411 [*Réfutation d'Helvétius*, written in the early 1770s, published in 1875]. This edition will be referred to hereafter by the initials AT.
89. *Oeuvres esthétiques*, pp.97-98. In the article 'Théosophes' Diderot described such a moment of 'exaltation [and] inspiration' as 'a state of orgasm and intoxication', *Encyclopédie*, XVI, 260b.
90. *Oeuvres esthétiques*, p.135.
91. J. Chouillet, 'Diderot: poet and theorist of the Homer and Ossianist revival', *British Journal of 18th century Studies* 5 (1982), p.227. Macpherson himself was influenced by P.-H. Mallet's *Monuments de la mythologie et de la poésie des anciens Scandinaves* (1756) which made no distinction between Scandinavians and Celts. Diderot subsequently translated some of Ossian.
92. *Encyclopédie*, V, 276a ['Eclectisme'].
93. Ibid., XVI, 253b-54a ['Théosophes'].
94. Ibid., IV, 1061b ['Distraction']; *Le Neveu de Rameau*, ed. J. Fabre (Geneva, 1950), p.85 [written between the 1760s and 1780s, published (in German) in 1805 and (in French) in 1821]. Keats writes about 'negative capability' in his letter of 21 December,

1817, *Letters of John Keats*, ed. R. Gittings (Oxford, 1975), p.43; see also the letters of 22 November, 1817 and 19 February, 1818, ibid., pp.36-37 and 65-67.

95. On *enthousiasme*, see *Oeuvres esthétiques*, pp.97 and 252; on *aliénation*, see *Neveu de Rameau*, p.83 and *Encyclopédie*, XVI, 260b ['Théosophes'].

96. Ficino had used *alienatio* as well as *furor* in describing states of inspiration and vision, see above, p.46.

97. *Eléments de physiologie*, ed. J. Mayer (Paris, 1964), p.296 [first published in 1875], and AT, II, 341.

98. AT, X, 251 [*Salon de 1765*], and AT, II, 341.

99. AT, X, 342 and 417; *Correspondance*, ed. G. Roth (Paris, 1955-70), IV, 56 (18 July, 1762).

100. *Neveu de Rameau*, p.72, and AT, X, 342.

101. AT, XI, 124 [*Salon de 1767*].

102. *Correspondance*, IV, 81 (31 July, 1762).

103. *Neveu de Rameau*, pp.5, 10, 93 and 105.

104. Ibid., pp.44 and 60-61.

105. Ibid., pp.81 and 86.

106. Ibid., pp.13-14.

107. *Oeuvres esthétiques*, pp.306, 330 and 330 [written from 1769, published 1830].

108. Ibid., pp.309, 318 and 332.

109. Ibid., pp.306, 336, 342 and 376.

110. Ibid., p.341.

111. Ibid., p.309.

112. Ibid., p.362.

113. On this subject see H. Dieckmann, *Cinq leçons sur Diderot* (Paris, 1959), pp.33-34.

114. Cicero, *De natura deorum*, III, 70.

115. AT, III, 159. On this work see my article 'Portrait de l'auteur, accompagné d'un fantôme: l'*Essai sur les règnes de Claude et de Néron*', *Diderot: les années dernières*, ed. P. France and A. Strugnell (Edinburgh, 1984), pp.43-62; and on this problem in relation to Diderot's other writings see K. Heitmann, *Ethos des Künstlers und Ethos der Kunst* (Münster Westfalen, 1962).

116. OC, III, 19 and 21.

117. *Correspondance complète*, ed. R.A. Leigh (Geneva & Oxford, 1965-98), II, 87.

118. See my article 'Reading Rousseau's First Discourse', *Studies on Voltaire and the 18th century*, 249 (1987), pp.262ff.

119. OC, III, 118.

120. OC, III, 429.

121. OC, I, 5.

122. OC, I, 5.

123. OC, I, 128.

124. OC, I, 641.

125. OC, I, 172.

126. OC, I 163 and 427.

127. OC, III, 8.

128. OC, I, 5.

129. OC, I, 5.

130. OC, I, 36, 641 and 1153 [*Rêveries...*].

131. OC, I, 1148 and 1153.

132. OC, I, 1140.

133. Voltaire: 'The quarrels of writers benefit literature, as the quarrels of the powerful and the complaints of the weak are necessary to liberty under a free government', cited in T. Besterman, *Voltaire* (Third edn., Oxford, 1976), p.550.

134. OC, I, 1123.

135. OC, I, 362-63.

136. OC, I, 171-72.

137. OC, I, 427.

138. OC, V, 72-74.

139. *Essay concerning human understanding*, II, xxi, 29ff.

140. Diderot, *Oeuvres philosophiques*, p.231 [*Pensées sur...la nature*, § LI]; for other examples, see G.W. Leibniz, *Nouveaux Essais...*, Bk.II, Ch.21, § 36, and C.A. Helvétius, *De l'esprit*, Discours III , Ch.5.

141. J. Harris, *Three Treatises on Art* (London, 1744), pp.24ff.

142. *Essays*, p.246 ('Of the Standard of Taste').

143. Voltaire, *Histoire de l'empire de Russie sous Pierre le Grand*, ed. M. Mervaud et al. (Oxford, 1999), p.552; Raynal, *Histoire des Deux Indes* (Geneva, 1783), I, 21 and VII, 123.

144. OC, I, 41.

145. *Confessions*, I, i.

146. OC, I, 1047.

147. The picture illustrated the opening sentence of the second part of the *Discours*: 'an ancient tradition, which passed from Egypt to Greece, stated that a god who was hostile to the peace of mankind invented the sciences' (OC, III, 17).

148. OC, III, 288. This idea, which had Stoic antecedents, occurred often in Protestant writings; see for example Defoe, *Robinson Crusoe* (Harmondsworth, 1965), p.186; Mary Wollstonecraft, *Vindication of the Rights of Woman* (Harmondsworth, 1985), pp.99 and 304; likewise, Mandeville, *Fable*, I, 106.

149. *Encyclopédie*, VII, 905b and 906a ['Grecs, Philosophie des'].

150. *Werke*, ed. E. Trunz (Hamburg, 1948-60), X, 48 [*Dichtung und Wahrheit*]. References to this edition, the Hamburger Ausgabe, will be indicated by the initials HA.

151. Kant, *Kritik der Urteilskraft*, § 46.

152. Wordsworth, *Essay, Supplementary to the Preface* [to *Poems*, 1815], in *William Wordsworth*, ed. S. Gill (Oxford, 1984), pp.657-58. As Wordsworth indicated, he owed this idea to Coleridge; his first formulation of it had been in a letter to Lady Beaumont, dated 21 May, 1807, (see *Selected Prose*, ed. J.O. Hayden (Harmondsworth, 1988), p.321).

153. HA, IV, 178 [*Prometheus* (written 1773, published 1835), lines 71-72]. See, on this work, N. Boyle, *Goethe: the poet and the age*, Vol.1: *The poetry of desire* (Oxford, 1991), pp.162ff.

154. Ibid., [line 77].

155. HA, I, 45 ['Prometheus' (written 1774, published 1785), lines 15-17].

156. HA, I, 178 [*Prometheus*, line 86].

157. Ibid., [lines 90-95].

158. Byron, *Childe Harold's Pilgrimage*, Canto III, stanza 6, lines 1-2.

159. HA, IV, 179-80 [*Prometheus*, lines 138-48].

160. HA, IV, 182-83 [*Prometheus*, lines 242-45]. This passage provides the final stanza to the poem 'Prometheus', HA, I, 46.

161. HA, I, 370 ['Vermächtnis', line 33]. For an analysis of the early poems in relation to the subject of this study see J. Schmidt, *Das Geschichte des Genie-Gedankens in der*

deutschen Literatur, Philosophie und Politik (Darmstadt, 1986), pp.193ff, especially his discussion of *Wanderers Sturmlied*, pp.199ff.

162. *Goethes Briefe*, ed. K.R. Mandelkow et al. (Hamburg, 1962-67), I, 246 (to Charlotte von Stein, 10 December 1777).

163. Ibid., I, 355 (to J.C. Lavater, 7 May 1778).

164. Ibid., I, 181 (to J.G. Herder, 25 March 1775).

165. Ibid., I, 234 (to Auguste Gräfin zu Stolberg, 17 July 1777).

166. Ibid., I, 177 (to Auguste Gräfin zu Stolberg, 13 February 1775).

167. HA, XIII, 45-47 ['Die Natur'].

168. HA, IX, 583 [*Dichtung und Wahrheit*].

169. HA, IX, 284 and see p.287 [Ibid].

170. *Goethes Briefe*, I, 9 (to Ludwig von Buri, 2 June 1764).

171. HA, X, 529-30 ['Selbstschilderung'].

172. HA, VI, 117 [*Werther*].

173. HA, III, 367 [*Urfaust*, lines 29-30].

174. *Gespräche mit Eckermann*, 10 February 1829; ed. F. Bergemann (Baden-Baden, 1981), p.290.

175. Ibid., 2 April 1829, p.310; likewise, HA, XII, 487 [Maxime no.863].

176. HA, III, 348 [*Faust*, Part II, lines 11575-76].

177. HA, III, 18 [*Faust*, Prologue, line 317].

178. *Gespräche*, 10 February 1829; p.290.

179. See Schiller's letter to Körner (2 February 1789), cited in his *On the Aesthetic Education of Man*, ed. E.M. Wilkinson and L.A. Willoughby (Oxford, 1967), p.xxxvi; also, Mme de Staël's observations in *De l'Allemagne* (Paris, 1968), I, 190-91 ['Goethe'].

180. *Roman Elegies and The Diary*, tr. D. Luke (London, 1988), pp.40-41 ('Mehr als ich ahndete, das Glück, es ist mir geworden').

181. HA, I, 61-62. ['Kenner und Künstler', lines 10ff].

182. HA, I, 369 ['Eins und Alles', line 15].

183. HA, XI, 211 [*Italienische Reise*, 17 March 1787].

184. B. Constant, *Journal*, (16 February 1804), *Oeuvres*, ed. A. Roulin (Paris, 1957), p.235.

185. HA, I, 52; see on this passage R. Gray, *Poems of Goethe* (Cambridge, 1966), pp.58-59; see likewise HA, XII, 227 ['Zum Shakespeares-Tag'].

186. HA, IX, 539 [*Dichtung und Wahrheit*]. Goethe translated two works which illustrated this point – *Le Neveu de Rameau* and Benvenuto Cellini's *Autobiography*. For a vivid fictional example see the character of Cardillac in E.T.A. Hoffmann's story *Das Fräulein von Scuderi* (1819).

187. *Gespräche*, 28 March 1827, p.558.

188. HA, II, 12 ['Der Deutsche dankt', lines 10-11].

189. HA, XII, 372 [Maxime no.49]. This remark bears a certain resemblance to the observation of the Roman lawyer and proconsul Quintus Mucius Scaevola that there were three kinds of gods in the Roman tradition: those of the poets, the philosophers and the magistrates. The statement is recorded by Augustine, *De civitate Dei*, IV, 27, and quoted by Montesquieu, in his *Dissertation sur la politique des Romains dans la religion* [1716], *Oeuvres*, i, 86.

190. HA, XI, 332 [*Italienische Reise*, 27 May 1787].

191. *Gespräche*, 11 March 1828, pp.624ff; see also 6 December 1829, p.350; 2 March 1831, pp.438-39; 8 March 1831, pp.441-42.

192. HA, X, 175 [*Dichtung und Wahrheit*, Bk.XX].

193. HA, X, 177.

194. *Gespräche*, 2 March 1831, pp.438; see also 23 October, 1828, p.652.
195. Ibid., 11 March 1828, p.626 and 2 March, 1831, p.439.
196. HA, X, 546 [Unterredung mit Napoleon].
197. See H. Blumenberg, *Work on Myth*, tr. R.M. Wallace (Cambridge, Mass.), pp.465ff.

Chapter Seven

1. J. Boswell, *Life of Johnson*, (Oxford, 1953), pp.1110-11n.
2. *On the Sublime*, tr. D.A. Russell, *Ancient Literary Criticism* (Oxford, 1972), p.494, XXXVI, 1 and XXXV, 3.
3. See M. Hope Nicolson, *Mountain Gloom and Mountain Glory: the development of the aesthetics of the infinite* (Ithaca, 1959), pp.213ff and 270ff.
4. K. Thomas, *Man and the natural world* (London, 1983), pp.102ff and 121ff.
5. *Leviathan*, ed. C.B. Macpherson (Harmondsworth, 1968), pp.120-21 [Ch.6].
6. C.A. Patrides, *The Cambridge Platonists* (Cambridge, 1980), pp.4ff.
7. Newton, *Optics*, Query 28 (1706), cited in *The Leibniz-Clarke Correspondence*, pp.173-74.
8. E.L.Tuveson, *The Imagination as a means to grace* (Berkeley, 1960), p.67.
9. *Essay concerning human understanding*,ed. P.Nidditch (Oxford, 1979), p.55 [I, ii, 15].
10. Ibid, p.552 [IV, iii, 20]. The 'candle of the Lord' phrase, used by the Cambridge Platonists, derived from Proverbs 20, 27.
11. Ibid., p.440 [III,vi, 4]; although Locke does go on to say that the name 'man' does imply that 'reason is essential to it', p.441.
12. Ibid., pp.335ff. [II, xxvii, 9ff].
13. Anthony Ashley Cooper, Earl of Shaftesbury, *The Life, Unpublished Letters and Philosophical Regimen*, ed. B. Rand (London, 1900), p.403 (3 June, 1709).
14. Diogenes Laertius, *Lives of the Philosophers*, VII, 86-87; Marcus Aurelius, *Meditations*, V, 3.
15. Cicero, *De officiis*, I, xxxi, 110-14.
16. *Philebus*, 50c and *Phaedrus*, 245c-246a.
17. *Hamlet*, I, 3, 78-80.
18. *Characteristics of Men, Manners, Opinions, Times* (London, 1711), I, 264.
19. Ibid., II, 358.
20. Ibid., I, 280-81.
21. *Essay concerning human understanding*, p.100 [I, iv, 23].
22. *Characteristics*, II, 109-110.
23. Ibid., II, 279 and 283ff.
24. Ibid., II, 405.
25. Ibid., II, 366.
26. Ibid., II, 346 and 218.
27. Ibid., II, 344.
28. Ibid., II, 345.
29. Ibid., II, 245, 343, 349, 351-52 and 393.
30. Ibid., II, 386.
31. Ibid., I, 136, 142 and 145.
32. Ibid., I, 206.
33. Ibid., I, 207.
34. Ibid., I, 312-13. In this passage fancy is portrayed as a seductive female 'sollicitress' and 'enchantress', a recurrent theme in Shaftesbury's writings (see, for example, *Life*,

Letters and...Regimen, pp.208 and 211).

35. Ibid., I, 233ff.
36. Ibid., I, 207.
37. Ibid., I, 208.
38. Ibid., I, 207.
39. M.Akenside, *The Pleasures of the Imagination* (London, 1744), III, 410, 625, and 400.
40. *Characteristics*, II, 205.
41. Ibid., II, 189; and see I, 293ff.
42. Ibid., II, 294 and I, 304.
43. Ibid., I, 264.
44. Ibid., I, 185.
45. Ibid., II, 272 and see II, 395ff. On the significance of this notion see J. Stolnitz, 'Of the origins of "Aesthetic Disinterestedness"', *Journal of Aesthetics and Art Criticism* 20 (1961), pp.131-43.
46. Ibid., II, 427. On this concern for personal moral integrity see L. Klein, *Shaftesbury and the culture of politeness* (Cambridge, 1994), pp.74-90.
47. Ibid., III, 262n.
48. Ibid., III, 139-40.
49. *Conjectures on Original Composition*, p.42.
50. Ibid., pp.53-54.
51. Ibid., p.20.
52. Ibid., p.12.
53. Ibid., p.68.
54. D. Erasmus, *Collected Works*, Vol. 28, ed. A.H.T. Levi (Toronto, 1986), pp.40-42.
55. *Conjectures*, p.31.The Protestant character of Young's essay is also evident from his anti-Catholic remarks, such as 'true poesy, like true religion, abhors idolatry' (p.67), or 'the blind veneration of a bigot saluting the papal toe' (p.55).
56. *The Task*, Bk.I, line 749.
57. *Enquiry into the Life and Writings of Homer*, p.24.
58. R. Lowth, *Lectures on the sacred poetry of the Hebrews*, tr. G. Gregory (London, 1787), I, 156-57. The work had originally been published in Latin in 1753.
59. Ibid., I, 154.
60. Ibid., I, 158.
61. Ibid., I, 169.
62. Ibid., I, 169.
63. Ibid., I, 79 and II, 14ff.
64. A. Gerard, *An Essay on Genius* (London, 1774), pp.29 and 31ff.
65. Ibid., pp.49 and 50.
66. Ibid., p.52.
67. Ibid., p.241.
68. Ibid., p.81.
69. Ibid., p.37, and see pp.71ff.
70. Ibid., p.49.
71. Ibid., p.49.
72. Ibid., p.318.
73. *Conjectures*, p.73.
74. Ibid., p.22.
75. Ibid., p.39.This idea had also occurred in Young's poem *Nights Thoughts on Life, Death and Immortality* (1741-45) in the final book (V) 'The Relapse', where Genius

'pleads exemption from the laws of sense; / Considers reason a leveller; / And scorns to share a blessing with the crowd', V, 265ff.

76. *Conjectures*, p.61.

77. Locke, *Essay concerning human understanding*, p.683, [IV, xvii, 14]. See likewise Milton, *Paradise Lost*, V, 487ff.

78. *Hamlet*, II, 2, 303ff: 'What piece of a work is man...in action how like an angel, in apprehension how like a god'. See also *A Midsummer Night's Dream*, V, 1,4ff and *Paradise Lost*, VIII, 354.

79. G.W. Leibniz, *Principes de la nature et de la grace*, § 14; *Philosophische Schriften*, ed. C.J. Gerhardt (Berlin, 1875-90), VI, 604.

80. Leibniz, *Monadologie*, § 83; *Philosophische Schriften*, VI, 621.

81. A. Baumgarten, *Aesthetica* , [1750-58] , §§ 38 and 44; and see his *Metaphysica*, §648. Baumgarten had first used the term 'aesthetic' in his *Meditationes philosophicae*...(1735), §116, and his ideas became widely known through the writings of his pupil G.F. Meier's *Anfängsgründe aller schönen Wissenschaften* (Halle, 1748); see §§ 217 and 221 of that work (I, 511 and 521) on the need for *Proportion* among both *Erkenntniskräfte* and *Begehrungskräfte* to achieve what Meier calls '*das aesthetische Temperament eines schönen Geist*' (I, 521).

82. M. Mendelssohn, *Betrachtungen über die Quellen und die Verbindungen der schönen Künste...*, [1757] *Gesammelte Schriften*, ed. F. Bamberger et al. [1929] (Stuttgart, 1971), I, 171.

83. J.G. Sulzer, 'Analyse du Génie', *Histoire de l'Académie Royale des Sciences et Belles Lettres: Année 1757* (Berlin, 1759), pp.393, 398-99 and 403.

84. F.G. Resewitz, *Versuch über das Genie* (1759), cited in P. Grappin, *La Théorie du génie dans le préclassicisme allemand* (Paris, 1952), p.131. See also on this subject C.R. Bingham, *The Rise and development of the idea of genius in 18th century German literature* (D.Phil. dissertation, Oxford, 1958).

85. G.E. Lessing, *Hamburgische Dramaturgie* no.34 [25 August, 1767], *Gesammelte Werke*, ed. P. Rilla (Berlin, 1968), VI, 175.

86. J.G. Herder, 'Shakespeare', *Werke*, ed. W. Pross (Munich, 1984-), I, 541-42; as a 'Creator' with 'divine power' or 'grasp' see pp.535-36 and 539. For similar remarks see J.M.R. Lenz, 'Anmerkungen übers Theater' [1774], in *Sturm und Drang: Kritische Schriften*, ed. E. Loewenthal (Heidelberg, 1949), pp.720-22, and J.C. Lavater, *Physiognomische Fragmente* [1774-78], ibid., pp.817, 819 and 823.

87. Goethe, 'Von deutscher Baukunst', *Werke* (Hamburger Ausgabe), XII, 13-14.

88. Goethe, 'Nach Faconet und über Falconet', HA, XII, 24.

89. Herder, 'Ossian', *Werke*, I, 482, and 502-3. On this movement in general see R. Pascal, *The German Sturm und Drang* (Manchester, 1953), and, on the religious dimension, pp.87ff. and 131ff.

90. J.G. Hamann, *Aesthetica in nuce* [1762], ed. S.-A. Jorgensen (Stuttgart, 1968), pp.113ff, on the senses, and p.103, on the childlike; *Hamann's Socratic Memorabilia*, ed. and tr. J.C. O'Flaherty (Baltimore, 1967), p.166, on sensibility, and pp.168-72, on naivety. See also O'Flaherty's Introduction, pp.21-22, on the importance to Hamann of human sexuality.

91. Genesis, 2, 20, commented on by Philo, *Allegorical interpretation of Genesis*, Bk.I, § 150, and see, for example, Milton, *De doctrina Christiana*, ch.15, and *Paradise Lost*, VIII, 352-4.

92. Letter to Nicolai (25 August, 1769), *Gesammelte Werke*, IX, 327.

93. *Über den Beweis des Geistes und der Kraft* [1777], *Gesammelte Werke*, VIII, 14.

94. References to Kant's writings are in the standard format: initials of the German titles are used for the three *Critiques* — *Kritik der reinen Vernunft* as KrV, *Kritik der praktischen Vernunft* as KpV, and *Kritik der Urteilskraft* as KU; other titles are given in abbreviated form. Volume and page numbers are to the Akademie Ausgabe (*Gesammelte Schriften*, Berlin, 1900-42), referred to as AA, with the usual exception of the first *Critique*, for which page numbers of the first edition (A) and second edition (B) are provided. I have benefited greatly from the the translations of N. Kemp Smith, L.W. Beck, J. Meredith, M. Gregor and other Kant scholars. The references here are to the essay 'Was ist Aufklärung?', AA, VIII, 35-36 and 40.

95. 'Idee zu einer allgemeinen Weltgeschichte...', Third and Ninth Thesis, AA, VIII, 19 and 30.

96. Ibid., Fourth and Fifth Thesis, AA, VIII, 20-22.The development of moral autonomy also involves pain, KpV, AA, V, 73.

97. KU, Introduction, Sect. VII (AA, V, 190) and IX (V, 197), and KU, § 9 (V, 218 and 219), § 23 (V, 244) and § 57 (V, 344).

98. KU, § 46 (V, 307), § 47 (V, 309), and § 49 (V, 318).

99. KU, § 49 (V, 314-15).

100. KU, § 47 (V, 318).

101. KU, § 86 (V, 443).

102. KU, Introduction, Sect. IX, (V, 195).

103. KU, § 23 (V, 245).

104. KU, General Comment (closing Bk.I), (V, 240).

105. KU, § 46 (V, 307).

106. KU, § 2 (V, 205ff).

107. KU, General Comment (following § 29), (V, 271ff).

108. KU, § 87 (V, 450).

109. KrV, A249/B307, and see KU, § 77 (V, 405ff).

110. KU, § 57 Comment 1 (V, 342ff).

111. See note 107.

112. KU, § 42, pp.298ff.

113. KU, § 59, (V, 353).

114. See G. Tonelli, 'Kant's Early Theory of Genius (1770-79)', *Journal of the History of Philosophy* 4 (1966), pp.109-31 and 209-24.

115. KrV, Bxvi.

116. 'Idee zu einer allgemeinen Geschichte...', Third Thesis, AA, VIII, 19-20. In both epistemological and ethical contexts Kant occasionally used the verb *schaffen* (to create) to describe this (e.g. KpV, A273/B751, *Die Metaphysik der Sitten*, AA VI, 439 and *Anthropologie...*, AA, VII, 321). Since in the former context the process is both involuntary and unconscious the word is inappropriate; but there may perhaps be some significance in the fact that he used it (unlike Hume, see below Ch.9, note 99).

117. See M.H. Abrams, 'Art-as-Such: The Sociology of Modern Aesthetics', and 'From Addison to Kant: Modern Aesthetics and the Exemplary Art', *Doing Things with Texts* (New York, 1989), pp.135-87.

118. KU, §§ 13 and 14 (V, 223ff).

119. KU, § 11 (V, 221).

120. KU, §§ 2 and 5 (V, 205 and 210).

121. KU, § 5 (V, 209).

122. See P. Kristeller, 'The Modern System of the Arts', *Journal of the History of Ideas* 12 (1951) and 13 (1952), reprinted in *Renaissance Thought II* (New York, 1965), pp.163-227.

123. *On the Aesthetic Education of Man* [1795], tr. and ed. E.M. Wilkinson and L.A. Willoughby (Oxford, 1967), XVII.1, p.205.

124. Ibid., XXVII.10, p.215.

125. Ibid., XXII.1, p.151 (translation modified) and II.5, p.9; (see also IX. 4, p.57; XX. 4 and note, pp.141-43; XXI. 5 and 6, pp.147-49).

126. For differing views of what precisely that future would be, see the comments of Wilkinson and Willoughby, ibid., pp.cxciff, and J. Chytry, *The Aesthetic State* (Berkeley, 1989), pp.94ff.

127. *System of Transcendental Idealism* [1800], tr. P. Heath (Charlottesville, 1978), Part VI, Sect.3, pp.229-30.

128. Ibid., Part VI, Sect.1, p.223.

129. Ibid., Part VI, Sect.2, pp.226-27.

130. See A. Wiedmann, *Romantic Art Theory* (Henley-on-Thames, 1986), pp.66ff., and F. Beiser, *Enlightenment, Revolution and Romanticism* (Cambridge, Mass., 1992), pp.228ff.

131. W.H. Wackenroder, *Herzensergiessungen eines kunstliebenden Klosterbruders* [1797], cited in M.H. Abrams, 'Kant and the theology of art', *Notre Dame English Journal* 13 (1981), pp.95 and 94.

132. *Über das Verhältnis der bildenden Künste zu der Natur* [1807], in F.W. Schelling, *Texte zur Philosophie der Kunst*, ed. W. Beierwaltes (Stuttgart, 1982), p.57.

133. Ibid., p.63.

134. The proverb was adapted from J.G. Seume's poem 'Die Gesänge'; see G. Büchmann, *Geflügelte Worte und Zitatenschatz* (Stuttgart, 1961), pp.164-65.

135. E.W. Broome, *The Rev. Rowland Hill* (London, 1881), p.93.

136. *Religion innerhalb der Grenzen...*, II, General Remark; AA, VI, 86.

137. *Anthropologie...*, § 67, AA, VII, 242. For a similar example of ancient wisdom in new terms see Novalis' reformulation (in *Die Christenheit oder Europa*) of the music of the spheres as 'the eternal *creative* music of the universe' (italics added), *Werke*, ed. G. Schulz (Munich, 1969), p.508.

138. Aristotle, *Poetics*, 1459a and 1454b.

139. Horace, *Ars poetica*, 400.

140. Gellius, *Noctes Atticae*, XI, 2, 5 (see Chapter 3, note 166).

141. *An Essay on the history of civil society* (Cambridge, 1995), p.175.

142. C. Garve, 'Betrachtung einiger Verschiedenheiten in den Werken der altester und neuern Schriftsteller, besonders der Dichter' (1779), *Popularphilosophische Schriften*, ed. K. Wolfel (Stuttgart, 1974), p.28.

143. Ibid., pp.37-38.

144. Ibid., pp.77ff.

145. Horace, *Ars poetica*, 394-96.

146. Compare his 'The Bard' and 'Elegy in a Country Curchyard'; see also R. Folkenflik, 'The Artist as Hero in the 18th century', *Yearbook of English Studies* 12 (1982), pp.96ff.

147. *Le Siècle de Louis XV*, Ch. 32, ed. A. Adam (Paris, 1966), II, 54.

148. *Oeuvres esthétiques*, (*Entretiens sur le Fils naturel* [1757]), p.105.

149. *Du théâtre ou nouvel essai sur l'art dramatique* (Amsterdam, 1773), pp.vi, 39-40, 45 and 135.

150. *Encyclopédie*, V, 642b ['Encyclopédie'].

151. *Choix de discours de réception à l'Académie française* (Paris, 1808), II, 69 and 73.

152. *Encyclopédie*, III, iv.

153. See the 1743 essay 'Le Philosophe' (which became the basis for the article on this

subject in Volume Twelve of the *Encyclopédie*), in H. Dieckemann (ed.), *Le Philosophe* (St. Louis, 1948).

154. In 1787 Ruhlière claimed that 'what we have called "the empire of public opinion"' had been a development of the second half of the century; since 1749 'men of letters' had had the ambition to be the mouthpiece and arbiters of public opinion, and 'the desire to instruct' had become more common than 'the desire to please', *Correspondance littéraire,...par Grimm, Diderot...*, ed. M. Tourneux (Paris, 1877-82), XV, 84 (4 June, 1787).

155. W. Blackstone [1769], cited in E. Hellmuth (ed.), *The Transformation of Political Culture: England and Germany in the late 18th century* (Oxford, 1990), p.479. In addition to this volume, see on this subject J.R. Censer and J. Popkin (eds.), *Press and Politics in Pre-Revolutionary France* (Berkeley, 1987); R. Chartier, *Les Origines culturelles de la révolution française* (Paris, 1990), pp.27ff; J.A.W. Gunn, *Beyond Liberty and Property* (Montreal, 1983); and H. Bödeker (ed.), *Über den Prozess der Aufklärung in Deutschland in 18 Jahrhundert* (Göttingen, 1987).

156. 'Was ist Aufklärung?', AA, VIII, 37.

157. 'Über den Gemeinspruch...', AA, VIII, 304.

158. C. Duclos, *Considérations sur les moeurs de ce siècle*, ed. F.C. Green (Cambridge, 1939), pp.138-39. See likewise A.-L. Thomas, 'De l'homme de lettres considéré comme citoyen' [1767], *Choix de discours de réception à l'Académie française* (Paris, 1808), I, 359ff.

159. Jean-Francois, Marquis de Chastellux, *De la felicité publique* (Bouillon, 1776), II, 109 [Sect.III, Ch.3].

160. This statement occurs in one of Diderot's anonymous contributions to Raynal's *Histoire des deux Indes*, (Geneva, 1783), IX, 117 [Bk.XIX, Ch.2].

161. Quoted in C.G. Stricklen, 'The *philosophes*' political mission...1750-89', *Studies on Voltaire and the 18th century* 86 (1971), p.177.

162. See P. Bénichou, *Le sacre de l'écrivain: 1750-1830* (Paris, 1973), pp.17ff. and passim; and J.A. Leith, *The Idea of art as propaganda in France, 1750-1799* (Toronto, 1965), especially pp.57ff.

163. L. Wekhrlin, *Graues Ungeheuer* [1784], cited in R. Vierhaus, 'Der aufgeklärte Schriftsteller', in H. Bödeker (ed.), *Über den Prozess der Aufklärung...*, p.54.

164. E. Sieyès, *Qu'est-ce que le Tiers état?*, ed. R. Zapperi (Geneva, 1970), p.125.

165. Ibid., p.164.

166. Ibid., pp.125-26. The view had featured in the *cahiers* compiled over the previous year; see M.B. Garrett, *The Estates-General of 1789* (London, 1935), pp.162-63.

167. Sieyès, *Tiers état*, p.149.

168. Ibid., p.171.

169. Ibid., p.177.

170. Ibid., p.173.

171. T. Paine, *Rights of Man*, ed. E. Foner (Harmondsworth, 1985), p.176.

172. M. Robespierre, 'Déclaration des droits...' [24 April, 1793], §1, *Oeuvres*, ed. M. Bouloiseau et al. (Paris, 1910-67), IX, 464.

173. B. Constant, *De la liberté des anciens comparée à celle des modernes*, (Paris, 1819).

Chapter Eight

1. Johnson's view appears to have been representative; see D. Spadafora, *The Idea of Progress in 18th century Britain* (New Haven, 1990), pp.6-7.

2.   J. Priestley, *Essay on the First Principles of Government, Theological and Miscellaneous Works* (London, 1817-32), XXII, 8-9.

3.   J.-L. Carra, *Esprit de la morale et de la philosophie* (1777), cited in R. Darnton, *Mesmerism and the end of Enlightenment in France* (Cambridge, Mass., 1968), p.110.

4.   G.E. Lessing, *Die Erziehung des Menschengeschlechts*, § 85, *Gesammelte Werke*, ed. P. Rilla (Berlin, 1968), VIII, 612.

5.   See on this subject G. Ladner, *The Idea of Reform* (Cambridge, Mass., 1959).

6.   E.L. Tuveson, *Millenium and Utopia* (Berkeley, 1949), pp.93ff and 116ff.

7.   Boswell, *Life of Johnson*, p.704 (22 March, 1776).

8.   William Worthington [1743], cited in R.S. Crane, 'Anglican Apologetics and the Idea of Progress, 1699-1745', *The Idea of the Humanities* (Chicago, 1967), I, 239.

9.   M.-J.-A.-N. Caritat, Marquis de Condorcet, *Esquisse d'un tableau historique des progrès de l'esprit humain*, ed. M. and .F. Hincker (Paris, 1966), p.77. The work was published in 1795.

10. Ibid., pp.243-44.

11. Ibid., pp.77, 221, 255 and 274.

12. Ibid., p.284.

13. *Some Thoughts concerning Education*, ed. J.W.and J.S. Yolton (Oxford, 1989), p.83 [§ 1].

14. Ibid., pp.83-84 [§ 2].

15. D. Spadafora, *The Idea of Progress...*, pp.145ff.

16. J. Priestley, *Hartley's Theory of the Human Mind...*(London, 1775), pp.202ff.

17. Ibid., pp.204-5.

18. Ibid., p.338.

19. Ibid., p.347. See likewise Hartley's Preface to his *Observations on Man, his Frame, his Duty and his Expectations* (London, 1749), I, vii-viii.

20. This statement occurs in Hartley's Conclusion to his *Observations...*(1749 edn) II, 453, which is marked not by the confidence shown by Priestley but rather by a deep sense of anxiety: 'the present circumstances of the world are extraordinary and critical, beyond what has ever yet happened', p.455, and see pp.439ff.

21. C. Macaulay, *Letters on Education* (London, 1790), pp.7 and 53. The same idea had appeared in a novel *The Child of Nature, improved by chance* (published in 1774): 'nature never made a murderer, a thief, a perjurer, and all the villains we hear of [owe their existence] to society only', cited in R.V. Sampson, *Progress in the Age of Reason* (London, 1956), p.53.

22. A.-R.-J. Turgot, *Oeuvres*, ed. G. Schelle (Paris, 1913-23), I, 215-16 and 285, first published in Du Pont de Nemours' edition of his writings (1808-11).

23. Ibid., pp.276 and 220.

24. Ibid., pp.131ff and 208.

25. Ibid., p.133.

26. Ibid., pp.283-85.

27. See R.L. Meek, *Social Science and the Ignoble Savage* (Cambridge, 1976), pp.9-27.

28. *Eloge de Gournay* (1755), *Oeuvres*, I, 604.

29. Ibid., I, 133.

30. St. Ambrose, cited in A. Lovejoy, 'Milton and the Paradox of the Fortunate Fall', *Essays in the History of Ideas* (Baltimore, 1948), p.288; Milton, *Areopagitica, Complete Prose Works* (New Haven, 1953-82), II, 515.

31. *Essay on Man*, Bk.II, line 292.

32. Hume, *Essays Moral, Political and Literary* (Indianapolis, 1985), p.280.

33. E. Benveniste, 'Civilisation, Contribution à l'histoire d'un mot', *Problèmes de linguistique générale* (Paris, 1966), pp.336-45; J. Fisch, 'Zivilisation, Kultur', *Geschichtliche Grundbegriffe*, ed. O. Brunner et al. (Stuttgart, 1972-97), V, 679-774; J. Starobinski, 'The Word "Civilisation"', *Blessings in Disguise*, tr. A. Goldhammer (Cambridge, Mass., 1993), pp.1-35.

34. *The History of the Decline and Fall of the Roman Empire*, ed. J.B. Bury (London, 1925), IV, 177-79.

35. Ibid., p.175.

36. Ibid., p.181.

37. Condorcet, *Esquisse...*, p.242.

38. J.G. Herder, *Über den Ursprung der Sprache*, *Werke*, ed. W. Pross (Munich, 1984-), II, 323.

39. *Geschichte der lyrischen Dichtkunst*, *Werke*, I, 25.

40. Ibid., I, 25.

41. Ibid., I, 28 and 37.

42. 'Shakespeare', ibid., I, 538-39.

43. I. Iselin, *Philosophischen Mutmassungen über die Geschichte der Menschheit* (Sec.edn. Zurich, 1768), I, 11 and 13.

44. Ibid., I, 53. On Iselin see P.H. Reill, *The German Enlightenment and the Rise of Historicism* (Berkeley, 1975), pp.65ff.

45. Herder, *Auch eine Philosophie der Geschichte*, *Werke*, I, 631 and 643ff.

46. Ibid., I, 617-18 and 613.

47. Ibid., I, 642.

48. Ibid., I, 643 and 677.

49. Ibid., I, 614, 616 and 632.

50. Ibid., I, 633-34.

51. Ibid., I, 613.

52. A. Lovejoy, *The Great Chain of Being* (Cambridge, Mass.), 1936, p.52.

53. Herder, *Werke*, I, 632.

54. Ibid., I, 636.

55. Ibid., I, 660-61.

56. Ibid., I, 678.

57. Ibid., I, 538.

58. *King Lear*, IV, I, 36-37.

59. *Von Erkennen und Empfindung*, *Werke*, II, 714.

60. *Sämmtliche Werke*, ed. B. Suphan (Berlin, 1877-1913), (referred to hereafter as Suphan), XIII, 46 and 114; XIV, 213.

61. Ibid., XIII, 148, 154-55 and 171; and see XIV, 213 – 'The divinity helps us only through our industry, reason and powers (*Kräfte*)...It formed man and said: "Be my image (*Bild*), a God on earth! Command and rule! [And] whatever noble and excellent things you can create out of nature, bring forth!'

62. Ibid., XIII, 178.

63. Ibid., XIII, 350-51.

64. Ibid., XIII, 184 and 154ff.

65. Ibid., XIV, 215 and 243.

66. *Werke*, I, 542.

67. Suphan, XIII, 175 and 420.

68. Ibid., XIV, 218.

69. Ibid., XIV, 219 and 223.

70. Ibid., XIV, 227 and 233-34.

71. Ibid., XIV, 239.
72. See R. Vierhaus, 'Bildung', *Geschichtliche Grundbegriffe*, I, 508ff.
73. Quoted in W.H. Bruford, *Culture and Society in Classical Weimar, 1775-1806* (Cambridge, 1975), p.236 (translation amended).
74. Suphan, XIII, 394.
75. Epictetus, *Discourses*, II, 8; Plotinus, *Enneads*, I, 6; Michelangelo, 'Non ha l'ottimo artista alcun concetto', *Rime*, ed. S. Barelli (Milan, 1975), no.151; Spenser, *An Hymn in Honour of Beauty* (especially stanzas 6 and 7).
76. *Theory of Moral Sentiments*, VI.iii.25.
77. *Principles of Moral and Political Science*, pp.227 and 225.
78. See Reill, *German Enlightenment and the Rise of Historicism*, pp.161ff and 215ff.
79. G. Leclerc, Comte de Buffon, *Des Epoques de la nature*, ed. G. Gohau (Paris, 1998), p.220; H. Davy, *A Discourse...on chemistry* (London, 1802), p.16.
80. *Common Sense* [1776], *The Thomas Paine Reader*, ed. M. Foot and I. Kramnick (Harmondsworth, 1987), p.80 and 109; R. Price, 'Observations on the Importance of the American Revolution' [1785], *Political Writings*, ed. D.O. Thomas (Cambridge, 1991), p.118.
81. See R. Koselleck, *Futures Past* tr. K. Tribe (Cambridge, Mass., 1985), p.279: 'the concept "progress (*Fortschritt*)" was first minted toward the end of the 18th century'. For a more extensive treatment of this subject see Koselleck's article 'Fortschritt', *Geschichtliche Grundbegriffe*, II, 351ff.
82. W. von Humboldt, *Idee zu einem Versuch, die Grenzen der Wirksamkeit des Staates zu bestimmen, Gesammelte Schriften*, ed. A. Leitzmann (Berlin, 1903-36), I, 171.
83. *Collected Works*, ed. K. Coburn et al. (Princeton, 1969-), I, 235.The lecture was published in *The Watchman* in 1796 with this passage reading: 'Man...is urged to develop the powers of the Creator and by new combinations of those powers to imitate his creativeness', *Collected Works*, II, 132. This may be the earliest instance of the word 'creativeness' in English; the first date given by the OED is 1820.
84. *The Theory of the Four Movements*, tr. I. Patterson (Cambridge, 1996), p.87.
85. *The Idler* no.60 (9 June, 1759), *Works of Samuel Johnson* (New Haven, 1963-), II, 186. On this subject see R. Wellek, 'The Price of Progress in 18th century reflections on literature', *Studies on Voltaire and the 18th century*, 155 (1976), pp.2265ff.
86. *Complete Writings*, ed. G. Keynes (Oxford, 1976), pp.621 and 777.
87. Known since its first publication in 1917 as 'The Oldest System-Programme of German Idealism', this fragmentary text has been published in a critical edition, under the title *Mythologie der Vernunft*, ed. C. Jamme and H. Schneider (Frankfurt, 1984). It is included in the first volume of the twenty volume Suhrkamp edition of Hegel's writings, *Werke*, ed. E. Moldenhauer and K.M. Michel (Frankfurt, 1970), which is used for references here. The phrase cited is *Werke*, I, 234.
88. Ibid., p.235.
89. Ibid., p.236.
90. Ibid., pp.235-36.
91. Ibid., p.206 [*Die Positivität der christlichen Religion*].
92. This remark occurs in the fragment *Der immer sich vergrössende Widerspruch*, cited in H.S. Harris, *Hegel's Development: towards the sunlight 1770-1801* (Oxford, 1972), p.443.
93. *Werke*, I, 483-84 [*Die Verfassung Deutschlands*].
94. Ibid., pp.557-58, 555 and 580.
95. *Sämtliche Werke*, ed. G. Lasson (Leipzig, 1928-38), XX, 213ff [*Jenaer Realphilosophie* II (1805/6)]; see N. Waszek, *Hegel and the Scottish Enlightenment*

(Dordrecht, 1988), pp.87ff. and *passim*.

96. Ibid., pp.217-18.On the significance of these formulations see M. Riedel, *Between Tradition and Revolution: the Hegelian Transformation of Political Philosophy*, tr. W. Wright (Cambridge, 1984), pp.17ff and 119ff.
97. *Werke*, VII, pp.351 and 350 [*Philosophie des Rechts*].
98. *Sämtliche Werke*, ed. Lasson, XIX, 240 [*Jenaer Realphilosophie* I (1803/4)].
99. All references to the *Phänomenologie des Geistes* (hereafter PhG) will be to the page numbers in *Werke*, III, followed by the paragraph number in the translation by A.V. Miller (Oxford, 1977), which is generally used here. These citations are PhG, p.130/ §160 and p.46/§47.
100. *Werke*, VII, 504. See likewise PhG §§ 310, 403 and 693. On Hegel's concept of *Geist* see C. Taylor, *Hegel* (Cambridge, 1975), pp.87ff.
101. *Macbeth*, III, iv, 138-9.
102. PhG, p.8/§ 11.
103. PhG, p.31/§ 27.
104. PhG, p.23/§ 17.
105. PhG, p.24/§ 20.
106. For a graphic overview of the work see J. Rée, *Philosophical Tales* (London, 1987), p.85.
107. In his lectures on the history of philosophy Hegel showed a high regard for the thought of Proclus, see *Werke*, XIX, 466ff.
108. *Werke*, XX, 476 [*Geschichte der Philosophie*].
109. *Werke*, XVII, 54 [*Philosophie der Religion*].
110. Ibid., p.56.
111. Ibid., pp.100ff. However, this does not lead Hegel in any way to (as it were) rehabilitate Prometheus, whom he sees as ministering only to natural needs and devoid of any spiritual dimension; see *Werke*, XVII, 107-8 and XIV, 54-57 [*Ästhetik*].
112. PhG, p.61/§ 65.
113. PhG, p.36/§ 32 and see p.24/§ 19.
114. PhG, p.72/§ 78.
115. *Werke*, VII, 47.
116. PhG, p.583/§ 798.
117. *Werke*, XII, 28 [*Philosophie der Geschichte*].
118. Ibid., p.32.
119. Ibid., pp.34ff.
120. Ibid., pp.45ff.
121. Ibid., p.49.
122. Ibid., p.97.
123. Ibid., p.529.
124. Ibid., pp.39ff and 55ff.
125. Ibid., p.57. On Hegel's attitude to Prussia see A.W. Wood, *Hegel's Ethical Thought* (Cambridge, 1990), pp.12-13, 242 and 257-58.
126. *Werke*, VII, 24.
127. Ibid., p.458, and pp.341, 346, 358-59, 381 and 411.
128. See S. Avineri, *Hegel's Theory of the Modern State* (Cambridge, 1972), pp.96-98, 157 and 240.
129. *Werke*, p.439 and 404; see also p.440.
130. *Werke*, XII, 12.
131. *Werke*, VIII, 90 [*Enzyklopädie*].
132. PhG, p.72/§ 77.

133. *Werke*, XII, 49.
134. PhG, pp.63-65/§§ 68 and 69.
135. PhG, p.18/§ 11; p.32/§ 28; p.65/§ 70.
136. PhG, p.73/§ 78. It should be noted that for Hegel this process was of course not in the least harmonious, and his use of the term has plausibly been seen as being sometimes ironic and (in its use as a chapter heading, at PhG § 484) sarcastic; see J. Shklar, *Freedom and Independence: a study of Hegel's...Phenomenology...* (Cambridge, 1976), pp.44 and 152.
137. *Werke*, XII, 28.
138. See J. Toews, *Hegelianism* (Cambridge, 1980), pp.85ff.
139. *Werke,* XII, 28.
140. *Reflections on the Revolution in France*, [1790] ed. C.C. O'Brien (Harmondsworth, 1968), p.189.
141. Koselleck, *Futures Past*, pp.32ff and 200ff.
142. Ibid., p.35.
143. *The Excursion*, IX, 25; *Poetical Works*, ed. E. de Selincourt (Oxford, 1936), p.689.

Chapter Nine

1. *Sartor Resartus*, ed. K. McSweeney and P. Sabor (Oxford, 1987), p.92.
2. *Poetical Works*, ed. E. de Selincourt (Oxford, 1936), p.374.
3. K. Tribe, *Genealogies of Capitalism* (London, 1981), pp.101ff.
4. J. Cottle, 'Malvern Hills' [1798], cited in R. Lonsdale (ed.), *The New Oxford Book of 18th century Verse* (Oxford, 1984), p.832.
5. Wordsworth, 'The Excursion' [1814], IX, 156ff and VIII, 298; *Poetical Works*, pp.691 and 685.
6. *The Philosophy of Manufactures* (London, 1835), p.339.
7. E.A. Wrigley, *People, Cities and Wealth* (Oxford, 1987), pp.10 and 36ff.
8. *The Wealth of Nations*, I.xi.n.9 and II.v.12.
9. See B. Fontana, *Rethinking the politics of commercial society* (Cambridge, 1985), p.95.
10. T.R. Malthus, *An Essay on the Principle of Population* [1798] (Oxford, 1993), p.39.
11. These were central themes of Ricardo's *On the Principles of Political Economy and Taxation* (1817). Smith was in favour of high wages; see WN I.viii.16, 36 and 59.
12. *Sir Thomas More: or Colloquies...*(London, 1829), p.19.
13. Ibid., pp.32, 132ff and 413. The work appeared in the year of Catholic Emancipation and a year after the repeal of the Test and Corporation Acts, which had excluded dissenters from holding government office.
14. Ibid., p.60.
15. Ibid., p.94.
16. Ibid., pp.198-99.
17. Ibid., p.171.
18. Ibid., p.170.
19. Ibid., p.169.
20. Ibid., pp.174 and 197.
21. Ibid., p.35.
22. 'Southey's Colloquies' [1830], *Critical and Historical Essays*, ed. F.C. Montague (London, 1903), I, 235.
23. Ibid., I, 215.
24. Ibid., I, 216.

25. Ibid., I, 216-17 and 239; see also p.242.
26. Ibid., I, 217.
27. Ibid., I, 245
28. Ibid., I, 245.
29. Epitomised by Macaulay in his essay 'Lord Bacon' [1837], as 'Utility and Progress' or 'Fruit and Progress', *Essays*, II, 196 and 201.
30. 'Southey's Colloquies', Ibid., I, 244.
31. Ibid., I, 244 and *History of England* [1849] (London, 1896), I, 219.
32. *Essays*, I, 245.
33. Malthus wrote of demand's 'creative power', *Essay on...Population*, p.42.
34. J. Bisset, 'Ramble of the Gods through Birmingham' [1800], *New Oxford Book of 18th century Verse*, pp.873-38.
35. E. Elliott, 'Steam at Sheffield' [c.1835], cited in J. Warburg (ed.), *The Industrial Muse* (London, 1958), p.20.
36. 'The Excursion', VIII, 87; *Poetical Works*, p.682.
37. R. Owen, 'Plan for the Relief of the Poor' [1817], *A New View of Society and Other Writings*, ed. G. Claeys (Harmondsworth, 1991), p.222.
38. T. Hodgkin, *Labour Defended against the claims of Capital'* [1825] (London, 1964), pp.82 and 104. The Biblical reference was to Paul's Epistle to the Galatians, VI, 7.
39. G. Mudie [1823], cited in G. Claeys, *Machinery, Money and the Millenium* (Cambridge, 1987), pp.76 and 77; the following year Owen wrote that 'riches are created solely by the industry of the working classes', ibid., p.62. For an earlier example of this view see the quotation from the *Gorgon* (1818) in E.P. Thompson, *The Making of the English Working Class* (Harmondsworth, 1968), p.849.
40. T. Hodgkin, *Labour Defended...*, p.56.
41. [W. Thompson], *Labour Rewarded* (London 1827), p.114.
42. J. Gray, *A Lecture on Human Happiness* [1825] (London, 1931), pp.8, 29, 15 and 27.
43. *The Philosophy of Manufactures*, p.16.
44. Ibid., p.13.
45. Ibid., pp.14 and 16.
46. Ibid., p.279.
47. Ibid., pp.282 and 108.
48. *Critical and Miscellaneous Essays* (London, 1869), II, 341.
49. Ibid., II, 327 and 330.
50. *Sartor Resartus*, p.44.
51. Ibid., p.48.
52. Ibid., p.56.
53. Ibid., p.129.
54. Ibid., p.138.
55. Ibid., p.120.
56. Ibid., p.56.
57. Ibid., p.31.
58. Ibid., p.180.
59. Ibid., p.42.
60. Ibid., pp.76 and 71.
61. Ibid., p.149.
62. Ibid., p.186.
63. 'Chartism', *Essays*, VI, 165.
64. *Past and Present, Works* (Centenary edn, London, 1897-1901), X, 153.
65. Ibid., pp.184 and 170.

66. Ibid., p.192.
67. *Yeast*, (London, 1901), pp.70-71.
68. *Self-Help* (London, 1958), pp.115, 170-71 and 229.
69. Ibid., p.58.
70. *Industrial Biography: iron workers and tool makers* (London, 1863), p.183. Curiously, as the epigraph to the previous chapter Smiles cites a French work on mechanics which stated the opposite: 'l'invention n'est-elle pas la poésie de la science?...Il faut être poëte pour créer', ibid., p.162. In 1795 Thomas Brindley had been described as having 'original genius', the power to 'create and invent', which poets had 'exclusively arrogated to themselves', cited in H. Jennings, *Pandaemonium 1660-1856* (London, 1987), p.68.
71. *Sir Thomas More: or Colloquies...*, I, 196-97.
72. 'Civilisation', *Collected Works*, ed. J.M. Robson et al. (Toronto, 1963-91), XVIII, 129.
73. 'Tocqueville on Democracy', ibid., XVIII, 169 and 199.
74. *Parliamentary Papers* [1806], cited in *Nature and Civilisation*, ed. A. Clayre (Oxford, 1977), p.67. On this subject see Hazlitt's comments on 'a genius for business' and a 'genius for action' in his essay 'On Thought and Action' [1821], *Selected Writings*, ed. D. Wu et al. (London, 1998), VI, 90ff.
75. *On Heroes, Hero-Worship and the Heroic in History* [1840], *Works*, V, 118.
76. *Past and Present, Works*, X, 205.
77. Ibid., pp.190-91.
78. *On Heroes..., Works*, V, 1.
79. Ibid., V, 27-28.
80. F. List, *Le Système naturel d'économie politique* [1837], tr. W.O. Henderson (London, 1983), pp.180ff. and *Das Nationale System der Politischen Ökonomie* [1841], tr. S.S. Lloyd (London, 1885) pp.136ff. See also C. von Clausewitz, *Vom Kriege* [1832], tr. J.J. Graham (Harmondsworth, 1982), pp.202-3 and 249.
81. *Past and Present, Works*, X, 273, and see p.296 on a 'chivalry of labour'.
82. Ibid., p.271.
83. Ibid., p.291.
84. *On Heroes..., Works*, V, 12 (and 15).
85. 'Chartism', *Essays*, VI, 146.
86. Ibid., VI, 144.
87. *On Heroes..., Works*, V, 175.
88. J.G. Fichte, *Werke*, ed. I.H. Fichte (Berlin, 1845), VI, 406.
89. *Anthropologie*, AA, VII, 321.
90. *Wissenschaftlehre* [1797], tr. P. Heath and J. Lachs (as *The Science of Knowledge*) (Cambridge, 1982), pp.38 and 83.
91. *On Heroes..., Works*, V, 155.
92. B. Vickers (ed.), *English Renaissance Literary Criticism* (Oxford, 1999), p.192: poets 'be (by manner of speaking) as creating gods'.
93. *Poetical Works*, ed. Selincourt, pp.735 and 737-38.
94. Ibid., p.750.
95. *Sir Thomas More: or Colloquies..*, p.418.
96. *Poetical Works*, p.738 [1800] and p.754 [1815].
97. Ibid., p.590: 'Prospectus', line 55.
98. Ibid., p.593: 'The Excursion', I, lines 169 and 194.
99. E. Young, *Night Thoughts*, VI, 423-24; J. Thomson, *The Seasons*, 'Autumn, line 960. (Addison had explained the matter in *The Spectator* no.413 (24 June, 1712); see on this subject M.H. Nicolson, *Newton demands the muse* (Princeton, 1966), pp. 22ff.) Hume

had raised the question, in his *Treatise*, of whether the mind in its normal operations had 'creative power' (*Treatise of Human Nature* (Oxford, 1978), p.84); in his *Enquiry concerning human understanding*, however, he had dismissed the idea (*Enquiry...* (Oxford, 1902), pp.19 and 69).

100. *The Prelude* [1805], II, 381-82, *William Wordsworth*, ed. S. Gill (Oxford, 1984), p.401.
101. *Poetical Works*, pp.683-84: 'The Excursion', VIII, lines 200-206 and 90.
102. Ibid., p.684: VIII, lines 207ff.
103. *Biographia Literaria*, ed. J. Engel and W.J. Bate (Princeton, 1983) (referred to hereafter as BL), I, 211.
104. R. Wellek, *Immanuel Kant in England: 1793-1838* (Princeton, 1931), pp.6ff.
105. See BL, Introduction, pp.cxviiff, and the annotations to the text.
106. These statements occur in the lecture 'On Poesy or Art', first printed in *Literary Remains* (1836), and then included in the edition of *Biographia Literaria* by J. Shawcross (Oxford, 1907), II, 253-63. Coleridge's surviving notes are printed in CC, V:2, *Lectures 1808-1819: On Literature*, ed. R.A. Foakes (Princeton, 1987), pp.217-27. References here are given to both the 1907 edition (referred to as Shawcross) and CC, V:2. The passage cited is Shawcross, II, 257and 259 / CC, V:2, 220 and 223.
107. BL, I, 304 and II, 83-84. On the central importance of religion for Coleridge, and also his need to validate the position of the isolated intellectual, see M. Butler, *Romantics, Rebels and Reactionaries* (Oxford, 1981), pp.72ff.
108. Ibid., I, 77 and 80.
109. Ibid., I, 111 and 117.
110. Ibid., I, 289.
111. Ibid., II, 15-16.
112. 'On Poesy or Art'; recorded in Shawcross, II, 258, but not in CC, V:2.
113. Ibid., Shawcross, II, 253 / CC, V:2, 217.
114. Ibid., Shawcross, II, 258 and 254 / CC, V:2, 221 and 218.
115. *Aids to Reflection*, CC, IX, 184ff.
116. BL, I, 273.
117. Ibid., I, 224 and see II, 5 n.4.
118. Ibid., I, 283.
119. Horaces, *Ars poetica*, 330-31; Boileau, *L'Art poétique*, IV, 167ff; Diderot, *Oeuvres esthétiques*, p.829; Blake, *Complete Writings*, p.776.
120. R. Porter, *Mind forg'd manacles* (London, 1987), pp.98ff, describing the shift from madness seen as possession by external forces to madness as an imbalace of mental powers, sees this period as one in which the association of madness and poetic achievement declined. However, there seems to have been no shortage of examples to fuel a continuing debate on the matter, as Porter recognises in his *Social History of Madness* (London, 1987), pp.63-64.
121. See BL, I, 30ff (especially 33 and 36-37), and 224; also CC, IX, 411-12 (on Virgil). It was of course not necessary to share Coleridge's metaphysics or aesthetics to hold this view; see, for example, William Godwin, *Enquiry concerning Political Justice* (Harmondsworth, 1985), pp.307-10.
122. The remark was made by Lady Caroline Lamb; see P. Grosskurth, *Byron: the flawed angel* (London, 1997), p.162.
123. 'Moore's Life of Byron' [1831], *Critical and Historical Essays*, I, 341. In this essay Macaulay may have expressed surprise but elsewhere he observed how frequent in the lives of extraordinary men was 'the union of high intelligence and low desires', 'Francis Bacon', ibid., II, 166.
124. *Lay Sermon* [1817], CC, VI, 199.

125. Ibid., IV, 189 and 206.
126. *Aids...*, CC, IX, 26.
127. *On the Constitution...*, CC, X, 46. See B.Knights, *The Idea of the Clerisy in the 19th century* (Cambridge, 1978), pp.39ff.
128. Ibid., CC, X, 59 and 48.
129. Ibid., CC, X, 69.
130. Ibid., CC, X, 52.
131. 'Coleridge', *Collected Works*, ed. J.M. Robson et al. (Toronto, 1963-91), X, 121.
132. Ibid., X, 155.
133. 'On Genius', ibid., I, 333.
134. Ibid., X, 140 and 95.
135. *Autobiography* [published 1873], *Collected Works*, I, 113.
136. Ibid., p.177.
137. 'Tocqueville...', Ibid, XVIII, 194.
138. *On Liberty and other writings*, ed. S. Collini (Cambridge, 1989), p.56.
139. *Collected Works*, X, 138.
140. *On Liberty*, p.58. These words were quoted from Wilhelm von Humboldt's *Ideen zu einem Versuch, die Grenzen der Wirksamkeit des Staats zu bestimmen*, first published in 1852 and translated into English in 1854, under the title *The Sphere and Duties of Government*. Mill could equally well have quoted from Carlyle's essay 'Jean Paul Friedrich Richter' [1827]: 'the great law of culture is: Let each become all that he was created capable of being...and show himself at length in his own shape and stature...A harmonious development of being [is] the first and last object of all true culture', *Essays*, I, 16-17.
141. *On Liberty*, p.60.
142. Ibid., pp.63 and 64-65.
143. *Culture and Anarchy and other writings*, ed. S. Collini (Cambridge, 1993), p.192.
144. Ibid., pp.61, 78-79 and 192.
145. Ibid., pp.190 and 207.
146. Ibid., p.190.
147. CC, X, 42-43.
148. *Culture and Anarchy*, p.84.
149. Ibid., pp.73 and 75; see also p.149.
150. Ibid., p.185.
151. Ibid., p.210.
152. Ibid.,pp.138-39.
153. Ibid., pp.130, 66 and 95.
154. Ibid., p.99.
155. Ibid., p.28. The text of this 1993 edition is the same as that printed in *Complete Prose Works*, ed. R.H. Super (Ann Arbor, 1960-77), III, 260. As explained in Chapter One, note 22, I have followed the first editions of the essay in using Arnold's original phrase 'true function of man' rather than the later version of 'highest function of man' (which is adopted by Collini and Super).
156. 'Heine' [1864], *Complete Prose Works*, III, 109.
157. Ibid., pp.111ff.
158. *Culture and Anarchy*, pp.95, 90, 78 and 193.
159. 'A New History of Greece', *Complete Prose Works* V, 269-71, on the decisive influence of Delphi and the 'Apolline religion'.
160. *Culture and Anarchy*, p.79.
161. See his essay 'Marcus Aurelius', *Complete Prose Works*, III, 133ff.

162. *Culture and Anarchy*, p.181.

163. 'Plan...' [1817], *A New View of Society*, p.222.

164. Ibid., pp.6 and 298; see also pp.254, 257, 263, 264 and 298.

165. Ibid., p.194.

166. This was the title of the journal promoting Owen's ideas, published from 1835 to 1846.

167. *Common Sense, The Thomas Paine Reader*, ed. M. Foot and I. Kramnick (Harmondsworth, 1987), p.109.

168. *Rights of Man*, ed. E. Foner (Harmondsworth, 1985), pp.268 and 162.

169. 'A Letter to the Bishop of Llandaff' [1793], *Selected Prose*, ed. J.O. Hayden (Harmondsworth, 1988), p.143.

170. G. Wood, *The Creation of the American Republic* (Chapel Hill, 1969), pp.331 and 27; the latter, quoting the Philadelphia Packet (15 January, 1776) is strikingly similar to Paine's statement (note 171), and may possibly have been connected with him, since he was at that time in Philadephia editing the Pennsylvania Magazine.

171. *Common Sense*, p.104.

172. *Rights of Man*, p.176.

173. *Collected Works*, XI, 273-74 and 324, and see *On Liberty and other writings*, p.213 [*The Subjection of Women*]. In the latter work (pp.184ff.) Mill argued against the view that women lacked any innate ability 'in speculation or creative art', and the previous year Bagehot had made a similar case for the as-yet-unknown 'creative power of women', see R.D. Edwards, *The Best of Bagehot* (London, 1993)), pp.224ff.

174. Ibid., XVIII, 89-90.

175. 'Address...' [1817], *A New View of Society*, p.172.

176. *Life of Robert Owen by Himself* [1857], in A.L. Morton, *The Life and Ideas of Robert Owen* (London, 1969), p.84.

177. *New View of Society*, pp.175 and 280.

178. *Life of Robert Owen...*, p.84.

179. 'The Catechism of *les Industriels*' [1823], in *The Political Thought of Saint-Simon*, ed. G. Ionescu (Oxford, 1976), p.188.

180. See S. Lukes, *Individualism* (Oxford, 1973), pp.4ff.

181. Cited in G. Claeys, *Citizens and Saints* (Cambridge, 1989), p.103.

182. PhG, §§ 207ff, on 'The Unhappy Consciousness', and (on ancient Greek religion) *Werke*, XIV, 101 and 104, and XVII, 117-19.

183. *Das Wesen des Christentums*, ed. W. Schuffenhauer (Berlin, 1956), I, 22, 75, 77 and 195.

184. Ibid., I, 19 and 49; *Gesammelte Werke*, ed. W. Schuffenhauer (Berlin, 1967-), IX, 243 [*Vorläufige Thesen zur Reformation der Philosophie* (1843)] and IX, 265 [*Grundsätze der Philosophie der Zukunft* (1843)].

185. Feuerbach, cited in J. Toews, *Hegelianism*, p.359; M. Bakunin, 'Die Reaktion in Deutschland' [1842], quoted in *Statism and Anarchy*, ed. M. Shatz (Cambridge, 1991), p.xvi.

186. B. Bauer, *Die gute Sache der Freiheit...*[1842], *Die Hegelsche Linke*, ed. H. and I. Pepperle (Leipzig, 1985), p.500; R. Gottschall, 'Mahnung' [1843], in *Der deutsche Vormärz*, ed. J. Hermand (Stuttgart, 1967), p.147; M. Hess, *Die europäische Triarchie* [1841], *Philosophische & Sozialistische Schriften 1837-50*, ed. A. Cornu and W. Mönke (Berlin, 1961), p.86.

187. A. Ruge, 'Der Mensch, eine Skizze' [1843], *Sämmtliche Werke* (Mannheim, 1848), VI, 364.

188. Ibid., 367.

189. J. Keats, 'On first looking into Chapman's Homer', lines 11-14. In fact Cortes never saw the Pacific at Darien; Keats confused him with Balboa; see *The Poems of John Keats*, ed. M. Allott (London, 1970), p.62.

190. *Das Wesen des Christentums*, pp.335 and 339.

191. K. Marx and F. Engels, *Werke*, (Berlin, 1956-68), III, 2 [*Die deutsche Ideologie*] and XL, 516 [*Ökonomisch-philosophische Manuskripte*]. (Between 1968 and 1981 this volume was an Ergänzungsband to the *Werke*; it became volume XL in 1985.) I am indebted to the translation of the latter writings by G. Benton and R. Livingstone, (in Marx, *Early Writings* (Harmondsworth, 1975)), as also to that of the *Grundrisse* by M. Nicolaus (Harmondsworth, 1973), and I have given references to their editions in brackets, with the initials EW and G respectively (although I have not always followed them). The reference here is EW, p.328.

192. *Werke*, XIII, 8-9 [*Zur Kritik der Politischen Ökonomie*]. The word isusually translated as 'mode of production', but this phrase often seems to obscure more than it illuminates.

193. Ibid., XL, 546 and 544 (EW, pp.357 and 355); in his review of Carlyle's *Past and Present* Engels made this point explicitly in terms of a wholly human 'free, independent creation (*Schöpfung*)', *Werke*, I, 546.

194. Ibid., XL, 451 (EW, p.265); see also XL, 538-39 (EW, pp.349-500).

195. Ibid., XL, 553-54 (EW, p.365); and II, 89 [*Die heilige Familie*]; Engels, *The Condition of the Working Class in England*, tr. F. Kelley-Wischnewetsky, revised by Engels [1887] (Oxford,1993), pp.135-36, 220ff and 263.

196. *Werke*, XL, 584 (EW, p.395).

197. Ibid., XL, 511 (EW, p.323).

198. Ibid., XL, 451.

199. Ibid., XL, 531 (EW, p.342); and IV, 467 [*Manifest der Kommunistischen Partei*].

200. Ibid., III, 37 and see p.75.

201. Ibid., III, 70-71.

202. *Grundrisse der Kritik der politischen Ökonomie* (Berlin, 1953), p.387 (G, p.488).

203. Ibid., p.204 (G, p.297).

204. Ibid., p.206 (G, p.298).

205. Ibid., pp.505 and 387 (G, pp.611 and 488).

206. Ibid., p.507 (G, p.614). On the central importance and normative status of this idea in Marx's thought, see J. Elster, *Making Sense of Marx* (Cambridge, 1985), pp.51, 54, 71, 79 and 83. Despite the problems to which he admits this gives rise (pp.88-90 and 522-27) Elster nevertheless regards this to be 'the most valuable and enduring element of Marx's thought' (p.521).

207. *Grundrisse*, p.505 (G, p.611).

208. *Werke*, III, 379.

209. Ibid., III, 33 and 424; *Grundrisse*, pp.75 and 593 (G, pp.158 and 706).

210. *Werke*, XL, 462-63 and III, 21.

211. See S.S. Prawer, *Karl Marx and World Literature* (Oxford, 1976), pp.98, 318, 374 and 414.

212. S.S. Prawer, *Karl Marx and World Literature*, pp.82, 288 and 411; S. Morawski, *Marx and Engels: On Literature and Art* (New York, 1974), pp.42 and 44.

213. S. Morawski, ibid., pp.13ff; P.J. Kain, *Schiller, Hegel and Marx* (Montreal, 1982), pp.83-91; J. Chytry, *The Aesthetic State* (Berkeley, 1989), pp.241 and 265-66.

214. *On the Aesthetic Education of Man*, ed. and tr. E.M. Wilkinson and L.A. Willoughby (Oxford, 1967), p.8.

215. Ibid., pp.100 and 104-108.

216. Ibid., p.204.

217. Although Fichte did not (like the young Hegelians) write of 'conscious action' per se, his writings continually assert the connection of thinking with willing and moral action; see, for example, *Sämmtliche Werke*, ed. I.H. Fichte (Berlin, 1845-46), II, 220ff, 248-49, 254ff and 263 [*Die Bestimmung der Menschen*].

218. A. Cieskowski, *Prolegomenon zur Historiosophie* (Berlin, 1838), pp.16ff; M. Hess, *Philosophische...Schriften*, pp.83 and 86; E. Bauer, *Die Hegelsche Linke*, pp.699-700: 'true history commences [when] it becomes *conscious*', and see p.200, n.186.

219. H. Stuke, *Philosophie der Tat* (Stuttgart, 1963), p.82.

220. *Werke*, XL, 545 (EW, p.356).

221. See for example S.S. Prawer, *Karl Marx and World Literature*, pp.364-65.

222. In general this follows from his insistence on polytheism (e.g. *Das Wesen des Christentums*, I, 190, and *Gesammelte Werke*, IX, 248); more precisely, from the role of anger, pain or unhappiness in generating what is new, (see his *Theogonie*, *Gesammelte Werke*, VII, 3ff, 47 and 54). On some aspects of this see M. Wartofsky, *Feuerbach* (Cambridge, 1977), pp.321ff.

223. *The Theory of the Four Movements*, tr. I. Patterson (Cambridge, 1996), p.87.

224. *New View of Society*, pp.213 and 280.

225. W. Thompson, *Labour Rewarded* (London, 1827), p.111 and see pp.26 and 36.

Chapter Ten

1.   J.J. Winckelmann, *Gedanken über die Nachahmung der Griechischen Werke...* [1755], *Kleine Schriften und Briefe*, ed. W. Senff (Weimar, 1960), p.44; E. Curtius, *Griechische Geschichte* (Berlin, 1857-67), I, 429ff; see also pp.399ff. on Delphi.

2.   G. Grote, 'Institutions of Ancient Greece', *Westminster Review* 5 (April, 1826), pp.274 and 277-78, and *A History of Greece* (London, 1846-56), II, 105; L. Preller, *Griechische Mythologie* (Leipzig, 1854), I, 21; see also K.O. Müller, *Prolegomena zu einer wissenschaftlicher Mythologie* (Göttingen, 1825), pp.243-44.

3.   All references are to the *Kritische Gesamtausgabe: Werke* (hereafter KGW) edited by G. Colli and M. Montinari (Berlin, 1967-95). In addition, for those works which Nietzsche wrote (from the late 1870s) set out in sections and numbered paragraphs, I have given the section (where applicable) in roman and the paragraph in arabic numerals, with titles indicated in the now conventional manner as follows: A = *The Antichrist*, BGE = *Beyond Good and Evil*, D = *Daybreak*, EH = *Ecce Homo*, GM = *The Genealogy of Morality*, GS = *The Gay Science*, HAH = *Human, All Too Human*, TI = *Twilight of the Idols*, Z = *Thus Spoke Zarathustra* (references for which are not to sections and paragraphs but to the page numbers of the translation by R.G. Hollingdale (Harmondsworth, 1969); I have benefited in general from Hollingdale's translations). For the early works I have given the original titles; for unpublished works I have given the letter N (for *Nachlass*) with the date. The reference here is to KGW, III/1, 20 [*Die Geburt der Tragödie*].

4.   Ibid., 31 and 34-5.

5.   Ibid., 46.

6.   Ibid., 147.

7.   Ibid., 86.

8.   Ibid., 110-11.

9.   KGW, III/2, 254. [*Über der Pathos der Wahrheit*].

10. C. Wagner, *Die Tagebücher* (Munich, 1976), I, 102. The date of this entry (3 June, 1869) falls between Nietzsche's first and second visits (17 May and 5 June).
11. KGW, III/1, 43 [*Die Geburt der Tragödie*].
12. Ibid., 64.
13. Ibid., 63.
14. Ibid., 105.
15. KGW, III/2, 260-61 [*Der griechische Staat*].
16. Ibid., 261.
17. Ibid., 278ff [*Homers Wettkampf*].
18. Ibid., 266.
19. KGW, IV/1, 154-55 [N, 1875].
20. Ibid., pp.136 and 103; KGW, III/2, 277 [*Homers Wettkampf*].
21. KGW III/2, 311 [*Die Philosophie im tragischen Zeitalter*].
22. Ibid., 318-19.
23. Ibid., 303-4 and 301.
24. Ibid., 302.
25. KGW III/1, 354 [*Schopenhauer als Erzieher*] and IV/1, 122 [N, 1875].
26. KGW, III/4, 21[N, 1872-73].
27. KGW, IV/3, 178 [HAH, I, 1].
28. KGW, III/2, 373 [*Über Wahrheit und Lüge*].
29. Ibid., 374.
30. Ibid., 376-77.
31. KGW, III/4. 47 [N, 1872-73].
32. This was the subtitle of Nietzsche's proposed work *Der Wille zur Macht*, KGW, VIII/2, 32 and 434; he retained it in different places after he had abandoned that work, see KGW, VIII/3, v-vi.
33. KGW, VI/1, 17 [Z, p.49].
34. KGW, V/2, 180 [GS, 179] and VI/1, 35[Z, p.61].
35. KGW, IV/2, 79 [HAH, I, 68] and IV/3, 294 [HAH, III, 227].
36. See for example KGW, V/1, 263-64 [D, 423], and there is possibly an element of this in the famous paragraph on the death of God, V/2, 158-60 [GS, 125], even though the words are put in the mouth of a 'mad person'.
37. KGW, VI/2, 15 [BGE, 9].
38. Ibid., 122-23 [BGE, 200].
39. KGW, VI/3, 114-15 [TI, IX, 14].
40. KGW, VI/2, 274 and 284 [GM, I, 2 and 10].
41. Ibid., 284 and 280 [GM, I , 10 and 7].
42. Ibid., 289 and 302 [GM. I, 11 and 16].
43. Ibid., 326 and 329 [GM, II, 11].
44. Ibid., 318 [GM, II, 7].
45. Ibid., 352 [GM, II, 24].
46. KGW, VI/1, 32 [Z, p.60].
47. Ibid., 143 [Z, p.137].
48. Ibid., 9 and 96 [Z, pp.42 and 102].
49. Ibid., 254 [Z, p.223].
50. Ibid., 358, 20 and 175 [Z, pp.301-2, 52 and 161].
51. Ibid., 244 [Z, p.215].
52. Ibid., 106 [Z, p.111].
53. KGW VII/1, 139 [N, 1882-83].

54. KGW, III/1, 63ff [*Die Geburt der Tragödie*]; KGW, III/2, 277ff [*Homers Wettkampf*] and VI/2, 289 [GM, I, 11]; KGW, V/1, 226 [D, 306] and V/2, 258 [GS, 344] and VIII/3, 134 [N, 1888].

55. KGW, V/2, 168-69 [GS, 143] and VI/2, 174 [BGE, 230].

56. KGW, VI/2, 309 [GM, II, 2].

57. KGW, VI/2, 289 [GM, I, 11] and VI/2, 123 [BGE, 200].

58. KGW, III/1, 324 [*Von Nutzen...Historie*]; KGW, IV/2, 361 [HAH, I, 617] and IV/3, 151 [HAH, II, 332].

59. KGW, V/2, 64 [GS, 19] and VIII/3, 87.

60. KGW, III/2, 366 [*Philosophie in tragische Zeitalter*]; KGW, IV/1, 103 [N, 1875]; KGW, IV/2, 144-45 and 151 [HAH, I, 147 and 159].

61. KGW, V/1, 22-23 and 29 [D, 14 and 20].

62. KGW, VI/3, 168 [A, 2] and 277 [EH, II, 1]; KGW, IV/2, 206 [HAH, I, 241]; see also his 'Tractatus politicus', KGW, VIII/2, 267-69 [N, 1887-8].

63. KGW, VI/2, 40-41 [BGE, 26]. He also developed a keen interest in Baudelaire; see the extensive extracts from the latter's writings, KGW, VIII/2, 317-29 and 332-34 [N, 1888].

64. KGW, VI/3, 145-46 [TI, IX, 49].

65. KGW, VI/1, 20 [Z, p.51].

66. Ibid., 262 [Z, p.229].

67. KGW, VIII/1,124 [N, 1885-86].

68. KGW, VI/2, 364 (and see 361) [GM, III, 6 and 4].

69. KGW, VIII/2, 315 [N, 1887-88].

70. KGW, VI/3, 298 [EH, III, 1].

71. KGW, VI/3, 347 [EH, IX, 8] and V/2, 417 [N, 1881].

72. F. Schiller, *Werke* (Nationalausgabe, Weimar, 1943-), XX, 424-25.

73. A. Smith, *The Theory of Moral Sentiments*, VII.ii.1.31: ' men of letters...are generally during their life so obscure and insignificant that their adventures are seldom recorded by contemporary historians'.

74. See, for example, E. Kris and O. Kurz, *Legend, Myth and Magic in the Image of the Artist* (London, 1979).

75. *The Young Duke*, (London, 1831), II, 227.

76. *Critical and Historical Essays*, ed. F.C. Montague (London, 1903), I, 314.

77. Ibid., 341.

78. W. Hazlitt, *Selected Writings*, ed. D. Bromwich et al. (London, 1998), II, 306 and VII, 136.

79. *Coriolanus*, V, iii, 35-36.

80. See C. Grana, *Modernity and its discontents* (New York, 1967) and M.R. Brown, *Gypsies and other Bohemians* (Ann Arbor, 1985).

81. *La Comédie humaine*, ed. P.-G. Castex et al. (Paris, 1976), III, 144.

82. Ibid., III, 217-18.

83. Ibid., III, 141.

84. C. Baudelaire, *Oeuvres complètes*, ed. C. Pichois (Paris, 1975-76), II, 494-96 [*Salon de 1846*].

85. Ibid., 533 [*De l'essence du rire* (1855)].

86. Ibid., 543.

87. Ibid., 322 [*Notes nouvelles sur Edgar Poe* (1856)].

88. Ibid., 333ff. Poe's views were set out in his essay *The Poetic Principle* (1850).

89. *Oeuvres complètes*, I, 134 ['*Le Voyage*'].

90. Ibid., II, 326 and 710-11 [*Le Peintre de la vie moderne* (1863)].

91. C. Grana, *Modernity and its discontents*, pp.20 and 33ff; G.H. Bell-Villada, *Art for Art's sake and the Literary Life* (Lincoln, Nebraska, 1996), pp.45ff.

92. E. Hobsbawm, *The Age of Capital* (London, 1975), p.336; M.R. Brown, *Gypsies and other Bohemians*, pp.9-10.

93. See M. Beebe, *Ivory Towers and Sacred Founts* (New York, 1964) and Bell-Villada, *Art for Art's sake...*

94. *Oeuvres complètes*, I, 276 [*Le Spleen de Paris*].

95. *Der Einzige und sein Eigentum*, ed. A. Meyer (Stuttgart, 1981), pp.51-52, 76, 356; 51 ('humanity'), 115 ('rational order'), 135 ('social duty').

96. Ibid., p.378.

97. Ibid., p.353.

98. Ibid., p.14.

99. Ibid., p.256.

100. Ibid., p.367.

101. Ibid., p.219.

102. Ibid., p.391.

103. Ibid., pp.146 and 298.

104. Ibid., p.225.

105. Ibid., p.5.

106. KGW, IV/3, 160 [HAH, II, 366].

107. KGW, VI/1, 293 [Z, p.252].

108. KGW, VI/2, 152 [BGE, 213].

109. Ibid., 234 [BGE, 269].

110. Ibid., 167; *Beyond Good and Evil*, [225] tr. R.G. Hollingdale (Harmondsworth, 1990), p.155.

111. KGW, V/2, 243 [GS, 335].

112. KGW, III/1, 355 [*Schopenhauer als Erzieher*].

113. KGW, VI/1, 175 and 177; [Z, pp.161 and 162-63].

114. KGW, VI/3, 366 [EH, XIV, 4] and VI/2, 32 [BGE, 23] (where Nietzsche uses *Haushalt* rather than *Ökonomie*, but with the same sense).

115. KGW, III/2, 261 [*Der griechische Staat*]; KGW, V/2, 311[GS, 377]; KGW, VI/2, 215 and 317 [BGE, 257 and GM, II, 6].

116. KGW, VI/1, 47 [Z, p.69].

117. KGW, VIII/1, 304 and VIII/2, 129.

118. See, for example, Shaftesbury, *Characteristics...*(London, 1711), II, 134 and 388-89; but the phrase was equally used without any religious connotations, e.g. by Mandeville or Hume or Darwin.

119. KGW, VI/3, 170 [A, 6] and VI/2, 217 [BGE, 259].

120. KGW, V/2, 311 [GS, 377]; KGW, VI/2, 144 and 203 [BGE, 208 and 251].

121. KGW, V/2, 132 and 277-78 [GS, 99 and 356]. See on this subject M. Tanner, 'Nietzsche and Genius', *Genius: the history of an idea*, ed. P. Murray (Oxford, 1989), pp.136-37.

122. KGW, VI/1, 227 [Z. p.202].

123. KGW, VI/3, 242 [A, 57].

124. KGW, VI/2, 215ff and 273 [BGE, 257 and GM, I, 2], and VI/3, 132 [TI, 37].

125. KGW, VI/2, 172 [BGE, 229].

126. KGW, IV/2, 19-20 and 102 [HAH, I, 1 and 107].

127. KGW, VI/2, 317 [GM, II, 6].

128. KGW, VII/3, 315 [N, 1885]; the text continues, 'where a *creative* way of thinking is in command'.

129. KGW, VIII/1, 85 [N, 1885-86].
130. KGW, V/2, 311 [GS, 377] and VI/2, 128 [BGE, 203] and VI/3, 311 [EH, IV, 4. On this subject see S. Ascheim, *The Nietzsche Legacy in Germany, 1890-1990* (Berkeley, 1992), pp.316ff. and D.W. Conway, *Nietzsche and the political* (London, 1997), pp.34 ff.
131. KGW, VI/3. 366 [EH, XIV, 4].
132. Gore Vidal (1976), cited in the *Oxford Dictionary of Modern Quotations* (Oxford, 1991), p.221. Nietzsche made a similar observation, KGW, V/1, 36 [D, 30].
133. KGW, VIII/1, 118.
134. In his essay 'Of Innovations', Francis Bacon observed that 'those things which have long gone together are as it were confederate within themselves; whereas new things piece not...they trouble by their inconformity', *Francis Bacon*, ed. B. Vickers (Oxford, 1996), p.388.
135. KGW, VI/2,149-50 [BGE, 212].
136. KGW, VIII/1, 320-21 [N, 1886-87].
137. KGW, VIII/1, 321 [ibid.].
138. KGW, V/2, 219-20 [GS, 300 and 301].
139. See on this subject B. Magnus, 'The Use and Abuse of *The Will to Power*', in *Reading Nietzsche*, ed. R.C. Solomon and K.M. Higgins (New York, 1988), pp.218-35.
140. B. Constant, *Journal* (16 February, 1804), *Oeuvres*, ed. A. Rollin (Paris, 1957), p.235.

Chapter Eleven

1. H. Bergson, *L'Évolution créatrice* (Paris, 1907).
2. J. Schumpeter, *Theorie der wirtschaftlichen Entwicklung* (1911); the reference here is to the second edition (1926) *The Theory of Economic Development*, tr. R. Opie (Cambridge, Mass., 1934), pp.92-93. It was, however, only in the last two decades of the twentieth century that the entrepreneur generally came to be called 'creative'; see, for example, G. Gilder, *Wealth and Poverty* (London, 1982), pp. ix, xiv, 20, 30 ff, 45 ff. and 251 ff.
3. B. Russell, *Principles of Social Reconstruction* (London, 1971), pp.6 and 161ff; for ancient examples see Seneca, *Epistulae morales*, IX, 7, and also St. Matthew's Gospel, 16, 26.
4. C. Spearman, *Creative Mind* (1931), N.D. Hirsch, *Genius and creative intelligence* (1931).
5. Inscription on the south face of the Musée de l'homme, Palais de Chaillot, Paris (1937).
6. J.Z. Young, *Doubt and certainty in Science* (Oxford, 1951), pp.61, 108 and 160-61; N. Chomsky, *Problems of Knowledge and Freedom* (London, 1972), p.46.
7. R. Reagan, *Speaking my mind* (London, 1990), p.417; T. Benn, *Arguments for Socialism* (London, 1979), p.17.
8. Z. Brezinski, *The Listener*, 14 June, 1979; L. Segal, *Is the future female* (London, 1987), p.2.
9. *Frankfurter Allgemeine Zeitung*, 5 December, 1994, p.9
10. S. Freud, 'New Introductory Lectures' [1932], *Complete Psychological Works*, tr. J. Strachey (London, 1953-77), XXII, 80.
11. P. Rieff, *Freud: the mind of a moralist* (London, 1959), pp.35 and 89ff.
12. KGW, V/2, 145, 159 and 256 [GS, 108, 125 and 343].
13. KGW, V/2, 309 [GS, 324], and VI/2, 4 and 10 [BGE, Preface and 2].

14. KGW, V/2, 232 [GS, 324].
15. KGW, V/2,233[GS, 324].
16. Ibid., 218 [GS, 299]. For an account of Nietzsche's thought in these terms see A. Nehamas, *Life as Literature* (Cambridge, Mass., 1992); for a discussion of this reading see B. Lester, 'Nietzsche and Aestheticism', *Journal of the History of Philosophy* 30 (1992), 275-90. For a philosophical defence of domestic Nietzscheanism see R. Rorty, *Contingency, Irony, and Solidarity* (Cambridge, 1989), pp.27 ff, 67-68, 96-97; on some of its limits, see pp.119-21 and 197, as well as his *Achieving our Country* (Cambridge, Mass., 1998), pp.96ff.
17. KGW, V/2, 210 [GS, 290].
18. *New Yorker*, 7 November, 1988.
19. On significance in general, see C. Taylor, *The Ethics of Authenticity* (Cambridge, Mass., 1991), pp.35ff and 82.
20. *Briefwechsel*, ed. G. Colli and M. Montinari (Berlin, 1977-93), III/1, 463 (24 December, 1883). Nietzsche read Emerson (in translation) from the age of seventeen; on this subject see G.J. Stack, *Nietzsche and Emerson: an elective affinity* (Athens, Ohio, 1992).
21. KGW, V/2, 303 [GS, 370] and VI/3, 341 [EH, IX, 6].
22. B. Magnus and K.M. Higgins, 'Nietzsche's works and their themes', *The Cambridge Companion to Nietzsche* (Cambridge, 1996), pp.43 and 48.
23. R. Hughes, *The Shock of the New* (London, 1980), p.402.
24. KGW, VI/2, 364 [GM, III, 6]; see also KGW, V/2, 300-1 and 303 [GS, 369 and 370], and especially KGW, VI/2, 234 [BGE, 269].
25. KGW, V/2, 81-82 [GS, 40 and 42].
26. KGW, III/1, 161 [*David Strauss der Bekenner*].
27. W. Blake, *Complete Writings*, ed. G. Keynes (Oxford, 1976), p.153; B. Constant, *Oeuvres*, ed. A. Roulin (Paris, 1957), pp.234-35.
28. *Midsummer Night's Dream*, V, I, 17.
29. KGW, V/2, 206 [GS, 283]).
30. There is one usage of 'creative' which has negative connotations, namely the phrase 'creative accounting', (defined in the *Observer Encyclopedia of Our Times* (17 November, 1996), p.33, as '*creative*, that is, as in virtually criminal…while never [being] actually illegal'). What we do not have — and what we need — is a sense of 'creative' that is ambivalent.
31. M.H. Abrams, *The Mirror and the Lamp* (Oxford, 1973), pp.30ff and 50ff.
32. J. Habermas, *The Philosophical Discourse of Modernity*, tr. F. Lawrence (Cambridge, 1987), p.7.
33. J. Schumpeter, *Capitalism, Socialism and Democracy* (London, 1943), p.83. This formulation was anticipated by Mandeville in his poem *The Fable of the Bees* (1705), lines 36-37: '…other millions were employed / To see their handiwork destroyed'.
34. Apollodorus, *The Library*, I, 7, 1, tr. J.G. Frazer (London, 1921), I, 51; and see Frazer's note, pp.51-53.

Index